Lok Sabha Elections 1999

Last of the Millennium

J.C. Aggarwal
N.K. Chowdhry

SHIPRA

(First Published in India in 2000)

Rs. 1500; US$ 60

ISBN: 978-81-7541-051-0

2021 Impression PoD

Lok Sabha Elections –1999
(Last of the Millenium)

Published by:
SHIPRA PUBLICATIONS
LG 18-19, Pankaj Central Market,
I.P. Ext., Patparganj, Delhi 110092
Ph. 91 11 22235152/ 6152; 9650028065
info@shiprapublication.com
www.shiprapublication.com

Preface

Lok Sabha elections, so far thirteen in number since independence, are a pointer to the fact that Parliamentary democracy has, as an institution, struck roots in the Indian polity. It assumes great significance taking into account the latest happenings, *i.e.* military rule, in neighbouring Pakistan. It is however, not enough that all we have to say is that democracy has survived. It must also establish itself as the instrument for promoting the greatest good of the greatest numbers.

The era of single party dominance seems to have come to an end. There was the time when Chief Ministers in States were shifted in and outed at the discretion of the party High Command at New Delhi. The regional parties are no longer satisfied with power within their own States. They want a determined say in the policy making at the Central level. On their own, they cannot provide the numbers and hence the need for coalition politics.

The BJP was for long considered as the untouchable among the political parties. From 1984 onwards when its strength in Lok Sabha was reduced to just two members, the party has been revising its political strategies. By 1996 it was clear that on its own the party may not be able to command an absolute majority whatever be its agenda. If it stuck to Hindutva Agenda, it would find no takers outside the Hindi belt. On the other hand if it decided to put aside the issues that gave it an identity,, it would be under pressure from its party cadres. The dilemma was resolved in the personality of the leader, Atal Bihari Vajpayee. He decided to put on the back burner the contentious issues and evolve a National Agenda. Regional parties opposed to the Indian National Congress, felt that they had little to fear from the BJP so far their own base was concerned finally decided to come under the unbrella of the National Democratic Alliance.

The 13th Lok Sabha elections were contested on the NDA manifesto, the BJP having tactically decoded to have none of its own agenda. It selected its allies carefully this time, and the alliance paid dividends. The Congress realised much later that it did not have the appeal to earn enough seats that would enable the party to form a government on its own strength. Halfway through the elections, the

Congress party also decided to form coalitions but by this time it had very little choice left.

Unnerved by the success and mass appeal of the NDA, the left parties decided to be with the Congress where it had nothing to show. As a last ditch effort the Congress did ally with Laloo Prasad in Bihar and Jayalalitha in Tamil Nadu. Laloo's charisma had faded and he, himself, lost the election. The AIADMK was humbled by the DMK. And the Congress tally in the Lok Sabha dropped down to an all time low.

The NDA had come out with a comfortable majority. It formed the government much to the humiliation of the Indian National Congress. Surprisingly the INC insists on ascribing this failure to everything except its charismatic president, Sonia Gandhi. The party had tried to project people like Manmohan Singh who might lead the government but he also lost the election to the BJP stalwart Vijay Kumar Malhotra. So the party has once again fallen back to its only charismatic Sonia Gandhi who won both elections and now would be in the Lok Sabha functioning on her own. Her performance as Leader of the Opposition will hereafter determine the prospects of Congress in the years to come.

It is difficult to draw generalisations from the results. All the same, performance as perceived by the voters has emerged as the most contributing factor. Incumbency seems to have lost relevance. The BJP is now acceptable in almost all parts of the country while the Congress has revived in States like Uttar Pradesh and Karnataka. The country needs a stable and performing government. The future of the country and the NDA allies will depend upon performance as there is no substitute for good governance. Atal Bihari Vajpayee, who has taken the oath third time in less than four years, as Prime Minister (though he accepted in his book '*Decisive Days*' that it is difficult to run coalition government) has to match now his performance skills with his oratory. The voters have given their verdict. Now it is for the political parties to live upto their expectations and show results.

A book of this nature has to rely on a number of secondary sources. While all possible efforts have been made to give correct and objective data, it is possible that some minor error might have crept in inadvertently for which we crave the indulgence of the readers. While presenting this book, we have taken help from a large number of books, newspapers, magazines, information agencies and individuals. Their list is too long but we are thankful to all of them.

J.C. Aggarwal
N.K. Chowdhry

Contents

4 *Poll Miscellany*

33 - 40

5 *Constituency-wise Results*

Analysis and Comments

41 - 115

6 *Last Election of the Millennium*

Records, Analysis and Highlights

116 - 139

List of Tables

Abbreviation

AC	Arunachal Congress
AIADMK	All India Anna Dravida Munnetra Kazhagam
AGP	Asom Gana Parishad
AIIC(S)	All India Indira Congress (Secular)
ASDC	Autonomous State Demand Committee
BJP	Bharatiya Janata Party
BSP	Bahujan Samaj Party
CPI	Communist Party of India
CPM	Communist Party of India (Marxist)
DMK	Dravida Munnetra Kazhagam
FBL	All India Forward Bloc
HPDP	Hill State People's Democratic Party
HVP	Haryana Vikas Party
INC	Indian National Congress
JD	Janata Dal
JKN	Jammu & Kashmir National Conference
JMM	Jharkhand Mukti Morcha
JP	Janata Party
KEC	Kerala Congress
KEC(M)	Kerala Congress (M)
MAG	Maharashtrawadi Gomantak
MNF	Mizo National Front
MPP	Manipur People's Party
MUL	Muslim League Kerala State Committee
NTRTDP (P)	NTR Telugudesam Party (Lakshmi Parvathi)
PMK	Pattali Makkal Katchi
RPI	Republican Party of India
RSP	Revolutionary Socialist Party
SAD	Shiromani Akali Dal
SAP	Samata Party
SDF	Sikkim Democratic Front
SHS	Shivsena
SP	Samajwadi Party
TDP	Telugu Desam Party
TMC(M)	Tamil Maanila Congress (Moopanar)
UDP	United Democratic Party
UGDP	United Goans Democratic Party

1

Dissolution of the Twelfth Lok Sabha

The Background

In the twelfth Lok Sabha the Bharatiya Janata Party (BJP) had 179 members at the time of constitution of the Lok Sabha. Atal Bihari Vajpayee was sworn in as the Prime Minister on March 19, 1998 with the support of more than twelve political parties.

The BJP-led Coalition Government survived till April 17, 1999. It had a tough time pleasing and displeasing its allies, some of whom made demands which were in some cases extremely unreasonable.

The Villain of the Fall

The maximum friction in operation came from Ms. Mamata Banerjee of West Bengal Trinamul Congress (7 members) and Ms. Jayalalitha of AIADMK (18 members). While Mamata Banerjee clamoured for special treatment to West Bengal from outside the government, the AIADMK wanted the dismissal of DMK government in Tamil Nadu. More than that Ms. Jayalalitha wanted corruption cases against her and other party members to be dropped or at least be soft pedalled.

Handling Mamata Banerjee was mostly within manageable limits. But, meeting Ms. Jayalalitha's demands was near impossible. BJP had to look far beyond a doubtful five year stay in government at the mercy of AIADMK supremo. It had all along stood in opposition to the use of Art. 356 for dismissing rival State governments.

Jayalalitha had already started feeling the heat. The noose around her was getting tighter. Atal Bihari Vajpayee could not oblige. So she was compelled to seek some other alliance.

Subramaniam Swamy arranged a meeting between two ambitious leading ladies, Sonia Gandhi and Jayalalitha over a cup of tea, in Delhi. Jayalalitha not only announced this meeting a political tremor but also ensured it to be so. On April 14, 1999, she met the President and declared that her party was no longer supporting the BJP led coalition Government.

Leaders of the Left parties, other opposition parties and Sharad Pawar as leader of the Opposition in Lok Sabha called on the President and asked Mr. Narayanan to ask Vajpayee to seek Vote of Confidence.

The Lok Sabha was being reconvened on April 15, '99. It was clear that in case a vote of confidence was not sought, there would be endless opposition. Accordingly on April 15, the Prime Minister moved a motion and briefly asked the Opposition to spell out how it had ensured alternative arrangements. Mr. Laloo Prasad Yadav said that the alternative would be forged in one minute (earlier he had said five minutes).

The crucial confidence vote was held on April 17. The BJP lost the motion by one vote.

The Main Characters in the Drama

Saifuddin Soz, the National Conference Member of Parliament from J&K, defied the party directive and brought down the BJP led Coalition Government at the Centre. His one vote cast 'at the call of his conscience' dealt the stunning blow. Only last year, the National Conference had bailed out the BJP during the trust motion by abstaining from voting. Soz was one of the three members of National Conference who had abided by the directive from Farooq Abdullah. However, this time he had different feelings. BJP could not be backed being a communal party. National Conference, as representative of the people of J&K, could not compromise on its basic ideal of secularism as the State had joined India for its secular character.

'Kashmiri Muslims can hold their head high, now that they have thrown communalists out of power'. The NC, however, did not subscribe to Soz's conscience voting. He ought to have resigned the day the party aligned itself with the BJP and sought fresh mandate from the people.

Saifuddin was keen to carve out a constituency for himself among Indian Muslims. Today he stands expelled from the NC.

Farooq Abdullah had his reasons for aligning with the BJP. He said, "We cannot afford a confrontation with the Centre being a small State with little resources and heavily dependent on Central assistance for security and development."

Soz's parting of ways with the NC had more to do with the losing popularity of the party. In the 1998 eletions, he just managed to win from the Baramullah constituency. The people of Kashmir were no longer lured by the autonomy plank on which the NC had fought the 1996 elections.

Girdhar Gomang was a memeber of the Lok Sabha but had taken over as Chief Minister of Orissa in February. In a similar situation, the Chief Minister of Bengal, Siddharth Shankar Roy had not been allowed to vote in the House even though he continued to be a Member of Parliament (MP).

There was a long debate about his right to vote as an MP. Finally the Speaker ruled that he would leave it to the conscience of Gomang. Since Gomang had come to the House just to cast his vote, he exercised his vote against the government.

Mayawati of BSP artfully dodged the BJP government. She posed as a courteous donor promising that its five MPs would abstain from voting. However, on the crucial day, she voted against the government. That was nothing new for Mayawati. Her philosophy is simple. On its own strength, the BSP can never come to power. So let there be frequent elections. Everytime, there is an election, she and the BSP can go to the Dalits and tell them how they were time and again being fooled by the Manuwadis.

Ms. Jayalalitha the AIADMK supremo with eighteen members had just one point agenda. The Centre ought to dismiss her rival, the DMK government in Tamil Nadu. At the back of this demand lay the fact that the noose had been tightening around her neck for nearly forty corruption cases lodged against her and the AIADMK leaders. It is alleged that having failed to secure the dismissal of the DMK government, she withdrew her party support to the Vajpayee-led coalition Government.

Withdrawal Symptoms

1998

March : Jayalalitha delays for three days her letter of support because she wants Subramaniam Swamy as the Finance Minister. Jaswant Singh rushes to Chennai. She relents.

April : Jaya refuses to attend meeting of the coordination committee when Sedapatti Muthiah is told to resign after charges were framed against him by a court. She has Buta Singh from the Cabinet but fails to get R.K. Hegde's and Jethmalani's heads.

July : Jaya says Advani is a security threat and suffers from selective amnesia. She says L.K. Advani, Home Minister had, in the runup to the polls, promised to dismiss the DMK Government, George Fernandes, Defence Minister molifies her.

August : Government is warned of serious consequences if the original Cauvery accord is not notified. Despite this, Cauvery accord is reached among riparian States. Fernandes and Pramod Mahajan are sent to buy peace with Jaya, who appeared set to pull out with her TN allies, the PMK, MDMK, Janata Party and TRC. She does not withdraw. But a few days later she accuses a PMO functionary (without naming him) of being bribed by a newspaper baron to transfer ED chief Bezbaruah.

September : Snubs the Prime Minister in Chennai by skipping the birth anniversary celebrations of Dravidian leader Annadurai, organised by the MDMK.

December : AIADMK participates in the all India strike sponsored by Left and other Opposition parties.

1999

February : Corruption cases against her and associates are transferred by the Centre from three special judges to other courts to placate her. But the peace is shortlived. She challenges the Government on the dismissal of Navy Chief, Vishnu Bhagwat.

March : Jaya demands the reinstatement of Bhagwat, a JPC probe into the Bhagwat/ Fernandes issue and the shifting of Fernandes to a "less sensitive" Ministry.

April 3 : Announces that Government has to accede to her three demands for continued support. All her demands are rejected.

April 14 : President is handed a letter saying that AIADMK no longer supports the Vajpayee Government.

The Congress party had all along been declaring that it was not interested in destabilising the government. Once AIADMK withdrew support, Congress was the first to ask for Vajpayee's resignation.

The countdown came on April 17. High drama had preceded the final moment.

Voting Pattern on Confidence Motion

Those voting against —	**270**	**Those voting in favour —**	**269**
Congress	137	BJP	182
CPM	32	Samata	12
SP	20	Telugu Desam	11
AIADMK	17	BJD	9
RJD	16	Akali Dal	8
CPI	8	Trinamool	7
Janata Dal	6	DMK	6
RSP	5	Shiv Sena	6
BSP	5	PMK	4
RPI	4	INDL	4
TMC	3	MDMK	3
FB	2	Lok Shakti	3
IUML	2	National Conference	2
Janata	1	Maneka Gandhi	1
Majlis (Oai)	1	TRC (Ramamurty)	1
ASDC	1	RJP (Anand)	1
Arunachal Con (M)	1	Arunachal Cong	1

AIIC (Ola)	1	HVP	1
SJP	1	SDF	1
NC (Soz)	1	Independents	3
Kerala Cong	1	(Satnam Singh, Lallungmauna and S. Biswamuthiary)	
UMF	1		
Buta Singh	1	MSCP	1
PWP	1	Nominated	2

R. Muthiah of AIADMK did not vote, Kim Gangte (CPI) and Kalti Devi (RJD) were absent.
Total stength-544, including Speaker, vacancies-2.

The BJP did not disclose till the end how it would forge the required majority, Many developments took place between the arrival of Ms. Jayalalitha in Delhi and the day of final voting.

Harkrishan Singh Surjeet had assumed the role of the principal architect of the toppling game. He took the Opposition or at least the parties that were with the Left for granted. This was offence enough for the DMK and the BJP was quick to exploit DMKs anger. DMK had other compulsions too. If an alternative coalition was to be led by the Congress, Ms. Jayalalitha and her AIADMK were bound to occupy important positions in return for what they had done to topple the Vajpayee-led coalition and paving way for the Congress. The DMK could not co-exist with the AIADMK. So the choice for the six member DMK was very limited. It had to support the BJP. TMC was no less opposed to AIADMK. But its leader G.K. Moopanar decided to extend support to Congress even though opposition led by the Congress included the AIADMK.

Indian National Lok Dal with 4 members had withdrawn support to the government on the issue price of Urea. However on April 16, the INLD leader Om Prakash Chautala announced that he had decided to support the BJP government. Two individual members Anand Mohan Singh (Rashtriya Janata Parishad) and Shanker Singh Vaghela walked over to the BJP.

It is beleieved that among those who decided to walkover to the BJP camp included Kalpanath Rai although he was among those who had demanded Vajpayee's resignation a few days earlier.

The TDP of Andhra Pradesh stood by the BJP-led Government.

The National Conference, except for one of its member Saifuddin Soz, stood with the government.

The death blow came from the BSP. It is believed that Ms. Mayawati had contacted with Mrs. Sonia Gandhi on the night of April 16. She believed that if the Congress came to power, the UP government under Kalyan Singh would be toppled by using powers under Art. 356. The Congress had earlier done that over 90 occasions and one more would make no difference to its record.

It is not known what bargain was agreed between the two. What is known is that Ms. Mayawati had only the previous day described both the BJP and the Congress as snakes and cobras.

The BSP with five memebers had, on April 16, decided that it would abstain during the vote of confidence. The fact that she stabbed in the back on the crucial day was her revenge for what had happened to her in Uttar Pradesh at the hands of BJP.

The electronic voting machine first showed 256 votes for the government and 263 for the opposition. The practice of manual voting through slips was then resorted to. A little after 2 P.M. the Speaker declared that the motion of confidence had not been carried through. The government had secured 269 votes against 270 secured by the opposition. The result was not on expected lines and surprised not only the truling front but opposition parties also. Even the common man did not believe it.

Forming an Alternative Government

Sonia Gandhi was authorised by the Congress Party to conduct negotiations with the Opposition leaders after the Vajpayee-led BJP Coalition Government failed to secure the confidence of the Lok Sabha.

She told the President that she had the support of 272 MPs. On April 21, she asked for two days time from R.K. Narayanan, President. But all that she could muster by April 23 was just 233 members.

Mulayam Singh, Samajwadi Party (SP) leader had not disclosed his cards while bringing about the fall of the Vajpayee-led coalition. But once it had been achieved, the opposition was no longer united. Among the United Front members, (the way they had been pulled down by the Congress), bitterness against the Congress was still fresh in memory. Mulayam Singh, on the other hand, was unwilling to commit political harakiri by allowing Congress to form a government of its own and then completely capture his Muslim vote bank in Uttar Pradesh. While BJP was the enemy, Congress was the rival. The SP Secretary Amar Singh was quick to dub Congress as communal. Mrs. Sonia Gandhi had no chance of becoming the Prime Minister succeeding Vajpayee except by allowing partnership in the coalition government. Congress very well knew that it would in such a situation be facing the same difficulties and demands from coalition partners that had made effective functioning difficult for the Vajpayee-led government. Ms. Jayalalitha had already made it known that in return for her support, she would expect favours from the Congress party if it were to be in Government.

Mulayam Singh is one name that stands out when it comes to discussing the strategic miscalculation by the Congress and its inability to muster up 272 MPs to support an alternative Prime Minister.

Much before the confidence vote, the SP, was keen to establish its proprietory claims on 10 Janpath. The party's secretary had sought an appointment with Sonia Gandhi for a suitable date when she would release Mulayam Singh's biography. The fax remained unresponded. That was the first snub.

There were many more subsequent calls to 10 Janpath but none was favoured with a response. The indifference revived the memory of many more snubs that had been cast at the party on earlier occasions. The Congress, at Haridwar, had announced that it would have no truck with a casteist party. The hint was clear and specific. Arjun Singh had dubbed them as 'migratory birds' and more than anything else, Congress at Pachmarhi had declared that it would not support any coalition government. The Congress was only for heading a minority government to which all others were expected to lend support from outside. The SP and Mulayam Singh had no use for such an arrangement.

Matters finally crystalized on April 22. Mulayam Singh made it clear to the power-broker Surjeet of CPI(M) that he would not bow to the dictates of Congress that 'shook' hands by the day and abused them by night'.

The prospects of Congress alone forming government had been sealed. Mulayam Singh was however shrewd enough not to be seen as a spoiler. He would accept a PM from the opposition if he could be controlled. The name suggested was that of Deve Gowda. All other parties in the secular alliance were expected to ratify the proposal. It did not happen and the dissolution of the 12th Lok Sabha now seemed to be a certainty.

The period between April 23 to April 25 had been one of hectic political activity. Various proposals were mooted and even discussed with the President. The Congress Working Committee met late on April 25 and concluded that Mrs. Sonia Gandhi would present the list of 239 MPs who had agreed to support a Congress-led minority government. The final decision would rest with the President.

The CPI(M) politburo, on the same day, rejected the proposal mooted by Ms. Jayalalitha and Mulayam Singh for an alternative government led by the Third Front. The proposal was authorised by V.P. Singh, who was convalescing in London. The Third Front did not have the numbers and therefore rejected the proposal.

Yet another proposal related to the recall of Vajpayee. Media reports indicated that supporters of the BJP led alliance had met the President indicating that they had the support of 270 members and as such should be given another chance to form the government. The view was supported by a number of constitutional experts who met the President and informed him that nothing in the Constitution barred the recall of Vajpayee. However, the President, it is believed told Jaswant Singh that the BJP should acquire more strength. He seemed to be insisting on the number 272 which the BJP was in no position to muster. The curtain was finally rung down.

The Dissolution Final

On April 26, 1999, the following communique was issued by Rashtrapati Bhavan :

The Rashtrapati Bhawan Communique

Consequent on the outcome of the Motion of Confidence in the Council of Ministers which was put to vote in the Lok Sabha on April 17, 1999, Atal Bihari Vajpayee, Prime Minister, submitted his resignation and that of the Council of Ministers to the President, that afternoon. The President accepted the resignation and requested the Prime Minister to continue in office until alternative arrangements were made. The Honourable Speaker met the President later that afternoon and gave him the details of the votes cast by individual MPs.

The same afternoon, the President received, a delegation led by George Fernandes, Convener of the Coordination Committee of the BJP and its allies which put forward its point of view that the President should not appoint a Prime Minister who will not be able to secure a credible majority and will also conceivably, lose the confidence of the House, becoming head of yet another caretaker government. This was followed up, by a letter from George Fernandes enclosing a copy of Resolution adopted at a meeting of the BJP-led Alliance partners and parties asserting that the only viable alliance that could be sworn-in was that led by Atal Bihari Vajpayee.

Intensive consultations: The President began intensive consultations with legal and constitutional experts on April 18, 1999. On April 19, 1999 Prof. P.J. Kurien, MP and Oscar Fernandes, MP met the President and gave him copies of Resolutions of the CPP and the CWC authorising Smt. Sonia Gandhi to take all further action in this regard. The President wrote to Smt. Sonia Gandhi on April 20, 1999 inviting her to hold discussions with him the next day.

In commencing these consultations, the President had two major objectives: (1) the need to avoid ordering a mid-term election and (2) the importance of seeing whether a party, or a combination of parties, could provide a workable, viable alternative government with the prospect of stability for a substantial period of time if not for the remaining term of the Twelfth Lok Sabha.

After her meeting with the President on April 21, 1999, Smt. Sonia Gandhi made a public statement to the effect that the Congress had a total support of 272 MPs and intended to form a government on its own with outside support. She indicated that, as required, she would contact those parties and individuals who were supporting the Congress, obtain letters of support from them, and would be conveying the outcome of her efforts to the President in two days time.

The President's consultations with legal and constitutional experts including the Attorney General for India continued meanwhile. He also held discussions on April 22, 23 and 24, 1999 with the following parties and individuals: H.K.S. Surjeet, general secretary, CPI (M) and Jyoti Basu, Chief Minister, West Bengal, A.B. Bardhan, general secretary CPI, Ms. J. Jayalalitha, general secretary, AIADMK, R.S. Gavai, MP, Ramdas Athawale, M and Prof. Jogendra Kwade, MP (all of Republican Party of India). Debabrata Biswas, general secretary, Amar Roypradhan and Bir Singh Mahato from All India Forward Bloc and Pankaj Jaikishan, general secretary and Debabrata Badopadhyay, Member (Central Committee) from Revolutionary Socialist Party, Mulayam Singh Yadav, president and Amar Singh general secretary Samajwadi Party, Ms Mayawati, Bahujan Samaj Party, Subramaniam Swamy, Janata Party, G.K. Moopanar, president, Tamil Maanila Congress, Buta Singh, MP (LS). Ram Jethmalani, Minister of Urban Affairs and Employment, Laloo Prasad Yadav, president, Rashtriya Janata Dal and Sharad Yadav, president, Janata Dal.

Left support : The leaders of CPI (M) and CPI conveyed to the President their unconditional support to the government led by the Congress. Leaders of the RPI, AIADMK, Janata Party and RJD gave him letters indicating their support to a government led by a Congress. G.K. Moopanar reiterated his party's support to the idea of a Congress-led government.

Mulayam Singh Yadav who called on the President on April 23, 1999 gave a letter stating that his party comprising 20 MPs would not support a government led by the Congress, even as they continued to oppose any government led by the BJP. Representatives of the All India Forward Bloc and the RSP who met the President reiterated their stand of equi-distance from the Congress and the BJP. Mayawati conveyed to the President that the Bahujan Samaj party was watching the situation and would decide at the appropriate time.

Smt. Sonia Gandhi, who had indicated at her first meeting with the President on April 21, 1999 that she would revert in two days, called on the President on April 23, 1999 with a list of 233 MPs belonging to the Congress, led by other parties and individuals, who would extend support for the formation of a Congress government. It was put to her that the number did not add up to the requisite strength. Smt. Gandhi conveyed to the President that she would continue discussions with parties and individuals who voted against the Motion of Confidence on April 17, 1999. She was requested to complete the exercise and convey the outcome thereof to the President as early as possible. On April 24, 1999, Sharad Yadav, President of the Janata Dal conveyed to the President his Party's support to any secular government at the Centre. Jayalalitha also met the President and apprised him of the efforts being made among the non-BJP parties to arrive at an agreement on an alternative government of the Third Front. The President received a call by I.K. Gujral, former Prime Minister, who gave his perspective on the situation. Chandra Shekhar, former Prime Minister conveyed his views by telephone.

BJP, allies' plus Jaswant Singh, Minister of Foreign Affairs, Murasoli Maran (DMK) and Vaiko (MDKM) called on the President and urged upon him the need for the consultations process to (i) conclude early and (ii) include the claim of the BJP and its allies to be invited. The President informed them that (a) the process of consultations would end shortly, and (b) he had an obligation to exhaust the first round of consultations with those who had voted against the Motion of Confidence on April 17, 1999 and after that, if those consultations failed to result in an alternative government, take up the BJP's claim. On Jaswant Singh's enquiry if the ruling alliance would be part of the consultation process if they could show accretion of strength, the President replied in the affirmative.

Congress view : On April 25, 1999 Smt. Gandhi called on the President and informed him that in the time given to her, she had tried her best but had not been able to make much further progress. The president told her that since his search was for a viable government which could secure vote of Confidence in the Lok Sabha, inviting the Congress when its support base in the Lok Sabha remained well short of the ruling coalition's proved strength of 269, was out of the question. Smt. Gandhi also informed him that it was the categorical and unanimous view of the Congress Working Committee that it could not support Third Front Government.

Jyoti Basu, H.K.S. Surjeet and Sitaram Vechury called on the President and explained the CPI (M)'s stand on the question of an alternative government and observed that, under the circumstances, no forward movement for a non-BJP led government was possible.

The Prime Minister met the President at 8.40 pm on April 25, 1999. The President conveyed to him that (a) the non-BJP parties had not succeeded in coming up with an alternative; and (b) no accertion in the number supporting the BJP-led alliance had been brought to his notice either. He gave the Prime Minister his assessment that the Twelfth Lok Sabha was not capable of yielding a government with a reasonable prospect of stability.

The recourse to dissolution on the defeat of a minority/coalition government arises when it appears to the President that a stable government cannot be formed without a general election. Dissolution is indicated if an alternative government with working majority which can be expected to carry on for a reasonable period of time is not feasible. The President informed the Prime Minister that in his perception the dissolution of the Twelfth Lok Sabha had therefore become necessary.

The Prime Minister responded by saying that he would discuss the position in Cabinet the following day.

Cabinet recommendation : The Cabinet met at 12 noon on April 26, 1999 and recorded a Minute recommending to the President that he may dissolve the Twelfth Lok Sabha so that a fresh mandate could be obtained from the people as early as possible. The minute converged with the President's own analysis of the situation.

The President could not but observe that the ruling alliance had lost its majority because of a lack of cohesion within its ranks when trying to form an alternative government. In this situation, the President reached the conclusion that the time had arrived for the democratic will of the people to be ascertained once again, so that a government can be formed which can confidently address the urgent needs of our people.

The President has, by presidential order under sub-clause(b) of clause 2 of Article 85 of the Constitution of India dissolved the Twelfth Lok Sabha today.

The official notification in respect to the date for the constitution of the new Lok Sabha will, in accordance with the recommendations of the Election Commission, be published in due course. The President wishes to thank legal and consitutional experts, political leaders and others who have given him their valuable advice and suggestions.

Search for an Alternative : The Plan and Why it Misfired

It was a little after 2 p.m. that the Speaker announced the result of the confidence vote - 269 votes for the government and 270 for the opposition. The immediate consequence was that the Cabinet met and decided to submit its resignation to the President which the latter accepted.

The Congress had been toying with the idea of leading a government. After a great deal of thought, the Congress arrived at the conclusion that it had three alternatives:

First, a Congress government, possibly led by Mrs. Sonia Gandhi with the outside support of all the opposition parties;

Second, allow someone like Deve Gowda, to head a government of the opposition with outside support from the Congress;

Third, a Congress-led coalition government.

To bring round the opposition parties, who might be wavering on the account of there being no definite alternative arrangement, Arjun Singh who had emerged as the closest adviser of the Congress president in this matter, told the media on April 16 that the Congress would not be averse to forming a coalition government. This was presumed to satisfy diverse elements like the RLM, which fears that the Congress Party is trying to poach on its monopoly of Muslim vote in Uttar Pradesh and Bihar, the AIADMK supremo, Ms. Jayalalitha and her closest adviser, Subramaniam Swamy and Ms. Mayawati of the BSP whom perhaps Arjun Singh had in view in his April 16 pronouncement, although the turn-around of the BSP came subsequently.

From the beginning, the Congress Party which generally believes that it has a divine right to rule India, has been feeling like fish out of water, having to support two United Front Governments from outside in 1996 and 1997 and sit in the opposition in 1998 and part of 1999, has been willing to wound but afraid to strike. Its postures that the party did not want to destabilise the Vajpayee government was not taken at its face value at least by the BJP, because it was always waiting for the AIADMK to pull out of the alliance.

Finally, when Ms. Jayalitha obliged the Congress Party, the leaders of the Congress decided to take the plunge and join hands with the opposition in mounting the toppling operation. All the while, the leaders of the Congress were conscious of the fact that the party had serious differences with a number of opposition bloc in the Lok Sabha, wanted the Congress to lead an alternative government and Surjeet and Jyoti Basu, West Bengal Chief Minister and one of the top leaders of the CPI-M had been repeatedly urging Mrs. Sonia Gandhi to take the initiative in the matter.

The CPI had been going alongwith the CPI-M although it had differences with the radical and larger Communist partner. However, the two small parties, the Revolutionary Socialist Party, RSP and the Forward Bloc, FB, which were members of the Left group and had seven members between them in the Lok Sabha, were as much opposed to the Congress as to the BJP. They voted with the opposition in throwing out the government, but made repeated pronouncements of their opposition to a Congress government. Surjeet was believed to be active in persuading the two recalcitrant parties.

The Uttar Pradesh group of Mulayam Singh Yadav's Samajwadi Party, was at loggerheads with the Congress because it regarded the Congress as stealing its Muslim vote in the State which is crucial in several constituencies. Often, Mulayam Singh had said that the Congress was his enemy number one and there had been open clashes between him and the UP Congress chief, Salman Khursheed. Laloo Prasad Yadav, on the other hand, thought he was less vulnerable because the Congress had not made much headway in his Bihar State, although the local Congress was opposed to Laloo Prasad's RJD and his wife's government, as much as the Congress in West Bengal and Kerala were opposed to the local CPI-M.

The hardest nut to crack was perhaps the AIADMK of Ms. Jayalalitha who wanted her pound of flesh in the form of important portfolios for herself and her supporters in the AIADMK and for Subramaniam Swamy. If they were not satisfied with the arrangement, Ms. Jayalalitha could pull down the Congress government any time as she had done in the case of Vajpayee.

So far as Ms. Mayawati was concerned, she had said that she would support the government of the Congress Party from outside. The question was what reliance one could place on her word. Congress would find it difficult to accommodate her in Uttar Pradesh where her price would be the head of Kalyan Singh.

There were pitfalls in forming a coalition government which seemed to be the only viable of the three alternatives before the Congress Party. The Deve Gowda alternative could not be used because it would recall what happened to Chandra Shekhar in 1991 when Mrs. Sonia Gandhi's husband, Rajiv Gandhi, had withdrawn support in just four months after instigating Chandra Shekhar to break away from the Janata Dal of V.P. Singh and form a separate government. As for forming a Congress government with the opposition supporting it from outside, Mulayam Singh Yadav and Ms. Jayalalitha would not at all agree to the arrangement because Yadav wanted the Defence portfolio and Ms. Jayalalitha another important portfolio like Home or External Affairs.

Mrs. Sonia Gandhi, had staked her claim and said that she had the support of 272 members in a House of 543, including the Speaker, which could mean that the Congress had majority support. She asked for two days' time on April 21 from the President, but on April 23, she was only able to claim the support of 233 members. When she met the media after her first meeting with Mr. Narayanan, she was very enthusiastic about her success and said that Jyoti Basu, West Bengal Chief Minsiter and a top leader of the CPI-M, did not want to become Prime Minister himself and she knew of the difficulties likely to be created by Mulayam Singh Yadav, president of the Samajwadi Party.

Mrs. Gandhi was at that stage trying to form a Congress-led minority government, with the outside support of a number of parties, groups and individuals, among whom were the supporters of the Congress in the confidence vote which the BJP-led governemnt lost on April 17. The options before the Congress, as already explained, were either to form a minority Congress Government with outside support of the Left, RLM and other groups; formation of a Congress coalition which would make it possible for people like Ms. Jayalalitha and Subramaniam Swamy as well as Mulayam Singh Yadav to participate in the government; or finally, in a repetition of the 1996-97 United Front experiment, the Congress supporting from the outside a United Front government led possibly by Jyoti Basu of the CPI-M.

The Congress was determined in the beginning to form a minority government of its own. The Samajwadi Party was completely opposed to this. Mulayam Singh Yadav did not disclose his hand in the beginning. He was one of the strongest in demanding the dismissal of the Vajpayee-led government and was also helping Surjeet and others in egging on Mrs. Sonia Gandhi to take the initiative in toppling the Vajpayee government. It was, therefore, expected by many that he would come forward to support the Congress in its plan to form a government of its own.

The Congress had several reasons for opting for this course of forming its own government with the outside support of what are known as "like-minded parties". One of this was that it had extended support to the United Front governments in 1996 and 1997 and it was now their time to return the compliment. The bitter memories of the withdrawal of support by the Congress first from the Deve Gowda Government and then frcm the Gujral Government of the United Front, were still fresh in the minds of many, but the Congress expected that this would be forgotten.

Old hostility between Yadav and the Congress however came to the fore as it did when the Congress party won the Assembly elections in Delhi, Rajasthan and Madhya Pradesh and threatened to encroach on the Muslim vote bank of Yadav. At that time, Yadav had described the Congress as equally communal as the BJP. In this context, it would be easy to understand Mulayam Singh's attitude towards the Congress and his refusal to allow Mrs. Sonia Gnadhi to become the Prime Minister.

After the Congress had difficulties in gathering support of diverse elements, particularly after the attitude of Mulayam Singh Yadav was known, the BJP and its allies felt that they were not without a chance to form a government once again.

Party managers took the signature of 269 members who had voted for the government in the confidence debate on April 17 and this was forwarded to the President although it was not known who their 270th member was, as claimed by Mr. Pramod Mahajan. Mrs. Sonia Gandhi had the support of 233 members. This meant that of the MPs who voted against the Vajpayee Governemnt, 20 members of the Samajwadi Party, six of the Janata Dal, seven of the RSP and Forward Bloc, five of the BSP, and Chandra Shekhar were all opposed to Mrs. Sonia Gandhi becoming the Prime Minister.

On its part, the BJP had to win over two or three more members or secure the BSP's decision to once more abstain in any trial of strength in the Lok Sabha. Efforts in this direction continued, but the BSP's leader in Parliament, Ms. Mayawati was not expected to lend her support or abstain without extracting a price for that. Her price, was the Chief Ministership of Uttar Pradesh, which Kalyan Singh of the BJP had to vacate.

The President simultaneously carried out consultations with a number of group leaders and perhaps met individuals at their request. The CPI-M leaders, Harkishan Singh Surjeet and Basu who met him on April 21, said they supported the Congress party and this was broadly the line taken by the CPI leader, Bardhan. Laloo Prasad Yadav, president of the RJD and former Chief Minister of Bihar, differed radically with Mulayam Singh Yadav and volunteered to support the Congress party from outside.

On April 21, supporters of the BJP led alliance, headed by L.K. Advani, the Home Minister and including all the allies of the BJP-led government, with the DMK also present, met the President and indicated that they had support of 270 members and should be reckoned as a likely formation for forming a new government.

A number of Constitutional experts, some of whom met the President also, expressed the view that there is nothing in the Constitution which prevents him from calling Vajpayee again if he can prove the support of a majority of the Lok Sabha.

There was resentment in a substaintial section of the political spectrum as well as the media over the President giving what is considered a long rope to the Congress and in particular giving Mrs. Sonia Gandhi some more time after the end of her two-day period on April 23.

In retrospect it may be said that the President was only keen to avoid another election so soon. He wanted to explore all possibilities before he came to the conclusion that fresh elections to the Lok Sabha were inevitably the only alternative. There was no constitutional bar to Vajpayee being called to form the government after he had once resigned. There was the precedent of Gujarat (1970) when the Congress (0) government was reinstated by the Governor after the Chief Minister had resigned. But the BJP was unable to satisfy the President that they had the requisite number. Media reports suggest that the President would have expected anything around 272 rather than 270.

The Congress had been able to muster just 239 M.Ps. The President had no options left. A mid-term poll remained the only alternative. All manoeuvers for a non BJP led majority had failed.

Why did the plan misfire? The question has been debated at length.

Much before the AIADMK supremo decided to part company with the BJP led alliance, the AICC spokespersons parted day after day that 'Congress would not destabilise the government. Sonia Gandhi's original plan was to take up first the much neglected task of internal organisational consolidation. The idea was that once the party had succeeded in repairing its internal cracks, it would be in a better position to face the coming State Assembly elections particularly in Andhra and Karnataka. This strategic course, the Congress could not follow. Ms. Jayalalitha deflected the party. The Congress cadres did not have the patience to wait. They saw Ms. Sonia Gandhi as a very ordinary politician. Subsequent events confirm that rather than Jayalalitha's anger, it was the Congress and their President that were perceived as agents of destabilisation.

Could the polls be held earlier? Atal Bihari Vajpayee had this to say in his interview to Outlook.

When do you think the mid-term polls should be held—June or September?

They should be held as quickly as possible. And the earliest is June.

Do you prefer a June election or will you leave it to the Election Commission?

We prefer a June election. And we feel that the Election Commission will/should also reach the same decision.

But will the revision of electoral rolls be over by then?

If it isn't, it can be stopped. This has been done in the past. Polling is possible in June. Otherwise I will be running a lame-duck government for too many months.

Isn't it going to be terrible hot in June?

Yes, it will be hot but elections have been held in June earlier. People can come and vote in the morning and evening (when it is relatively cooler) and the polling time can also be extended late into the evening.

The Congress is saying that you want an early poll to take advantage of the 'sympathy factor'...

And those who are opposing it are doing so to prevent us from getting any advantage of this sympathy wave !

What's your feeling? Is there a sympathy wave in your favour? What's your feedback?

Log dukhi hain, with the manner in which the government was toppled. Our feedback is that people believe the government was removed through manipulation. By one chief minister's vote who shouldn't have been there, at that. And that this should not have happened.

But isn't it a fact that the Congress will make stability an issue and say that 'look, no non-Congress government can last its term?

People have seen what kind of government the Congress has provided. And anyway, the Congress has toppled the governments which have gone over the last few years—Chandra Shekhar, Deve Gowda, Gujral. In fact, they have created the instability.

State Assmbly election results have given the message to the political parties in very certain terms 'Perform or Perish'.

2
Events and Manifestos

The Trailor—Assembly Elections in Four States

In the Lok Sabha elections 1998, the BJP had led in as many as 330 of the total 620 Assembly segments that went to the polls on November 25, 1998. However, their overall tally in a State like MP plunged to a pathetic 120.

What went wrong with the BJP, a party that has perpetually forged ahead in the political horizon after 1984? The fact that the BJP,.to its credit, has political stalwarts like Atal Bihari Vajpayee, L.K. Advani, Jaswant Singh, Yaswant Sinha et al, who enjoy unsullied reputation not only among the people but strangely among their political foes also, needs no further elaboration. At the same time, what emerged manifestly as a major factor contributing to their defeat is that the BJP had taken the people for granted.

The euphoria that swept the nation receded within months after the BJP assumed power, when people in the capital had to live without water and electricity for days together. That apart, there was a growing sense of insecurity among the Delhiites following regular bomb blasts, including the one in front of the Police Headquarters. Third, the overall price rise in vegetables and mustard oil made the common man's life difficult. It is a warning to all the political parties as a whole that there can be no straying from issues that affect the common man.

The disenchantment with BJP was reflected in a characteristic way: In Delhi, the BJP, seat strength plummeted to 15 from 49 whereas in Rajasthan it was 33 from 96. In Madhya Pradesh it could muster only 120 seats. In sharp contrast, the Congress increased its tally in Delhi from 14 to 51, in Rajasthan it was up from 76 to 150 and, surprisingly, it added one more seat in MP, taking its total to 173. Conversely, in Mizoram, the Congress tally was 6 out of the Assembly strength of 40.

In three of the four States—Delhi, Rajasthan, Madhya Pradesh and Mizoram where elections were held on November 25, 1998—new leaders were sworn-in as Chief Ministers following the shift in power after the Assembly elections, which was termed as mini-general elections.

Ms. Sheila Dikshit, who swept the Congress (I) to a comfortable position, was made the Chief Minister of Delhi. The 61-year-old Ms. Dikshit is the fifth Chief Minister and the first woman Congress Chief Minister of the Union Territory. A product of Miranda House, Delhi University, she was the first preference of the Congress President, Ms. Sonia Gandhi. Ms. Dikshit is a seasoned politician. Earlier, she was the Minister of State for Parliamentary Affairs in Rajiv Gandhi Cabinet.

In Madhya Pradesh, the Congress put up a spectacular performance under the leadership of Digvijay Singh, who became Chief Minister for the second consecutive term. He was administered the oath of office and secrecy by Governor, Bhai Mahavir on December 1, 1998. Singh 52, is the 21st Chief Minister of the State. He had taken over as the Chief Minister for the first time in December 1993 after an extended spell of the President's Rule in the State in the wake of post-Ayodhya riots.

Ashok Gehlot, Rajsthan PCC (I) President, who led the party to an impressive victory, was sworn-in as the new Chief Minister of the State. Gehlot, 47 has the distinction of holding the office of PCC chief for the third consecutive term, honesty and simplicity being his hallmark. Gehlot was picked up by late prime minister Rajiv Gandhi as a youth leader. The State Governor, N.L. Tibrewal administered the oath of office to Gehlot on December 1, 1998.

In Mizoram, the Mizo National Front (MNF) President Zoramthanga was sworn-in as the Chief Minister of Mizoram, on December 3, 1998 Zoramthanga is the leader of the United Legislature Party comprising the MNF and Mizoram People's Conference (MPC).

Table 2.1 : Assembly Poll Outcome 1998

State	Congress		BJP		Janata Dal		Independent and Others	
	1993	1998	1993	1998	1993	1998	1993	1998
*Delhi (70)	14	51	49	15	4	1	3	2
**Rajasthan (200)	76	150	96	33	6	3	22	11
Madhya Pradesh (320)	174	173	117	120	11	11 (BSP)	18	16
Mizoram (40)	18	6	14	21 (MNF)	0	12 (MPC)	8	1 (Ind)

*Elections held 69 seats.
**Elections held 197 seats.

The Poll Process

Table 2.2 : Time Table for 1999 Elections

Poll Date	Number of Constituencies going for polling	Last date for filing nominations	Last date for withdrawal of candidature
Sep 5	146	Aug 18	Aug 21
Sep 11	20*	Aug 19	Aug 23
Sep 11	103	Aug 24	Aug 27
Sep 18	79	Aug 28	Sep 1
Sep 25	74	Sep 6	Sep 9
Oct 3	11**	Sep 10	Sep 17
Oct 3	110	Sep 14	Sep 17

*20 constituencies in Kerala
**11 constituencies in Orissa

Table 2.3 : No. of Poll Days in States/UTs

States/UTs	No. of poll days
AP, Bihar, J&K	Three
MP and UP Karnataka, Maharashtra, Manipur Orissa, Rajasthan and Tamil Nadu	Two
All other States and UTs	One

Table 2.4 : Lok Sabha Election Schedule

States and	Sep				Oct	States and	Sep				Oct
Union Territories	5	11	18	25	3	Union Territories	5	11	18	25	3
Andhra Pradesh (42)	13	15	14			Nagaland (1)				1	
Arunachal Pradesh (2)					2	Orissa (21)				10	11
Assam (14)					14	Punjab (13)	13				
Bihar (54)			19	19	16	Rajasthan (25)	10	15			
Goa (2)	2					Sikkim (1)					1
Gujarat (26)	26					Tamil Nadu (39)	19	20			
Haryana (10)	10					Tripura (2)					2
Himachal Pradesh (4)				4		Uttar Pradesh (85)			30	24	31
Jammu & Kashmir (6)	2	2	2			West Bengal (42)					42
Karnataka (28)	15	13				A & N Islands (1)	1				
Kerala (20)		20				Chandigarh (1)	1				
Madhya Pradesh (40)		14	14	12		Dadra & Nag. Hav. (1)	1				
Maharashtra (48)	24	24				Daman & Diu (1)	1				
Manipur (2)				1	1	Delhi (7)	7				
Meghalaya (2)				2		Lakshadweep (1)					1
Mizoram (1)				1		Pondicherry (1)	1				

Total number of constituencies: 543.
Figures in brackets indicate number of constituencies.

The unduly long span gave the surveys and exit polls a free run. Did the results of such poll surveys exercise influence on voting patterns for elections held on a subsequent date remains debateable.

Promises Galore—The Election Manifestos

Stability—The Common Factor

The election manifestos issued by the various political parties for the General Elections 1999 were unique in more than one way.

Garibi Hatao was no longer the popular slogan. All political parties seemed to have realised the futility of promising square meals for all. Nor was there any focus on affordable shelters, leave aside housing for the millions without a roof over their heads. The emphasis was on stability. The contenders seemed to be contended with continuing in the playfield for all time rather than scoring goals.

The BJP this time was part of the National Democratic Alliance. There was no separate manifesto issued by the BJP although later it was realised that there should have been one. Repeatedly, on different forums the BJP was grilled on its oft repeated promises and issues—Ram Mandir, Common Civil Code and the integration of the State of Jammu and Kashmir. Everytime the answer was that the BJP agenda was the same as the National Agenda of the NDA.

The composition of NDA was explained by Outlook in its August 16 issue in the following words:

Composition of the National Democratic Alliance

Once upon a time, there was a BJP. The Shiv Sena, its only "natural ally". Then the Akali Dal signed on—two "communal" forces being better than one. The socialists, Fernandes leading the Samata Party and Hegde the Lok Shakti, walked into their parlour to fight their own demons (Laloo and Deve Gowda) better. Likewise, the Mamata-led Trinamool Congress, the devil in her case being the CPI (M). The alliance acquired the looks of a winner, so the Dravidian parties decided to take turns; first the AIADMK was a partner and now the DMK has taken its place with the MDMK, PMK and TRC in tow. The same is true of Haryana where Bansi Lal hopped on, later replaced by Om Parkash Chautala's INLD. The smaller parties gravitated towards the party in power—the Arunachal Congress and National Conference are prime examples—as did independents and one-man parties. Come elections '99 this flexifront called BJP plus allies was rechristened the NDA. But the number of its constituents keeps changing. Take Mamata, a "friend" of the NDA and in a poll tie-up with BJP, but her resignation from the NDA still holds. The Telegu Desam, now in secret parleys with the BJP, supported Vajpayee in Parliament and has occasionally sent representatives to NDA meets without being an official constituent. Even if there is no agreement on seats, it is certain to bail out the BJP if needed. The AGP, which supports the BJP, wasn't included mainly because it won no seats in the '98 polls. Allies like the JBSP and Loktantrik Congress in UP, the Himachal Vikas Party and the MGR ADMK and MGR Kazhagam in Tamil Nadu as well as some of the smaller parties from the Northeast like the Manipur Congress may have to be inducted if they win seats and demand a place. For a party that once revelled in its "splendid isolation", the BJP's come a long, long way.

The Congress Election Manifesto

The Congress highlighted 'stability and experience'. There were old repeated promises with the hope that the electorate would continue to take those promises seriously even though those promises were rarely redeemed when the Congress Party had been in power for over four decades.

The Congress came down heavily on coalition governments. These were termed as opportunistic and unprincipled.

The Press briefing after the formal release of the Manifesto was reported by *The Times of India* in the following words :

Talking to the press after the release of the manifesto, Ms. Sonia Gandhi left the issue of party's prime ministerial candidate open. In fact, at the manifesto release function, she gave the pride of place to Manmohan Singh, giving the impression that he could be elected Prime Minister if the Congress came to power.

Apparently to take the wind out of the BJP's campaign against her foreign origin, Ms. Gandhi seems to be projecting Dr. Manmohan Singh, who has been made the party candiate from South Delhi constituency even though he is a Rajya Sabha member. Deviating from past practice, no working committee member was present with the Congress president on the dais, except Shivraj Patil, chairman of the manifesto committee, Pranab Mukherjee, chairman publicity committee, and Dr. Manmohan Singh.

Asked why the Congress was not projecting her as the prime ministerial candidate, Ms. Gandhi said: "I have said it before and am saying it again that after the elections, Congress Members of Parliament will choose the prime ministerial candiate."

The manifesto promised to promote secularism, create one crore new jobs annually, enact a new reservation law to end ambiguities, strengthen panchayati raj institutions and double annual expenditure on poverty alleviation and social development.

The coalition experiment, according to the Congress, was bereft of ideology, adding that such a government was riddled with intra-party and inter-party differences. "The choice is between a coalition that has failed miserably and a cohesive Congress alternative," it added.

If the election results are any indicators, the Congress over-estimated its capacity to come to power on its own strength. State Assembly elections held nine months ago were treated as trailor. Unluckily for the Congress, the trailor had been a hit but the real show flopped.

The NDA Manifesto

Three days later the NDA came out with its manifesto. It proposed a five year term as fixed for all elected bodies along with a legislation to prevent foreign born Indians from holding high offices.

There was the promise to set up the Lok Pal with adequate powers to bring even the office of the Prime Minister under its purview.

There was also the proposal to replace the existing provision of no-confidence motion with the German type system of 'constructive vote of non-confidence.'

The promise of a new law to ensure that "the high offices of State—legislative, executive and judicial—are held only by natural(ly) born Indian citizens" seemed to be a direct response to demands from within the BJP-led alliance to bar Congress president Sonia Gandhi from becoming Prime Minister in future. The manifesto promised electoral reforms to check defections, corruption and criminalisation of politics and to prevent electoral malpractices.

A National Judicial Commission would be set up to recommend judicial appointments in the high courts and the Supreme Court and to draw up a code of ethics for the judiciary.

If elected to office, the NDA will appoint a commission to review the Constitution "in the light of the experiences and developments since 1996". Blaming the previous governments for the "neglect" of the defence sector, the manifesto proposed to correct the "imbalance" and ensure adequate budgetary support to meet the needs of the forces.

"In today's unipolar world, it is of paramount importance that India constantly maintains and strengthens the state of preparedness, morale and combat effectiveness of our armed forces." It recommended the "establishment of a credible nuclear deterrence" as per the advice of the National Security Council.

Addressing another long-pending issue, the NDA agreed to "take effective measures for eliminating all pensionary anomalies" of the defence personnel. The necessary legislative and administrative measures would be adopted to allow proxy voting by the armed forces.

Taking note of the raging revolution in information technology across the globe, the manifesto vowed to make India a "software superpower" and promised a national informatics policy with short, medium and long-term perspectives.

'The NDA commits itself to establishing a civilised, humane and just civil order which does not discriminate on grounds of caste, religion, class, colour, race or sex.'

"We will truly and genuinely uphold and practise the concept of secularism consistent with the tradition of *sarva panth samadara* (equal respect for all faiths) and on the basis of equality of all."

'The interests of SCs, STs and backward classes would be adequately safeguarded through appropriate legal, executive and societal efforts and through large-scale education and empowerment.'

"We will provide legal protection to existing percentages of reservation in government jobs and education institutions at the Centre and state levels.

If required, the Constitution will be amended to maintain the system of reservation." Stating that the NDA was committed to extending the SC/ST reservations for another ten years, the manifesto said that the necessary legislative measures would be taken to sanctify reservation percentages above 50 per cent, as followed by certain states.

Nationalist Congress Party (NCP)

The issue of Sonia's foreign origin had led to a split in the Congress Party. The group led by Sharad Pawar was not reconciled to the idea of her being the Prime Minister over riding the claims of senior party leaders like Pawar himself. P.A. Sangama had joined hands on the issue and the split group formed the Nationalist Congress Party.

The base of the newly formed party was limited to Maharashtra where Pawar had a certain degree of clout, specially with the sugar lobby.

Pawar was keen to maintain its distance from both the parent body, the Congress and the BJP which it termed as 'communal' in no uncertain terms.

The party released its manifesto simultaneously in New Delhi and Mumbai.

Citing Babasaheb Ambedkar as the constitutional authority, the NCP promised that it would take appropriate legal measures to bar person's of foreign origin from accessing top posts of the land.

There were two points similar to the BJP manifesto released earlier. The NCP also promised constitutional amendment to provide a fixed term for the Lok Sabha in order to bring about political stability in the country.

If the BJP advocated the German model, the NCP has said that the country could opt for the Scandinavian model where the Parliament has to first elect the prime minister who will secure majority of the House and then take oath of office. The prime minister shall not be removed from office unless an alternative prime minister is elected first.

The manifesto also suggested electoral reforms based on the recommendations of the Law Commission, especially to secure probity and standards in public life. It also promised transformation of administration into "a neutral, transparent and accountable entity".

Among the other assurances, the NCP promised a separate ministry for the development of the minorities and said that the Minorities Commission will be given constitutional status. The party also assured creation of an exclusive and full-fledged ministry for women's development.

The party took pains to explain why its leaders broke away from the Congress. "Never before in the history of any political party in the country, may be in the world, has any leader with no experience, no track record of public service, having so little understanding of complex national problems, was recipient of such cooperation, support and institutional loyalty, as Ms. Gandhi has been."

However, the NCP lamented that Ms. Gandhi "concentrated all powers in her hands, stifling internal debate in the Congress Working Committee, especially when it came to her own role. Her approach to politics and her style of wielding political authority came as a rude shock".

The NCP particularly blamed Ms. Gandhi for failing to tackle serious issues and taking crucial decisions. It cited as example the manner in which the Vajyapee government was brought down, the way the 12th Lok Sabha came to be dissolved and the country "pushed into yet another costly general elections". The NCP was critical of the BJP as well, accusing it of "communalism and bigotry" and terming the record of the Vajpayee government as "dismal".

It is rightly said that politicians have no interests other than self interest. The post-election developments seem to confirm the dictum. NCP has allied with the Indian National Congress to form the State government in Maharashtra. In Meghalaya Sangama did not hesitate to ally with BJP to settle scores with the Congress.

Alliance with BJP could have put the NCP in power as an ally in Maharashtra and Pawar in the Central cabinet. But Bal Thackery would have nothing to do with Pawar and the BJP could not afford to lose him as an ally.

The DMK

Among the State level parties, the DMK had something exclusive to say in its Manifesto.

It vowed to continuously take steps for scrapping Art. 356. 'It was against the principle of federalism and democracy'.

"Article 356 is merely a carbon copy of Article 35 enacted in 1935 by the British. As a first step, the Centre is duty-bound to immediately amend the article based on the judgement in the Bommai case by the constitution bench of the Supreme Court," the DMK said in its election manifesto.

Reiterating the party's commitment to protect minorities, the manifesto said: "No harm will be caused to anyone due to religious fanaticism and if at all any harm is caused, the DMK will rise to protect the affected and will not be reluctant to make any kind of sacrifice".

The DMK found it unacceptable that reservations were not to exceed 50 per cent and that the economically better-off creamy layer among the backward classes was ineligible for reservation. "These concepts are contrary to social justice. The power to determine percentage of reservation should be delegated to state governments.

The DMK had to be extra cautious in its proclamations. It was part of the BJP led NDA and yet it did not want to be seen as an ally of BJP perceived as anti-muslim in its own State. Similarly, the party had to project itself as the defender of SC/Backward interests. These compulsions were reflected in the manifesto.

Janata Dal

Perpetual divisions had been the fate of the Janata Dal ever since its formation as a distinct political group. This time it was Janata Dal (Secular) emerging as an entity separate from the Janata Dal (U). The Janata Dal (S) had been carved out with the former Prime Minister H.D. Deve Gowda as the nucleus.

The JD(S) promised to provide reservation in government jobs for minorities and Dalit Christians apart from undertaking a special recruitment drive to fill the backlog of reservations for Dalits.

The party said it would align with like-minded forces to build a "self reliant, prosperous, egalitarian and just and secular India". Deve Gowda had told journalists that his party would spring a "surprise" in Karnataka in the polls, but in Parliament it would prefer to sit in the opposition benches after the elections. He said he would confine himself to Karnataka where the party was contesting 224 assembly seats.

The JD (S) promised to allocate 49 per cent of investible resources for agriculture and rural development. The manifesto said the party would provide remunerative prices for agricultural produce on the basis of equitable price balance between agriculture and industrial produce.

A system of insurance of crops and cattle and against natural calamities would be worked out. A scheme to provide compensation for farmers would be worked out and fertiliser subsidy continued and the party would establish a Rs. 500 crore agriculture price stabilisation fund. The party would take a balanced approach towards globalisation process keeping Indian interests in mind, the manifesto stated.

Incidentally, Deve Gowda lost the election. So much for the credibility of his promises to the voters.

The BJP

The BJP, the leading constituent of the NDA had not issued a separate Manifesto. At every forum, its leaders proclaimed that their agenda was the same as that of the NDA.

However on August 30, the BJP dished out its own Manifesto. It decried the Janata Dal for its infighting (in Karnataka) and indifference to development of the State.

The BJP Manifesto was targetted basically for the Karnataka voters.

The Hindustan Times made the following observations in this respect:

The manifesto, while targetting former Prime Minister H. D. Deve Gowda for his alleged interference in the governance of the State, was forced into complete silence on the rule of Chief Minister J. H. Patel.

In fact, the BJP faced embarrassing moments from its own cadres to queries over its relationship with Patel's faction of the Janata Dal. The problem was more acute as the BJP in the last five years, until a few weeks back when Patel joined hands with it, was preparing to go all out against the Patel Government.

According to BJP sources who prepared its manifesto, the release was delayed as the critical references to Patel had to be deleted. At the same time, the Deve Gowda faction needed to be criticised.

The result: a mere paragraph on the alleged faults of Deve Gowda.

Besides this, the BJP in its manifesto promised to improve the infrastructure of the State including power, roads and irrigation for agriculture.

The Economic Programme

With the installation of the NDA government at the centre, the economic programme promised in the Manifesto deserves some special attention. N. Chandra Mohan contrasted the economic policies outlined this time with the agenda for National Governance in 1998.

There were broad elements of continuity between the BJP-led National Democratic Alliance's National Agenda for Governance (NAG) and the NAG of March 1998, the major differences on the economic front were only qualitative in nature. Reflecting the experience of 13 months of governance, the constraints of an overzealous, inward-looking, *swadeshi* brigade's point of view on economic matters were missing in the NAG of 1999.

That document was not an annual budget which could be tinkered with, but was a five-year plan of sorts, as it represented the highest common denominator of objectives behind which the BJP's rainbow coalition of political allies stood united. The tone of 'back to business' as usual was indicated in the vast identical portions of the economic part of NAG of 1998 and 1999.

The big changes in the NAG of 1999 were the forceful declarations that "*swadeshi* is not reinventing the wheel": it meant enabling domestic corporates to compete with MNCs. Domestic trans-nationals should develop. That liberalisation is not something that should be shunned but accepted. India could not do without foreign direct investment (FDI). A target of $10 billion a year of FDI was necessary to commensurate with India's growth objectives. A Fiscal Responsibility Act is necessary.

The NAG of 1999 did not suggest a return to protectionism—in the sense of Ambassador and Fiat cars being protected for four decades and Maruti's for two decades. The tone of NAG 1999 in fact suggests more of a practical middle path: not State versus markets. Not capitalism versus socialism. Not Left or Right. Only that government and industry must work together. There is a fresh section on trade and commerce which stated that India's interests must be robustly asserted at the WTO. The Nobel laureate Amartya Sen's shadow is also obvious in the references to a strategic pro-poor policy which treats those in poverty as a net resource replete with their own ideas and experience.

The Third Front constituents had not much to say. The Left seemed convinced that whatever its ideological compulsions, there was no going back from liberalisation in the country. There was little that it could dish out as an alternative model for the one it had all along stuck to had collapsed in the country of its birth—the USSR. China had started collaborating with US capital and Indian labour had in no State responded to the Communist call. The areas of influence were limited to West Bengal, Tripura and Kerala and as such the Left was in no position to talk about policies that would have an all India appeal. SP and BSP in U.P. had emerged restrengthened but both parties centred round individuals rather than national programmes. Their appeal lay in their personal agendas in the name of castes and not any economic programmes for the country.

Election Manifestos seem to have become more of a ritual than anything of substance in the elections. Local and regional considerations, besides the contestants' personalities weigh in the voters mind much more than the ideology or promises made by the political parties at the national level. The one usefulness of these documents however remains intact. No party can afford a summersault if it comes to power.

3

Issues—Campaign Trail

Performance Ratings and Poll Results of States

There was a flood of poll surveys and exit polls this time. The projection of seats/likely to be won by various political parties was too varied.It also fluctuated from phase I to phase V of the poll. Psephology however came out as a very imperfect science if at all it could be termed as one. The different agencies had varying sample size and did not conform to any established norms. The results were as varying as their methodology and size of samples.

Except for one agency, everyone gave the NDA a majority. There were major upsets as the results came in but the poll pundits had readymade excuses. Astrologers and Satta Bazar worked on their own predictions but the voter defied them all.

One area in which the survey did come out fairly well was the satisfaction level of the voters with the performance of State governments. This was the poll survey conducted by GVL Narsimha Rao of Development and Research Services.

In Andhra Pradesh the satisfaction level was 64%. The party in power, the TDP did well in the Lok Sabha elections. Gujarat had shown a satisfaction level of 57% and the Lok Sabha results were near congruent to these findings.

Madhya Pradesh was out of trend. The satisfaction level recorded was 51% but the results did not bear it out. Tamil Nadu with 51% satisaction level stood by the DMK. Rajasthan was equally disappointing. The satisfaction level was 48% against dissatisfaction at 38%. But the Lok Sabha results did not reflect the survey findings. In West Bengal the dissatisfaction was 44% against 48% satisfaction but this nearly balanced situation did not reflect in the results. The Trinamul Congress and BJP did register gains but not in the proportions reflected in the survey. Maharashtra had given a dissatisfaction level of 49%. The satsifaction level was well below (44%). The ruling party lost giving place to a Congress NCP alliance. Uttar Pradesh had shown a dissatisfaction level of just 51%. It was marginal but the losses in terms of Lok Sabha seats were much higher. Dissatisfaction was also foreseen in Punjab (58%) and this was well reflected in the Lok Sabha results that went against the ruling BJP-Akali coalition. Karnataka voters had shown 61% dissatisfaction and no wonder the Congress came to power with an absolute majority leaving the fractured JD far behind. People were not happy (dissatisfaction level 58%) in Orissa and also in Bihar (dissatisfaction 70%) and the verdict was against the party in power at the State. The survey had also found Atal Bihari's rating as the best leader for the Prime Ministerial post as 57% against Sonia's at only 27% in August. The margin had been reduced later but Vajpayee continued to remain ahead. One did not need psephology to have come to this conclusion.

Sonia Gandhi: The Foreign Origin Factor

Should a person of foreign origin have the right to contest and hold the high office of the Prime Minister? The Congress party regarded it as a non-issue as long as Sonia delivered votes for the party.

The State Assembly elections in which the Congress defeated the incumbent BJP Governments in Rajasthan, and Delhi and retained its position in Madhya Pradesh closed the foreign origin issue so far as her own party was concerened. However Sharad Pawar and the former Speaker P.A. Sangama could not reconcile to the idea. She was acceptable as long as she headed the party. But if she were to be the Prime Minister, there was no scope for their political ambitions.

The BJP, although it did not make much of the issue, did not feel comfortable with the idea of a person of foreign origin becoming the Prime Minister of India. To them it was an insult to the capability of 100 million Indians. Most other Indians too had their reservations although the 1999 elections were in no way a referendum on the issue. Examples from a number of foreign countries can be cited where there is a bar on naturalised citizens holding high offices. In Finland, naturalised citizens can enter Parliament after three years of stay in the country but that is where they have to stop.

Section 5/Art. 2 of the US Constitution provides that only a person born in USA can become the President. He/She must also be 35 years of age and residing on US territory for a minimum of 14 years prior to the date of filing the nomination. However naturalised citizens can get elected to House of Representatives and the Senate after having 7 and 9 years of residence in respective cases.

American Secretary of State, Madeline Albright was born in Czechoslovakia and married to an American. She could be a Secretary but not the President.

Art. 54 of the German Constitution also requires that for election to the office the President, a candidate must be German born, 40 years of age and be qualified to vote for parliamentary elections.

Deepak Obhrai was born to Indian parents in Tanzania. He was educated in India and is an MP in Canada. Herb Dhaliwal is a Canadian Minister Kassem Utteem, the President of Mauritius is a descendant of migrants from eastern Uttar Pradesh.

There are however some conditions peculiar to Sonia. She married an Indian, came to India but retained her Italian citizenship for over a decade till her husband resigned from the job of a pilot in the Indian Airlines. Her name was erroneously entered in the voters list even when she held Italian citizenship and was not even a naturalised citizen of India. The mistake was subsequently corrected.

All through her stay she has remained isolated from the hub of India's main stream. Even when she makes an effort to speak in Hindi, one can make out that she is not natural in her flow of words. Her interaction with the common Indian masses are heavily guarded and limited to what she is required to read or whatever she can see from the helicopter while on an election tour. She has no experience of social work except meetings of the Trusts which she heads by virtue of her family connections. Sonia Gandhi's claim to high offfice is based exclusively on her family connections and the fact that she has been able to put a halt to bickerings at the top. Indian masses have accepted her as the Indian Bahu. Is she entitled to inherit the legacy of the Nehru-Gandhi family or not remains an open question.

The Filth in Electioneering

The 1999 election was marked with near vulgar personal villifications during the campaign. There were no issues to be presented before the electorate. Neither party had anything distinctive to offer. Party propaganda was as such hard hitting as well as mixed with fictional charges to the extent that it was near impossible for the ordinary voter to discriminate between fact and fiction.

The process of hitting the opponents below the belt had become prominent with Sadhvi Rithambra's cassette doing the round during the past BJP election campaign. It had logic and also abuse. 'We are willing to accept them (Muslims) as uncles and cousins but they won't accept we have a common grand father'. So she coined the term *'Babar ki aulad'* referring to Indian Muslims who were not reconciled to their Hindu ancestory.

Even V.P. Singh could not resist the temptation. In his election meetings, he would show a pocket calculator and say 'The secret account number in which Bofors pay offs were deposited in the Swiss Banks are here'.

The BSP had resorted to upper caste bashing with the slogan '*Tilak, Taraju* aur *Talwar* (signifying, Brahmins, Vaishya and the Kshatriyas)—*inko maro jute char'*. The 1999 election, however, touched a new low in personal remarks against the opposing candidates.

In the earlier elections, barring a few examples quoted above, dirty words were limited to the lower rungs of the political parties. The top leaders took care to maintain some standards of decorum even while criticizing their adversaries. This time there were no holds barred and the worst electioneering came from the top. When the press and the EC showed their displeasure, the parties resorted to putting up front organisations that cropped up overnight.

Pramod Mahajan, Minister for Information and Broadcasting had in one of his speeches talked of importing Monica Lewinsky (or for that purpose Bill Clinton or Tony Blair) to run the country, if foreigners could be better trusted. The Congress was quick to say that the comparison was aimed at their leader Sonia Gandhi. Pramod Mahajan denied the allegation but by then the dirty tricks departments in all the political parties had started working over time.

The Congress had put Kapil Sibbal as its spokesman. Sibbal went on to charge the Prime Minister with 'sleeping while the enemy came'. The PM was charged with actively conniving and consorting with the Pakistani invaders, a charge that no Indian would in his senses accept against the BJP or its leader Atal Bihari.

Sonia Gandhi had been counteracting the criticism against her Itlaian origin by repeating that she was married in India, became a widow in India and brought up two children in this country. She did not have much to talk about her contribution to India's social life or participation in poverty alleviation programmes at any level. She had retained her Italian citizenship all along until her husband Rajiv Gandhi left Indian Airlines. As an Indian national she was barely sixteen years old. Defence Minister George Fernandes questioned her candidature by asking, 'What is Sonia Gandhi's contribution to the nation?' He added 'She did contribute two children to the hundred crore population.'

The BJP spokesman Arun Jaitley came up with the apprehension (in case Congress came to power and Sonia became the Prime Minister) 'Next we will have some Kargil intruder wanting to be Prime Minister.' Sonia's explanation about her nationality was that the day she came as a daughter-in-law, she became an Indian. The rest was just a technical question.

The Finance Minister Yashwant Sinha did not want to be seen unconcerned or above the rhetorics. He talked of hereditary prime minsitership—Nehru, Indira and then Rajiv. 'Tomorrow it will be Robert Vadera (Sonia's son-in-law). The Shiv Sena Chief put all poison in his sling. Sonia had been dubbed as a reader while Atal Bihari was hailed as a leader. Her inability to speak without reference to her written speeches was ridiculed by saying, suppose someone replaced one single page of her written speech with a subzi bazar list? She will probably read it out word for word.' The mud slinging was not limited to Sonia. Sharad Pawar was compared to Elizabeth Taylor. 'He marries, divorces, remarries and again divorces'. The barb came from Pramod Mahajan.

Nitish Bhardwaj, who had played Krishna in the popular TV serial was pitted against Laxman Singh (brother of Digvijay Singh) from Raigarh. The Chief Minister wished it was an actress (rather than Nitish) who could have at least 'entertained' his brother.

Biju Janata Dal was the target of attack from Congress in Orissa. The Excise Minister Suresh Kumar Routray touched a new low in his campaign against Naveen Patnaik 'Naveen is neither a man nor a woman. How can you trust somebody who is not even sure of his gender'.

Jayalalitha in Tamil Nadu campaigned against BJP with the song that translated in Hindi meant, 'Oh Vajpayee, you have cheated me/us'. (*Yeamathi poittingale ayya, Vajpayee ayya*).

Karunanidhi hit back with the same level of indecency. 'If a woman says she has been cheated (by a man) we can only draw awkward conclusions'.

In this battle, there seemed to be no exceptions. Jyoti Basu called Mamata a 'lunatic' and in reply Mamata threatened to convert CPI (M) headquarters in Calcutta into a modern hospital.

Atal Bihari felt really hurt at the accusations and counter—accusations. 'In my long political life, never have I seen anybody in the opposition make such personal remarks against me'. Sonia attributed the slander campaign against her to their (BJP) bent of mind and attitude towards women.

Sponsored Advertisements

The slanging matches were not limited to election speeches. The leading newspapers carried big adverstisement from intermediatory front organisations. The BJP propaganda advertisements came from Purva Sainik Sewa Parishad. Someother front organisations included Lok Abhiyan, and All-India Kashmiri Pandit Conference. The total expenditure on print campaign could have touched the Rupees seven crore figure.

The Congress did not take up Sonia's foreign origin issue in its advertisements directly. It highlighted the sugar from Pakistan imports/which according to the Congress paid for the weapons used in Kargil. (Sugar had been put under Open General License when Narasimha Rao was the Prime Minister) 'What can we expect from a party that needs to import its own leader.

No guesses were needed to identify the real advertisers in such cases. Proxy advertisements may have been resorted to so that political parties could keep themselves absolved from responsibility of the contents.

Print campaigns were not limited to advertisements. The Congress party could not digest the findings of opinion polls that had put it well behind the NDA led by BJP.

The Lokmat-IMS-CMCR poll predicted that the Congress would emerge as the single largest party. The credentials of the agency were suspect. The EC guidelines on polls meant nothing to the political parties who were out to try every weapon in their armoury.

Issues in Slanging Matches

Three issues had dominated the slanging matches. There was the issue of Sonia's foreign origin. The BJP termed Sonia's projection as India's Prime Minister an insult to nation's self respect and also a security threat. Other BJP leaders had highlighted her inexperience in public life as a serious criteria that made her ineligible for the high office.

As caretaker government, the BJP government had taken a major decision with regard to the Telecom Policy. The Congress argued that backtracking on the original terms of contract with private parties had deprived the government with revenue of Rs. 1,500 crore. The BJP argued that the industry was sinking and the old policy had to be abandoned to rescue the industry. Pranab Mukherjee of the Congress and the CPI(M) Somnath Chatterjee had in personal communications pleaded the cause of existing cellular operators but backtracked when it did not suit them politically.

On Kargil, the Congress charged BJP government with being negligent. The BJP, on the other hand, termed the Congress rhetoric as anti-national and providing substance to Pakistani propaganda.

Point

Where was Rahul Gandhi when soldiers were dying at Kargil? At Wimbeldon with his girl friend: ***Bal Thackeray***

Apart from being a daughter-in-law Sonia should list her other contributions if any: ***George Fernandes***

When Sonia says she will die for her motherland, she means her mother-in-laws land: ***Pramod Mahajan***

I read she is singing a song while campaigning. Jayalalitha may end up dancing in her next campaign: ***M. Karunanidhi***

Thum to thehre pardesi, Sath kya nibaho gi. Subah pehli flight se, Italy bhag jao gi: ***BJP song***

A responsible oppositon does not play political games while the nation is at war:***Lok Abhiyan***

The Congress is ready to allow soldiers to die for the country but not ready to allow them to vote for the country: ***Purva Sainik Sewa Prishad***

Counter Point

To Advani goes the award of the pettiest mind in BJP: ***Kapil Sibal***

Only one point brought Vajpayee closer to J.H. Patel. Wine and Women: ***Ghulam Nabi Azad***

The bomb exploded 6 km away and Vajpayee wet his dhoti in fear: ***Mulayam Singh Yadav***

Karunanidhi is a rotten egg. The foul smell is now crossing all limits: ***J. Jayalalitha***

We haven't pulled you down, We haven't grabbed your chair. You have fallen on your own, Oj Vajpayee Oh. ***AIDMK song***

Whom do we believe—The RSS or Sardar Patel? ***Communalism Combat***

The Unusual Tricks

Many unusual tricks were employed by the rival parties this time. Through personal contacts in *Hindustan Times*, BJP (read Pramod Mahajan) was able to secure in advance the text of a proposed paid advertisement inserted by the Congress. A rebuttal in the name of PSSP appeared simultaneously along with the Congress advertisement on Kargil.

The BJP taunted that the Congress was leaking like a sieve. (That is how they got the text of the advertisement in advance). It was not an intelligence failure, quipped the Congress. The ruling party is tapping our telephones and jamming our calls.

Yet another example of clever manoeuvering was the availability of aircrafts for campaigning. The travel arrangements made by the Congress went away when the aircrafts booked by the party were secured by the BJP.

Little did Rajiv know that his '*Nani yad diladenge*' was the beginning of much worse things to come in the next decade. Even the fighting forces and Chiefs were not spared this time. The EC could just appeal and so did the Prime Minister. But the political parties had other priorities. The Congress knew it had little to offer on its own. It could only pick holes in BJPs performance. The BJP knew Ms. Sonia had charisma, more so among the illiterate and rural voters. Therefore the need to higlight the issue relating to her foreign origin and inexperience. But was it necessary to turn the political arena into a mud pit with every contender free to throw as much as he or she wished at the rival? The answer lies in the electoral performance of the contenders.

Manmohan Singh on RSS Hand in '84 Riots

Congress leader Manmohan Singh raised a fresh controversy by claiming that the RSS had a hand in the 1984 riots. He also charged Prime Minister A. B. Vajpayee with doublespeak and alleged that the economy was facing renewed uncertainty. On the bull run on the stock market, he said: "Something is wrong." He also outlined a four-pronged package to revive the economy, including financial sector reforms.

Vajpayee on Abuses in Campaigns

Reiterating that the PMO had no role to play in the sugar import from Pakistan, Atal Bihari Vajpayee continued his tirade against malicious personal attacks during election campaign.

There was enough stock of sugar in the country and there was no need for any import, Vajpayee said. If there were no imports, how could there by a scam. Vajpayee said, "The entire world is watching us and our electoral process". Without naming anybody, he called upon leaders of political parties to refrain from making personal remarks. "Abuses have no place in our campaigning," he said.

Launching a frontal attack on the Congress for ushering in an era of instability in the country at the Rajkot rally, the Prime Minister said the power-hungry party had engineered the fall of numerous governments at the Centre and in states. "They are past masters in the toppling game," he remarked.

Criticising the Congress, the Prime Minister said, "My friends in the Opposition did not like the way we stood up to international pressure soon after the Pokhran II experiments. We would have crumbled under pressure but we withstood the test of time thanks to our scientists and technologists". Vajpayee said, "We never did anything for the chair. We had the national interest at heart and did not lust for power. We had waited for 40 long years and were ready to wait for long," Vajpayee said amid cheers.

On the Kargil issue, Vajpayee said, "Pakistan is known to be an aggressor" and therefore, some serious decisions were needed to keep the borders secure. "Pakistan wanted to snatch some of our land, but the jawans ensured not an inch of land was taken away," he said.

Not in Good Taste

* The Congres is like Ravana and they have unleashed Ms. Sonia, the Surpanakha (Ravana's sister who was humiliated by Lakshman) on the country.
—HRD Minsiter M.M. Joshi in Mysore (*Asian Age*)
* We may have to ask even the Prime Minister how, without being married, he has a son-in-law? Who's son-in-law? Who is married to whom?
—Congres leader Ghulam Nabi Azad on ETV (*The Pioneer*)
* *Aulad nahi, damaad hai* (PM has no children, but he has a son-in-law).
—Rajesh Khanna in Rothak (*Asian Age*)
* Sharad Pawar is like Elizabeth Taylor. He marries, divorces, remarries and again divorces.
—Pramod Mahajan in Mumbai (*Asian Age*)
* Mrs. Jayalalitha is a *Vishkanya*. Anyone who touches her, does not survive.
—Pramod Mahajan in Vidarbha (*Hindustan Times*)
* What is her (Sonia's) contribution to the nation? The two children she gave birth to. She has contributed two people to the 100 crore population of our country. Is there anything else?
—George Fernandes in Bangalore and Bellary (*Indian Express*)
* We respect Sonia as a *bahu* of the Nehru-Gandhi family. We also know that she was the favourite *bahu* of the late Indiraji. But is that good enough for us to let a foreign born person like Ms. Sonia to become our PM? If we are so keen on having foreigner as a PM, why not have Tony Blair or Bill Clinton or even Miss Monica Lewinsky.
—Pramod Mahajan in Vidarbha (*Hindustan Times*)

Paid Advertisements by Upfront Organisations

Congress Party's Credentials to Champion

The Cause of Women
Naina Sahni Tandoor Murder Case
Romesh Sharma's Escapades
Jessica Lal Murder Case
Lucknow Party Office Rape Case
Anjana Mishra Gang Rape Case
Who are they trying to fool?

Lok Abhiyan

Remember the scams? Urea Scam, Sugar Scam, Fodder Scam, Share Scam, Bofors Scam, JMM Bribery Scam... when power was abused, suitcase by suitcase, reducing political offices to a license to loot. And today the one thing that unites his opponents: how to escape the Prevention of Corruption Act. And here is Atal Bihari Vajpayee. Five decades in public life, not a single blot. Because he is committed. Not to himself. To his nation.

To cleanse the nation of corruption that is eating into our very vitals, put your mark against his name. It is a mark that will cleanse the system. Vote for a cleaner polity. Vote for probity. Vote for the very symbol of honesty.

Vote for Atal Bihari Vajpayee. The leader you can trust. In war. In peace.

- ❖ In 1977-1979, the Jan Sangh (which eventually became the BJP) refused to give up its ties to the RSS. George Fernandes, a minister in the coalition government, led the protest against the Jan Sangh's "dual membership." Ultimately, the coalition government led by Morarji Desai collapsed.
- ❖ In 1989-1990, the BJP embarked on a rath yatra that caused communal riots across the country. The BJP's wantonly communal act was a response to V. P. Singh's irresponsible politics of caste. Eventually, the BJP withdrew support and the coalition government collapsed.
- ❖ In 1996, the BJP foolishly formed a minority government in the hope it could wean away many of the parties that formed the United Front. However, no party was comfortable with the BJP's communal agenda. The Vajpayee government collapsed in 13 days.
- ❖ In 1997-1999, the BJP decided to put its communal agenda "on the backburner." Despite the deception, the "hidden agenda" kept popping up... in Gujarat, in Orissa...as fanatics of the Sangh Parivar operated at will....destroying tribal places of worship, killing missionaries, harassing minorities. Caught between its communal cadres and its prickly allies, the Vajpayee government collapsed in 13 months.

Deception is the hallmark of the BJP's brand of politics.

The people of India deserve a politics that acts as a catalyst of economic change and social transformation.

Bring back the Congress.
Stop this deceptive brand of politics.

Table 3.1 : Congress—Mother of all scams

Period	Name of Scams	Approx
1987	Bofors Gun Deal	65 crore
1991	Airbus Deal	200 crore
1992	Securities Scam	3000 crore
1994	The Real Sugar Scam	1200 crore
1995	Havala Case	65 crore
1995	Telecom Scam	3 crore
1995	Urea Scam	133 crore
1996	JMM Bribery Case	3.5 crore
1996	Bihar Fodder Scam	1200 crore

The Sugar Import

The Vajpayee Government had allowed the import from Pakistan of 5.54 lakh tonnes of sugar during the first ten months of the current season. This despite the knowledge that the surplus at the end of the ongoing season (October 1 to September 30) would be as high as 63 lakh tonnes. The imports carried a nominal duty of 27.5 per cent. The demand by Indian sugar producers that the import duty be raised was turned down by the Prime Minsiter's Office.

The projection for the 1998-99 season was 14 lakh tonnes, against an annual domestic consumption of 146 lakh tonnes. The country had already a carry-over stock of 55 lakh tonnes of sugar at the beginning of the season and the surplus stock of September 30 is exptected to be 63 lakh tonnes.

Import of sugar is allowed under OGL, and conentionally government worldwide hike the import duty when there is a glut, so that its domestic industry is not hurt. But the PMO rejected, not once but thrice, the proposal of even its own Minister (S.S. Barnala) to raise the import duty to 40 per cent.

The most distressing factor was that at a time when Pakistan was hit by economic sanctions and its economy was in a shambles, the Vajpayee Govt handed it over on a platter a bonanza of Rs. 900 crore, between October last and July this year. The period includes the entire duration of the conflict.

Who Imported Sugar from Pakistan? Sugargate

The BJP named the owners of the Delhi-based Kundan Rice Mills to refute the Congress allegation that the Prime Minster's Office was involved in a sugar import deal with Pakistan.

BJP general secretary K. N. Govindacharya said, "Its owners are no Ottavio Quattrochis. It is an unknown Garg family of Naya Bazar, Chandni Chowk—a private party that imports sugar."

He was responding to Congress spokesperson Kapil Sibbal's claim of August 30 that the Kundal Rice Mills signed contract with 'Pakistan's ISI-controlled Army Welfare Trust for import of 80,000 metric tonnes of sugar last February.

The BJP had come out with the name of the owners even though the PMO had nothing to do with the import bacause the Congress had attempted to create a mystery over its onwership in an attempt to trace links to the Prime Minister.

"Kundan Rice Mills was till the other day an unknown name. So it was not easy for the BJP to find out the identity of its owners". "Our question is how is the Prime Minister's Office, or for that matter the Congress or the electorate, concerned about this matter?" Sugar imports at zero duty were in place since 1994 when they were allowed by the Narasimha Rao Government. Our Government had nothing to do with it. In fact, it was the Vajpayee Government which imposed customs duty initially at five per cent, which was subsequently raised to 20 per cent and 25 per cent." Asked why the Vajpayee Government allowed trade between India and Pakistan even during the Kargil conflict, the BJP spokesperson said, "Trade policies were framed earlier to the conflict."

Govind Acharya pointed out that the Congress was questioning the integrity of the Army top brass by taking up the cause of a Brigadier, who was upset with his transfer, to show that the victory at Kargil was a defeat.

"Earlier, when India was fighting a military war in Kargil and a diplomatic battle against Pakistan, the Congress kept on hurling charges that ran contrary to the national spirit."

"After India won the war", the entire world acknowledged India's splendid victory, the Congress described it as a defeat. At India's moment of pride, the Congress chose to sulk."

From The Pulpit of Jama Masjid

Bukhari: Defeat both Cong, BJP

The Shahi Imam of Jama Masjid, Syed Abdulla Bukhari, appealed to the Muslims to make every possible effort to defeat the Congress and the Bharatiya Janata Party in the parliamentary elections.

The politicians had time and again used the Muslims for their electoral gains. The political instability in the country would continue till the interests of the Muslim community were addressed.

"If we succeed in defeating those parties which have never worked for our interests, they will be compelled to seek our support. Their defeat will be our victory."

"With Muslim support, the Congress continuously remained in power from 1947 to 1977. In return the party gave us injustice, joblessness and poverty."

The Congress and the BJP were held responsible for the demoliton of the Babri Masjid. "The demolition was a well-planned conspiracy of the two parties... And no Muslim can forgive them for this act."

"The Congres had decreased the Muslim representation in Parliament during the past 12 Lok Sabha elections. The number of Muslim MPs in the previous Lok Sabha was just 27. And as per the population ration, the number of Muslim MPs should not be less than 70."

"The party had once again ignored the power of the Muslim voters. "Of the two hundred fifty candidates, the Congress has given tickets to only nine Muslims."

Of the 3.5 lakh electorate in Chandni Chowk, about 1.5 lakh voters belong to the Muslim community. East Delhi has about 7.5 lakh Muslim voters. He said it was surprising that the Congress had not given a single ticket to any Muslim in Delhi... "Support Janata Dal (Secular) candidate Shoaib Iqbal in Chandni Chowk. Don't vote for Congress and BJP in East Delhi. Chose any secular candidate."

Congress and Kargil

Prime Minister Atal Bihari Vajpayee directly blamed the Congress for the Kargil crisis, saying Pakistan exploited the political instability that the party had created. He was addressing a rally in this town, where Congress president Mrs. Sonia Gandhi was facing the BJP's Mrs. Sushma Swaraj in a battle that had become the symbol of the election at large.

Vajpayee promised to revive the Bill promising 33 per cent reservation to women in Parliament and State Assemblies, if his party was re-elected with the requisite majority. He also appealed to the "court of the people" to examine the manner in which the Congress had "ousted" his government.

With just 48 hours left for campaigning, the BJP played its final card by bringing Vajpayee to Bellary. He attracted an impressively big crowd, though it did not appear entirely spontaneous.

The PM's 40-minute speech appeared to have gone down well. But a section of the crowd became restive, apparently because his speech was in Hindi. A hastily-arranged interpreter helped settle the audience, and cheerleaders applauded at the right places. Vajpayee's speech was preceded by Mrs. Swaraj's speech in Kannada and TDP chief Chandrababu Naidu's address in Telugu (there is a big Telugu-speaking segment here).

Vajpayee made much of the "power-obsessed" Congress' "conspiracy" to unseat his government. On Kargil, he said: "Pakistan saw that the government had fallen and the LS was dissolved. It thought this was a good time to act, and invaded Kargil. This was the consequence of the instability created by the Congress."

4

Poll Miscellany

Electronic Gadgetry in Elections 1999

In select constituencies, it was no longer stamping the ballot paper and then stuffing it down the ballot box. In place was a small gadget known as Electronic Voting Machine (EVM).

Not everybody knew this during the assembly elections last year.

Last year, EVMs were used on an experimental basis in the New Delhi constituency. This time, all seven constituencies in Delhi were put to the button.

EVMs were used in a large number of urban constituencies all over the country.

One can't go wrong with these machines. The button is large and prominent, you can't miss it and you can't press it twice. Mind you—if you press the wrong button, your vote will be registered in the name of some other candidate. You can do nothing to rectify your mistake.

The machine has vertical list with names of candidates along with the party they belong to together with the election symbol. Against each name is a red light that glows when an oval blue button next to it is pressed.

A long beep—tells you that you got it right.

The voting machine consists of two units—a control unit and balloting unit. Both run on batteries and are compact enough to be carried in two suitcases.

While the balloting unit plays the role of a ballot paper, the control unit, monitored by the presiding officer, is your ballot box.

The control unit is kept with the presiding officer at a polling booth who will monitor the casting of votes. After each vote is cast, there will be a beep (12 seconds long) and till the presiding officer resets the "ballot" button for the next voter, no one can cast another vote.

Each machine can cater upto a maximum of 16 candidates. At the most four machines can be interlinked as per the requirement of each constituency.

To prevent tampering or bogus voting, there are certain in-built safeguards. The machine has been designed in such a manner that not more than five votes can be cast in one minute. This has been precisely done to check bogus voting.

How does your vote get registered in the machine? When the ballot button is pressed, it is immediately recorded in a memory chip in the control unit.

In the control unit is the all-important "stop" button. Once pressed, this will inactivate the balloting unit completely.

So, in the event of booth capturing, all the presiding officer will need to do is press the "stop" button. Thereafter, no more votes will be registered but the votes already polled will remain in memory. As per procedures, the presiding officer will press this button when the polling draws to a close later in the evening.

With these machines, the counting of votes has been made exceptionally simple.

The control unit has a "result" button which can display the number of votes polled against each candidate, in a matter of moments. But the access to this button is sealed even before the actual polling begins.

Only on the day of counting, the seal is broken in the presence of the counting agents of the political parties and the vital button pressed for results.

If something goes wrong with any machine, it could be immediately replaced by a new one by the mobile squad of the Election Commission.

What could actually go wrong with the machine? "Nothing." Its memory will go only if the control unit is burnt for it suffers extensive damages. Rest be assured. Nothing can go wrong with this devise.

Opinion and Exit Polls—The Supreme Court Verdict

On August 20, 1999 the Election Commission came out with a notification prohibiting the telecast of opinion poll results and advertisements by political parties through the electronic media.

The first challenge to the order came from a private satellite channel. It filed a petition in the Madras High Court seeking to declare the notification as illegal and void.

It was contented on behalf of the petitioner that the notification went against the freedom of expression of political parties and individuals. The notification amounted to discrimination between newspapers and the electronic media. The Madras High Court stayed the operation of the Election Commission notification.

On similar petitions filed by the TDP and a private channel, the Andhra High Court had declared the notification as unreasonable and discriminatory. Do the guidelines set by the Election Commission have the force of law passed by the Parliament? Do these guidelines infringe upon the fundamental rights to information and the right to expression under a garb? The question was finally settled by a Constitution Bench of the Supreme Court.

While the government contested the notification, the Janta Dal (United) pleaded that publication of the results of the exit poll after one phase could influence the electorate slated to vote in the other phases. Many of these were sponsored by vested interests and their results, if projected before the masses just before the elections, could serve to prejudice them. The ban on advertising through the electronic media was supported on the ground that only the rich parties could afford such advertisements and the relatively smaller parties were disadvantageously placed.

The Election Commission's case was that the ban on publication should be made absolute between the evening of September 3 and the last date of the five phase poll. The exit poll results should not be published before October 3. The EC sought Courts directions to the Centre and other states to enforce its guidelines on opinion/exit polls and political advertisemnts. The Chief Election Commissioner M.S. Gill must have had second thoughts on the validity of the notification for he was quick to point out that 'there is no problem or personal agenda or any hang-ups involved'. The Commission was only trying to protect the fragile structure of democracy by banning opinion polls. Any breach of the guidelines would in the ultimate analysis be destructive of the constitutional rights of the citizens guaranteed under Art. 324 as well as the fundamental right guaranteed under Art. 14.'

It was clear that the guidelines did not have the statutory backing. However the Supreme Court had observed that Articles 103 and 192 read with Section 8a of the Representation of the People Act cast an obligation on the Head of the State to adhere to the recommendations of the Commission. 'The Commission wanted the orders issued by them to be interpreted by the Supreme Court.'

During the hearing, one of the Judges had specifically observed that the balance of equity between the freedom of speech and Commission's right to regulate it for free and fair polls had to be kept in mind while looking into the various aspects of the Commission's power to pass such guidelines.

Are these restrictions necessary to provide a level playing field to all the contestants? Does it not amount to denying the T.V. Channels their right to practice any trade and business?

One of the Commissioners had, on an earlier occasion, maintained that the silent, illiterate electorate neither have access to TV sets nor capacity to read newspapers. If that was the case put up by one of the Commissioners, the notification could not be accepted in toto.

The crunch came on September 14th. According to the report filed by the Legal Editor of *The Times of India*, The Election Commission on September 14, withdrew its controversial guidelines banning the publication and telecast of opinion and exit polls during the elections following the Supreme Court ruling that the Commission had no power to issue such an order.

During the hearing of petitions relating to the scope of EC's powers under Article 324 of the Constitution, Commission's counsel Harish Salve informed the Court about the withdrawal of the guidelines. He said that "having regard to what has transpired in the Court today, the EC has decided to and will recall these guidelines..."

The statement came in the wake of the Court's observation that "As voters and citizens we might regret we have to sign a judgement which will curtail your powers. But if we have to do it, it is because of these guidelines."

A five-judge Constitution Bench headed by Justice S.P. Bharucha asked the Commission to issue a notification recalling the guidelines within a day or two. Salve assured the court that a formal notification recalling these guidelines, issued first on February 21, 1998, and reiterated on August 20 this year, would be issued in a day or two.

Dismissing the commission's petition seeking enforcement of the guidelines, the Bench comprising Justice Bharucha, Justice B.N.Kirpal, Justice S.S.M. Quadri, Justice V.N. Khare and Justice D.P. Mohapatra said it was without merit but clarified that the Court did not examine whether the guidelines violated the fundamental right to free speech and expression.

As the hearing started, the judges persistently asked the Commission how it had the power to issue such an order without thinking about its enforcement. "Your (EC's) guidelines will remain a guideline: It is not binding (on anybody)," the Court told Mr Salve.

As Salve contended that publication of exit or opinion polls would impinge upon free and fair elections, the court said, "At the end of the day, you (EC) may go home with a perception that you have far less powers than the public perception of it."

On the counsel's plea that the publication of such survey polls would create a problem, the court said, "The problem is of your own creation. You should have seen what your powers are before issuing such guidelines."

Referring to the Commission's prayer for a direction to the Union government to enforce the guidelines, the Court remarked, "It is absurd to say that EC will issue the guidelines but if somebody violates them, the Supreme Court will take action."

"If you had assumed that you had powers to issue such guidelines, why are you doubting the very same powers by coming to the Court and seeking their enforcement?" the court wondered. Asked how the government would enforce the guidelines in case the apex Court were to give such a direction, Mr Salve said, "Once the Supreme Court declares these guidelines to be valid, everybody will obey."

An anguished court observed, "What you wish to do is to make the Supreme Court act in aid of the Commission and declare the guidelines as law. This is a presumption on the part of the Commission."

"Why are you seeking a declaration to that effect from us? This is not the way directions are issued to the government. You have no power (to issue such a guideline). It is as simple as that," the court added.

The judges also said that "the Election Commission, which commands respect, has been reduced to this to come to the court to seek execution of its guidelines". Arguing for *Frontline* magazine, senior advocate Shanti Bhushan said that Article 324 gave no legislative power to the EC. If any law banning the publication of exit or opinion polls was to be passed, it had to be first debated in Parliament, he said.

Bhushan said exit and opinion polls give vital information to the electorate to vote intelligently in order to avoid a hung verdict. However, he agreed with the Court that the Commission was empowered to give directives to its subordinate officers for fair conduct of elections.

Additional Solicitor-General C.S. Vaidyanathan said Article 19 could only be curtailed through a legislation and since EC had no power to legislate, it could not issue guidelines which would curtail the right to speech.

The Election Commission's concern for providing a level playing field is understandable. But it should not have overlooked its basic limitations. It cannot create laws. That function lies with the Parliament. If the political parties do not agree to be transparent, there is nothing that the Commission can do about it since it is the prerogative of the legislatures to make laws that could be enforced. Executive fiats can be no substitute for Acts of Parliament. This is so simple as that.

The Election Commission is very much like the umpire on the field. The rules of the game have already been set. The Refree cannot change them, whatever his intentions. If they discriminate between the players on the field, the refree cannot do anything about them. The remedy lies in someone else's domain.

Election Commission, since the time of Seshan has often aspired for a place in history. That place is only for the politicians. The refree may sometimes aspire for the applause that comes to the batsman hitting a sixer or scoring a century or a bowler performing a hat trick, but that would always be in vain. His importance on the field begins with the match and ends with the end of the match. Seshan learnt this lesson almost immediately after his term. M.S. Gill may take a little longer.

Ideologies of Political Parties and General Elections

In the pre-Independence era, Indian National Congress was the first political party. Its one point agenda was freedom from British rule. Ideology as such did not rank high although the party did adopt non-violence as its strategy. There were many other social ideals to be achieved but those could not be termed as strictly ideological.

The Muslim League was another organisation with some political cohesion. It was more a religious outfit and the partition and creation of Pakistan emerged on their agenda much later after it became apparent that the Britishers might at last leave the country. The Hindu Mahasabha rarely got the support of Hindu masses to the extent the Muslim League did. In terms of cadres there have been the Communists and the RSS that deserve special mention. These two have 'ideologies' although in the present scenario even these seem to have softened down. The Communists have not much to show after the collapse and disintegration of USSR while the RSS would push only to the extent the BJP led coalition does not go out of power.

The Janata Party of 1977 comprised the Communists, the Jana Sangh, the Socialists, the Kulaks, and Congress old timers. It was born out of Mrs. Indira Gandhi's efforts to impose a family dictatorship in India. Democracy, it seemed was threatened and generated blind anti-Congressism. Later came the Janata Dal. But it split on Mandal issue and later the demolition of Babri Masjid alienated most other groups from the BJP.

The alienation was short lived for politicians in India do not know how to live without political power. Ideals are good as long as they serve as a means to political power or a share therein but if they come in the way of personal political ambitions, they are given a go-by at the first opportunity. There are no exceptions. If political survival is threatened the Indian politician would go to any limits. The BJP was at one time untouchable being branded as a rank communalist party. The Congress in Kerala had no problem associating with the Muslim League if that helped the party to be in power. The Congress gave secularist certificates to the party although the party never said those things.

Coming back to BJP men like Hegde or JH Patel could align with BJP where it was politically convenient. As the Congress gave a clean chit to the Muslim League arguing that it was different from the pre-independence Muslim League, so do the present day socialists and secularists say about BJP under Atal Bihari. The BJP has at no stage disclaimed its affiliations with RSS and the RSS has never diluted its Hindutva Agenda. This one trait—unprincipled opportunism among India's politicians has created many undesirable features in Indian polity. The worst among them is the criminalisation of politics. If grabbing power remains the only end, the criminals provide the most effective means. Muscle power and money power are products of rank opportunism among the Indian politicians. No wonder no party is willing to get its sources of finance known to public. Everyone has soiled hands.

Prime Ministers of India of 1990s

V.P. Singh	2.12.89-10.11.90	344 days
Chandra Shekhar	10.11.90-21.6.91	224 days
P.V. Narasimha Rao	21.6.91-16.5.96	1792 days
Atal Bihari Vajpayee	16.5.96-1.6.96	13 days
H.D. Deve Gowda	1.6.96-21.3.97	325 days
I.K. Gujral	21.3.97-19.3.98	333 days
Atal Bihari Vajpayee	19.3.98-17.84.99	395 days
Atal Bihari Vajpayee	Continued to act as P.M. and was again sworn in on October 13, 1999.	

What the NDA Allies Expect

DMK:	Solution to Cauvery issue on its terms
TDP:	No short changing his State—the A.P.
INLD:	No tough measures that may make Chauthala unpopular (like hike in diesel price)

Assembly and Lok Sabha Polls Together

Andhra Pradesh:	TDP and BJP together bagged 192 out of a total of 294 seats. The NDA alliance also bagged 32 of the 42 Lok Sabha seats. Good governance yielded congruent results.
Maharashtra:	Shiv Sena and BJP together could manage only 125 out of 294 Assembly seats. Congress and NCP formed the government with a tally of 75 and 58 seats. In the Lok Sabha elections the Shiv Sena had a tally of 15 seats while the BJP had 13 seats making a total of 28 out of 48 seats. The performance represents a shaky position for the NDA alliance.
Karnataka	Congress secured 132 out of the 224 total Assembly seats. The BJP and JD(U) trailed well behind with just 63 seats. The BJP led alliance was down from 13 to 9 seats in the Lok Sabha elections. Congress and allies raised their tally from 9 in 1998 to 18 in 1999. The voters are averse to infighting and the JD split was totally unapproved by the electors.

All in the Election Game

The present Lok Sabha poll was not the longest

The 1951 poll extended from Oct. 25 to Feb. 21, 1952

The 1957 poll extended frm Feb. 24 to June 9

The 1962 poll extended from Feb. 16 to June 6

The highest number of rallies was addressed by Sonia Gandhi (160). Shatrughan Sinha trailed behind with 134 while Atal Bihari Vajpayee addressed 108 rallies.

The 620.4 million voters had to choose 538 Members of parliament out of 4,648 candidates. It costed Rs. 845 crore.

Highlights of Election Results

BJP and Allies polled 41.3% votes registering a positive swing of 1.2

Congress and Allies polled 34.7% votes registering a positive swing of 3.4

Others had a vote share of 23.9% registering a negative swing of 5.0.

India Today—Insight post-poll survey among 22,326 voters across 94 assembly segments provided the following insight into how the country might have voted during the 1999 polls.

The BJPs patrons included Upper Caste, SC/ST as well the OBCs. The highest percentage (52) was in respect of upper castes.

More males than females favoured saffron. The patronage was almsot equally distributed among the young, middle aged and the seniors.

The Congress Tally Fell

Leadership	Year	No. of Seats	Year	No. of Seats
Under Indira Gandhi	1971	352	1977	154
Under Rajiv Gandhi	1984	415	1989	197
Under Sonia Gandhi	1998	140	1999	112

While P.V. Narasimha Rao and Sitaram Kesri had to quit for failure, no such thing happened in case of the Gandhis. P.V. Narsimha Rao resigned in 1996 and Sitaram Kesri was forcibly removed from office even though the party had retained its earlier tally.

State Level Performance of Political Parties: Some Trends

In Sikkim, the Sikkim Democratic Front led by Pawan Kumar Chamling swept the poll bagging 24 out of the 32 seats. Sikkim Sangram Parishad secured 7 seats while 1 seat was won by the independent.

Arunachal Pradesh Assembly results showed an absolute preference for the Congress. The party got more than two third majority in a 60 member house. The other contesting political parties included Nationalist Congress and Arunachal Congress besides the Independents.

In Andhra Pradesh, N. Chandrababu Naidu led his Telugu Desam Party to a spectacular victory by defeating the Indian National Congress.

In Karnataka, the Congress got a decisive mandate, The BJP, JD (S) and JD (U) trailed far behind with the AIDMK just registering its presence. The JD dissensions came as a boon to the Congress. The State Congress chief S.M. Krishna was sworn in as the Chief Minister. A hung verdict in Maharashtra was followed by a hectic lobbying by both the BJP-Shivsena alliance and the INC and the Pawar led Congress.

Politics makes strange bed fellows. Pawar had been expelled from the Congress for having raised the issue of Sonia's foreign origin. But the events in Maharashtra forced the INC to ignore all the harsh words that had been traded between the INC and Sharad Pawar led group. The Congress had no option and having fared so badly in the Lok Sabha—it was over anxious to be part of the government in Maharashtra irrespective of what had transpired between Sonia baiters and Sonia loyals. The INC agreed to have its nominee as the Chief Minister while the NCP had to be content with the post of Deputy Chief Minister. Chagan Bhujhal of the NCP became the Deputy while Vilasrao Deshmukh became the Chief Minister of Maharashtra. The Janata Dal (S), the SP and the PWP are the other allies in the INC-NCP alliance.

State Assembly and Lok Sabha Results in North East

In Sikkim, the Sikkim Democratic Front was swept to power with over two third majority. The SDF also won the solo Lok Sabha seat.

In Arunachal Pradesh both Lok Sabha seats were won by the Indian National Congress. The Congress won majority in the 60 member Assembly nearly decimating the Nationalist Congress, Arunachal Congress and the Independents.

Vote by Categories

The Urban voters showed a definite preference for BJP (42) against just 35 in respect of rural voters. In terms of religion, the BJP vote was made up of 41% Hindus. It also included 10% Muslims.

The Congress regained its ground among the SC/ST (31) as also among the OBCs (23). Its share was almost evenly balanced between male and female voters and also between the rural and urban voters.

Among the Muslims the share was 45%, the highest. All age groups seemed to be almost equally responsive to the Indian National Congress.

The performance of the BJP and Allies during 1998 was rated good by 56% of the voters covered in the survey.

Sonia fought against the foreign origin label sticking. 45% voters believed that foreign origin should debar a person from becoming the P.M.

The voters seemed emphatic about the Lok Sabha term. Among the voters covered in the survey 77% believed that the term should be fixed for 5 years.

Significant Events Associated with 13

1919 April 13	Worst ever Jallianwala Bagh massacre committed by the British rulers at Amritsar (Punjab) in Pre-independence India
1952 May 13	First session of Indian Parliament held with Jawaharlal Nehru as Prime Minister and Rajendra Prasad as President.
1962 May 13	Dr. Rajendra Prasad relinquished office. Dr. S. Radha Krishnan assumed office as President of India.
1967 May 13	Dr. S. Radha Krishnan relinquished office. Dr. Zakir Hussain assumed office as President of India.
1996— 13 days	Atal Bihar Vajpayee remained Prime Minister and resigned after the discussion on Motion of No Confidence.
1998 —13 months	Atal Bihari Vajpayee functioned as P.M. and resigned after losing vote of confidence by one vote.
1999— Oct. 13	Atal Bihari Vajpayee sworn in as Prime Minister for the third time.

5

Constituency-wise Results

Analysis and Comments

The outcome of Lok Sabha Polls as reflected in different States provide very significant material for those interested in study and analysis of popularity trends of political parties over the years.

Students of Indian politics and research scholars will be interested in constituency-wise results for these provide an insight into voters perception of the performance and acceptability of various political parties. The data is also important as it tells upon matters like voters apathy or otherwise to the prevailing system of elections. Comparisons of victory margins reflect the growing or declining popularity of parties and individuals. Apart from the number of seats won or lost over the previous elections, the data generated is useful in assessing whether the political base of the party is expanding or shrinking. The political parties have now started using the data thus generated for selection of candidates. Sharing of seats with political allies and for determining the thrust areas of their electioneering.

ANDHRA PRADESH (42)

The main contenders were the TDP, INC and the BJP. The Congress got 5 while the BJP 7 seats. AIMIM won the Hyderabad seat and all others (29) were bagged by the TDP.

The Andhra elections to the Lok Sabha (42 seats) were important in as much as it demonstrated the supremacy of performance over incumbency as the determining factor. Medak from where Indira Gandhi had at one time sought revival in politics voted for the BJP. Renuka Chowdhry of the INC won from Khammam constituency.

Total seats	
1952	= 25
1957 & 1962	= 43
1967 & 1971	= 41
1977 onwards	= 42

Party Performance

The big winner of 1999 is Chandrababu Naidu. He returns to power in Andhra Pradesh looking, if anything, stronger than he was five years ago. His handsome haul of Lok Sabha seats makes him the BJP's most weighty ally in the National Democratic Alliance. In short, he enjoys real clout in Hyderabad and New Delhi and has a real opportunity to further his reform agenda. The Telugu Desam's performance in both the Assembly and Lok Sabha polls sparkles against the generally dull outcome of a contest which, when it has no left parties standing where they were in 1998, has left them much worse off.

The TDP has bucked a strong anti-incumbent wave which, with only two or three exceptions, has humbled ruling parties time and again over the past five years. The predictions were that the TDP had more to lose than gain from its poll alliance with the BJP: it was assumed that the loss of the Muslim vote would do serious damage. It was said Naidu's cyber-dreams had wrought no miracles in the administration or rural life and the economic reform was impossible to sell to the people. Such pessimism has been wrong.

So striking are the results in Andhra Pradesh that many state chieftains will want to make a trip to Hyderabad to study Naidu's methods and tactics. More than one factor contributed to the TDP's success. It was essentially a two-horse race between the TDP-BJP alliance and the Congress. Judging by the defeat of a number of Congress stalwarts, voters seem to have voted with their heads. It is tempting to think that is exactly where the TDP's appeal lies, in the head, and people have made a practical choice. If so, the results are a vindication of Naidu's belief that the people do understand what he is trying to do when, rather than dole out subsidised rice, he computerises the administration at break-neck speed, and aggressively courts information technology companies and other private enterprise, and pushes for power stations. Perhaps people have come to realise that new opportunities down the road are a better deal than the free rice and dhotis they used to be promised at election time.

There is not too much to show as yet outside Hyderabad and one or two other cities for Naidu's enthusiasm for economic liberalisation. Certainly judging by the migrations to other states triggered by drought in Anantapur and Chittoor districts, the government has paid insufficient attention to basics like emergency employment schemes. But the message that the TDP is changing the way of doing things may be getting through. Naidu's reformist zeal has already persuaded many from the World Bank to private domestic and foreign investors to invest in the state. Perceptions are important and the perception is that Andhra Pradesh welcomes new project proposals, will process them intelligently and fast and do everything possible to provide the necessary infrastructure. Naidu now appears to have won strong backing from the people of the state for economic reform. He will have to work twice as hard to product the results people expect from his government. [*Indian Express*]

Constituency-wise Results — 1999 and Winners of 1998

Adilabad : 10,94,871* (7,70,154) - S. Venugopalal Chary (TDP) : 3,90,308
Mohd. Sultan Ahmed (INC) : 2,80,585; C. Shanker Rao (CPI) : 35,113; Kodali Venkat Narayan Rao (IND) : 22,141; Ch. Dayananad (RPI) : 10,466; Sumathi Reddy (Anna TDP) : 3,859; Md. Chanda Pasha (IND) : 1,130; Invalid : 26,552
In 1998, S. Venugopala Chary (TDP) won by a margin of 33,534 votes.

Amalapuram (SC) : 9,08,137* (6,63,249) - Mohana Chandra Balayogi Ganti (TDP) : 3,68,476*
Gollapaali Surya Rao (INC) : 2,49,597; Akumarthi Surya Narayana (MCPI-S.S. Srivastava) : 26,487; Yesu Ratnam Saka (ATDP) : 16,769; Akumarthi Aseervadham (AJBP) : 1,920; Invalid : 0
In 1998, Ganti Mohana Chandra Balayogi (TDP) won by a margin of 90,240 votes.

* Total Electorates
Figures in ( ) are Votes polled

* Elected speaker of the Lok Sabha on 22.10.1999 for the second term.

Anakapalli : 10,36,504* (7,63,648) - Ganta Srinivasa Rao (TDP) : 3,92,984 Gurunadha Rao Gudivada (INC) : 3,34,520; Appala Trinadha Rao Bhisetti (ATDP) : 13,918; Srinivas Rao Choday (NTRTD) : 3,562; Invalid : 18,664 In 1998, G. Gurunadha Rao (INC) won by a margin of 13,644 votes.

Anantapur : 12,26,301* (7,72,471) - Kala Sreenivasulu (TDP) : 3,78,488 Anantha Venkata Rami Reddy (INC) : 3,57,386; A. Ramachandra Chowdary (ATDP) : 14,823; Others : 2,142; Invalid : 19,632 In 1998, Ananta Venkata Rami Reddy (INC) won by a margin of 82,224 votes.

Angole : 11,90,279* (7,76,640) - Karanam Balarama Krishna Murthy (TDP) : 3,92,840; Sreenivasulu Reddy (INC) : 3,70,892; Byrapuneni Suryanarayana (ATDP) : 6,394; Others : 6.514; Invalid : 0 In 1998, Magunta Sreenivasulu Reddy (INC) won by a margin of 20,866 votes.

Bapatla : 10,77,805* (7,27,256) - D. Ramanaidu (TDP) : 3,99,596 Jesudas Seelam (INC) : 3,07,139; Venkateswarlu Katharu (ATDP) : 4,852; Others : 2,838; Gurava Reddy Vali (NTRTD) : 1,256; Invalid : 11,575 In 1998, Janardhana Reddy Nedurumalli (INC) won by a margin of 40,476 votes.

Bhadrachalam : 10,85,474* (7,59,883) - Dumpa Mary Vijaya Kumari (TDP) : 2,93,593; T. Ratnabai (INC) : 2,56,490; Ramaiah Sode (CPI) : 1,22,496; Pangi Satyanarayana (NTRTDP-LP) : 24,425; Others : 31,552; Invalid : 31,327 In 1998, Ramaiah Sode (CPI) won by a margin of 59,440 votes.

Bobbili : 9,50,559* (7,16,703) - Botcha Satyanarayana (INC) : 3,39,768 Smt. Aruna Padala (TDP) : 3,35,947; Dasari Manjula (AJBP) : 16,425; Enumala Appa Rao (IND) : 2,010; Invalid : 22,553 In 1998, Kondapalli Pydithalli Naidu (TDP) won by a margin of 26,912 votes.

Chittoor : 11,40,219* (8,53,197) - Noothana Kalva Ramakrishna Reddy (TDP) : 4,19,208; R. Gopinath (INC) : 4,00,570; G. Abdul Rawoof (ATDP) : 12,972; Others : 2,656; Invalid : 17,791 In 1998, Nuthanakalava Ramakrishna Reddy (TDP) won by a margin of 80,081 votes.

Cuddapah : 10,90,670* (7,38,831) - Vivekananda Reddy Y.S. (INC) : 3,67,833 Kandula Rajamohan Reddy (TDP) : 3,41,236; Others :13,785; Invalid : 15,977 In 1998, Y.S.Rajasekhar Reddy (INC) won by a margin of 53,620 votes.

Eluru : 11,42,811* (8,52,429) - Bolla Bulli Ramlaiah (TDP) 4,35,884; Maganti Venkateswara Rao (Babu) (INC) : 3,73,653; Others : 24,932; Invalid : 17,960 In 1998, Maganti Venkateswa Rao (INC) won by a margin of 25,019 votes.

Guntur : 12,39,906* (7,81,299) - Yemparala Venkateswararao (TDP) 3,99,065 Rayapati Sambasiva Rao (INC) : 3,58,735; Others : 14,016; Bhashyam Narasaiah (Anna TDP) : 9,438; Invalid : 45

Hanamkonda : 11,18,854* (7,56,578) - Chada Suresh Reddy (TDP) : 3,75,285 M. Kamaluddin Ahmed (INC) : 2,89,504; Kalidas Madatha (CPI) : 37,904; Others : 10,080; Ambati Suryanarayana (AJBP) : 7,006; Dharmapuri S. Rajaram Yadav (SP) : 3,831; Kosanam Satyanarayana (NTRTDP-LS) : 1,688; Smt. A.V. Vijaya Lakshmi (NCP) : 1,168; Invalid : 30,112 In 1998, Chada Suresh Reddy (TDP) won by a margin of 45,491 votes.

Hindupur : 11,51,503* (7,92,868) - B.K. Parthasarathi : 4,32,575
S. Gangadhar (INC) : 2,97,938; Others : 30,538; P. Ravi Chandra (ATDP) : 8,003; Invalid : 23,814
In 1998, S. Gangadhar (INC) won by a margin of 26,138 votes.

Hyderabad : 15,67,033* (10,83,871) - Sultan Salahuddin Owaisi (AIMIM) : 4,48,165; Baddam Bal Reddy (BJP) : 3,87,344; Konda Laxma Reddy (INC) : 2,00,642; Others : 19,412; Jaiprakash Singh (ATDP) : 13,041; Invalid : 193
In 1998, Sultan Salahuddin Owaisi (AIMIM) won by a margin of 71,612 votes.

Kakinada : 11,71,879* (8,12,541) - Mudragada Padmanabham (TDP) : 4,35,811
Thota Subba Rao (INC) : 3,14,376; Boddu Krishna Mohan (ATDP) : 44,466; Nayanalasetty Murthy (CPI-ML-Liberation) : 8,855; Pachipala Rama Prakash (IND) : 6,210; Pentapati Chandra Sekhara Rao (IND) : 1,502; Muthyala Rama Linga Chowdary (AJBP) : 1,321; Invalid : 0
In 1998, Krishnam Raju U.V. (BJP) won by a margin of 67,798 votes.

Karimnagar : 12,59,224* (8,39,871) - Chennamaneni Vidyasagar Rao (BJP) : 3,98,437; Anand Rao Chalimeda (INC) : 3,79,067; Smt. Sankepally Suma (Anna TDP) : 11,222; Gajabheemkar Vittal (NTRTDP-LP) : 8,827; Others : 3,720; Invalid : 38,598
In 1998, Chennamaneni Vidyasagar Rao (BJP) won by a margin of 95,997 votes.

Khammam : 12,28,810* (9,47,819) - Renuka Chouwdary (INC) : 3,28,596; Baby Swarna Kumari Maddineni (TDP) : 3,20,198; Gugloth Dharma (CPI-M) : 1,84,422; Others : 83,355; Invalid : 31,248
1998, Nadendla Bhaskar Rao (INC) won by a margin of 11,664 votes.

Kurnool : 11,63,375* (7,72,089) - Kambhalapatil Krishna Mur (TDP) : 3,85,688
Kotla Vijaya Bhaskara Red (INC) : 3,61,201; Others : 2,179; ADI Narayana Reddy. H (PPI) : 1,680; Invalid : 21,341
In 1998, Kotla Vijayabhaskara Reddy (INC) won by a margin of 12,836 votes.

Machilipatnam : 10,06,262* (7,29,190) - Brahmanaiah Ambati (IDP) : 3,87,533
Sambasiva Rao Kavuru (INC) : 3,04,537; Rajendra Prasadu Puttagunta (AJBP) : 12,071; Kameswararao Dodda (PPI) : 7,721; Invalid : 17,328
In 1998, Kavuru Sambasiva Rao (INC) won by a margin of 81,092 votes.

Mahabubnagar : 12,49,455* (1,32,285) - A.P. Jitender Reddy (BJP) : 63,822
Mallikarjun (INC) : 60,132; Others : 2,952; Invalid : 5,379
In 1998, S. Jaipal Reddy (JD) won by a margin of 22,641 votes.

Medak : 12,19,960* (8,63,584) - A. Narendra (BJP) : 4,00,244
M. Baga Reddy (INC) : 3,78,161; Others : 28,148; Allaram Ratnaiah (MCPI) : 10,483; Tirunagari Muraliohar (AJBP) : 8,248; Invalid : 38,300
In 1998, M. Baga Reddy (INC) won by a margin of 16,480 votes.

Miryalguda : 12,06,212* (9,26,426) - Jaipal Reddy Sudini (INC) : 4,01,437
Rangashai Reddy Yadevelli (TDP) : 3,43,960; Ch. Seetharamulu (CPI-M) : 1,31,386; Yerra Johnson (MCPI-SSS) : 14,068; Others : 13,569; Invalid : 22,006
In 1998, Baddam Narsimha Reddy (INC) won by a margin of 14,498 votes.

Nagarkurnool (SC) : 12,12,541* (8,43,230) - Manda Jagannath (TDP) : 4,31,095
Mallu Ravi (IND) : 3,64,195; Others : 16,382; Invalid : 31,558
In 1998, Dr. Mallu Ravi (INC) won by a margin of 19,675 votes.

Nalgonda : 14,17,117* (7,47,071) - Gutha Sukender Reddy (TDP) : 3,05,522
Kanukula Janardhan Reddy (INC) : 2,79,778; S. Sudhakar Reddy (CPI) : 1,34,994; Others : 4,639; Invalid : 22,138

In 1998, Suravaram Sudhakar Reddy (CPI) won by a margin of 24,455 votes.

Nandyal : 11,16,163* (7,48,102) - Bhuma Nagi Reddy (TDP) : 3,91,655 Gangula Prathapa Reddy (INC) : 3,19,046; Telugu Ramanjaneyulu (NTRTDP-LP) : 1,517; Others : 13,931; Invalid : 21,953

In 1998, Bhuma Nagi Reddy (TDP) won by a margin of 4,650 votes.

Narasapur : 10,21,712* (7,04,453) - Uppalapati Venkata Krishnam Raju (BJP) : 4,21,099; Kanumuru Bapiraju (INC) : 2,55,151; Rudraraju Satyanarayana Raju (R.S.) CPM) : 28.203

In 1998, Kanumuru Bapiraju (INC) won by a margin of 47,970 votes.

Narasaraopet : 12,62,560* (8,78,186) - Janardhanareddy Nedurumal (INC) : 4,32,266; Lal Janbasha S.M. (TDP) : 4,18,384; Invalid : 27,536

In 1998, Konjeti Rosaiah (INC) won by a margin of 47,718 votes.

Nellore (SC) : 11,65,164* (7,85,977) - Rajeswaramma Vukkala (TDP) : 3,81,166 Panabaka Lakshmi (INC) : 3,40,713; Thummalagunta Prapancha Bhanu Raju (CPM) : 30,856; Others : 17,097; Invalid : 16,145

In 1998, Panabaka Lakshmi (INC) won by a margin of 46,527 votes.

Nizamabad : 11,29,775* (7,76,775) - Ganga Reddy Gaddam (TDP) : 3,73,260 S. Santhosh Reddy (INC) : 3,69,824; Others : 4,755; Shakkari Konda Dharmapuri (Anna TDP) : 4,504; Invalid : 24,432

In 1998, Gangareddy Gaddam (TDP) won by a margin of 32,752 votes.

Parvathipuram : 9,11,611* (6,36,856) - Dadichiluka Veera Gowri Sankararao (TDP) : 3,04,000; Kishore Chandra Suryanarayana Deo Vyricherila (INC) : 2,90,719; Others : 18,922; Invalid : 23,215

In 1998, Vijaya Ramaraju Setrucharia (TDP) won by a margin of 23,277 votes.

Peddapalli : 13,32,496* (8,89,480) - Smt. C. Suguna Kumari (TDP) : 4,03,397 G. Venkat Swamy (INC) : 3,88,136; Yerrala Gattaiah (CPI) : 41,379; Others : 20,997; Invalied : 35,571

In 1998, C. Suguna Kumari (TDP) won by a margin of 6,174 votes.

Rajampet : 9,46,152* (6,78,817) - Gunipati Ramaiah (TDP) : 3,22,107 Annaiahgari (INC) : 2,94,937; Mahaboob Basha Shaik (ATDP) : 22,473; Others : 21,041; Invalid : 18,259

In 1998, Annaiahgari Sai Pratap (INC) won by a margin of 47,840 votes.

Rajamundry : 11,37,216* (8,23,716) - Satyanarayana Rao S.B.P.B.K. (BJP) : 4,11,956; Chitturi Ravindra (INC) : 3,51,925; Bommidi Ram Mohana Rao (AJBP) : 15,727; Velagala Satti Reddy (ATDP) : 10,932; Others : 5,746; Invalid: 27,430

In 1998, Girijalavenkata Swamy Naidu (BJP) won by a margin of 9,912 votes.

Secunderabad : 1769,797* (9,70,791) - Bandaru Dattareya (BJP) : 5,06,626 Nadendla Bhasker Rao (INC) : 4,09,000; Mohd Adam Malik (MBT) : 13,461; K.S. Ganesh Rao (JD-S) : 12,949; Others : 12,315; Invalid : 16,440

In 1998, Bandaru Dattatreya (BJP) won by a margin of 1,85,910 votes.

Siddipet : 16,24,566* (10,72,820) - M. Rajaiah (TDP) : 5,83,346 Nandi Yellaiah (INC) : 4,29,625; N.A. Krishna (ATDP) : 16,944; Others : 12,617; Invalid : 30,288

In 1998, Malyala Rajaiah (TDP) won by a margin of 11,025 votes.

Srikakulam : 9,85,232* (6,75,943) - Yerrannaidu Kinjarapu (TDP) : 3,73,851 Kanithi Viswanadham (INC) : 2,76,969; Appala Naidu Golive (AJBP) : 7,280; Invalid : 17,843

In 1998, Kinjarapu Yerrannaidu (TDP) won by a margin of 86,365 votes.

Tenali : 9,60,395* (6,59,306) - Umareddy Venkateswarulu (TDP) : 3,39,800
P. Shiv Shankar (INC) : 2,66,771; Nageswara Rao Parchuri (CPM) : 35,860; Others : 3,170; Invalid : 13,705
In 1998, P. Shiv Shanker (INC) won by a margin of 12,160 votes.

Tirupathi (SC) : 11,99,978* (8,24,420) - N. Venkataswamy (BJP) : 3,86,478
Chinta Mohan (INC) : 3,73,981; T. Gunasekhar (ATDP) : 12,311; Others : 17,667; Invalid : 33,983
In 1998, Chintha Mohan (INC) won by a margin of 9,346 votes.

Vijayawada : 13,84,257* (9,29,476) - Gadde Rama Mohan (TDP) : 4,82,968
P. Upendra (INC) : 3,95,902; Kolli Nageswara Rao (CPI) : 36,902; Sudhakara Reddi Lakkireddi (NTRTDP-LP) : 986; Others : 12,718
In 1998, Upendra Parvathaneni (INC) won by a margin of 30,074 votes.

Visakhapatnam : 14,20,538* (9,12,789) - M.V.V.S. Muthy (TDP) : 4,42,036
T. Subbarami Reddy (INC) : 4,03,117; Ch. Narsinga Rao (CPM) : 26,610; Navish Yadav (T.N.V. Murthy) (SP) : 9,377; Apparao Gudivada (IND) : 2,263; Nanduri Pani (IND) : 1,458; Invalid : 27,928
In 1998, Subbarami Reddy T. (INC) won by a margin of 61,517 votes.

Warangal : 11,32,718* (8,53,607) - Bodakunti Venkateshwarlu (TDP) : 3,85,593
T. Kalpana Devi (INC) : 3,72,227; Others : 39,522; Gollapelly Nagaiah (CPI-M): 30,622; Thakur Desh Raj Singh (AJBP) : 4,025; Invalid : 21,618
In 1998, Azmeera Chandulal (TDP) won by a margin of 24,809 votes.

1998

Party	Seats won	Vote share
Congress	22	38.5%
T.D.P.	12	32.0%
BJP	4	18.3%
Others	4	11.2%

ARUNACHAL PRADESH (2)

Both Lok Sabha seats were won by the Indian National Congress

Constituency-wise Results — 1999 and Winners of 1998

Arunachal East : 2,63,250* (1,96,263) - Wangcha Rajkumar (INC) : 1,10,792
Tapir Gao (BJP) : 69,389; Chau Khouk Manpoong (AJBP) : 10,163; Invalid : 5,919
In 1998, Wangcha Rajkumar (AC) won by a margin of 27,437 votes.

Arunachal West : 3,45,924* (2,44,966) - Jarbom Gamlin (INC) : 1,31,483
Omak Apang (AC) : 70,760; Toko Kach (NCP) : 33,076; Invalid : 9,647
In 1998, Omak Apang (AC) won by a margin of 45,105 votes.

---

* Total Electorates
Figures in ( ) are Votes polled

ASSAM (14)

The BJP enetered with a tally of two wins. The victories came from Gawahati and Nowgong. The Reserved Kokrajhar seat was won by the independent candidate Sansuma Khunggur Bwismuthiary. The INC won 10 out of the total 14 seats. Tarun Gogoi of INC won from Kaliabor. One seat went to CPI-MLL

Number of Seats	
1952 and 62	- 12
1967 onwards	- 14

Constituency-wise Results — 1999 and Winners of 1998

Autonomous District (ST) : 3,96,324* (3,86,609) - Jayanta Rongpi (CPI-ML) : 2,08,730; Biren Singh Engti (INC) : 1,48,832; Others : 29,047
In 1998, Jayanta Rongpi (ASDC) won by a margin of 1,04,864 votes.

Barpeta : 10,21,799* (7,67,914) - A.F. Golam Osmani (INC) : 3,25,838 Ramani Kanta Deka (BJP) : 2,36,476; Uddhab Barman (CPM) : 1,41,272; Others : 12,491; Invalid : 11,581
In 1998, A.F. Golam Osmani (UMFA) won by a margin of 2,24,507 votes.

Dibrugarh : 9,44,304* (5,78,810) - Paban Singh Ghatowar (INC) : 2,70,863 Ajit Chaliha (BJP) : 2,03,747; Biju Phukan (AGP) : 75,932; Others : 7,132; Invalid : 21,136
In 1998, Paban Singh Ghatowar (INC) won by a margin of 1,41,122 votes.

Guwahati : 13,54,405* (8,58,028) - Bijoya Chakravarty (BJP) : 3,84,771 Bhubaneswar Kalita (INC) : 3,09,533; Durga Das Boro (AGP) : 1,19,034; Others : 24,090; Invalid : 20,600
In 1998, Bhubaneswar Kalita (INC) won by a margin of 1,28,173 votes.

Jorhat : 10,02,056* (6,49,354) - Bijoy Krishna Handique (INC) : 3,04,690 Janaki Nath Handique (BJP) : 2,05,330; Deba Kumar Gogoi (NCP) : 2,530; Invalid : 18,610
In 1998, Bijoy Krishna Handique (INC) won by a margin of 1,62,009 votes.

Kaliabor : 11,10,183* (7,79,600) - Tarun Gogoi (INC) : 3,73,542 Keshab Mahanta (AGP) : 2,06,150; Bhadreswar Tanti (BJP) : 1,67,331; Others : 11,687; Invalit : 20,890
In 1998, Tarun Gogoi (INC) won by a margin of 2,32,345 votes.

Karimganj (SC) : 9,42,838* (6,95,538) - Nepal Chandra Das (INC) : 3,36,799 Parimal Suklabaidya (BJP) : 2,94,540; Kushi Kanta Das (CPM) : 34,250; Others: 14,117; Invalid : 15,832
In 1998, Nepal Chandra Das (INC) won by a margin of 10,466 votes.

Kokrajhar (ST) : 11,67,813* (9,10,953) - Sansuma Khungur Bwismuthiary (IND) : 3,34,367; Theodore Kisku Rapaz (URMCA) : 2,46,942; Gangadhar Ramchiary (PDF) : 1,72,432; Premsingh Brahma (INC) : 65,234; Anil Murmu (IND) : 63,427; Kanakeswar Narzary (UBNLF) : 7,611; Invalid : 20,940
In 1998, Sansuma Khungur Bwiswmuthiary (IND) won by a margin of 41,432 votes.

---

* Total Electorates
Figures in ( ) are Votes polled

Lakhimpur : 10,57,604* (7,67,004) - Ranee Narah (INC) : 2,55,925
Sarbananda Sonowal (AGP) : 2,01,402; Udai Sankar Hazarika (BJP) : 1,84,533; Ronoj Pegu (IND) : 89,963; Others : 12,000; Invalid : 23,181
In 1998, Ranee Narah (INC) won by a margin of 1,20,782 votes.

Mangaldoi : 11,79,715* (8,58,489) - Madhab Rajbangshi (INC) : 2,83,749
Munindra Singha Lahkar)BJP) : 2,67,315; Birendra Prasad Baishya (AGP) : 1,54,711; Rabi Ram Brahma (IND) : 1,10,610; Others : 15,973; Invalid : 26,131
In 1998, Madhab Rajbangshi (INC) won by a margin of 1,30,577 votes.

Nowgong : 11,13,153* (7,80,508) - Rajen Gohain (BJP) : 3,28,861
Nripen Goswami (INC) : 2,93,433; Muhi Ram Saikia (AGP) : 1,03,497; Others : 22,502; H.R.A. Choudhury (UMF) : 13,405; Invalid : 18,810
In 1998, Nripen Goswami (INC) won by a margin of 37,834 votes.

Silchar : 8,26,446* (6,07,228) - Santosh Mohan Deb (INC) : 3,29,256
Kabindra Purakavastha (BJP) : 2,21,504; Abdul Muhib Mazumdar (IND) : 29,060; Others : 7,323; Subhas Mohan Dev (NCP) : 5,737; Invalid : 14,348
In 1998, Kabindra Purkayastha (BJP) won by a margin of 19,566 votes.

Tezpur : 9,71,023* (7,04,449) - Moni Kumar Subba (INC) : 2,30,884
Ram Prasad Sarmah (BJP) : 2,05,178; Kosheswar Bora (AGP) : 2,03,141; Others : 36,805; Invalid : 28,441
In 1998, Moni Kumar Subba (INC) won by a margin of 1,30,349 votes.

1998

Party	Seats won	Vote share
Congress	10	38.9%
BJP	1	24.5%
ASDC	1	2.2%
Others	2	34.4%

BIHAR (54)

The State had the Janata Dal (United) and the Rashtriya Janata Dal besides the BJP and the INC as the main contenders. The BJP was able to secure 23 of the total 54 seats. Laloo Yadav lost to Sharad Yadav from Madhepura while George Fernandes won from Nalanda on JD (U) ticket. Ram Vilas Paswan was back from Hajipur while Kirti Azad won the Darbhanga seat. Hazaribagh voted Yashwant Sinha (BJP) while M. Sahabuddin was back from Siwan as the RJD candidate. The RJD was successful only in 7 constituencies out of a total of 54 and marked a great set back for Laloo Prasad who was at one time perceived as invincible in Bihar. The Janata Dal (U) bagged 18 seats, Indian National Congress 4, and others 2 seats.

RJD and INC had contested as allies.

"Democratic justice has finally caught up with Laloo Prasad Yadav. Ten years after the total destruction he began delivering by way of revolution to the people of Bihar, the long arm of the electorate has snuffed out, albeit extremely belatedly, his cynical, self-serving vision of social justice. It would perhaps be premature to write an obituary for the performer with a sola topi hairdo, but the break-up of his formidable Yadav-Muslim votebank has shattered the myth of his invincibility. "*Rome Pope ka, Madhepura Gope ka* (Rome belongs to the Pope, Madhepura to the Yadav)," went a popular saying.

Madhepura has voted for a Yadav alright, but for a man from Madhya Pradesh, not the great Yadav leader from Patna's 1 Anne Marg. Yet, even when Laloo emerges from the stupor his electoral defeat has banished him to, it is doubtful that he will come to grips with the legacy he has bequeathed to the Republic of Bihar.

It is a legacy of perfidy, of hollow populism and of reigning anarchy. The irony is rife. A disciple of Jayaprakash Narayan, Laloo cruised to the helm of affairs in Bihar on the anti-corruption plank. Today, however, when he is not enchanting the chattering classes by fattening fish to take on the opposition, news items about him are splattered with phrases like the fodder scandal and the bitumen scam. Never one to be miserly with sweeping promises or absurd similes, he assured Bihar's rickshawalas of Maruti vans and roads smooth as Hema Malini's cheeks to ply them on. Today under his proxy raj motorable roads are conspicuous by their very absence, and development is limited to the odd electricity pole punctuating an arid countryside. And social justice? It is merely a cruel euphemism for exploitative socio-economic hegemony and periodic midnight visitations by rival private militias. Laloo may have regaled the multitudes with exhortations like a plea to vote for him so that they could all accompany him to Delhi for a cup of tea in Connaught Place, but for thousands of Dalits in his jungle raj even the act of wearing chappals is a taboo which can be breached only by risking reprisal.

Whether the churning that has been set in motion by the Madhepura upset heralds an early fall of the Rabri Devi regime or not, it will now be extremely difficult for Laloo to recoup the ground surrendered this unusually harsh monsoon season. That his social coalition has unravelled is evident, given the winning uppercaste-backward-Dalit-tribal alliance forged by the BJP Janata Dal (U) combine. If the Bihar vote calls for a spot of introspection by Laloo, it also makes it incumbent on the opposition to follow up their sweep in the general elections by going to the people with a blueprint for the reconstruction of civil society. It is time the people were given a chance to associate the slogan social justice with land reforms, development and an administration that delivers education, health care and law and order." [*Indian Express*]

Constituency-wise Results — 1999 and Winners of 1998

Araria (SC) : 10,41,534* (6,48,975) - Sukdeo Paswan (RJD) : 3,08,579
Parmanand Rishidev (BJP) : 3,06,410; Others : 23,657; Invalid : 10,329
In 1998, Ramji Das Rishideo (BJP) won by a margin of 33,937 votes.

Arrah : 11,23,985* (6,89,363) - Ram Prasad Singh (RJD) : 2,64,132
H.P. Singh (JD-U) : 1,71,804; Rameshwar Prasad (CPI-ML-L) : 1,41,936; Rang Bahadur Singh (IND) : 87,263; Others : 16,576; Invalid : 7,652
In 1998, H.P. Singh (SAP) won by a margin of 58,164 votes.

Aurangabad : 10,91,703* (6,83,925) - Shyama Singh (INC) : 3,17,418
Sushil Kumar Singh (JD-U) : 2,47,002; Raja Ram Singh (IND) : 83,970; Ganesh Prasad (BSP) : 15,005; Others : 11,228; Invalid : 9,302
In 1998, Sushil Kumar Singh (SAP) won by a margin of 86,293 votes.

Bagaha (SC) : 10,28,623* (5,79,316) - Mahendra Baitha (JD-U) : 2,61,498
Purnamasi Ram (RJD) : 2,06,747; Kanchchan Baitha (CVP) : 56,561; Nand Jee Ram (CPI-ML-L) : 28,208; Others 17,256; Invalid : 9,046

* Total Electorates
Figures in ( ) are Votes polled

In 1998, Mahendra Baitha (SAP) won by a margin of 45,743 votes.

Balia : 9,96,729* (5,06,250) - Ramjivan Singh (JD-U) : 1,69,443
Ashok Kumar (RJD) : 1,57,411; Shatrughan Prasad Singh (CPI) : 1,39,836; Others : 32,695; Invalid : 6,865
In 1998, Raj Vanshi Mahto (RJD) won by a margin of 52,384 votes.

Banka : 10,64,171* (6,35,956) - Digvijay Singh (JD-U) : 2,33,453
Giridhari Yadav (IND) : 2,12,045; Shakuni Choudhary (RJD) : 1,60,678; Others: 20,117; Invalid : 9,663
In 1998, Digvijay Singh (SAP) won by a margin of 11,291 votes.

Barh : 10,94,939* (7,59,653) - Nitish Kumar (JD-U) : 3,62,016
Vijay Krishna (RJD) : 3,60,681; Shashi Devi (CPI-ML-L) : 21,128; Others : 6,833; Invalid : 8,995
In 1998, Nitish Kumar (SAP) won by a margin of 15,170 votes.

Begusarai : 11,11,018* (6,41,348) - Rajo Singh (INC) : 3,18,244
Shyam Sundar Singh (JD-U) : 2,98,294; Others : 18,729; Invalid : 6,081
In 1998, Rajo Singh (INC) won by a margin of 52,907 votes.

Bettiah : 10,98,738* (6,96,181) - Madan Prasad Jaiswal (BJP) : 3,43,027
Mataur Rahman (RJD) : 3,03,377; Triveni Tiwary (CPI) : 23,317; Dharmesh Prasad Verma (SJP-R) : 11,901; Others : 7,418; Invalid : 7,141
In 1998, Madan Prasad Jaiswal (BJP) won by a margin of 41,901 votes.

Bikramganj : 11,35,485* (7,42,514) - Kanti Singh (RJD) : 3,46,259
Vashisht Narayan Singh (JD-U) : 3,11,491; Arun Singh (CPI-ML-L) : 52,384; Narendra Singh Kushwaha (BSP) : 14,801; Others : 9,983; Invalid : 7,596
In 1998, Bashisht Narayan Singh (SAP) won by a margin of 7,851 votes.

Buxar : 10,21,614* (6,09,414) - Lal Muni Choubey (BJP) : 2,35,968
Shivanand Tiwary (RJD) : 2,24,362; Tej Narayan Singh (CPI) : 67,916; Mitranand Singh (CPI-ML-L) : 36,385; Sobh Nath Ram Anokha (BSP) : 32,957; Others : 5,161; Invalid : 6,665
In 1998, Lal Muni Choubey (BJP) won by a margin of 84,316 votes.

Chapra : 10,02,998* (7,78,714) - Rajiv Pratap Rudi (BJP) : 3,90,477
Hira Lal Rai (RJD) : 3,46,924; Bachchu Prasad Biru (BSP) : 12,378; Lal Babu Rai (JD-S) : 11,689; Others : 8,607; Invalid : 8,639

Chatra : 10,15,249* (4,26,241) - Nagmani (RJD) : 2,19,783
Dhirendra Agrawal (BJP) : 1,64,684; Mahavir Prasad Yadav (BSP) : 11,264; Others : 21,048; Invalid : 9,472
In 1998, Dhiendra Agarwal (BJP) won by a margin of 33,375 votes.

Darbhanga : 10,43,030* (7,66,168) - Kirti Azad (BJP) : 3,95,549
Md Ali Ashraf Fatmi (RJD) : 3,40,001; Baidyanath Yadav (CPI-ML-L) : 9,978; Bishwanath Mandal (BSP) : 5,471; Others : 7,292; Invalid : 7,877
In 1998, Md Ali Ashraf Fatmi (RJD) won by a margin of 36,108 votes.

Dhanbad : 14,33,667* (7,71,044) - Rita Verma (BJP) : 3,66,065
A.K. Roy (MCO) : 3,51,839; Kansari Mandal (JMM) : 18,617; Others : 24,940; Invalid : 9,583
In 1998, Rita Verma (BJP) won by a margin of 1,78,689 votes.

Dumka (ST) : 9,51,282* (5,54,237) - Babu Lal Marandi (BJP) : 2,01,141
Rupi Soren Kisku (JMM) : 1,96,493; Ramesh Hembram (INC) : 1,34,625; Others : 13,241; Invalid : 8,737

In 1998, Babulal Marandi (BJP) won by a margin of 12,556 votes.

Gaya : 10,56,767* (6,47,949) - Ramji Manjhi (BJP) 3,19,517
Rajesh Kumar (RJD) : 2,98,745; Others : 18,171; Invalid : 11,516
In 1998, Krishna Kumar Chaudhry (BJP) won by a margin of 36,446 votes.

Giridih : 11,15,439* (5,40,464) - Ravindra Kumar Pandey (BJP) : 2,48,417
Rajendra Prasad Singh (INC) : 2,28,630; Shiva Mahato (JMM-U) : 48,802; Others : 12,150; Invalid : 2,465
In 1998, Ravindra Kumar Pandey (BJP) won by a margin of 68,791 yotes.

Godda : 10,87,651* (6,41,987) - Jagdambi Prasad Yadav (BJP) 2,21,181
Suraj Mandal (JMM) : 1,41,298; Furkan Ansari (INC) : 1,08,850; Sanjay Kumar (CPI) : 86,430; Javed Iqbal Ansari (RJD) : 60,092; Others : 15,690; Invalid : 8,446
In 1998, Jagdambi Prasad Yadav (BJP) won by a margin of 75,680 votes.

Gopalganj : 11,77,203* (7,50,762) - Raghunath Jha (JD-U) : 3,65,107
Kali Prasad Pandey (RJD) : 3,28,983; Satraj Singh (CPI-ML-L) : 29,990; Chhathu Sah (BSP) : 11,058; Others : 6,706; Invalid : 8,918
In 1998, Abdul Ghafoor (SAP) won by a margin of 68,605 votes.

Hajipur (SC) : 10,64,323* (7,90,448) - Ram Vilas Paswan (JD-U) : 4,34,609
Ramali Ram (RJD) : 3,29,105; Others : 15,887; Invalid : 10,847

Hazaribagh : 12,13,800* (6,00,310) - Yashwant Sinha (BJP) : 2,83,956
Akalu Ram Mahto (RJD) : 1,01,314; Teklal Mahto (JMM-U) : 71,346; Ramendra Kumar (CPI) : 55,615; Ishwar Ram Paswan (INC) : 36,929; Deoki Nandan Vedia (CPI-ML-L) : 20,898; Fagu Besara (JMM) : 12,687; Others : 9,136; Invalid : 8,429
In 1998, Yaswant Sinha (BJP) won by a margin of 1,56,691 votes.

Jamshedpur : 11,60,646* (6,35,251) - Abha Mahato (BJP) : 2,85,232
Ghanashyam Mahato (INC) : 1,63,744; Sunil Kumar Mahato (JMM) : 80,417; Dulal Mnshi (CPI) : 56,354; Sudhir Mahato (JMM-U) : 36,065; Others : 6,416; Invalid : 7,023
In 1998, Abha Mahato (BJP) won by a margin of 97,433 votes.

Jahanabad : 11,05,969* (7,86,107) - Arun Kumar (JD-U) : 3,33,332
Surendra Prasad Yadav (RJD) : 3,16,045; Ramadhar Singh (CPI-ML-L) : 99,325; Ramashraya Prasad Singh (IND) : 16,878; Others : 9,702; Invalid : 10,825
In 1998, Surendra Prasad Yadav (RJD) won by a margin of 58,907 votes.

Jhanjharpur : 10,52,589* (6,84,147) - Devendra Prasad Yadav (JD-U) : 3,75,852
Surendra Prasad Yadav (RJD) : 2,48,038; Chitranjan Sah (BSP) : 29,245; Others: 21,281; Invalid : 9,731
In 1998, Surendra Prasad Yadav (RJD) won by a margin of 37,270 votes.

Katihar : 10,39,396* (6,42,852) - Nikhil Kumar Choudhary (BJP) : 2,80,911
Madan Mohan Singh Nishad (BSP) : 1,44,059; Mubarak Hussain (INC) : 1,41,575; Tariq Anwar (NCP) : 48,900; Others 20,113; Invalid : 7,294
In 1998, Tariq Anwar (INC) won by a margin of 20,441 votes.

Khunti (ST) : 8,28,500* (4,12,090) - Kariya Munda (BJP) : 1,87,484
Sushila Kerketa (INC) : 1,61,222; N.E. Horo (JKP) : 52,981; Ghanshyam Singh Munda (FBL) : 3,151; Invalid : 7,252
In 1998, Kariya Munda (BJP) won by a margin of 39,949 votes.

Kishanganj : 11,29,025* (7,27,839) - Syed Shahnawan Hussain (BJP) : 2,58,035
Taslimuddin (RJD) : 2,49,387; Maulana Asranul Haque (NCP) : 1,97,478; Others : 12,735; Invalid : 10,204
In 1998, Taslimuddin (RJD) won by a margin of 6,488 votes.

Kodarma : 11,62,500* (6,02,557) - Tilakdhari Pandit Singh (INC) : 2,73,808
Ritlal Prasad Verma (BJP) : 2,63,630; Nazmul Hasan (CPI-ML-L) : 21,100; Mumtaj Ansary (NCP) : 19,587; Others : 16,872; Invalid : 7,560
In 1998, Ritlal Verma (BJP) won by a margin of 97,909 votes.

Lohardaga : 9,39,788* (3,69,875) - Dukha Bhagat (BJP) : 1,63,658
Indra Nath Bhagat (INC) : 1,59,835; Bishwanath Bhagat (JMM) : 28,245; Others : 11,776; Invalid : 6,361
In 1998, Indranath Bhagat (INC) won by a margin of 19,397 votes.

Madhepura : 9,97,083* (6,60,906) - Sharad Yadav (JD-U) : 3,28,760
Laloo Prasad (RJD) : 2,98,441; Others : 21,272; Invalid : 12,433
In 1998, Laloo Prasad (RJD) won by a margin of 51,983 votes.

Madhubani : 10,99,522* (7,17,312) - Hukumdeo Narayan Yadav (BJP) : 3,28,616
Shakil Ahmad (INC) : 2,66,001; Bhogendra Jha (CPI) : 99,394; Others : 12,937; Invalid : 10,364
In 1998, Sgakeel Ahmad (INC) won by a margin of 16,487 votes.

Maharajganj : 9,82,199* (7,05,705) - Prabhunath Singh (JD-U) : 3,98,485
Mahachandra Prasad : 2,94,412; Chandraketu Singh (IND) : 4,413; Invalid : 8,405
In 1998, Madan Prasad won by a margin of 41,901 votes.

Monghyr : 11,47,663* (7,12,195) - Brahma Nand Mandal (JD-U) : 3,46,615
Bijoy Kumar Bijoy (RJD) : 3,24,800; Others : 33,863; Invalid : 6,917
In 1998, Bijoy Kumar Bijoy (RJD) won by a margin of 4,065 votes.

Motihari : 11,13,078* (6,85,679) - Radha Mohan Singh (BJP) : 3,38,696
Rama Devi (RJD) : 3,17,026; Prabhat Kumar Singh (AJBP) : 11,774; Others : 9,566; Invalid : 8,617
In 1998, Rama Devi (RJD) won by a margin of 88,809 votes.

Muzaffarpur : 10,68,341* (7,30,490) - Captain Jai Narain Prasad Nishad (JD-U) : 3,63,820; Mahendra Sahni (RJD) : 3,03,100; Vijay Shukal (IND) : 34,613; Others : 17,994; Invalid : 10,963

Nalanda : 11,80,372* (8,78,541) - George Fernandes (JD-U) : 4,64,458
Gaya Singh (CPI) : 3,58,637; Surendra Ram (CPI-ML-L) : 42,612; Others : 5,872; Invalid : 6,962
In 1998, George Fernandes (SAP) won by a margin of 1,15,670 votes.

Nawada (SC) : 11,73,464* (8,59,271) - Sanjay Paswan (BJP) 4,53,943
Vijay Kumar Choudhary (RJD) : 3,69,858; Gajendra Manjhi (CPI-ML-L) : 11,288; Others : 15,263; Invalid : 8,919
In 1998, Malti Devi (RJD) won by a margin of 14,384 votes.

Palamau (SC) : 10,80,276* (5,16,661) - Braj Mohan Ram (BJP) : 2,71,651
Jorawar Ram (RJD) : 1,86,532; Rampati Ram (BSP) : 34,809; Kishore Kumar (CPI-ML-L) : 11,594; Renu Devi (JP) : 4,368; Invalid : 7,707
In 1998, Braj Mohan Ram (BJP) won by a margin of 80,825 votes.

Patna : 14,73,430* (8,12,307) - C.P. Thakur (BJP) : 3,79,370
Ram Kripal Yadav (RJD) : 3,32,478; Ramanand Yadav (IND) : 47,682; Saroj Choubey (CPI-ML-L) : 20,476; Others : 22,101; Invalid : 10,200

In 1998, C.P. Thakur (BJP) won by a margin of 52,606 votes.

Ranchi : 11,32,046* (5,83,745) - Ram Tahal Choudhary (BJP) : 3,79,261
K.K. Tewari (INC) : 1,38,084; Prem Chand Mahto (JMM) : 39,021; Others : 20,724; Invalid : 6,655
In 1998, Ram Tahal Chowdhary (BJP) won by a margin of 1,43,293 votes.

Rosera (SC) : 10,75,902* (7,34,149) - Ram Chandra Paswan (JD-U) : 4,20,564
Pitamber Paswan (RJD) : 2,77,648; Others : 25,502; Invalid : 10,435
In 1998, Pitamber Paswan (RJD) won by a margin of 43,283 votes.

Saharsa : 11,41,819* (7,32,053) - Dinesh Chandra Yadav (JD-U) : 3,92,926
Surya Narayan Yadav (RJD) : 2,98,433; Niraj Kumar (BHJC) : 12,969; Dinesh Prasad Sinha (AJBP) : 11,479; Lalan Choudhary (IND) : 5,790; Invalid : 10,456
In 1998, Anup Lall Yadav (RJD) won by a margin of 54,169 votes.

Samastipur : 12,17,806* (8,01,021) - Manjay Lal (JD-U) : 3,68,776
Ashok Singh (RJD) : 3,56,088; Ram Japit Rai (IND) : 17,602; Vinod Chaudhary (CPI-ML-L) : 16,724; Gajendra Prasad Himanshu (LS) : 14,253; Others : 17,595; Invalid : 9,983

Sasaram (SC) : 11,44,806* (6,62,269) - Munni Lal (BJP) : 2,57,223
Ram Keshi Bharati (RJD) : 2,38,547; Chandrika Das (BSP) : 82,861; Chhedi Paswan (NCP) : 46,449; Ravishanker Ram (CPI-ML-L) : 14,320; Others : 13,915; Invalid : 8,954
In 1998, Munni Lal (BJP) won by a margin of 88,728 votes.

Sheohar : 10,82,838* (7,25,420) - Md. Anwarul Haque (RJD) : 3,47,279
Anand Mohan (BPSP) : 3,44,744; Others : 23,913; Invalid : 9,484
In 1998, Anand Mohan (RJP) won by a margin of 88,904 votes.

Singhbhum (ST) : 8,46,408* (4,82,318) - Laxman Giluwa (BJP) : 231,237
Vijay Singh Soy (INC) : 1,48,926; Champai Soren (JMM) : 71,527; Lakshman Soy (UGDP) : 11,153; Others : 8,657; Invalid : 10,818
In 1998, Vijay Singh Soy (INC) won by a margin of 10,830 votes.

Sitamarhi : 11,26,655* (7,54,419) - Nawal Kishore Rai (JD-U) : 4,10,515
Suryadeo Rai (RJD) : 3,09,298; Others : 22,889; Invalid : 11,717
In 1998, Sitaram Yadav (RJD) won by a margin of 24,184 votes.

Siwan : 9,90,207* (7,09,886) - M. Sahabuddin (RJD) : 3,85,059
Amar Nath Yadav (CPI-ML-L) : 2,55,226; Akhlaque Ahmad (JD-U) : 53,333; Others : 8,610; Invalid : 7,658
In 1998, Md. Shahabuddin (RJD) won by a margin of 1,20,484 votes.

Vaishali : 10,50,090* (7,20,498) - Raghuvansh Prasad Singh (RJD) : 3,08,458
Lovely Anand (BPSP) : 2,63,066; Shashi Kumar Rai (IND) : 1,12,450; Others : 25,778; Invalid : 10,746

GOA (2)

The success of BJP at both the seats established beyond doubt its acceptance as a national level party with no hard-core Hindutva stigma. The results must have surprised even the BJP itself.

Constituency-wise Results — 1999 and Winners of 1998

Mormugao (South Goa) : 4,95,208* (2,18,851) - Ramakant Angle (BJP) : 1,06,064
Joaquim Alemao (INC) : 91,607; Wilfred D'Souza (NCP) : 10,529; Others :

4,723; Invalid : 5,928

In 1998, Sardinha Francisco Caetano (INC) won by a margin of 7,850 votes.

Panaji (North Goa) : 4,13,592* (1,91,093) - Shripad Naik (BJP) : 1,04,,958

Ramakant Khalap (INC) : 68,237; Others : 17,790; Invalid : 108

In 1998, Ravi Sitaram Naik (INC) won by a margin of 417 votes.

GUJARAT (26)

The State had been a strong hold of the BJP. The party retained 20 out of the 26 Lok Sabha seats. The Congress alliance with Vaghela did not pay dividends. Its tally was a mere 6 seats. However, Shankarsin Vaghela himself was elected on INC ticket from Kapadvanj constituency.

	Total Seats
1962	22
1967 & 1971	24
1978 onwards	26

Since 1977 the voter turnout has been below the National average.

"On the face of it, the Lok Sabha elections in Gujarat have meant a gain of only one seat for the BJP, whose tally rose to 20 out of 26. But it is the exchange of seats between the BJP and the Congress that should make the latter sit up.

The Congress is shocked that five of its seven traditional seats, which stayed with it even in its worst days, have been snatched by the BJP. Four of the six won by Congress are new, but the party had hoped to retain its seven seats and add a few more.

Kargil has not helped the BJP as much as the failure of the Congress of capitalise on issues like the state government's handling of the water crisis and the humiliation of minorities. The Congress strategy of fielding 15 Patels to counter BJP's "Patel-ism" failed. In the process, it lost out on its traditional vote-banks. And, thanks to factionalism, it could not take advantage of the RJP's merger with the party.

Four of the five seats which the Congress lost are tribal seats, where the saffron brigade's Dangs "experiment" was successful in spliting the tribal *adivasi* votes into Hindus and Christians. "Here," says political analyst Dinesh Shukla, "The Congress should have had its ear to the ground." Madhusudan Mistry, former state RJP president, agrees that the BJP had managed to extricate mileage while the Congress never attacked the issue wholistically.

Before the elections, BJP stategist Sanjay Joshi had said that the Christian issue would, in fact, help the party, for it "brought a new Hindu re-awakening and there would be surprises." And it happened. It isn't rhetoric when Chief Minister Keshubhai Patel says, "From Backward Classes to minorities, everyone has reposed confidence in the BJP."

Mistry believes the Congress could have prevented this if "it had come out with concrete programmes for its traditional vote-banks, instead of toying with the Patel lobby." Shukla says, "The Hindu-Christian divide didn't affect tribals in Sabarkantha (also in north Gujarat) while the Backwards got together in the Scheduled Caste seats of Dhandhuka and Patan." For this, he gives credit to Vaghela, whom Congress is yet to accept as a leader because of factionalism.

While the Janata Dal (Gujarat) group feels side lined because decisions remain with the PCC president C.D. Patel-Amarsin Chaudhary group, the RJP is seen as another group, which enjoys the backing of former External Affairs Minister Madhavsingh Solanki, and its leader a threat to the old guard.

But C.D. Patel says the Congress suffered because polling was held in the first round when Kargil and dethroning of the Vajpayee Government were fresh.

The same reasons that helped the Congress in north Gujarat are cause for the BJP to worry. It lost Mehsana, held by A.K. Patel since 1984, and Patan, represented by Gujarati film singer Mahesh Kanodiya. "The BJP entered Gujarat with Mehsana and held on to the region till 1999. It has suddenly got marginalised," says Shukla. Even Keshubhai Patel admits, "Except in north Gujarat, the results are as we expected."

Meanwhile, though the BJP may hate to admit it, anti-minority violence in the tribal heartland of Gujarat has paid richer dividends than it could ever imagine. For the first time in 52 years, not a single ST seat has gone into the kitty of the Congress, which had come to take tribal backing for granted.

The BJP, which was holding Valsad, has wrested Chhotaudepur, Dahod and Mandvi from the Congress. The last two seats have not been ever represented by any party other than the Congress. While Mistry admits the anti-incumbency factor could have gone against them, the candidates are reluctant to think so. Says Damor, "Hindu-Christian *vaatma koi dam nathi*. The tribals have forgotten Dangs and Randhikpur. We ran short of cash. There were no workers to campaign in the last few days. [*Darshan Desai and Milind Ghatwai*]

Constituency-wise Results — 1999 and Winners of 1998

Ahmedabad : 13,20,159* (5,27,737) - Pathak Harindrakumar Ramchandra (BJP) : 2,80,696; Dani Girishbhai Popatbhai (INC) : 2,27,728; Others : 19,313
In 1998, Harin Pathak (BJP) won by a margin of 1,36,812 votes.

Amreli : 8,74,521* (4,16,331) - Sanghani Dilipbhai Nanub (BJP) : 2,17,670 Thummar Virji Keshavbhai (INC) : 1,81,346; Others : 8,472; Invalid : 8,843
In 1998, Dileep Sanghani (BJP) won by a margin of of 1,22,173 votes.

Anand :10,47,272* (5,60,270) - Patel Dipakbhai Chimanbhai (BJP) : 2,73,683 Chavda Ishvarbhai Khodibhai (INC) : 2,70,022; Others : 4,328; Invalid : 12,237
In 1998 Chavda Ishvarbhai Khodabhai (INC) won by a margin of 38,056 votes.

Banaskantha : 11,06,766* (6,03,011) - Haribhai Parthibhai (BJP) : 3,08,313 G. Bhairavdanji Khetdanji (INC) : 2,82,337; Others : 2,598; Invalid : 9,763
In 1998, Chaudhari Haribhai Parathibhai (BJP) won by a margin of 84,755 votes.

Baroda : 14,38,964* (5,96,475) - Smt. Jayaben Bharatkumar (BJP) : 3,22,758 Patel Urmilaben Chimanbhai (INC) : 2,30,109; Gohil Upendrasinh Pratapsinh (NCP) : 27,813; Others : 4,346; Invalid : 11,449
In 1998, Thakhar Jayaben Bharatkumar (BJP) won by a margin of 52,417 votes.

Bhavnagar :10,23,921* (4,45,003) - Rana Rajendrasinh Ghanshyamsinh (BJP) : 2,65,446; Gohil Dilipsinh Ajitsinh (INC) : 1,64,093; Others : 5,226; Invalid : 10,238
In 1998, Rana Rajendrasinh Ghanshyamsinh (BJP) won by a margin of 79,206 votes.

Broach : 10,96,772* (5,91,308) - Mansukhbhai Dhanjibhai Vasava (BJP) : 2,90,195 Vasava Amarsinh Ramsinh (INC) : 2,43,055; Bhagat Anil Bhai Chhitubhai (JD-U) : 36,999; Others : 10,786; Invalid : 10,273

---

* Total Electorates
Figures in ( ) are Votes polled

In 1998, Chandubhai Deshmukh (BJP) won by a margin of 11,606 votes.

Bulsar (ST) : 11,51,087* (5,96,255) - Manibhai Ramjibhai Chaudhari (BJP) : 3,00,161; Uttambhai Harjibhai Patel (INC) : 2,73,404; Others : 8,502; Invalid : 14,188

Chhota Udaipur (ST) : 9,62,525* (5,25,320) - Rathva Ramsinh Patalbhai (BJP) : 2,48,970; Naranbhai Jemalbhai Rathawa (INC) : 2,42,772; Others : 13,538; Invalid : 15,040

In 1998, Naranbhai Jemalabhai Rathawa (INC) won by a margin of 61,015 votes.

Dhandhuka (SC) : 10,29,973* (4,72,739) - Verma Ratilal Kalidas (BJP) : 2,29,754 Parmar Manhar Karsandas (INC) : 2,24,531; Others : 7,912; Invalid : 10,542

In 1998, Varma Ratilal Kalidas (BJP) won by a margin of 16,395 votes.

Dahod (ST) : 10,28,979* (4,77,760) - Katara Babubhai Khimabhai (BJP) : 2,32,288 Somjibhai Damor (INC) : 2,19,857; Others : 11,359; Invalid : 14,256

In 1998, Damor Somjibhai Punjabhai (INC) won by a margin of 1,14,280 votes.

Gandhinagar : 18,33,606* (7,41,073) - Lal Krishna Advani (BJP) : 4,53,127 T.N. Seshan (INC) : 2,64,200; Others : 23,746

In 1998 Advani Lal Krishna (BJP) won by a margin of 2,76,701 votes.

Godhra : 10,20,262* (4,83,245) - Solanki Bhupendra Sinh Prabhatsinh (BJP) : 2,80,684; Patel Shantilal Parshotamdas (INC) : 1,85,662; Others : 6,798; Invalid: 10,101

In 1998, Patel Shanthilal Parshotam Das (INC) won by a margin of 39,248 votes.

Jamnagar : 9,58,418* (3,61,424) - Koradiya Chandresh Valjibhai (BJP) : 1,90,669 Patel Raghavji Hansrajbhai (INC) : 1,54,950; Others : 7,014; Invalid : 8,791

In 1998, Koradiya Chandreshbhai Valjibhai (BJP) won by a margin of 60,119 votes.

Junagadh : 10,79,568* (5,03,447) - Chikhaliya Bhavnaben Devrajbhai (BJP) : 2,66,809; Chavda Pethalji Nathabhai (INC) : 2,19,961; Others : 5,483; Invalid : 11,194

In 1998, Chikhaliya Bhavnaben Devrajbhai (BJP) won by a margin of 90,311 votes.

Kaira : 10,54,781* (4,94,597) - Prabhatsinh Chauhan (BJP) : 2,58,024 Dinsha Zaverbhai Patel (INC) : 2,24,307; Others : 2,973; Invalid : 9,293

In 1998, Dinsha Patel (INC) won by a margin of 40,215 votes.

Kapadvanj : 11,24,201* (6,74,671) - Vaghela Shankarsinh Laxmansinh (INC) : 4,13,193; Chauhan Jaysinh Mansinh (BJP) : 2,47,812; Others : 3,571; Invalid : 10,095

In 1998, Chauhan Jaysinhji Manshingji (BJP) won by a margin of 51,294 votes.

Kutch : 8,72,937* (3,93,536) - Gadhvi Pushpadan Shambhudan (BJP) : 1,91,533 Babubhai Meghji Shah (INC) : 1,87,218; Others : 5,013; Invalid : 9,772

In 1998, Gadhvi Pushpadan Shambhudan (BJP) won by a margin of 61,025 votes.

Mandvi (ST) : 10,63,704* (6,16,838) - Patel Mansinhbhai Kalayanji (BJP) : 3,29,172; Gamit Chhitubhai Devjibhai (INC) : 2,63,341; Others : 17,097; Invalid : 7,228

In 1998, Chhitubhai Devjibhai Gamit (INC) won by a margin of 16,486 votes.

Mehsana : 11,04,439* (6,36,366) - Patel Atmaram Maganbhai (INC) : 3,40,445 Patel Amratbhai Kalidas (BJP) : 2,84,710; Others : 2,423; Invalid : 8,788
In 1998, A.K. Patel (BJP) won by a margin of 1,25,334 votes.

Patan (SC) : 10,03,826* (4,85,924) - Rashtrapal Pravichandra Somabh (INC) : 2,46,798; Kanodiya Maheshkumar Mithabhai (BJP) : 2,29,671; Others : 2,558; Invalid : 6,897
In 1998, Kanodia Maheshkumar Mithabhai (BJP) won by a margin of 1,29,519 votes.

Porbandar : 8,94,299* (3,31,908) - Javiya Gordhanbhai Jadavbhai (BJP) : 2,10,627 Manvar Balvantbhai Bachubh (INC) : 1,09,267; Others : 5,962; Invalid : 6,052
In 1998, Javiya Gordhanbhai Jadavbhai (BJP) won by a margin of 1,25,323 votes.

Rajkot : 13,79,914* (5,58,473) - Kathiriya Vallabhabhai (BJP) : 3,12,941 Radadiya Vithalbhai Hansraj (INC) : 2,26,194; Others : 7,095; Invalid : 12,243
In 1998, Karthiriya Vallabhbhai Ramjibhai (BJP) won by a margin of 3,54,187 votes.

Sabarkantha : 11,19,855* (6,72,677) - Chaudhry Nishaben Amarsinh (INC) : 3,34,565; Patel Kanubhai Ravjibhai (BJP) : 3,20,189; Others : 6,407; Invalid : 11,516

Surat : 19,50,958* (6,29,199) - Rana Kashiram Chhabildas (BJP) : 4,23,773 Pachchigar Rameshchandra Rupen (INC) : 1,74,576; Others : 17,381; Invalid : 13,469
In 1998, Kashiram Rana (BJP) won by a margin of 3,03,164 votes.

Surendranagar : 9,70,544* (4,78,757) - Makvana Savsibhai Kanjibhai (INC) : 2,18,463; Others : 6,123; Invalid : 9,803
In 1998, Dave Bhavnaben Kardam Jumar (BJP) won by a margin of 9,654 votes.

1998

Party	Seats won	Vote share
BJP	19	48.3%
Congress	7	36.5%

HARYANA (10)

The BJP and Indian National Lok Dal shared 5 seats each. The INC strtagey of first bailing out Bansilal and then ditching him proved to be a bad move.

Number of seats

1967 and 1971	- 9
1977 onwards	- 10

Vajpayee's charisma, coupled with the failure of the Congress to fill the gap created by the alienation of former chief minister Bansi Lal from the masses in Haryana, helped the INLD-BJP combine to achieve the landslide victory in the state.

The last-minute support of Congress to Bansi Lal to thwart Om Prakash Chautala from coming to power, and its subsequent withdrawal, seems to have cost the Congress dearly as it failed to retain even the three seats it won last time and got completely wiped out. Factionalism and infighting in the party also contributed to the rout of the

Congress which had won nine seats in 1996.

The Congress's bid to thwart Chautala proved counter-productive. Chautala succeeded in riding the anti-Bansi Lal tide by providing the electorate with a formidable alternative combine after aligning with the BJP.

Sensing the anti-Bansi Lal mood, the BJP also moved smartly withdrawing support to him. Interestingly, feeling the pulse of the electorate, Chautala tied up with the BJP and even gave it five seats, while in 1996, he was not willing to give even four seats, which forced the BJP to align with HVP then.

The anger of the public against Bansi Lal was evident from the fact that his son Surender Singh lost badly, even in the Tosham assembly segment which has been represented and nurtured by Bansi Lal all along - where the Congress managed to achieve some lead. Analysts feel that Bansi Lal could not stand up to his image of being a development-oriented man. The failure of prohibition, coupled with his failure to keep the promise of 24-hour power supply, besides other issues, proved costly for him.

The last-minute tie-up with BSP also did not help Bansi Lal, due to which the BSP lost its Ambala seat too which it won last time. From having drawn a blank in the 1996 poll, Chautala emerged stronger by strengthening his position from four seats last time to winning all the seats in alliance with the BJP in the state.

In fact, the alliance achieved leads in 85 out of the 90 assembly segments falling in the 10 Lok Sabha constituencies, with the Congress leading in only five assembly constituencies of Mahendergarh, Ferozepur Jhirka, Nuh, Taoru and Tosham.

The BJP-INLD combine got 58.25 per cent votes while the Congress could get only 34.93 per cent, leaving Bansi Lal's HVP with a paltry 2.71 per cent and BSP with 1.95 per cent.

Though the Congress managed to increase its votes this time from 26.02 per cent in 1998 and 22.64 per cent in 1996, HVP and BSP lost their vote banks heavily. They had got 11.6 per cent and 7.68 per cent respectively in the last poll. On the other hand, the BJP hogged a total voting percentage of 18.89 per cent in 1998 while Chautala's INLD got 25.9 per cent votes last time.

Though Sonia's foreign origin factor did not seem to have worked in Haryana, the influence of Vajpayee among both the urban and rural elecorate worked, going by the heavy margins of victory. This also showed that the individual candidate did not matter much in the state this time and many political lightweights and non-entities also made it with big margins.

With people getting fed up with the policies of Bansi Lal, Chautala reversed some of the unpopular decisions taken by the Bansi Lal Government and made some populist promises soon after coming to power, which made the alliance win over the electorate.

The campaigning done by Vajpayee in Rohtak, Karnal and Fetehabad seemed to have made a strong impact on the masses. On the other hand, campaigning by Sonia Gandhi in Hissar and Kurukshetra did not prove to be of much help to the Congress.

With the state having lost a number of soldiers, the Kargil issue also seemed to have created a strong undercurrent among the electorate. The INLD-BJP combine even fielded a Kargil widow in the political arena, making her emerge victorious finally. This is however, termed by the opposition as "politicisation" of the Kargil issue. [*Sanjeev Chopra*]

Constituency-wise Results — 1999 and Winners of 1998

Ambala (SC) : 10,89,891* (6,97,909) - Rattan Lal (BJP) : 3,57,460
Phool Chand Mullana (INC) : 2,32,982; Aman Kumar Nagra (BSP) : 83,644; Others : 18,251; Invalid : 5,572
In 1998, Aman Kumar Nagra (BJP) won by a margin of 2,884 votes.

Bhiwani : 10,46,591* (7,40,291) - Ajay Singh Chautala (INLD) : 3,81,255
Dharambir (INC) : 1,77,849; Surender Singh (HVP) : 1,51,636; Others : 11,741; Parbhat (CPI-M) : 10,511; Invalid : 7,299
In 1998, Surender Singh (HVP) won by a margin of 9,711 votes.

Faridabad : 13,30,157* (7,55,003) - Ram Chander Bainda (BJP) : 3,67,842
Zakir Hussian (INC) : 3,33,594; Shyam Sunder Kapoor (HVP): 37,045; Others (SP) : 7,003; Invalid : 9,519
In 1998, Ram Chander Bainda (BJP) won by a margin of 15,343 votes.

Hissar : 10,22,705* (6,44,942) - Surender Singh Barwala (INLD) : 3,96,540
Birender Singh (INC) : 2,36,088; Others : 6,674; Invalid : 5,640
In 1998, Surender Singh Barwala (HLD-R) won by a margin of 80,491 votes.

Karnal : 11,29,777* (7,71,194) - I.D. Swami (BJP) : 4,33,733
Bhajan Lal (INC) : 2,85,879; Pardeep Kumar (BSP) : 26,860; Others : 24,629; Invalid : 93
In 1998, Bhajan Lal (INC) won by a margin of 52,061 votes.

Kurukshetra : 10,73,147* (7,30,321) - Prof. Kailasho Devi (INLD) : 4,38,701
Om Parkash Jindal (INC) : 2,75,091; Others : 9,965; Invalid L 6,564
In 1998, Kailasho Devi (HLD-R) won by a margin of 1,41,520 votes.

Mahendragarh : 12,36,921* (7,52,278) - Sudha Yadav (BJP) : 4,20,706
Inderjeet Singh (INC) : 2,81,566; Raghu (BSP) : 25,826; Others : 16,608; Invalid : 7,572
In 1998, Inderjit Singh (INC) won by a margin of 68,136 votes.

Rohtak : 9,30,507* (6,34,235) - Inder Singh (INLD) : 3,66,926
Bhupinder Singh (INC) : 2,22,233; Arvind Kumar Sharma (IND) : 27,265; Others : 11,654; Kanta (SP) : 5,295; Invalid : 862
In 1998, Bhupinder Singh (INC) won by a margin of 383 votes..

Sirsa : 10,99,694* (6,42,894) - Sushil Kumar Indora (INLD) : 4,21,199
Om, Parkash (INC) : 1,99,545; Babu Lal (SP) : 10,712; Others : 5983; Invalid : 5,455
In 1998, Sushil Kumar Indorea (HLD-R) won by a margin of 93,930 votes.

Sonepat : 10,52,361* (6,59,484) - Kishan Singh Sangwan (BJP) : 4,57,056
Chiranji Lal (INC) : 1,90,918; Others : 8,347; Kanwal Singh (NCP) : 1,844; Invalid : 1,319
In 1998, Kishan Singh (HLD) won by a margin of 1,37,324 votes.

1998

Party	Seats won	Vote share
HLD (R)	4	25.9%
Congress	3	26.0%
BJP	1	18.9%
HVP	1	11.6%
IND	1	17.6%

* Total Electorates
Figures in ( ) are Votes polled

HIMACHAL PRADESH (4)

Shanta Kumar (BJP) was elected from Kangra, giving the BJP a tally of 3 out of total of 4 seats. Dhani Ram won the Shimla (SC) seat as a candidate of the Himachal Vikas Congress.

Total Number of Seats	
1967 and 1971	9
1977 onwards	10

The charisma of Atal Bihari Vajpayee coupled with the leadership of Prem Kumar Dhumal enabled the BJP-HVC combine to register a spectacular victory in the Lok Sabha elections in the hill state of Himchal Pradesh and spell a doom for the Congress which has been routed.

Besides retaining all the three seats of Kangra, Mandi and Hamirpur which the BJP had wrested from the Congress in 1996, the combine managed to overthrow the Congress even from its well-fortified fortress of Shimla (Reserve). It is for the first time after 1977 that the BJP, along with its alliance partner, has swept the poll and increased its vote share to 59 per cent, a record 20 per cent higher than the Congress.

The magic of Vajpayee seems to have worked splendidly and uniformly in all the four seats, though he himself could not visit all these places for campaigning. On the contrary, the Congress last ditch effort to replace its sitting MP K.D. Sultanpuri, a six time winner and field three sitting MLAs and bringing Sonia Gandhi to campaign didn't prove to be of much help to the party.

The anti-incumbency weapon of the Congress misfired and it was the performance of the 18-month-old BJP-HVC coalition which paid visible dividends to the BJP. Moreover, the powerful apple lobby throwing its lot with the BJP, employees factor dormant, ex-servicemen and OBC refusing to get allured by the Congress posers also helped the combine make a clean sweep.

In spite of a low turnout of 57.13 per cent voters as compared to 65.32 per cent last time, the BJP-HVC combine secured a record 12.50 lakh votes against 4.06 lakh votes polled by the Congress. The victory margin of former chief minister Shanta Kumar in Kangra and Suresh Chandel in Hamirpur crossed the one lakh mark, even as Maheshwar Singh managed the highest margin of 1.31 lakh.

The real morale booster for the BJP and HVC came from Shimla, where Lt. Col. (retd) Dhani Ram Shandil beat former minister and sitting Congress MLA Gangu Ram Musafir in his maiden electoral battle. Except Rohru, the Assembly segment of former chief minister Virbhadra Singh, Shillai and Renuka, the HVC secured an impressive lead in all Assembly segments including Jubbal-Kotkhai-A stronghold of former chief minister Ram Lal Thakur.

Even senior Congress leaders, like Virbhadra Singh admits the party had never expected such a drubbing in the elections, reducing its area of influence to just four Assembly segments-one in Mandi and three others in Shimla.

For the BJP, the advantages perhaps were enormous. Entering the electoral battle from a position of advantage of being in power, the BJP tried to consolidate on gains effectively even as Congress lacked in resources, manpower and issues. Vajpayee's popularity blended with performance of Dhumal government pushed the Congress much behind. "We went to the people with the issues of Vajpayee and performance of our government at the Centre as well as in the state," Dhumal says.

In a state, which has a large share in the defence forces, and over 60 brave soldiers laid down their lives in the recent war, Kargil was bound to be an issue. Kangra district alone has over a dozen martyrs, including PVC Captain Vikram Batra and Lt Saurabh Kalia. The Congress's attempt to blame the BJP for Kargil and "killing" of soldiers, too, boomeranged.

Shanta Kumar's victory in Kangra by a record margin is reconsolidation of his position in the lower merged areas, after his charisma started fading away in 1992. The employees had turned against him and so had the apple growers. If his election to the Lok Sabha in 1996 marked his re-emergence, then this time he has succeeded in further consolidating his base.

In Hamirpur—the home district of the Chief Minister-Dhumal's own popularity in the area and Kargil remained a decisive issue. The Congress fielded former minister and party MLA Ram Lal Thakur, projecting him as the potential "winner" but its calculations went completely haywire. The victory margin of 1.29 lakh votes—an all time high, perhaps will remain a record in itself.

Maheshwar Singh's victory in Mandi also has come on predictable lines in the constituency which has remained a Congress bastion. Vajpayee's links with Kullu, part of the Mandi constituency, and Sukh Ram's support to the BJP together paved way for his re-election to the Lok Sabha for the third time. Except Rampur, the Congress candidate Kaul Singh Thakur could not get lead in any Assembly segment.

The apple-dominant Shimla (Reserve), where heavyweights like Virbhadra, Ram Lal Thakur and Vidya Stokes had called the shots, is perhaps the worst-ever shock for the Congress. [*Ashwani Sharma*]

Constituency-wise Results — 1999 and Winners of 1998

Hamirpur : 9,37,500* (5,59,678) - Suresh Chandel (BJP) : 3,36,172
Ram Lal (INC) : 2,06,925; Others : 12,343; Invalid : 4,233
In 1998, Suresh Chandel (BJP) won by a margin of 77,909 votes.

Kangra : 9,35,090* (5,56,916) - Shanta Kumar (BJP) : 3,25,066
Sat Mahajan (INC) : 2,24,324; Others : 3,460; Invalid : 4,066
In 1998, Shanta Kumar (BJP) won by a margin of 59,235 votes.

Mandi : 9,68,821* (5,28,636) - Maheshwar Singh (BJP) : 3,25,929
Kaul Singh (INC) : 1,94,904; Others : 4,407; Invalid : 3,396
In 1998, Maheshwar Singh (BJP) won by a margin of 1,31,832 votes.

Shimla (SC) : 9,45,063* (5,04,488) - Col. Dhani Ram Shandil (HVC) : 2,64,002
Gangu Ram Musafir (INC) : 2,17,072; Others : 19,090; Invalid : 4,324
In 1998, Krishna Dutt Sultanpuri (INC) won by a margin of 42,025 votes.

1998

Party	Seats won	Vote share
BJP	3	51.4%
Congress	1	41.9%

* Total Electorates
Figures in ( ) are Votes polled

JAMMU AND KASHMIR (6)

While general elections were held in rest of country in 1952, in Jammu and Kashmir the first general elections were held in 1967. Prior to that Lok Sabha Members used to be nominated. For J&K these were the Ninth and not the Thirteenth Lok Sabha Elections. Lok Sabha elections could not be held here in 1991 due to terrorist activities.

The Delimitation Commission was appointed in 1966. J&K was divided into parliamentary constituencies—Srinagar, Baramulah, Anantnag, Jammu, Udhampur and Ladakh. The BJP won from Udhampur and Jammu while the remaining four seats were bagged by the J&K National Conference.

In 1967 Shafi Quresi from Anantnag (Congress) and Kushak Bakula were elected unopposed from Ladakh. Earlier in the Assembly elections held in 1957, thirty six members out of a total of 44 were elected unopposed. All these belonged to National Conference. In 1998 the voting figures were not declared in Baramulah even after the conclusion of the elections. All that the government said was that it would not be in national interest to probe more into the reasons.

Prof. Saifuddin Soz had been declared elected by a majority of only 37,794 votes. The opponent Beg had alleged that the ballot boxes were filled after the voting was over. Among the victors this time is Omer Abdullah, son of Farooq Abdullah. The losers include Prof. Saifuddin Soz.

Star Constituency : Baramullah

It was a 'do or die' situation for the star contestant in Baramullah. Saifuddin Soz was running as an independent after being expelled from the National Conference party. His defiance of the partywhip and casting the single vote that brought down the Vajpayee government may have won Soz admirers at home and amongst the anti-BJP forces, but it vastly complicated his task of managing a fourth win from Baramullah, one of the largest districts J&K with 97 per cent of its population being Muslim.

Though he had the support of the Left, Congress and the Rashtriya Janata Dal, he still had to contend with a formidable rival, Muzzafar Hussain Baig this time representing the new Jammu and Kashmir People's Democratic party. A well known Supreme court lawyer with a considerable Pahari vote, Baig trailed with 30.79 per cent votes as against Soz's 43.38 per cent in 1998 elections. The National Conference put up Abdul Shaheen made great efforts to defeat Soz, and they are not without assets in this insurgency-torn district.

Constituency-wise Results — 1999 and Winners of 1998

Baramullah : 7,63,649* (2,12,180) - Abdul Rashid Saheen (JKN) : 84,243
Muzaffar Jissaom Bais (IND) : 48,130; Ghulam Nabi Mir (JKAL) : 25,697; Saif-ud-din Soz (IND) : 11,230; Mohammad Sultan (BJP) : 2,680; Others : 19,755; Invalid : 20,445

In 1998 Professor Saifuddin Soz (JKN) won by a margin of 37,794 votes.

Jammu : 14,48,144* (6,76,708) - Vishno Datt Sharma (BJP) : 2,89,412
Rajinder Singh Chib (JKN) : 1,47,393; Madan Lal Sharma (INC) : 1,26,356; Makhan Singh (BSP) : 53,665; Sardar Tarlok Singh (IND) : 15,598; Others : 33,497; Invalid : 10,787

* Total Electorates
Figures in ( ) are Votes polled

In 1998, Vaid Vishno Dutt (BJP) won by a margin of 1,27,901 votes.

Ladakh : 1,43,719* (1,17,671) - Hassan Khan (JKN) : 52,187

Thupatan Chhewang (INC) : 50,097; Others : 7,775; Sonam Paljor (BJP) : 5,801; Invalid : 1,811

In 1998, Syed Hussain (JKN) won by a margin of 30,557 votes.

Srinagar : 8,54,136* (1,01,933) - Umar Abdullah (JKN) : 55,542

Mehbooba Mufti (IND) : 18,683; Syed Mehdi (INC) : 18,453; Fayaz Ahmad Bhat (BJP) : 2,091; Others : 2,215; Invalid : 4,949

In 1998, Omar Abdullah (JKN) won by a margin of 70,839 votes.

Udhampur : 10,07,030* (4,03,210) - Prof. Chaman Lal (BJP) : 1,94,678

Jagjivan Lal (JKN) : 76,371; Balbir Singh (INC) : 75,838; Roop Lal (BSP) : 22,278; Prof. Bhim Singh (JKNPP) : 12,787; Others : 15,235; Invalid : 6,023

In 1998, Prof Chamanlal Gupta (BJP) won by a margin of 81,364 votes.

KARNATAKA (28)

The Janata Dal dissensions proved a boon to the INC. The party bagged 16 out of a total of 28 seats. Sonia Gandhi was elected from Bellary defeating Sushma Swaraj of the BJP. However Ghulam Nabi Azad did not quit as he had declared before elections in case the win was by less than a lakh majority. Like most politicians he said he accepted moral responsibility and went along with business as usual. The JD (U) got only 3 seats. The BJP bagged 7 seats but the Congress wave was much too strong for Sushma to have been able to defeat Sonia. All the same Sushma did exceedingly well considering Sonia's victory margin at Amethi.

Once again the voters made it known that they do not approve of internal dissensions in political parties.

	Total Seats
1952	11
1957 and 1962	26
1967 and 1971	27
1977 onwards	28

"It's nothing short of a miracle". This was how the spectacular victory was earned by the former Karnataka Chief Minister, S. Bangarappa, not only for himself in the Lok Sabha election as the Congress (I) candidate in the Shimoga district but also for his hand-picked candidates in six of the eight Assembly constituencies.

The fact that he could establish a lead in all the eight Assembly segments falsified the pre-poll assessments which apparently failed to take note of the "under currents" which contributed to his facile victory.

The manner in which he emerged victorious after losing the 1998 Lok Sabha election from the same constituency in which he was pushed to the third place appeared to show that his defeat then was a fluke and that what he has achieved this time is the hard proof of the fact that his political clout is still intact.

The late commencement of his campaigning which he actively started from September 5—hardly one week earlier to the polling—was a matter of worry for the party candidates in the Assembly constituencies as they heavily depended on his personality to gain support. But once he took up the campaigning it was a whistle stop exercies till the last day for campaigning.

However, what was unique in his campaigning was that he never sought the campaign by any outside party leader and managed it by himself giving an impression that he was capable of doing it on his own.

He defeated his nearest BJP rival, Mr. Ayanur Manjunath by a margin of about 95,000 votes in a straight fight while the Janata Dal (Secular) candidate and MLC, K.H. Srinivàs, was pushed to the third place.

Bangarappa, who continues to occupy the centre stage as far as the politics in his home district of Shimoga is concerned dominated the party affairs even before the elections were formally announced by effecting a sudden change in the Presidentship of the District Congress (I) Committee by installing his protege, Mir Aziz Ahmed, in that place when he found that the incumbent President, Ismail Khan, was not favourably disposed to his candidature.

Bangarappa had incurred the displeasure of the rank and file in the district unit of the party when he succeeded in getting the candidates of his choice nominated to all the eight Assembly constituencies. The caste composition of the candidates also came in for criticism by his own partymen who argued that by preferring three Lingayat candidates, three Eediga (a backward community to which Bangarappa belongs) out of a total of eight seats. Bangarappa had ignored other dominant communities like Muslims, Brahmins and Kurubas.

But he was least perturbed by such criticism and saw to it that his was the final say as far as the recommendation of the candidates to the party's High Command for the Assembly constituencies in the district was concerned. The selection of some of the candidates, particularly of G.D. Narayanappa (his co-brother) for the Hosnagar constituency, Mahalingappa for the Shikaripur constituency and H.M. Chandrasekharappa for the Shimoga constituency raised many eyebrows in the political circles.

But what was amazing was the manner in which Bangarappa ensured their victory particularly that of Mahalingappa who virtually became a "giant killer" by causing a major political upset by defeating the BJP from Shikaripur, B.S. Yediyurappa, and that of Chandrasekharappa who mauled yet another BJP leader, K.S. Eshwarappa, from, the Shimoga constituency.

It was evident that apart from the solid support of his community which has nearly a three lakh population, the Muslims and Lingayats extended their support to the Congress (I) candidates in the district.

With his commendable performance Bangarappa once again has proved that he is no more a spent force but very much a force to reckon with. [*Hindu*]

Constituency-wise Results — 1999 and Winners of 1998

Bagalkot : 11,27,911* (7,83,328) - Rudragouda Sanganago (INC) : 3,78,488
Ajaykumar Sambashiva (JD-U) : 3,02,054; Gannigera Ashoka Vir (JD-S) : 72,422; Invalid : 30,364
1998, Ajaykumr Sambasadashiv Samaik (LS) won by a margin of 83,632 votes.

Bangalore North : 18,26,440* (10,29,393) - C.K. Jaffer Sharief (INC) : 5,25,885
Muchael Fernandes (JD-U) : 3,50,000; C. Narayanaswamy (JD-S) 1,05,912; M Sundara Murthy (AIADMK) : 17.163; Others : 30,433
In 1998, C.K. Jaffer Sharief (INC) won by a margin of 72,447 votes.

Bangalore South : 14,84,954* (8,04,339) - Ananth Kumar (BJP) 4,10,161
B.K. Hariprasad (INC) : 3,44,104; B.T. Parthasarathy (JD-S) : 22,801; Others :

* Total Electorates
Figures in ( ) are Votes polled

15,630; Arumugam (ADMK) : 11,643
In 1998, Ananth Kumar (BJP) won by a margin of 1,80,047 votes.

Belgaum : 12,30,574* (8,23,929) - Amarasinha Vasantharao Patil (INC) : 3,83,444
Baba Gouda Patil (BJP) : 3,33,546; Poojari Siddappa (IND) : 48,584; Yellappa Datta Kamble (IND) : 16,193; Invalid : 42,162
In 1998 Babagouda R. Patil (BJP) won by a margin of 97,057 votes.

Bellary : 12,12,950* (8,46,380) - Sonia Gandhi (INC) : 4,14,650
Sushma Swaraj (BJP) : 3,58,550; Mahalingapa (JD-S) : 28,855; Invalid : 44,325
In 1998 K.C. Kondaiah (INC) won by a margin of 63,738 votes.

Bidar (SC) : 12,00,524* (7,61,143) - Ramachandra Veerappa (BJP) : 3,50,221
Narasinga Rao Suryav (INC) : 1,98,188; Doddi Shankar Rao (JD-S) : 1,12,423; Subhash Sikhindra Ba (BSP) : 49,802; Basappa Akalavadi (IND) : 19,045; Invalid : 31,464
In 1998, Ramachandra Veerappa (BJP) won by a margin of 1,84,633 votes.

Bijapur : 11,83,078* (7,45,901) - Basavanagouda Patil (BJP) : 3,48,816
Laxmibai Gudadinni (INC) : 3,12,177; Mallikarjuna Loni (JD-S) : 38,398; Basavaraj Sangappa Akashi (BSP) : 14,833; Invalid : 31,677
In 1998, Patil Mallanagouda Bansanagouda (INC) won by a margin of 52,822 votes.

Chamarajnagar : 12,10,440* (8,11,498) - V. Srinivas Prasad (JD-U) : 3,11,547
A. Siddaraju (INC) : 2,95,401; Govindaiah (JD-S) : 1,07,556; Kempa Siddaiah (KCVP) : 44,854; Invalid : 52,140
In 1998 A. Siddaraju (JD) won by a margin of 70,319 votes.

Chikaballapur : 11,89,155* (8,49,650) - R.KL. Jalappa (INC) : 4,22,570
N. Ramesh (JD-U) : 2,11,372; G. Venkatachalaiah (JD-S) : 1,31,586; Ajay Bharat Kattamma (IND) : 33,211; G.C. Bayya Reddy (CPM) : 17,434; S.R. Krishanam Raju (IND) : 2,297; Invalid : 31,180
In 1998, R.L. Jalappa (INC) won by a margin of 1,27,053 votes.

Chikkodi : 10,94,053* (7,68,499) - Ramesh C. Jigajinagi (JD-U) : 3,92,450
Pradeep Kumar Shankarananda Kanagal (INC) : 3,07, 860; Gopinath M. (BSP) : 13,664; Others : 13,831; Invalid : 25,121
In 1998, Jigajinagi Ramesh Chandappa (LS) won by a margin of 1,31,238 votes.

Chikmagalur : 10,50,637* (7,39,934) - D. C. Srikantappa (BJP) : 3,24,470
D. M. Putlegowda (INC) : 2,94,193; D.L. Vasantha Kiumari (JD-S) : 70,292; U Babu Mogera (IND) : 21,340; Venkatalakshmi (AIADMK) : 4,508; Invalid : 25,131
In 1998, D.C. Srikantappa (BJP) won by a margin of 52,496 votes.

Chitradurga : 11,77,238* (8,67,099) - Shashi Kumar (JD-U) : 3,70,793
C.P. Mudalagiriyappa (INC) 3,59,615; T.J. Mariappa (JD-S) : 1,01,399; Invalid : 35,292
C.P. Mudalagiriyappa (INC) won by a margin of 58,321 votes.

Davanagere : 20,77,324* (8,81,896) - G. Mallikarjunappa (BJP) : 3,98,969
Shamanur Shivashankarappa (INC) : 3,82,700; Mallappa (JD-S) : 64,705; Basavaraj (ADMK) : 3,704; Invalid : 31,818
In 1998, Shamanur Shiva Shankarappa (INC) won by a margin of 11,332 votes.

Dharwad North : 11,21,240* (7,52,119) - Vijay Sankeshwar (BJP) 3,45,197
Veeranna A. Mattikatti (INC) : 3,03,595; Ismail Kalebudde (JD-S) : 71,147; Invalid : 32,180

In 1998, Vijay Sankeshwar (BJP) won by a margin of 1,29,182 votes.

Dharwad South : 10,91,726* (7,68,791) - Prof. I.G. Sanadi (INC) : 3,55,523

Gulbarga : 12,80,838* (7,72,019) - Iqbal Ahmed Saradagi (INC) : 3,51,740 Basavaraja Patil Sedam (BJP) : 2,81,931; Malleshappa Avoor (JD-S) : 65,683; Vittala Hereu (BSP) : 35,452; Others : 4,135; Invalid : 33,078

In 1998, Baswaraj Patil Sedam (BJP) won by a margin of 1,31,798 votes.

Hassan : 12,16,816* (8,92,467) - G Puttaswamy Gowda (INC) : 3,98,344 H.D. Deve Gowda (JD-S) : 2,56,587; B.D. Basavaraj (BJP) : 1,71,604; Kovi Babanna (IND) : 16,397; M. Chikkegowda (IND): 15,694; Invalid : 33,841

In 1998, H.D. Devegowda (JD) won by a margin of 31,654 votes.

Kanakapura : 21,09,246* (12,76,465) - M. V. Chandrasekhara Murthy (INC) : 5,33,652; M. Srinivas (BJP) : 4,99,101; H. D. Kumara Swamy (JD-S) : 1,62,465; Veerappa (IND) : 33,327; N. Brahmananda (IND) : 6,253; Invalid : 41,667

In 1998, M. Srinivas (BJP) won by a margin of 16,441 votes.

Kanara : 11,01,871* (7,74,489) - Margaret Alva (INC) : 3,56,694 Ananth Kumar Hedge (BJP) : 3,46,053; Garadikar D. Nayak (JD-S) : 36,328; Others : 6,386; Invalid : 29,028

In 1998, Anant Kumar (BJP) won by a margin of 87,047 votes.

Kolar (SC) : 11,45,546* (8,61,018) - K. H. Muniyappa (INC) : 3,21,964 Mangamma Muniswamy (BJP) : 2,39,182; Balaji Channaiah (JD-U) : 1,87,261; M. G. Raman (JD-S) : 26,754; A. N. Venkataravanappa (IND) : 21,604; Others : 18,993; Invalid : 45,260

In 1998 K.H. Muniyappa (INC) won by a margin of 77,972 votes.

Koppal : 12,43,236* (7,98,764) - H.G. Ramulu (INC) : 3,50,599 Basavaraja Rayareddy (JD-U) : 3,38,287; Mallikarjuna Divatar (JD-S) : 56,084; Invalid : 53,794

In 1998, H.G. Ramulu (INC) won by a margin of 83,122 votes.

Mandya : 10,99,048* (8,31,319) - Ambarish (INC) : 4,18,044 Krishna (JD-S) : 2,65,853; D. Ramalingalah (BJP) : 82,489; Mahesh (BSP) : 21,547; Devappa (IND) : 12,468; Invalid : 30,918

In 1998 Ambareesh (JD) won by a margin of 1,80,523 votes.

Mangalore : 10,01,240* (7,33,255) - V. Dhananjaya Kumar (BJP) : 3,53,536 M. Veerappa Moily (INC) : 3,45,067; Lokeswari Vinaya Chandra (JD-S) : 20,980; Invaild : 13,672

In 1998, V. Dhananjaya Kumar (BJP) won by a margin of 6,907 votes.

Mysore : 13,02,550* (8,99,392) - Srikantadatta Narasimharaja Wodeyar (INC) : 3,38,051; C.G. Vijauashankar (BJP) : 3,24,620; B.S. Marillingaiah (JD-S) : 1,90,107; Somasundar Sastry (KCVP) : 28,158; M. Amjath Khan (AIADMK) : 18,439; Invalid : 17

In 1998, C.H. Vijayashankar (BJP) won by a margin of 1,03,024 votes.

Raichur : 12,25,596* (7,22,574) - Venkatesh Naik (INC) : 3,59,946 Abdul Samad Siddiqui (JU-U) : 1,07,704; Mahantesh Patil Atnu (JD-S) : 83,844; Invalid : 1,71,044

In 1998 A. Venkatesh Naik (INC) won by a margin of 78,278 votes.

Shimoga : 11,33,466* (8,21,424) - A. S. Bangarappa (INC) : 4,27,870 Ayanoor Manjunath (BJP) : 3,32,832; K.H. Srinivas (JD-S) : 38,432; Others : 7,914; Invalid : 24,376

In 1998 Ayanoor Manjunath (BJP) won by a margin of 1,59,907 votes.

Tumkur : 11,00,408* (8,00,018) - G.S. Basavaraju (INC) : 3,18,922
S. Mallikarjunaiah (BJP) : 2,54,985; C.N. Bhaskarappa (JD-S) : 1,90,295; V. Nagaraju (BSP) : 9,644; Invalid : 26,172
In 1998 S. Malikarjunaiah (BJP) won by a margin of 71,187 votes.

Udupi : 10,24,659* (6,93,191) - Vinay Kumar Sorake (INC) : 3,51,197
I. M. Jayarama Reddy (BJP) : 3,17,466; Srinivas (JD-S) : 12,375; Invalid : 12,153
In 1998 I.M. Jayarama Shetty (BJP) won by a margin of 56,568 votes.

1998

Party	Seats won	Vote share
BJP	13	27.0%
Congress	9	36.2%
Lok Shakti	3	11.6%

KERALA (20)

The CPI (M) had 8 out of a total of 20 seats. The INC too had 8 seats while the Muslim League bagged 2 seats — the Ponnani and Manjeri seat. G.M. Bantwala was back. Kerala Congress and Kerala Congress (M). had 1 seat each. The CPI drew a blank.

Total Seats

1952	12
1957 - 1962	18
1967-1971	19
1977 onwards	20

While its partners in the National Democratic Alliance (NDA) were an inestimable asset to the BJP in winning the numbers' game for the formation of a government at the Centre, the alliance proved to be a liability for the party in Kerala.

In spite of cobbling together an eight-party front under the banner of the NDA, the BJP, together with its allies, could increase its vote share in the State only by a negligible 0.3 per cent. In contrast, the BJP on its own could increase its vote share from 4.79 per cent in 1991 to 5.74 per cent in 1996 and 7.78 per cent in 1998.

The votes polled by its allies in the constituencies allotted to them in 1999 were far less than the votes secured by the BJP candidates in those constituencies in 1998.

The NDA partners, Janata Dal (U) and SRP, which contested in seven constituencies (Kollam, Mukundapuram, Kannur, Manjeri, Idukki, Alappuzha and Thrissur) polled 79,848 votes less than the BJP candidates in these constituencies in 1998.

Moreover, the BJP too fared worse than its 1998 performance in five constituencies—Kasargod, Vadakara, Muvattupuzha, Kozhikode and Kottayam—by polling 12,345 votes less.

In fact, the formation of the alliance itself was just a theatrical exercise, as most of its allies such as the Bharatiya Labour Party, NDP (Kidangoor), Bharat Vikas Party, and Socialist Republican Party were just letter-head organisations, with no noticeable presence or mass base. They proved to be spoilsports for the BJP.

This ghost of an alliance formed by the BJP in Kerala was jinxed from the beginning. The Bharat Vikas Party withdrew from the contest after the BJP refused to yield the Thiruvananthapuram seat to their party's leader and former Minister K. Sankaranarayana Pillai.

Some other allies who were allotted certain seats later felt shy of contesting and returned the seats to the BJP, putting it in an embarrassing and difficult position. It had to find candidates and make preparations for campaigning at the eleventh hour.

A long-forgotten party called the Socialist Republican Party was virtually resurrected by the BJP from its grave to contest against K. Karunakaran of the Congress and E. M. Sreedharan of the CPM in Mukundapuram. By doing so, the BJP provided grist to the campaign mill of the LDF, which alleged a Congress-BJP tie-up in Mukundapuram and Thiruvananthapuram for the mutual advantage of the Congress and BJP candidates in these constituencies. The LDF still argues on the strength of the election results in these two constituencies that such a covert understanding between the Congress and the BJP was in place. [*Indian Express*]

Constituency-wise Results — 1999 and Winners of 1998

Adoor : 10,06,963* (7,02,784) - Kodikkunnial Suresh (INC) : 3,37,003
Surendran Kunju Kunju (CPI) : 3,14,997; K. Raveendranath (BJP) : 43,926; Others : 2,260; Invalid : 4,598
In 1998, Chengara Surendran (CPI) won by a margin of 17,005 votes.

Alappuzha : 10,35,452* (7,92,966) - V.M. Sudheeran (INC) : 3,92,700
Murali (CPM) : 3,57,606; Thiruvarppu Parameswaran Nair (BJP) : 27,682; Others : 10,788; Invalid : 4,190
In 1998, V.M. Sudheeran (INC) won by a margin of 40,637 votes.

Badakara : 11,55,674* (8,58,222) - A.K. Premajam (CPM) : 4,04,355
P.M. Suresh Babu (INC) : 3,78,511; O.K. Vasumaster (BJP) : 62,593; Others : 12,179; Invalid : 584
In 1998, A.K. Premajam (CPM) won by a margin of 59,151 votes.

Chirayankil : 10,96,417* (6,90,941) - Varkala Radhakrishnan (CPM) : 3,09,304
M.I. Shanavas (INC) : 3,06,176; Padmakumar (BJP) : 63,889; Others 6,009; Invalid : 5,563
In 1998, Varkala Radhakrishnan (CPM) won by a margin of 7,542 votes.

Ernakulam : 11,80,911* (7,73,672) - George Eden (INC) : 3,94,058
Mani Vithayathil (IND) : 2,82,753; T.D. Rajalekshmi (BJP) 77,640; Others : 19,221
In 1998, George Eden (INC) won by a margin of 74,508 votes.

Idukki : 11,21,484* (7,78,859) - K. Francis George (KEC) : 3,65,313
Prof. P.J. Kurien (INC) : 3,56,015; Tomy Cheruvally (JD-U) : 35,497; Others : 17,079; Invalid : 4,955
In 1998, P.C. Chacko (INC) won by a margin of 6,258 votes.

Kannur : 11,20,318* (8,86,323) - A.P. Abdulla Kutty (CPM) : 3,28,390
Mullappally (INC) : 4,18.143; N. Hariharan (JD-U) : 26,069; Others : 7,578; Invalid : 6,143
In 1998, Mullappally Ramachandran won by a margin of 2,180 votes.

Kasaragod : 11,99,963* (9,30,990) - Thayambath Govindan (CPM) : 4,23,564
Khader Mangad (INC) : 3,91,986; P.K. Krishna Das (BJP) : 1,01,934; Others : 7,900; Invalid : 5,606
In 1998, T. Govindan (CPM) won by a margin of 48,557 votes.

---

* Total Electorates
Figures in ( ) are Votes polled

Kollam : 10,87,711* (7,40,657) - P. Rajendran (CPM) : 3,51,872
M.P. Gangadharan (INC) : 3,32,586; Prof. Jayalekshmi (JD-U) : 42,579; Others : 8,524; Invalid : 5,096
In 1998, N.K. Premachandran won by a margin of 71,762 votes.

Kottayam : 10,18,385* (7,33,607) - Suresh Kurup (CPM) : 3,44,296
P.C. Chacke (INC) : 3,33,697; K.R. Surendran (BJP) : 41,531; Others : 8,801; Invalid : 5,282
In 1998, Suresh Kurup (CPM) won by a margin of 5,447 votes.

Kozhikode : 11,24,074* (8,26,901) - K. Muraleedharan (INC) : 3,83,425
C.M. Ibrahim (JD-S) : 3,33,023; P.C. Mohanan Master (BJP) : 83,862; Others : 21,997; Invalid : 4,594
In 1998, P. Sankaran (INC) won by a margin of 18,657 votes.

Manjeri : 12,17,888* (8,16,421) - E. Ahamed (MUL) : 4,37,563
I.T. Najeeb (CPM) : 3,14,152; Mohiyudeen (JD-U) : 58,541; Invalid : 6,255
In 1998, E. Ahamed (ML) won by a margin of 1,06,009 votes.

Mavelikkara : 9,35,780* (6,67,088) - Ramesh Chennithala (INC) : 3,10,455
K. Nainan Koshy (IND) : 2,77,012; Raman Pillai (BJP) : 73,669; Others : 2,772; Invalid : 3,180
In 1998, Prof P.J. Kurien (INC) won by a margin of 1,261 votes.

Mukundapuram : 10,01,264* (7,92,212) - K. Krunakaran (INC) : 3,97,156
E.M. Sreedharan (CPM) : 3,44,693; M.S. Muraleedhran (SRP) : 30,779; Others : 12,950; Invalid : 6,634
In 1998, A.C. Jose (INC) won by a margin of 8,949 votes.

Muvattupuzha : 10,20,153* (6,92,278) - P.C. Thomas (KEC-M) : 3,57,402
P.M. Ismail (CPM) : 2,80,463; V.V. Augustine (BJP) : 47,875; Others : 2,524; Invalid : 4,014
In 1998, P.C. Thomas (KEC-M) won by a margin of 1,14,809 votes.

Ottappalam : 11,03,327* (7,83,018) - S. Ajaya Kumar (CPM) : 3,59,758
Pandalam Sudhakaran (INC) : 3,46,043; P.M. Velayudhan (BJP) : 70,851; Invalid : 6,366
In 1998, S. Ajayakumar (CPM) won by a margin of 19,800 votes.

Palakkad : 11,32,416* (8,13,885) - N.N. Krishnadas (CPM) : 3,72,536
M.T. Padma (INC) : 3,41,769; C.Uday Bhaskar (BJP) : 87,948; Others : 4,290; Invalid : 7,342
In 1998, N.N. Krishnadas (CPM) won by a margin of 25,022 votes

Ponnani : 11,46,335* (6,95,882) - G.M. Banatwalla (MUL) : 3,73,572
P.P. Suneer (CPI) : 2,43,094; K. Narayanan Master (BJP) : 66,427; Others : 6,830; Invalid : 5,959
In 1998, G.M. Banatwala (ML) won by a margin of 1,04,244 votes.

Thiruvanathapuram : 11,98,918* (7,51,002) - V.S. Sivakumar (INC) : 2,86,737
Kaniyapuram Ramachandra (CPI) : 2,71,455; O. Rajagopal (BJP) : 1,57,149; Others : 31,547; Invalid : 4,114
In 1998, K. Karunakaran (INC) won by a margin of 15,398 votes.

Thrissur : 10,73,123* (7,37,054) - A.C. Jose (INC) : 3,43,793
V.V. Raghavan (CPI) : 3,32,161; A.S. Radhakrishnan (JD-U) : 44,354; Others : 10,109; Invalid : 6,637
In 1998, V.V. Raghavan (CPI) won by a margin of 18,243 votes.

1998

Party	Seats won	Vote share
Congress	8	38.7%
CPM	6	21.0%
CPI	2	8.3%
MUL	2	5.0%
IND	2	27.0%

Voter turnout has always been above the national average.

MADHYA PRADESH (40)

The Congress had high hopes having won the Assembly elections less than a year ago. Madhya Pradesh has 40 seats. The INC could get only 11 seats. The BJP tally was 29. The Congress at the State level could not do anything worth the voters repeated confidence. Shyma Charan Shukla was elected from Mahasamund (INC), Uma Bharati (BJP) from Bhopal and Sunder Lal Patwa from Hoshangabad (BJP)

Total Seats	
1952	29
1957-1962	36
1967-1971	37
1977 onwards	40

All the three women nominees of the BJP for the Lok Sabha elections in Madhya Pradesh emerged successful while all four women Congress nominees lost.

The three women BJP winners are Union Minister Ms. Uma Bharti (Bhopal), Mrs. Sumitra Mahajan (Indore) and Mrs. Jayshree Banerjee (Jabalpur) all of whom registered victories with margins of more than one lakh votes each.

Of these three, Ms. Bharti and Mrs. Mahajan have also achieved the distinction of winning all five elections in a row since 1989.

Mrs. Mahajan has won all her polls from Indore, while Ms. Bharti won four from Khajuraho but this time shifted to Bhopal where also she trounced Suresh Pachouri of Congress by about 1.69 lakh votes.

For Mrs. Banerjee, it was her first victory in a Lok Sabha poll and this has come after she was denied a BJP ticket for the November 1998 Assembly elections in the State.

The four Congress loosers are Ms. Vimla Verma (Seoni), Mrs. Madhavi Choudhary (Sagar), Mrs. Chhabila Netam (Kanker) and Ms. Pushpa Singh (Raigarh).

Mrs. Chhabila is the wife of senior Congress leader, Aarvind Netam and she first won from Kanker in May 1996 for which her husband was denied a Congress ticket on the ground that his name figured in the hawala scam. [*PTI*]

Constituency-wise Results — 1999 and Winners of 1998

Balaghat : 9,16,845* (5,83,792) - Prahladsingh Patel (BJP) : 2,51,308
Udaysingh Pancheswar (BSP) : 29,733; Others : 14,003; Invalid : 2,88.748

* Total Electorates
Figures in ( ) are Votes polled

In 1998, Gaourishankar Chaturbhuj Bisen (BJP) won by a margin of 25,531 votes.

Bastar (ST) : 9,54,338* (3,75,604) - Baliram Kashap (BJP) : 1,55,421
Mahendra Karma (INC) : 1,34,684; Manish Kunjam (CPI) : 58,900; Others : 7,592; Invalid : 19,001
In 1998, Baliram Kashyap (BJP) won by a margin of 16,886 votes.

Betul : 10,20,873* (5,46,338) - Vijay Kumkar Khandelwal (BJP) : 2,72,512
Gufran Bhai (INC) : 2,08,040; Sunilam (IND) : 47,325; Others : 6,195; Invalid : 12,266
In 1998, Vijay Kumar (BJP) won by a margin of 39,666 votes.

Bhind : 13,04,284* (6,67,048) - Ram Lakhan Singh (BJP) : 2,70,766
Satyadev Katare (INC) : 2,17,192; Kedarnath (BSP) : 1,05,157; Shriram Bihari (SP) : 58,577; Invalid : 15,356
In 1998, Ram Lakhan Singh (BJP) won by a margin of 98,908 votes.

Bhopal : 15,75,999* (9,76,686) - Uma Bharti (BJP) 5,37,908
Suresh Pachori (INC) : 3,69,041; Shrawan Gourav (IND) : 19,710; Phool Singh (BSP) : 18,617; Aslam Sher Khan (NCP) : 6,044; Others : 25,176; Invalid : 190
In 1998, Sushil Chandra Verma (BJP) won by a margin of 1,93,932 votes.

Bilaspur (SC) : 11,07,061* (5,33,926) - Punnulal Mohale (BJP) : 2,74,860
Rameshwar Kosariya (INC) : 1,99,527; Goutiya Anjor Das Patel (BSP) : 37,138; Others : 14,283; Invalid : 8,118
In 1998, Punnulal Mohle (BJP) won by a margin of 48,615 votes.

Chhindwara : 10,55,473* (6,36,654) - Kamal Nath (INC) : 3,99,904
Santosh Jain (BJP) : 2,10,976; Others : 14,144; Invalid : 11,630
In 1998, Kamal Nath (INC) won by a margin of 1,53,399 votes.

Damoh : 12,40,502* (5,71,668) - Ramkrishna Kusmaria (BJP) : 2,46,909
Tilak Singh Lodhi (INC) : 2,33,190; Ashok Vir Vikam Singh (SP) : 41,134; Pradeep Patel (BSP) : 34,174; Others : 8,592; Invalid : 7,669
In 1998, Ramakrishna Kusmaria (BJP) won by a margin of 1,30,590 votes.

Dhar (ST) : 11,57,368* (6,98,836) - Gajendra Singh (INC) : 3,55,482
Harsh Chouhan (BJP) : 3,21,377; Others : 5,749; Invalid : 16,228
In 1998, Gajendra Singh (INC) won by a margin of 21,100 votes.

Durg : 13,29,627* (7,72,240) - Tara Chand Sahu (BJP) : 3,89,777
Pradeep Choubey (INC) : 3,45,259; Bhojram Darsena (BSP) : 14,378; Others : 11,296; Invalid : 11,530
In 1998, Tarachand Sahu (BJP) won by a margin of 68,718 votes.

Guna : 12,80,953* (6,89,151) - Madhav Rao Scindia (INC) : 4,43,965
Rao Deshraj Singh (BJP) : 2,29,537; Others : 5,991; Invalid : 9,658
In 1998, Rajmata Vijaya Raje Scindhiya (BJP) won by a margin of 1,02,998 votes.

Gwalior : 12,80,141* (6,16,741) - Jaibhan Singh (BJP) : 2,54,486
Chandra Mohan Nagori (INC) : 1,71,370; Phool Singh Baiya (BSP) : 1,16,678; Babu Singh (SP) : 34,406; Others : 39,764; Invalid : 37
In 1998, Madhavrao Scindia (INC) won by a margin of 26,279 votes.

Hoshangabad : 11,53,130* (6,86,887) - Sundar Lal Patwa (BJP) : 3,53,760
Rajkumar Patel (INC) : 3,09,313; Others : 13,310; Invalid : 10,504
In 1998, Sartaj Singh (BJP) won by a margin of 68,981 votes.

Indore : 14,78,108* (8,34,050) - Sumitra Mahajan (BJP) : 4,74,167
Mahesh Joshi (INC) : 3,42,852; Suresh Yadav (BSP) : 3,262; Others : 5,513; Invalid : 8,256
In 1998, Sumitra Mahajan (BJP) won by a margin of 49,852 votes.

Jabalpur : 12,24,308* (5,33,808) - Jaishree Banerjee (BJP) 3,00,648
Chandra Mohan (INC) : 1,90,894; Narbada Prasad Ahirvar (BSP) : 24,223; Others : 12,761; Invalid : 5,282
In 1998, Dada Baburao Paranjpe (BJP) won by a margin of 84,052 votes.

Janjgir : 12,43,586* (6,72,135) - Charandas Mahant (INC) : 2,78,931
Banshilal Mahto (BJP) 2,64,248; Jainarayan Chouksey (BSP) : 87,475; Mahetter Singh Kusaro (GGP) : 24,452; Othres : 7,817; Invalid : 8,212
In 1998, Charan Dash Mahant (INC) won by a margin of 44,586 votes.

Jhabua (ST) : 11,12,426* (6,20,445) - Kantilal Bhuriya (INC) : 3,71,842
Dileep Singh Bhuriya (BJP) : 2,22,465; Kailash Bhabar (AJBP) : 6,073; Invalid : 20,065
In 1998, Kantilal Bhuriya (INC) won by a margin of 82,373 votes.

Kanker (ST) : 10,36,456* (5,86,219) - Sohan Potai (BJP) : 3,18,040
Chhabila Arvind Netam (INC) : 2,29,849; Anjor Singh Thakur (CMM) : 15,526; J.R. Thakur (BSP) : 5,168; Others : 5,507; Invalid : 12,129
In 1998, Sohan Potai (BJP) won by a margin of 54,370 votes.

Khajuraho : 13,79,636* (7,46,601) - Satyavrat Chaturvedi (INC) : 3,35,861
Akhand Pratap Singh Yadav (BJP) : 2,54,724; Surendra Pratap Singh (SP) : 86,621; Umesh (BSP) : 36,316; Others : 20,319; Invalid : 12,760
In 1998, Uma Bharti (BJP) won by a margin of 1,03,849 votes.

Khandwa : 11,10,115* (6,31,014) - Nandkumar Singh Chauhan (BJP) : 3,64,161
Tanvant Singh Keer (INC) : 2,38,058; Mo Yusuf (BSP) : 5,062; Others : 13,426; Invalid : 10,307

Khargone : 11,56,776* (6,98,684) - Tarachand Patel (INC) : 3,54,133
Balkrishan (BJP) : 3,15,987; Bhagawan (BSP) : 9,268; Others : 6,511; Invalid : 12,785
In 1998, Rameshwar Patidar (BJP) won by a margin of 20,679 votes.

Mahasamund : 10,71,547* (6,92,070) - Shyamacharan Shukla (INC) : 3,40,635
Chandrashekhar Sahu (BJP) : 3,25,200; Others : 16,212; Invalid : 10,023
In 1998, Chandrasekhar Sahu (BJP) won by a margin of 47,732 votes.

Mandla (ST) : 10,01,407* (4,94,166) - Faggan Singh Kulaste (BJP) : 2,32,042
Devendra Tekam (INC) : 2,25,470; Hirasingh Markam (GGP) : 13,955; Others : 10,871; Invalid : 11,828
In 1998, Faggan Singh Kulaste (BJP) won by a margin of 13,512 votes.

Mandsaur : 13,43,327* (7,53,766) - Lakshaminarayan Pandey (BJP) : 3,95,928
Rajendra Singh Gautam (INC) : 3,40,443; Others : 8,995; Invalid : 8,400
In 1998, Lakshminarayan Pandey (BJP) won by a margin of 17,702 votes.

Morena (SC) : 12,58,860* (5,00,327) - Ashok Chhabiram (BJP) : 2,10,790
Gopal Das (INC) : 1,48,564; Pratim Prasad (BSP) : 1,03,727; Mata Prasad Chourasiya (SP) : 26,351; Others : 7,304; Invalid : 3,591
In 1998, Ashok Chhabiram (BJP) won by a margin of 68,121 votes.

Raipur : 11,77,144* (6,69,096) - Ramesh Bais (BJP) : 3,54,736
Jugal Kishore Sahu (INC) : 2,74,676; Pradeep Kumar (BSP) : 19,158; Others :

12,360; Invalid : 8,166
In 1998, Ramesh Raja (BJP) won by a margin of 83,379 votes.

Raigarh (ST) : 9,75,567* (5,79,451) - Vishnudeo Sai (BJP) : 2,76,244
Pushpadevi Singh (INC) : 2,70,471; Hemlata Ming (BSP) : 13,402; Others : 9,905; Invalid : 9,429
In 1998, Ajit Jogi (INC) won by a màrgin of 4,382 votes.

Rajgarh : 11,17,038* (6,73,385) - Laxman Singh (INC) : 3,54,234
Nitish Bharadwaj (BJP) : 2,88,541; Ramprasad (BSP) : 7,013; Others : 14,374; Invalid : 9,223
In 1998, Laxman Singh (INC) won by a margin of 52,241 votes.

Ranjandgaon : 10,16,619* (6,03,564) - Raman (BJP) : 3,04,607
Motilal Vora (INC) : 2,77,892; Others : 9,485; Invalid : 11,580
In 1998, Motilal Vora (INC) won by a margin of 52,241 votes.

Rewa : 13,69,793* (7,48,206) - Sunder Lal Tiwari (INC) : 2,75,115
Ramalakhan Singh Patel (BSP) : 2,10,964; Engineer Mithai Lal Kol (SP) : 35,957; Others : 26,108; Invalid : 8,430
In 1998, Chandra Mani Tripathi (BJP) won by a margin of 68,973 votes.

Shahdol (ST) : 11,99,849* (5,96,064) - Dalpat Singh (BJP) : 2,62,224
Ajit Jogi (INC) : 2,42,325; Jugal Kol (BSP) : 62,223; Lalaram Baiga (SP) : 8,757; Others : 8,278; Invalid : 12,257
In 1998, Gyan Singh (BJP) won by a margin of 39,734 votes.

Shajapur (SC) : 11,98,844* (7,63,615) - Thavarchand Gehlot (BJP) : 3,87,607
Radha Kishan Malviya (INC) : 3,52,941; Bhanwar Lal (BSP) : 7,405; B.K. Damale (SP) : 2,250; Others : 3,356; Invalid : 10,056
In 1998, Gehlot Thavarchand (BJP) won by a margin of 18,994 votes.

Sagar (SC) : 11,22,464* (5,43,932) - Virendra Kumar (BJP) : 2,93,357
Madhavi Chaudhary (INC) : 2,32,884; Others : 10,612; Invalid : 7,079
In 1998 Virendra Kumar (BJP) won by a margin of 1,48,204 votes.

Sarangarh (SC) : 10,88,186* (6,85,903) - P.R. Khute (BJP) : 2,81,769
Parasram Bhardwaj (INC) : 2,30,010; Dauram Ratnakar (BSP) : 1,48,659; Others : 14,446; Invalid : 11,019
In 1998, Parasram Bharadwaj (INC) won by a margin of 6,387 votes.

Surguja (ST) : 10,99,864* (5,91,785) - Khal Sai Singh (INC) : 2,97,776
Larang Sai (BJP) : 2,36,349; Jagmani Devi (CPI-M) : 11,985; Prof. Gopal Ram (IND) : 10,708; Dhansingh Dhurve (BSP) : 6,967; Others : 16,561; Invalid : 11,439
In 1998, Larang Sai (BJP) won by a margin of 20,620 votes.

Satna : 11,89,045* (6,25,336) - Ramanand Singh (BJP) : 2,17,932
Rajendra Kumar Singh (INC) : 2,14,527; Shukhalal Kushwaha (BSP) : 1,56,354; Narayan Tripathi (SP) : 9,370; Others : 19,677; Invalid : 7,476
In 1998, Ramanand Singh (BJP) won by a margin of 44,485 votes.

Seoni : 11,15,422* (5,97,341) - Ram Naresh Tripathi (BJP) : 2,82,891
Vimla Verma (INC) : 2,66,957; Kankar Munjare (JP) : 20,219; Others : 16,485; Invalid : 10,789
In 1998, Vimla Varma (INC) won by a margin of 1,12,809 votes.

Sidhi (ST) : 12,62,819* (6,14,501) - Chandra Pratap Singh (BJP) : 2,64,981
Tilakraj Singh (INC) : 2,60,126; Basanti Devi (BSP) : 51,289; Vishwanath Singh Markam (SP) : 10,657; Raghubeer Singh Masram (GGP) : 10,317; Others :

9,506; Invalid : 7,625

In 1998, Jagannath Singh (BJP) won by a margin of 46,533 votes.

Ujjain (SC) : 11,08,023* (6,73,657) - Satyanarayan Jatiya (BJP) : 3,60,103
Tulasi Silawat (INC) : 2,92,065; Babulal Thawaliya (BSP) : 6,582; Others : 5,401; Invalid : 9,560

In 1998, Satyanarayan Jatiya (BJP) won by a margin of 93,887 votes.

Vidisha : 11,72,014* (6,55,434) - Shivraj Singh (BJP) : 3,60,421
Jasvant Singh (INC) : 2,78,024; Others : 9,200; Invalid : 7,789

In 1998, Shivraj Singh (BJP) won by a margin of 1,37,858 votes.

1998

Party	Seats won	Vote share
BJP	30	45.7%
Congress	10	39.4%

MAHARASHTRA (48)

The Pawar split had its repurcussions in the State. The Nationalist Congress party formed by the Pawar split bagged just 6 seats. Shiv Sena won only 15 out of a total of 48 seats. The BJP won 13 seats. Thus, the combine got only 28 seats. The Congress got 10 seats inspite of the Pawar factor. Other got 4 seats.

The Pawar INC rift was patched up as the two combined to form the State Ministry. While Pawar knew he had no future as a split group. Sonia was no where near being the P.M. Sunil Dutt was elected from Mumbai (North-West) and so was Shivraj Patil from Latur, Sharad Pawar was elected from Baramati.

Smruti Koppikar had this to say about Kingmaker Pawar.

Those who have seen Sharad Pawar's politics from close quarters will testify this : he promises a lot but delivers little. Elections 1999 has been no different. He sought a make or break mandate for his fledgling Nationalist Congress Party (NCP) both in the Maharashtra Assembly and Lok Sabha. He is not quite made it in either.

In the process, Pawar achieved what he did on so many occasions earlier but is hardly remorseful about. He successfully stymied the Congress, leaving it dented enough so that it cannot come to power on its own and, in the process, allowed the Shiv Sena-BJP coalition to reap dividends. At the heart of it, it's the classic divide-and-rule policy-except that Pawar doesn't get to rule. In the 1995 Assembly elections and 1996 general election, Pawar worked his policy from within the party. This time, he was outside.

Free of an antagonistic leader like Sonia Gandhi and outside the Congress fold, he believed, lay his dream future—to be kingmaker if not king. The best of strategies often misfire. As it turns out, the BJP-led National Democratic Alliance can coast along comfortably in New Delhi without knocking at his door for support.

In his home state, he is still second fiddle to the Congress and cannot hope to wean away Congress-men to form an NCP-led government. If at all, it will be the other way around. NCP legislators may prop up a Congress government either by supporting it en bloc or some joining the parent party. Yet, NCP leaders do not believe Pawar made an error of judgement in queering his pitch out of the Congress. "He raised an issue and faced the consequences. There is no regret," says his lieutenant in Mumbai, Chhaggan Bhujbal.

At the end of all the hype and hoopla remains the fact that Pawar has never led a party or a coalition to vicotry in the state nor has he gifted his erstwhile party with a good show in the Lok Sabha since his bold experiment in 1978. In fact, figures show that he caused a gradual downslide in the number of seats whenever he led the party.

Few question his administrative abilities but many are beginning to wonder if the "strongman" status was exaggerated. Pawar has power, no doubt, but in specific regions of the state. Whether under the Congress umbrella or outside it, he has managed to get a vote share of about 23-25 per cent. But it's not enough to give him a command over the state. "Of couse, Pawar wields considerable influence but in a sense it is limited," says Prataprao Bhosale, PCC president and once a Pawar loyalist.

Elections 99 has shown that Pawar has limited appeal. Of course, he had less than six months to steer the NCP to a respectable slot. This time, more that ever, Pawar has to begin proving himself all over again.

Constituency-wise Results — 1999 and Winners of 1998

Ahmednagar : 11,47,107* (7,75,680) - Dilipkumar Mansukhlal Gandhi (BJP) : 2,78,508; Maruti Deoram Alias Dada Patil (NCP) : 2,50,051; Bhos Babasaheb Sahadu (INC) : 1,89,589; Shaikh Umar Abdul Latif (IND) : 10,131; Vithoba Hiraji Jadhav (MRC) : 3,579; Invalid : 43,822
In 1998, E.V. alias Balasaheb Vikhe Patil (SHS) won by a margin of 14,245 votes.

Akola : 11,45,140* (6,98,153) - Ambedkar Prakash Yashwant (BBM) : 2,72,243 Fudkar Pandurang Pundlik (BJP) : 2,63,527; Korpe Dr Santosh Kumar Wamanred (NCP) : 1,23,640; Maulana Warisuallakhan (IND) : 9,016; Others : 3,211; Invalid : 26,506
In 1998, Ambedkar Prakash Yashwant (RPI) won by a margin of 37,782 votes.

Amravati : 11,24,886* (6,98,150) - Gudhe Anant Mahadeoappa (SHS) : 3,19,916 R.S. Gavai (RPI) : 2,46,264; Kale Mohan Natthuji (NCP) : 71,801; Others : 25,752; Invalid : 34,417
In 1998, R.S. Gavai (RPI) won by a margin of 13,859 votes.

Aurangabad : 13,72,209* (9,06,312) - Chandrakant Khaire (SHS) : 3,83,144 A.R. Antule (INC) : 3,27,255; Baburao Pawar (NCP) : 1,34,831; Others : 9,043; Invalid : 52,039
In 1998, Ramkrishna Baba Patil (INC) won by a margin of 29,271 votes.

Baramati : 14,62,248* (9,22,819) - Pawar Sharadchandra Govindrao (NCP) : 5,10,928; Pratibha Lokhande (BJP) : 2,12,025; Prof. Ramkrishna More (INC) : 1,46,641; Hire Mohan Palande (ABHS) : 14,514; Invalid : 38,711
In 1998, Pawar Sharadchandra Govindrao (INC) won by a margin of 2,68,184 votes.

Bhandara : 9,23,256* (6,63,106) - Chunnilalbhau Thakur (BJP) : 2,91,355 Shrikant Jichkar (INC) : 2,87,536; Nimbarate Jagdish Kanhaji (NCP) ; 33,007; Harischandra Bhioram Salam (GGP) : 11,142; Dudhakuwar Jituji Raghuji (BSP) : 11,051; Others : 1,863; Invalid : 27,152
In 1998, Patel Praful Manoharbai (INC) won by a margin of 19,306 votes.

* Total Electorates
Figures in ( ) are Votes polled

Beed : 11,75,871* (8,51,591) - Jaysingrao Gaikwad Patil (BJP) : 3,32,946
Radhakrishna Sahebrao Patil (NCP) : 2,81,756; Ashok Patil (INC) : 1,62,478; Sk Jalal Sk Khairodin (IND) : 19,565; Chavan Namdeo Fakira (CPI) : 10,210; Others : 1,127; Invalid : 43,509
In 1998, Jaisingrao Gaikwad Patil (BJP) won by a margin of 6,103 votes.

Buldhana (SC) : 10,39,128* (7,43,613) - Adsul Anandrao Vithoba (SHS) : 2,94,922
Wasnik Mukul Balkrushna (INC) : 2,49,915; Sardar Sahebrao Ashruji (NCP) : 1,33,165; Chavan Baliram Motiram (IND) : 18,948; Lahane Vijay Bandu (IND) : 8,187; Invalid : 38,476
In 1998, Wasnik Mukul Balkrushna (INC) won by a margin of 53,557 votes.

Chandrapur : 11,24,263* (8,27,213) - Pugliya Nareshkumar Chunnalal (INC) : 3,28,522; Ahir Hansraj Gangaram (BJP) : 3,25,685; Potdukhe Shobha Sudhakar (NCP) : 87,304; Gunmukulwar Venkatash Ramayaji (GGP) : 39,467; Dumbere Mahadev Punaji (IND) : 7,560; Invalid : 38,675
In 1998, Puglia Nareshkumar Chunnalal (INC) won by a margin of 1,50,355 votes.

Chimur : 10,13,322* (7,80,590) - Diwathe Namdeo Harbaji (BJP) : 3,00,601
Jogendra Kawada (RPI) : 2,30,561; Patel Prafulbhai Manoharbhai (NCP) : 1,47,322; Shiwarkar Anil Laxman (IND) : 37,113; Gajabe Sudhakar Marotrao (IND) : 15,516; Others : 10,337; Invalid : 39,140
In 1998, Prof. Jogendra Kawade (RPI) won by a margin of 2,122 votes.

Dahanu (ST) : 14,34,676* (7,08,881) - Adv. Chintaman Wanage (BJP) : 2,40,866
Shingda Damodar Barku (INC) : 1,78.596; Nam Shankhar Sakharam (NCP) : 1,44,589; Ozare Rajaram Nathu (CPM) : 89,459; Zole Dattatraya Kalu (BSP) : 6,478; Invalid : 48.893
In 1998, Nam Shankar Sakharam (INC) won by a margin of 34,558 votes.

Dhule (ST) : 11,02,841* (6,26,242) - Ramdas Rupla Gavit (BJP) : 2,11,904
Chayre Bapu Hari (INC) : 1,98,919; Ahire D.S. Ahire Saheb (NCP) : 1,67,834; Bhil Gulab Dasharath (IND) : 4,437; Adv. More Madhav Bandu (BSP) : 3,177; Others : 7,614; Invalid : 32,357
In 1998, D.S. Ahire (INC) won by a margin of 57,713 votes.

Erandol : 10,82,949* (6,79,699) - Annasheb M.K. Patil (BJP) : 2,97,867
More Vasantrao Jivanrao (NCP) : 1,93,411; Prof. V.G. Patil (INC) : 1,32,902; Sk A Hakim Sk Raheman (IND) : 4,715; Invalid : 50,804
In 1998, Annsaheb M.K. Patil (BJP) won by a margin of 24,836 votes.

Hingoli : 10,33,943* (7,32,505) - Mane Shivaji Gyanbarao (SHS) : 2,97,284
Adv Pole Naik Madhavrao Bahenara (BBM) : 2,16,629; Suryakanta Patil (NCP): 1,75,224; Invalid : 43,368
In 1998, Suryakanta Patil (INC) won by a margin of 77,666 votes.

Ichalkaranji : 11,16,538* (8,10,616) - Mane Nivedita Sambhajirao (NCP) : 3,37,657; Alwade Kallappa Baburao (INC) : 3,24,845 Babu Alias Pundlik Krishna Ja (SHS) : 1,00,697; Others : 15,414; Invalid : 32,003
In 1998, Alwade Kallapa Baburao (INC) won by a margin of 12,194 votes.

Jalgaon : 11,01,166* (7,43,399) - Y. G. Mahajan Sir (BJP) : 3,34,020
Ulhas Vasudeo Patil (INC) : 1,20,951; Sk Shavir Sk Mangu (IND) : 2,289; Invalid : 41,914
In 1998, Ulhas Vasudeo Patil (INC) won by a margin of 56,814 votes.

Jalna : 11,01,890* (8,01,690) - Danve Raosaheb Dadarao Patil (BJP) : 3,32,620
Bangar Dnyandeo Ganpatrao (INC) : 2,08,711; Borade Vijayanna Sampatrao (NCP) : 1,73,337; Others : 11,796; Invalid : 75,226
In 1998, Pawar Uttamsinh Rajdharsinh (BJP) won by a margin of 1,808 votes.

Karad : 10,34,700* (7,60,026) - Shrinivas Dadasaheb Patil (NCP) : 3,50,504
Chavan Prithviraj Dajisaheb (INC) : 2,27,547; Mankumare Vasant Dnyandev (SHS) : 1,51,178; Patil Shrinivas Baburao (IND) : 4,701; Invalid : 26,096
In 1998, Chavan Prithviraj Dajisaheb (INC) won by a margin of 1,73,015 votes.

Khed : 10,70,955* (6,90,687) - Ashok Namdeorao Mohal (NCP) : 2,85,476
Bankhele Kisanrao Baburao (SHS) : 2,27,458; Kandage Ram Janardan (INC) : 1,38,151; Gavali Arun Gulab (ABHS) : 9,520; Others : 1,748; Invalid : 29,334
In 1998, Ashok Namdeorao Mohol (INC) won by a margin of 1,01,430 votes.

Kolaba : 11,56,635* (7,10,770) - Ramsheth Thakur (PWPI) : 2,74,361
D.B. Patil (SHS) : 2,31,264; Sable Pushpa Tukaram (INC) : 1,48,146; Puranik Ballad Govind (IND) : 6,473; Invalid : 50,526
In 1998, Ramsheth Thakur (PWPI) won by a margin of 9,126 votes.

Kolhapur : 10,71,553* (7,74,638) - Mandlik Sadashivrao Dadoba (NCP) : 3,46,459
Udaysingrao Gaikwad (INC) : 2,37,549; Maj. Gen. Shivajirao Shripatil Patil (SHS) : 1,63,866; Invalid : 26,764
In 1998, Mandik Sadashivrao Dadoba (INC) won by a margin of 61,598 votes.

Kopargaon : 9,52,599* (6,88,637) - E.V. Balasaheb Vikhe Patil (SHS) : 2,53,498
Solicitor Gulabrao Sakharam S (NCP) : 2,06,083; Adik Govindrao Wamanrao (INC) : 1,77,643; Gunjal Radhesham Shivram (CPI) : 10,651; Others : 5,063; Invalid : 35,699
In 1998, Tanpure Prasad Baburao (INC) won by a margin of 79,243 votes.

Latur : 10,96,607* (7,94,814) - Patil Shivraj Vishwanath (INC) : 3,14,213
Gopalrao Vitthalrao Patil (BJP) : 2,73,923; Pasha Patel (NCP) : 1,55,816; Others : 9,157; Invalid : 41,705
In 1998, Patil Shivraj Vishwanath (INC) won by a margin of 3,327 votes.

Malegaon (ST) : 10,83,230* (6,98,501) - Mahale Haribhau Shankar (JD-S) : 1,91,643; Gangurde Babanrao Lahanu (BJP) : 1,87,251; Kahandole Zamaru Mangau (INC) : 1,79,941; Gavit Chintaman Janu (CPM) : 69,142; Others : 25,590; Invalid : 44,934
In 1998, Kahandole Zamaru Mangau (INC) won by a margin of 61,196 votes.

Mumbai North : 22,22,232* (9,53,769) - Ram Naik (BJP) : 5,17,941
Chandrakant Gosalia (INC) : 3,63,805; Damodar Janardan Tandel (INC) : 25,132; Others : 11,651; Invalid : 35,240
In 1998, Ram Naik (BJP) won by a margin of 75,017 votes.

Mumbai North Central : 11,48,320* (5,28,342) - Manohar Gajanan Joshi (SHS) : 2,94,935; Raja Dhale (BBM) : 1,25,940; B.C. Kamble : 56,684; Shaikh Mohammad Faruque (IUML) : 17,454; Panda Sureshchandra (IND) : 10,549; Others : 22,729; Invalid : 51
In 1998, Ramdas Athawale (RPI) won by a margin of 25,232 votes.

Mumbai North East : 19,90,340* (9,29,549) - Kirit Somaiya (BJP) : 4,00,436
Adv. Gurudas Kamat (INC) : 3,93,160; Rammanohar V. Tripathi (NCP) : 1,02,513; Others : 19,902; Dattatray Bhojraj Waghmare (IND) : 13,406; Invalid : 132

In 1998, Gurudas Kamat (INC) won by a margin of 47,452 votes.

Mumbai North West : 15,53,015* (7,13,586) - Sunil Dutt Ragunath (INC) : 3,66,669; Madhukar Raghunath Sirpotdar (SHS) : 2,81,130; Ramesh Dube Mataprasad (NCP) : 41,947; Others : 10,668; Invalid : 13,172

Mumbai South : 7,19,281* (3,03,094) - Jayanwanti Mehta (BJP) : 1,44,945 Murli Deora (INC) : 1,34,702; Aziz Lalani (SP) : 19,128; Others 4,224; Invalid : 95

In 1998, Murli Deora (INC) won by a margin of 21,065 votes.

Mumbai South Central : 8,12,576* (3,67,643) - Mohan Vishnu Rawale (SHS) : 1,76,323; A. Majeed Memon Advocate (SP) : 97,287; Dada Samant (BBM) : 77,747; Gaikwad P. K. (IND) : 16,248; Invalid : 29

In 1998, Mohan Vishnu Rawale (SHS) won by a margin of 153 votes.

Nagpur : 15,51,367* (8,29,732) - Vilas Muttemwar (INC) : 4,24,450 Vinod Yaswantrao Gudadhe Patil (BJP) : 3,51,755; Prof Ashok Godghate (IND): 15,817; Prof. P.S. Changole (BSP) : 14,465; Others : 3,878; Invalid : 19,367

In 1998, Vilas Muttemwas (INC) won by a margin of 1,63,282 votes.

Nanded : 11,91,310* (7,83,847) - Patil Bhaskarrao Bapurao (INC) : 3,27,293 Dhanallrao Vyankatrao Deshmukh (BJP) : 2,94,718; Gunwant Patil Hangargekar (SBP) : 71,279; Others : 21,438; Gaikwad Sopan Nivrati (ABHS) : 17,637; Invalid : 51,482

In 1998, Patil Bhaskarrao Bapurao (INC) won by a margin of 47,287 votes.

Nandurbar (ST) : 10,79,466* (7,10,653) - Gavit Manikrao Hodlya (INC) : 3,18,338 Vasave Govind Pamu (NCP) : 1,87,567; Kuwarsing Fuiji Valvi (BJP) : 1,51,509; Bhuribai Mansing Shemle (CPM) : 13,625; Invalid : 39,614

In 1998, Gavit Manikrao Hodiya (INC) won by a margin of 65,711 votes.

Nashik : 13,44,755* (7,67,154) - Dhikale Uttamrao Nathuju (SHS) : 3,03,084 Patil Madhav Balwant (NCP) : 2,66,272; Gulave Gopalrao Ravlaji (INC) : 1,48,346; Others : 11,070; Invalid : 38,382

In 1998, Patil Madhav Balwant (INC) won by a margin of 1,02,392 votes.

Osmanabad (SC) : 9,36,324* (6,66,905) - Kamble Shivaji Vithalrao (SHS) : 2,52,135; Deokule Kanifnath (NCP) : 1,93,062; Arvind Kamble (INC) : 1,67,005; Vitthal Kundlink Raut (IND) : 15,670; Sanjaykumar Bhagwat Waghmare (BSP) : 5,315; Invalid : 33,718

In 1998, Arvind Tulshiram Kamble (INC) won by a margin of 47,018 votes.

Pandharpur (SC) : 11,06,361* (8,27,236) - Athawale Ramdas Bandu (IND) : 4,13,115; Kshirsagar Nagnath Dattatray (BJP) : 1,53,610; Thorat Sandipan Bhagwan (INC) : 1,11,903; Ghodke Dagdu Pandharinath (IND) : 99,242; Pritish Shivajirao Jalgaonkar (BSP) : 2,940; Invalid : 46,426

In 1998 Thorat Sandipan Bhagwan (INC) won by a margin of 97,432 votes.

Parbhani : 10,55,193* (7,05,772) - Jadhav Suresh Ramrao (SHS) : 2,54,019 Jamkar Raosaheb Bhausaheb (INC) : 2,10,354; Warpudkar Suresh Ambadasrao (NCP) : 1,79,443; Others 17,816; Invalid : 44,140

In 1998, Warpudkar Sureshrao Ambadasarao (INC) won by a margin of 45,493 votes.

Pune : 14,34,680* (7,49,215) - Pradeep Rawat (BJP) : 3,04,955 Joshi Mohan (INC) : 2,13,670; Tupe Vithal Baburao (NCP) : 1,98,738; Others : 15,291; Invalid : 16,561

In 1998, Tupe Vithal Baburao (INC) won by a margin of 93,218 votes

Rajapur : 7,90,537* (4,56,197) - Suresh Prabhakar Prabhu (SHS) : 2,21,523
Prof. Madhu Dandawate (JD-S) : 1,08,673; Major Sudhir Sawant Sitaram (INC): 1,03,556; Invalid : 22,445
In 1998, Suresh Prabhu (SHS) won by a margin of 65,042 votes.

Ramtek : 10,50,812* (6,89,659) - Subodh Moite (SHS) : 2,42,454
Purohit Banwari Lal (INC) : 2,30,765; Hajare Pandurang Jairamji (NCP) : 1,49,741; Others : 32,862; Invalid : 33,837
In 1998, Rani Chitralekha Bhosale (INC) won by a margin of 66,776 votes.

Ratnagiri : 8,72,263* (5,58,086) - Anant Gangaram Geete (SHS) : 2,93,834
Ziman Sujit Bhagoji (NCP) : 1,78,491; Rajaram Shinde (INC) : 62,029; Invalid: 23,732
In 1998, Anant Gangram Geete (SHS) won by a margin of 31,234 votes.

Sangli : 10,31,607* (7,35,332) - Prakash Bapu Vasantrao Patil (INC) : 3,81,162
Patil Madan Vishwanath (NCP) : 2,20,602; Dange Rajendra Alias Chiman Ramchander (BJP) : 97,273; Ganpati Tukaram Kamble G T (IND) : 7,320; Invalid : 28,975
In 1998, Patil Madan Vishwanath (INC) won by a margin of 73,239 votes.

Satara : 9,84,469* (7,03,005) - Laxmanrao Pandurang Jadhav (NCP) : 3,13,325
Hindurao N. Naik Nimbalkar (SHS) : 1,88,554; Khardekar Nimbalkar Yashawant (INC) : 1,59,953; Others : 7,429; Invalid : 33,744
In 1998, Abhayasinh Shahumaharaj Bhosale (INC) won by a margin of 1,81,476 votes.

Solapur : 10,26,004* (6,30,769) - Shinde Sushilkumar Sambhajirao (INC) : 2,86,578; Valyal Lingraj Balirayya (BJP) : 2,09,583; Abdulpurkar Aralappa Gangappa (NCP) : 1,02,803; Others : 4,482; Invalid : 27,323
In 1998, Shinde Sushilkumar Sambhajirao (INC) won by a margin of 1,04,405 votes.

Thane : 27,71,746* (9,34,027) - Prakash Paranjape (SHS) : 3,91,446
Nakul Patil (INC) : 2,91,763; Prabhakar Hegade (NCP) : 1,77,256; Wadhavinde Mahendra Keru (IND) : 37,145; Madhukar Vitthalrao Dekat (BSP) : 8,073; Invalid : 28,344
In 1998, Prakash Paranjpe (SHS) won by a margin of 2,49,579 votes.

Wardha : 10,79,968* (6,81,697) - Prabha Rao (INC) : 2,49,564
Suresh Ganpatrao Waghmare (BJP) : 2,42,502; Datta Meghe (NCP) : 1,52,856; Chidam Narayanrao Ramji (GGP) : 6,472; Invalid : 30,303
In 1998, Datta Meghe (INC) won by a margin of 83,083 votes.

Washim : 10,04,211* (6,77,971) - Bhawana Pundlikrao Gawli (SHS) : 2,44,820
Deshmukh Anantrao Vitthalrao (INC) : 2,05,225; Prof Javed Khan (NCP) : 1,54,030; Naik Raju Ramu (IND) : 24,859; Others : 10,481; Invalid : 38,556
In 1998, Naik Sudhakarrao Rajusing (INC) won by a margin of 1,08,590 votes.

Yavatmal : 10,07,603* (6,48,757) - Uttamrao Deorao Patil (INC) : 2,58,535
Haribhau Rathod (BJP) : 2,43,309; Rajabhau Thakre (NCP) : 77,968; Kishorbhau Tiwari (IND) : 19,076; Makram Sheetal Kavadooj (GGP) : 14,181; Laxmanbhau Kinkar (IND) : 2,319; Invalid : 33,369
In 1998, Uttamrao Deorao Patil (INC) won by a margin of 54,673 votes.

MANIPUR (2)

Manipur State Congress bagged the Inner Manipur seat. The second seat was vacant.

Inner Manipur : 6,57,928* (4,46,627) - Thounaojam Chaoba Singh (MSCP) : 1,53,387

Khadem Mani Singh (MPP) : 1,45,192; Nimai Chand Luwang (INC) : 1,34,297; Others : 9,810; Invalid : 3,941

In 1998, Thounaojam Chaoba Singh (MSCP) won by a margin of 16,187 votes.

MEGHALAYA (2)

Indian National Congress and Nationalist Congress Party (A.P. Sangama) shared one seat each.

Shillong : 7,24,401* (3,68,845) - Raty Ripple Kyndiah (INC) : 1,45,020

Stanlington D. Khongwir (UDP) : 1,07,197; Hopingstone Lyngdoh (HSPDP) : 40,301; Sounder S. Cajee (PDM) : 33,164; Thrang Hok Rangad (BJP) : 31,859; Invalid : 11,304

Tura : 4,53,861* (2,92,613) - P.A. Sangma (NCP) : 1,82.883

Atul C. Marak (INC) : 69,304; Monendro Agitok (BJP) : 29,990; Clifford Marak (GNC) : 4,561; Robin Rema (CPI) : 2,736; Invalid : 3,139

In 1998, P.A. Sangma (INC) won by a margin of 1,77,659 votes.

MIZORAM (1)

Mizoram (ST) : 4,48,638* (2,93,455) - Vanlalzawna (IND) : 1,71,557

Rokamlova (IND) : 1,02,898; Mulai Hlychho (MFD) : 8,444; Rualpawla (IND) : 4,508; Lallianzuala (RJD) : 2,132; P. Saidinga (EU) : 1,578; Lallawmsanga (LS): 669; Invalid : 1,669

In 1998, H. Lallungmuana (IND) won by a margin of 41 votes.

NAGALAND (1)

Nagaland : 9,55,914* (7,28,843) - K. Asungba Sangtam (INC) 5,16,119

Shurhozelie (INC) : 1,62,521; Neikhahoz (BJP) : 37,156; Akhai Achumi (LS) : 5,763; Roland (IND) : 3,486; Invalid : 3,798

In 1998, Asangba Sangtam (INC) won by a margin of 2,91,438 votes.

ORISSA (21)

INC could get just two out of a total of 21 seats. The incumbency factor acted negatively for the party. It was from Orissa that the one vote of the CM who was also an MP at the time of confidence vote that led to the fall of the BJP led coalition plunging the country into the 13th election for the Lok Sabha. The voters were not amused.

The BJD got 10 seats while the BJP bagged 9 seats.

N. Ramdas made the following media comments.

Is it end of the road for the Congress (I) in Orissa? If the results of the Lok Sabha election are any indicators, it will be very difficult for the Congress (I) to make its presence felt in the Orissa Assembly which is to go to polls early next year. The Congress (I) could retain only two of the five seats it had won during the last Lok Sabha elections.

---

* Total Electorates
Figures in ( ) are Votes polled

The BJD-BJP alliance bagged 19 of the 21 seats this time. While the BJD won 10 of the 12 seats it contested, the BJP emerged victorious in all the nine seats it contested. The Congress(I), which had fielded candidates in 20 seats could manage to retain its seats in the tribal dominated Koraput and Dhenkanal constituencies.

But the margin of victory in both the seats where the Congress (I) won is not a good sign for the party's future. In Koraput which the Congress (I) had been winning since the first Lok Sabha election in 1952 and from where the present Chief Minister, Giridhar Gomang, has been winning since 1971, his wife, Ms. Hema Gomang, could retain the seat by a margin of little over 12,000 votes. Koraput, being a traditional Congress(I) bastion, has shown signs that it may not be so anymore and the party may lose its hold there if the present trend continues.

This is for the second time that the BJD candidate, Jayram Pangi, is losing to the Congress(I). In the last elections, he had lost to Gomang. In the other seat which the BJD knowingly conceded to the Congress (I) was Dhenkanal where the Congress, candidate, K.P. Singh Deo, could manage to win by little over 3000 votes.

From the very beginning, the BJP wanted to have discussions on seat-sharing with the BJD on the winning prospects of the candidates. However, the BJD president under compulsions refused to have any dialogue fearing it would affect its dominating role. The BJD also refused to change its Dhenkanal candidate, Tatagatha Satpathy. The BJP was keen on fielding its candidate, Rudra Naraya Pani there, according to the wishes of the State unit which did not have the support of the party high command in Delhi. Pani filed two sets on nomination papers, one as BJP candidate and the other as Independent. With the State unit not being able to get the high command's nod, Pani continued to remain in the fray as an Independent. The presence of the Independent resulted in the Congress(I) gaining confidence and hoping for a comfortable victory. However, the Prime Minister, Atal Bihari Vajpayee, visited the constituency and boosted Satpathy's chances resulting in his polling a little over 2,45,000 votes. But Pani polled more than 90,000 votes which were crucial and proved expensive for Satpathy. Most of the independent candidates, except Pani, lost their deposits.

Other prominent defeats were those of the Congress (I) candidates Ms Jayanti Patnaik, wife of former Chief Minister, J.B. Patnaik, from the Berhampur constituency and Ranjib Biswal, son of Basant Kumar Biswal, Minister for Water Resources, from the Jagatsingpur constituency.

Patnaik had stayed put in Berhampur ever since the party high command agreed to his wife's candidature. But all his efforts proved futile as Ms. Patnaik could not retain the seat and the BJP candidate was elected. The Congress(I) had never lost the elections from Berhampur since 1961.

Basant Kumar Biswal, against whom there are many charges of corruption and who is still holding on to his protfolio after he patched up with J.B. Patnaik, suffered a major setback in the defeat of his son, Ranjib Biswal in Jagatsingpur. Ranjib Biswal lost to Trilochen Kanungo of the BJD by a margin of over 1,45,000 votes."

Constituency-wise Results — 1999 and Winners of 1998

Aska : 11,75,865* (4,85,318) - Naveen Patnaik (BJD) : 3,59,178

Duti Krushna Panda (CPI) : 1,02,442; Chakradhar Sahu (NCP) : 10,484; Others: 7,393; Invalid : 5,821

---

* Total Electorates

Figures in ( ) are Votes polled

In 1998, Naveen Patnaik (BJD) won by a margin of 86,211 votes.

Balasore : 12,42,578* (7,75,874) - M.A. Kharbela Swain (BJP) : 4,28,070
Subhankar Mohapatra (INC) : 2,91,698; Sambhunath Mohanty (CPI) : 26,586; Tapas Kumar Rath (JMM) : 14,813; Others : 7,602; Invalid : 7,105
In 1998, M.A. Kharbela Swain (BJP) won by a margin of 83,967 votes.

Berhampur : 11,59,468* (5,80,534) - Anadi Charan Sahu (BJP) 3,10,704
Jayanti Patnaik (INC) : 2,56,581; Others : 3,271; Invalid : 9,978
In 1998, Jayanti Patnaik (INC) won by a margin of 35,240 votes.

Bhadrak (SC) : 11,95,146* (6,84,182) - Arjun Charan Sethi (BJD) : 3,97,450
Panchanan Mandal (INC) : 2,75,017; Others : 6,671; Invalid : 5,044
In 1998, Arjun Charan Sethi (BJD) won by a margin of 33,563 votes.

Bhubaneswar : 13,18,560* (6,25,342) - Prasanna Kumar Patasani (BJD) : 4,14,429
Bibhuti Bhusan Singh Mardaraj (INC) : 1,80,468; Others : 30,445; Invalid : 0
In 1998 Prasanna Kumar Patasani (BJD) won by a margin of 1,27,908 votes.

Bolangir : 10,51,199* (6,42,631) - Sangeeta Kumari Singh Deo (BJP) : 4,04,988
Sarat Pattanaik (INC) : 2,24,009; Lalit Mohan Gandhi (AJBP) : 3,215; Invalid : 10,419
In 1998, Sangeeta Kumari Singh Deo (BJP) won by a margin of 1,58,529 votes.

Cuttack : 12,15,249* (6,24,984) - Bhartruhari Mahatab (BJD) : 4,07,603
Kanhu Charan Lenka (INC) : 2,02,286; Others : 9,917; Invalid : 5,178
In 1998, Bhartruhari Mahtab (BJD) won by a margin of 1,12,694 votes.

Deogarh : 11,68,931* (6,90,605) - Debendra Pradhan (BJP) : 3,76,412
Hemananda Biswal (INC) : 2,89,543; Pascal Barla (JMM) : 5,320; Others : 9,445; Invalid : 9,885
In 1998, Debendra Pradhan (BJP) won by a margin of 10,780 votes.

Dhenkanak : 11,18,853* (6,10,993) - Kamakhya Prasad Singh Deo (INC) : 248,824
Tathagata Satpathy (BJD) : 2,45,150; Rudra Narayan Pani (IND) : 97,180; Others : 12,909; Invalid 6,930
In 1998, Tathagata Satpathy (BJD) won by a margin of 32,511 votes.

Jagatsinghpur : 12,33,063* (7,63,694) - Trilochan Kanungo (BJD) - 4,39,888
Ranjib Biswal (INC) : 2,90,606; Akhaya Kumar Pradhan (CPI) : 26,975; Others: 953; Invalid : 5,272
In 1998, Ranjib Biswal (INC) won by a margin of 19,929 votes.

Jaipur (SC) : 11,71,211* (5,98,474) - Jagannath Mallik (BJP) : 3,51,057
Ram Chandra Mallick (INC) : 2,37,360; Others : 4,854; Invalid : 5,203
In 1998, Ramachandra Mallik (INC) won by a margin of 91,864 votes.

Kalahandi : 10,60,990* (6,54,702) - Bikram Keshari Deo (BJP) : 3,71,911
Bhakta Charan Das (INC) : 2,55,392; Biranchi Panda (SHS) : 10,169; Others : 5,016; Invalid : 12,214
In 1998, Bikram Keshari Deo (BJP) won by a margin of 1,19,914 votes.

Kendrapara : 11,21,183* (6,24,939) - Prabhat Kumar Samantaray (BJD) : 3,59,314
Archana Nayak (INC) : 2,57,175; Others : 3,947; Invalid : 4,503
In 1998, Pravat Kumar Samantray (BJD) won by a margin of 7,825 votes.

Keonjhar (ST) : 10,92,055* (6,29,384) - Ananta Nayak (BJP) : 4,16,956
Sobanta Singh Laguri (INC) : 1,94,403; Others : 6,636; Invalid : 11,389
In 1998, Upendranath Nayak (BJP) won by a margin of 86,275 votes.

Koraput (ST) : 11,20,784* (5,67,490) - Hema Gamang (INC) : 2,77,555
Jayaram Pangi (BJD) : 2,65,401; Kartika Gamango (CPI-ML) : 8,476; Invalid :

16,058
In 1998, Giridhar Gamang (INC) won by a margin of 81,516 votes.

Mayurbhanj (ST) : 9,64,354* (5,77,592) - Salkhan Murmu (BJP) : 3,00,747
Kamala Tiriya (INC) : 1,52,807; Bhadab Hansdah (JMM) : 92,727; Others : 21,566; Invalid : 9,745
In 1998, Salkhan Murmu (BJP) won by a margin of 74,319 votes.

Nawarangpur (ST) : 10,85,575* (6,76,874) - Parsuram Majhi (BJP) : 3,31,863
Chandra Sekhar Majhi (INC) : 3,15,712; Others : 5928; Invalid : 23,371
In 1998, Khagapati Pradhani (INC) won by a margin of 73,935 votes.

Phulbani (SC) : 11,26,908* (6,40,741) - Padmanav Behera (BJD) : 3,57,024
Mrutyunjjay Naik (INC) : 2,54,809; Bedabyas Suna (BSP) : 15,314; Ramakanta Naik (SHS) : 3,649; Invalid : 9,945
In 1998, Padmanava Behera (BJD) won by a margin of 91,072 votes.

Puri : 11,76,817* (6,66,936) - Braja Kishore Tripathy (BJD) : 3,83,060
Jayant Das (INC) : 2,51,315; Jagannath Mishra (CPM) : 13,026; Others 9,704; Khitish Biswal (CPI-ML) : 3,574; Invalid : 6,257
In 1998, Braja Kishore Tripathy (BJD) won by a margin of 52,545 votes.

Sambalpur : 11,90,344* (7,02,356) - Prasanna Acharya (BJD) : 3,98,597
Krupasindhu Bhai (INC) : 2,71,634; Rabindra Meg (BSP) : 13,904; Others : 8,302; Invalid : 9,919
In 1998, Prasanna Acharya (BJD) won by a margin of 24,769 votes.

Sundargarh (ST) : 11,98,357* (6,30,535) - Jual Oram (BJP) : 3,26,395
Christopher Ekka (INC) : 1,73,881; George Tirkey (JMM) : 1,00,447; Simon Lakra (CPI-M) : 13,318; Others : 3,537; Invalid : 12,957
In 1998, Jual Oram (BJP) won by a margin of 1,26,028 votes.

PUNJAB (13)

Once again inner dissidence cost the ruling party heavily. The INC got revived with 8 out of 13 seats. The BJP had to be content with just one seat (Vinod Khanna at Gurdaspur). The CPI had one seat while the two Akali factions shared 2 and 1 seat each. The SAD - BJP alliance was wrecked by the dissidence in the Akali camp.

Total Seats	
1952	18
1957 - 1962	22
1967 onwards	13

"The detailed analysis of the results, especially of the constituency-wise performance of each party, for the 13 Lok Sabha seats in Punjab, where the BJP led National Democratic Alliance, received a drubbing has some interesting indicators. It was clear that "Sikh vote bank" got fragmented, while the BJP lost its vote share by 11.32 percent as compared to its performance in the February 1998 elections.

For the first time in the history of the State, especially in the post 1984 era, the "Sikh vote Bank" stood fragmented. The votes polled by the ruling Shiromani Akali Dal (SAD) led by the Chief Minister, Parkash Singh Badal, the breakaway Sarb Hind Shiromani Akali Dal (SHSAD) of the former SGPC chief, G.S. Tohra and the SAD (Amritsar) led by the "hard-liner" Simranjit Singh Mann, put together was 36.64 percent. Badal's party got two seats, the SHSAD drew a blank, while Mann was successful from Sangrur.

Following the incidents in 1984, which included the army action "Operation

Bluestar" was conducted to flush out militants from the Golden Temple in Amritsar and the anti-Sikh carnage in Delhi and other parts of the country following the assassination of the then Prime Minister, Mrs. Indira Gandhi, Punjab witnessed the emergence of the "Sikh vote bank" phenomenon. This was a political development rooted in the "anti-Congressism" and was successful in replacing the traditional behaviour of the Akali vote bank, which had a communal inclination.

This year's results have indicated that though fragmented the Sikh vote bank still operates within the various shades of the Akali conglomerate. Contrary to the claims of the Congress, the memories of 1984 still haunt the Sikh voters, especially the peasants in the rural areas and traders in the cities. In the elections to the parliament in 1985, the SAD had polled 37.17 percent of the total valid votes, which has remained more or less unchanged, though the Akali Dal has faced varied fragmentation at different occasions. Earlier, the SAD had been accounting for just above 25 percent votes in different elections.

However, in the post terrorism period, especially in 1997, the state witnessed the emergence of concern for the "Punjabi identity", which resulted in the alliance between the SAD-BJP representing the convergence of the "Sikh vote bank" and the interests of the Hindu community in the state. In the February 1997 assembly polls and the Lok Sabha elections a year later, this alliance polled 46 and 44.6 percent votes respectively. In the present elections, the combine got just 37.74 percent.

In the three seats of Gurdaspur, Amritsar and Hoshiarpur, where it retained its previous candidates, the BJP suffered a loss to its vote bank to the tune of 11.32 percent as compared to its own performance last year. Even at Gurdaspur, where the actor turned politician, Vinod Khanna, managed a victory through a wafer thin margin, the party lost 9.55 percent of its vote share. In Amritsar, where the BJP state unit's president, Daya Singh Sodhi was seeking a re-election, lost the contest as the party vote share dropped by 11.2 percent.

On the other hand, the Congress, which romped home with an impressive victory at eight seats, got a boost of 4.15 percent. The party managed the best improvement in its vote share by regaining Jalandhar, which was represented by the former Prime Minister, I.K. Gujral, in the last Lok Sabha where the Congress polled 8.7 percent votes more than last year. Similarly at Amritsar, where the former External Affairs minister, R.L. Bhatia, regained the seat, the party accounted for an 8.37 percent jump in its votes. The party's candidate, Jagmeet Singh Brar, became the giant killer of the present polls, when he overcame Sukhbir Singh Badal, the only son of the Punjab Chief Minister, in a battle royal at Faridkot. The party gained by 1.27 votes only.

The failure of the Congress party high command to deal with the scourge of factionalism was quite visible at Patiala and Gurudaspur. Despite an impressive victory margin of nearly 80,000 votes, the party's vote share dropped by 0.76 percent. The seat was wrested by "Maharani" Parneet Kaur, the wife of the President of the state unit of the Congress and scion of the royal family of this erstwhile princely state, Capt. Amrinder Singh. At Gurdaspur, despite the party gaining 5.41 percent in its last year's vote share, the candidate could not manage a victory. Both these seats were witnesses to some bitter factional feuds.

The political analysts explain the Punjab election results by arguing that a sizeable number of voters from the Hindu community have moved away from the SAD-BJP alliance.

This category of voters has either become non-voters, or they have shifted back to the Congress. Moreover, the loss of about 25.57 percent votes suffered by the BSP is being interpreted that the voters from the Scheduled Castes have consolidated behind the Congress, which was aligned with the CPI and CPI (M) this time, as combine accounted for 44.35 per cent votes." [*Sarbjit Pandher*]

Constituency-wise Results — 1999 and Winners of 1998

Amritsar : 12,44,316* (5,96,536) - Raghunandan Lal Bhatia (INC) : 2,96,533
Daya Singh Sodhi (BJP) : 2,64,534; Bhupinder Singh Maan (SHSAD) : 17,581; Others : 10,952; Invalid : 6,936
In 1998, Daya Singh Sodhi (BJP) won by a margin of 91,140 votes.

Bhatinda : 12,17,731* (6,56,684) - Bhan Singh Bhaura (CPI) : 3,27,484
Chatin Singh Samaon (SAD) : 2,66,167; Gurdeep Singh (SHSAD) : 42,676; Others : 14,241; Invalid : 6,116
In 1998, Chatin Singh Samaon (SAD) won by a margin of 49,856 votes.

Faridkot : 12,24,531* (8,71,755) - Jagmeet Singh Brar (INC) : 4,18,454
Sukhbir Singh Badal (SAD) : 4,13,306; Others : 26,263;Rajinder Kumar Sharma (IND) : 13,673; Invalid : 59
In 1998, Sukhbir Singh Badal (SAD) won by a margin of 34,959 votes.

Ferozepur : 12,14,129* (7,56,925) - Zora Singh (SAD) : 3,00,236
Hans Raj (INC) : 2,85,375; Mohan Singh (BSP) : 1,53,213; Others : 11,276; Invalid : 6,825
In 1998, Zora Singh (SAD) won by a margin of 44,467 votes.

Gurdaspur : 11,22,008* (6,77,041) - Vinod Khanna (BJP) : 3,15,267
Sukhbans Kaur Bhinder (INC) : 3,13,868; Sucha Singh (SHSAD) : 35,665; Others : 5,769; Invalid : 6,472
In 1998, Vinod Khanna (BJP) won by a margin of 1,06,833 votes.

Hoshiarpur : 11,13,122* (5,85,866) - Charanjit Singh Channi (INC) : 2,56,211
Kamal Chaudhry (BJP) : 2,22,005; Rakesh Ram Gujjr (BSP) : 88,999; Others : 18,651; Invalid : 0
In 1998, Kamal Chaudhry (BJP) won by a margin of 65,332 votes.

Jalandhar : 11,41,005* (5,68,257) - Balbir Singh (INC) : 2,67,209
Prabhjot Kaur (SAD) : 2,32,543; Kuldip Singh Wadal (IND) : 38,649; Sant Sukhjit Singh (IND) : 10,845; Others : 13,543; Invalid : 5,468
In 1998, Inder Kumar Gujral (JD) won by a margin of 1,31,016 votes.

Ludhiana : 14,71,530* (6,74,419) - Gurcharan Singh Galib (INC) : 3,46,928
Amrik Singh Aliwal (SAD) : 2,41,682; Gurdarshan Singh Grewal (SHSAD) : 64,893; Others : 13,466; Invalid : 7,450
In 1998, Amrik Singh Aliwal (SAD) won by a margin of 9,212 votes.

Patiala : 13,10,354* (7,81,794) - Parneet Kaur (INC) : 3,60,125
Surjit Singh Rakhra (SAD) : 2,81,217; Prem Singh Chandumajra (SHSAD) : 89,268; Others : 51,184

Ropar (SC) : 12,66,744* (7,18,970) - Shamsher Singh (INC) : 3,26,651
Satvinder Kaur (SAD) : 2,49,270; Balbir Kaur (SHSAD) : 1,18,353; Others : 17,263; Invlid : 7,433
In 1998, Satwinder Kaur (SAD) won by a margin of 85,504 votes.

---

* Total Electorates
Figures in ( ) are Votes polled

Sangrur : 11,45,315* (7,16,182) - Simranjit Singh Mann (SAD-M) : 2,98,846 Surjit Singh Barnala (SAD) : 2,12,529; Ajit Singh (CPM) : 1,90,824; Others : 8,005; Invalid : 5,978

In 1998, Surjit Singh Barnala (SAD) won by a margin of 82.165 votes.

1998

Party	Seats won	Vote share
SAD	-	32,9%
BJP	3	11.7%
IND	2	55.4%

RAJASTHAN (25)

Rajasthan is yet another state that fell out of trend in the Lok Sabha elections 1999. BJP had been in power at the state level till it got a severe drubbing in the polls preceeding the Lok Sabha elections. The BJP got 16 and the Congress 9 seats.

It is customary for political parties to hold out carrots before the elections. Neither the party making the promises arc serious about them nor does the electorate take them for their word.

In case of Rajasthan there was an exception this time. The Congress, during campaign for Assembly elections promised the Jats the OBC status if voted to power. Rajasthan politics is markedly divided between the Jats and the Rajputs. The Jat leaders took the Congress promise seriously. Howerver nothing happened in this direction after the Congress assumed power in the State. When the Lok Sabha elections came, the Jats enbloc decided to teach the Congress a lesson. The BJP was once again ahead of the Congress in the number of seats won during the Lok Sabha elections 99.

The Chief Minister Ashok Gehlot was held squarely responsible for this neglect. In at least half a dozen seat the Jats plumped for the BJP having targetted the Congress at places where it was most vulnerable. The Jat Mahasabha acted like a catalyst.

The turn out in many constituencies where Muslims were in significant numbers was low. This also had its effect on the prospects of Congress candidates. In the 1996 elections, the BJP and the Congress had shared between themselves 12 seats each. The vote share of the BJP was 42.36 and that of the Congress 40.51. Gehlot had represented Jodhpur five times. This time however the seat was lost to BJP. In Jaipur, Girdhari Lal Bhargava increased his victory margin. Except for two Districts, the Jats have since been given the OBC status in Rajasthan.

The Press identified many factors behind the Congress debacle :

A shift in the loyalties of the traditional support base of Jat voters, anti-incumbency factor against the sitting MPs, the Kargil war, and, to some extent, the image of Atal Bihari Vajpayee seemingly have affected the ruling Congress party's fortunes in the current Lok Sabha elections judging by the result now available.

Even while admitting that the clean image of the Chief Minister, Ashok Gehlot, did not help the party much in the current elections - as there had been a general feeling that he had yet to come to grips with the day to day administration — it cannot be denied that most of the senior party leaders did not exactly show a positive attitude throughout the election campaign.

There are many complaints from among both the losers as well as winning candidates of the party that senior leaders not only did not cooperate but also were party to the spoiling game. The senior party leader, Rajesh Pilot, who had a lowest ever margin victory of 6902 votes from his traditional constituency Dausa this time would perhaps vouchasafe for this. A similar situation was there in Alwar, where the former queen, Mrs. Mahendra Kumari lost by a margin of 57,928 to the BJP's Jaswant Yadav.

Perhaps a classic example would be Balram Jakhar himself who lost from Sikar constituency by a margin of 28,173 votes to the sitting MP, Subash Maharia. Soon after the polling in the constituency — which took place in the first phase - Jakhar had in fact requested the Rajasthan PCC(I) chief, Girija Vyas to suspend two of the party MLAs representing two segments in the Lok Sabha seat. Vyas, reportedly postponed any action as it would have been counterproductive in the second phase of polling.

One may call it anti-incumbency against the sitting MP but opposition to candidates who were renominated mostly came from the partymen and local leaders. The defeat of Shankar Pannu in Ganganagar, Narendra Budhania in Churu, Ramnarain Meena in Kota, Mrs. Usha Meena in Sawai Madhopur, Dwaraka Bhairwa in Tonk and Meeta Lal Jain in Pali could be partly attributed to "kar seva" (a local euphemism for sabotage from within) from own partymen.

In Jodhpur Lok Sabha seat held five times in the past by the Chief Minister, Ashok Gehlot, it was Congressmen who had voted overwhelmingly for the BJP winner, Jaswant Bishnoi, to spite the young Chief Minister, who happens to be a member of the backward class. In Jodhpur the Chief Minister's detractors voted with a vengeance as the margin was 1.13 lakh, much beyond the expectations of the BJP leadership.

The Congress (I) candidate and former Speaker, P.C. Vishnoi lost in all segments, including Sardarpura where Gehlot had won a by-election about seven months back with over 40,000 votes margin. It would be remembered that the first public meeting of the Jat Mahasabha in support of the demand of backward status to Jats was held in Jodhpur soon after it was known that the new Chief Minister of the State would be Gehlot—and not one from the Jat fraternity of leaders.

One pertinent aspect about the partymen attempting to undo the prospects of the Congress candidates was that they were mostly the victims of the sitting MPs in the Assembly elections. The sitting MPs then had either tried to manipulate the tickets for their favourites or to defeat the party nominees once they found them not to their liking. One came across such complaints from Congress MLAs against Jakhar, Budhania, Shankar Pannu and others during the campaign period.

The Rajasthan PCC(I) chief, Girija Vyas, a victim of sabotage by partymen in the previous elections when she had lost from Udaipur, got the advantage of her position in the current polls. Not only that her detractors cooperated but even those dissidents from other Lok Sabha constituencies, who wanted to avoid a direct conforntation with the party's official candidates in their respective areas too converged on Udaipur region to join the campaign.

Constituency-wise Results — 1999 and Winners of 1998

Ajmer : 11,05,198* (5,93,638) - Rasa Singh Rawat (BJP) : 3,32,130
Prabha Thakur (W) (INC) : 2,44,456; Bharat (NCP) : 16,882; Invalid : 170
In 1998, Prabha Thakur (INC) won by a margin of 5,772 votes.

* Total Electorates
Figures in ( ) are Votes polled

Alwar : 11,56,697* (6,19,711) - Jaswant Singh Yadav (BJP) : 3,25,556
Mahendra Kumari (W) (INC) : 2,67,628; Har Sahai Meena (BSP) : 8,786; Others : 12,896; Invalid : 4,854
In 1998, Ghasi Ram Yadav (INC) won by a margin of 2,561 votes.

Banswara (ST) : 11,82,170* (6,57,182) - Tara Chand Bhagora (INC) : 3,79,775
Rajesh Katara (JD-U) : 2,63,511; Ivalid : 13,896
In 1998, Mahendrajeet Singh (INC) won by a margin of 1,14,517 votes.

Barmer : 14,13,173* (8,41,216) - Col Sona Ram Choudhary (INC) : 4,24,150
Manvendra Singh (BJP) : 3,92,010; Agrendra Kumar (BSP) : 4,393; Others : 9,286; Invalid : 11,377
In 1998, Col. Sonaram Chowdhary (INC) won by a margin of 85,540 votes.

Bayana (SC) : 10,91,258* (4,98,957) - Bahadur Singh (BJP) : 2,34,881
Jagnnath Pahadia (INC) : 2,01,549; Ram Niwas (BSP) : 43,443; Others : 15,087; Invalid : 3,997
In 1998, Ganga Ram Koli (BJP) won by a margin of 4,550 votes.

Bharatpur : 10,58,909* (5,77,462) - Vishvendra Singh (BJP) : 2,77,460
Jagat Singh (INC) : 1,80,442; Nasru Khan (BSP) : 81,628; Pt. Ram Kishan (SP): 18,941; Others : 15,186; Invalid : 3,805
In 1998, Kuwar Natwar Singh (INC) won by a margin of 68,453 votes.

Bhilwara : 11,36,950* (6,07,629) - Vijayendra Pal Singh (BJP) : 2,87,858
Rampal Upadhayay (INC) : 2,73,629; Gopal Lal Jat (IND) : 28,219; Others : 10,539; Invalid : 7,384
In 1998, Rampal Upadhyay (INC) won by a margin of 79,951 votes.

Bikaner : 17,61,949* (9,46,465) - Rameshwar Lal Dubdi (INC) : 4,93,638
Ram Pratap Kasania (BJP) : 3,99,129; Dilip Singh Marwal (BSP) : 24,013; Others : 18,958; Invalid : 10,727
In 1998, Balaram Jhakhar (INC) won by a margin of 1,90,625 votes.

Chittorgarh : 12,48,906* (8,20,414) - Shrichand Kriplani (BJP) : 4,11,275
Udai Lal Anjana (INC) : 3,73,898; Radha Bhandari (W) (CPI) : 18,512; Others : 5,244; Invalid : 11,485
In 1998, Udai Lal Anjana (INC) won by a margin of 25,377 votes.

Churu : 12,37,374* (6,85,728) - Ram Singh Kaswan (BJP) : 3,51,485
Narendra Kumar Budania (INC) : 3,04,676; Daulat Ram Pensia (BSP) : 10,214; Others : 13,959; Invalid : 5,394
In 1998, Narendra Budaniya (INC) won by a margin of 29,732 votes.

Dausa : 12,61,132* (7,52,102) - Rajesh Pilot (INC) : 3,72,263
Rohitash Kumar Sharma (BJP) : 3,65,361; Others : 5,941; Invalid : 8,537
In 1998, Rajesh Pilot (INC) won by a margin of 61,074 votes.

Ganganagar (SC) : 12,68,522* (6,69,982) - Nihal Chand (BJP) : 3,58,104
Er. Shankar Pannu (INC) : 2,62,218; Rawata Ram (CPI) : 19,442; Dharam Pal Kataria (BSP) : 16,569; Others : 8,757; Invalid : 4,892
In 1998, Sankar Pannu (INC) won by a margin of 42,761 votes.

Jaipur : 17,53,564* (8,08,535) - Girdhari Lal Bhargava (BJP) 4,56,720
Pt. Raghu Sharma (INC) : 3,14,930; Sandip Saxena (IND) : 13,074; Others : 23,698; Invalid : 113
In 1998, Girdhari Lal Bhargava (BJP) won by a margin of 1,38,971 votes.

Jalore (SC) : 12,45,605* (6,54,323) - Buta Singh (INC) : 3,30,652

Bangaru Laxman (BJP) : 2,94,728; Others : 18,128; Invalid : 10,815

Jhalawar : 10,69,287* (6,87,868) - Vasundhara Raje (BJP) : 4,09,574
Abrar Ahmed (INC) : 2,57,159; Others : 10,992; Invalid : 10,143
In 1998, Vasundhara Raje (BJP) won by a margin of 63,567 votes.

Jhunjhunu : 11,73,598* (6,73,939) - Sisram Ola (INC) : 3,30,198
Banwarilal Saini (BJP) : 2,53,850; Sumitra Singh (IND) : 72,258; Others : 12,678; Invalid : 4,955
In 1998,. Sisram Ola (AIIC-S) won by a margin of 37,859 votes.

Jodhpur : 13,96,538* (6,63,615) - Jaswant Singh Vishnoi (BJP) : 3,68,463
Poonam Chand (INC) : 2,55,166; Manaram (BSP) : 15,685; Others : 17,039; Invalid : 7,262
In 1998 Ashok Gehtot (INC) won by a margin of 5,444 votes.

Kota : 12,19,405* (6,36,319) - Raghuveer Singh Koushal (BJP) : 3,20,205
Ramnaryan Meena (INC) : 2,95,436; Others : 13,319; Invalid : 7,359
In 1998, Ram Narain Meena (INC) won by a margin of 17,428 votes.

Nagaur : 12,30,637* (7,11,110) - Ram Raghunath Choudhary (INC) : 2,67,914
Vijay Punia (BSP) : 2,19,445; Shyam Sunder Kabra (BJP) : 2,07,815; Others : 9,584; Invalid : 6,352
In 1998, Ramraghunath (INC) won by a margin of 1,06,399 votes.

Pali : 10,80,008* (5,40,142) - Pusp Jain (BJP) : 3,16,844
Mitha Lal Jain (INC) : 2,12,178; Panna Lal (BSP) : 2,816; Others : 948; Invalid : 7,356
In 1998, Mithalal Jain (INC) won by a margin of 27,436 votes.

Salumbar (ST) : 11,17,315* (5,76,990) - Bheru Lal Meena (INC) : 2,90,976
Mahaveer Bhagora (BJP) : 2,38,568; Megh Raj Tawar (CPI) : 22,417; Invalid : 14,532
In 1998, Bheru Lal (INC) won by a margin of 77,882 votes.

Sawai Madhopur (ST) : 11,76,727* (5,15,746) - Jaskaur (BJP) : 2,77,014
Usha (INC) : 2,18,133; Dhable Ram (BSP) : 10,738; Others : 5,627; Invalid : 4,234
In 1998, Usha (INC) won by a margin of 62,334 votes.

Sikar : 12,86,900* (7,55,152) - Subhash Maharia (BJP) : 3,41,445
Balram Jakhar (INC) : 3,13,272; Amra Ram (CPM) : 80,491; Others : 14,196; Invalid : 5,748
In 1998, Subhash Maharia (BJP) won by a margin of 41,322 votes.

Tonk (SC) : 11,37,748* (5,46,331) - Shyam Lal Bansiwal (BJP) : 2,87,265
Dwarka Prasad Bairwa (INC) : 2,38,907; Others : 13,290; Invalid : 6,869
In 1998, Dwarka Prasad Bairwa (INC) won by a margin of 57,469 votes.

Udaipur : 12,56,888* (7,09,576) - Girija Vyas (W) (INC) : 3,72,645
Shanti Lal Chaplot (BJP) : 3,18,554; Others : 8,887; Invalid : 9,490
In 1998, Shanti Lal Chaplot (BJP) won by a margin of 11,447 votes.

SIKKIM (1)

The Seat was won by the Sikkim Democratic Front candidate Bhim Pal Dahal.

TAMIL NADU (39)

The BJP allied with DMK while the INC allied with AIADMK. BJP's own tally was just 4 seats. The DMK was up in 12 seats. In comparison AIADMK won only 10 seats PMK won 5, MDMK 3 and others 3.

The INC managed just two seats with Mani Shanker Aiyyar elected from Mayiladuturai. The CPI (M) registered its presence in the State at Madurai only.

Total Seats

1952	- 75
1957-1962	- 41
1967 onwards	- 39

Suresh Nambath made the following observations.

"Tamil Nadu saw a north-south divide in the present Lok Sabha election which was one of the most closely-fought in the State's history. In the northern districts, it was a clean sweep for the DMK-led NDA, but in the south, the AIADMK front arrested the trend and made some gains.

The geographical divide coincides with the change in the caste configuration. With the DMK tying up with the Vanniar-based PMK, which boasts of a strong presence in the north, most of the seats in these areas went the NDA way. The Thevar-affilliation to the AIADMK enabled the party to retain its strongholds in the south where the Thevars are in a majority.

Apart from the three seats in Chennai, the NDA won almost all the constituencies in the north, where the Vanniar-based party, the PMK, had a strong presence: Bharmapuri, Krishnagiri, Tirupattur, Arakkonam, Tindivanam, Chengalpattu, Sriperumbudur, Vellore, Chidambaram and Cuddalore.

The only exception was Salem, where the AIADMK defeated the TRC, but here the NDA campaign was hampered by a pre-election dispute between the PMK and the TRC.

In the southern constituencies which saw Thevar consolidation, the AIADMK front won in Sivaganga, Ramanathapuram, Periyakulam, Tirunelveli, Tenkasi, Madurai and Dindigul.

The AIADMK was able to retain the support of Dalits in the reserved constituencies of Tenkasi and Rasipuram. The surprise, however, was in another reserved constituency, Nagapattinam, where the CPI, in the company of the AIADMK, was expected to do well. Indeed, Nagapattinam, with a large agricultural labour population, had voted against the wave, and for the CPI in both 1989 and 1998. But the seat went to the NDA in this election.

As there was no "wave" in this election, electoral arithmetic decided the fortunes of the main contestants. The DMK and the PMK together were a potent force in the northern districts. The MDMK, despite hiccups in the alliance with the DMK, was able to contribute significantly to the NDA's limited successes in the south.

In contrast, the AIADMK had only the Congress(I), weakened by the 1996 split, and the Left as allies. Although the Congress (I) regained some of the vote-share it had lost to the TMC, it was unable to alter the AIADMK front's fortunes in any dramatic way.

The CPI(M) and the CPI, with their pockets of influence, were not of much help to the AIADMK although there was good cadre coordination among these parties.

The AIADMK was able to retain its traditional stronghold, Gobichettipalayam and Palani in the west. In Myladuthurai, Mani Shankar Aiyar to the Congress (I) brought in his own votes to supplement the share of the AIAMDK and the Congress(I).

The TMC fared much worse than the AIADMK. Despite its pro-Dalit image, it made only minimal impact in this election. However, it polled more than the victory margin in many constituencies. But given its campaign point of equidistance from both the 'communalism of the BJP-DMK' and the 'corruption of the AIADMK' there is no saying whether it had hurt the DMK or the AIADMK more."

Constituency-wise Results — 1999 and Winners of 1998

Arakkonam : 11,20,043* (7,41,851) - Jagatharakshakan S. (DMK) : 3,46,520
K.V. Thangka Balu (INC) : 2,50,876; Velu, A.M. (TMC) : 1,21,386; Others : 7,341; Invalid : 15,728
In 1998, Gopal C. (AIADMK) won by a margin of 49,488 votes.

Chidambaram (SC) : 11,10,229* (7,32,994) - Ponnusamy E. (PMK) : 3,45,331
Thrirumavalavan R. (TMC) : 2,25,768; Sumathy Udayakumar T (INC) : 1,50,794; Others : 2,412; Invalid : 8,689
In 1998, Elumalai alias Ezhilmalai R (PMK) won by a margin of 7,955 votes.

Chingleput : 12,00,040* (6,99,911) - Moorthy, A.K. (PMK) : 3,30,551
Thirunavukkarasu, S.S. (AIADMK) : 3,17,740; Others : 21,052; Balaraman, C. (JD-S) : 18,028; Invalid : 12,540
In 1998, Kanchi Panneerselvam (AIADMK) won by a margin of 22,916 votes.

Coimbatore : 15,71,475* (8,74,,020) - Radhakrishnan,. C.P. (BJP) : 4,30,068
Nallakannu, R. (CPI) : 3,75,991; Balasubramoniyan, S.R. (TMC) : 45,205; Others : 18,203; Thirumoorthy, K. (AIFB) : 3,089; Palanisamy., R. (TDK) : 1,464
In 1998, Radhakrishnan, C.P. (BJP) won by a margin of 1,44,676 votes.

Cuddalore : 11,36,122* (7,24,354) - Adhi, Sankar (DMK) : 3,58,367
Damodharan M.C. (AIADMK) : 2,84,414; Venkatesan M.C. (TMC) : 65,467; Others : 1,496; Invalid : 14,610
In 1998, Dhamotharan M.C. (AIADMK) won by a margin of 27,129 votes.

Dharmapuri : 12,26,816* (7,27,866) - Elangovan, P.D. (PMK) : 3,40,162
Munusamy, K.P. (AIADMK) : 3,14,622; Rajendran, M.C. (TMC) : 26,682; Appavu Chetty, V. (IND) : 20,125; Selvam, C. (TDK) : 12,215; Others : 1,966; Invalid : 12,095
In 1998, Pary Mohan (PMK) won by a margin of 99,427 votes.

Dindigul : 11,94,616* (6,86,045) - Sreenivaasan, C. (AIADMK) : 2,94,794
Chandrasekar, S. (DMK) : 2,74,451; Chitthan, N.S.V. (TMC) : 69,713; Surendran, K (AIFB) : 32,342; Others : 2,103; Invalid : 12,642
In 1998 Sreenivaasan C., (AIADMK) won by a margin of 15,199 votes.

Gobichettipalayam : 10,66,276* (6,42,672) - Kaliappan, K. K. (AIADMK) : 2,99,184; Arjun, K.G.S. (DMK) : 2,69,172; Kuppuswamy, C.K. (TMC) : 48,304; Others : 9,528; Invalid : 16,484
In 1998, Cinnasamy, V.K. (AIADMK) won by a margin of 1,14,642 votes.

Karur : 11,70,582* (7,36,611) - Chinna Samy M. (AIADMK) 3,34,407
Palani Samy K.C. (DMK) : 3,31,560; Natrayan K. (TMC) : 45,539; Others : 8,199; Invalid : 16,906
In 1998, Thambi Durai, M (AIADMK) won by a margin of 43,673 votes.

Krishnagiri : 11,63,442* (6,97,254) - Vetriselvan, V. (DMK) : 3,47,737

---

* Total Electorates
Figures in ( ) are Votes polled

Thambi Durai M. (AIADMK) : 3,15,913; Vadivelu, G.A. (JD-S) : 13,154; Others : 4,408; Invalid : 16,042
In 1998, Munusamy (AIADMK) won by a margin of 49,349 votes.

Madras Central : 12,75,067* (6,17,900) - Murasoli Maran (DMK) : 3,64,565
Abdul Latheef, M. (AIADMK) : 2,27,616; Othres : 25,719
In 1998, Murasoli Maran (DMK) won by a margin of 71,727 votes.

Madras North : 20,41,314* (8,93,936) - Kuppusamy, C. (DMK) : 4,71,101
Soundarrajan, A. (CPM) : 3,11,312; Aaroon Rasheed, J.M. (TMC) : 81,192; Others : 15,868; Invalid : 14,463
In 1998, Kuppisamiy, C. (DMK) won by a margin of 69,093 votes.

Madras South : 20,74,128* (9,36,522) - Baalu, T.R. (DMK) : 5,62,221
Dhandayudhapani, V. (INC) : 3,22,037; Muktha V. Srinivasan (TMC) : 38,700; Others : 13,564
In 1998, Baalu. T.R. (DMK) won by a margin of 20,014 votes.

Madurai : 14,29,975* (7,47,919) - Mohan P. (CPM) : 3,27,971
Muthuramalingam Pon (DMK) : 2,90,756; Rambabu A.G.S. (TMC) : 89,956; Subramanian Swamy (JP) 20,484; Others : 18,752
In 1998, Subramanian Swamy (JP) won by a margin of 54,077 votes.

Mayiladuthurai : 10,30,626* (6,55,340) - Mani Shankara Aiyar (INC) : 3,24,384
Arulmozhi P.D. (PMK) : 2,84,253; Krishnamoorthy K. (TMC) : 34,998; Balasundram S. (CPI-ML) : 2,161; Invalid : 9,544
In 1998, Krishnamoorthy, K. (TMC) won by a margin of 42,456 votes.

Nagapattinam (SC) : 10,54,666* (6,96,279) - Vijayan A.K.S. (DMK) : 3,42,237
Selvarasu M. (CPI) : 3,19,771; Nadayalagan T. (PT) : 22,346; Balagur Durai (IND) : 1,158; Invalid : 10,767

Nagercoil : 10,57,712* (6,21,397) - Radhakrishanan P. (BJP) : 3,07,319
Dennis N. (INC) : 1,61,676; Jumaradoss (TMC) : 1,39,030; Others 4,070; Invalid : 9,302
In 1998 Dennis N. (TMC) won by a margin of 29,185 votes.

Nilgiris : 13,48,417* (7,42,722) - Mathan, M @ Master Mathan, M. (BJP) : 3,69,828
Prabhu, R. (INC) : 3,45,869; Chinnaraj C. (PT) : 7,612; Others : 5,689; Invalid : 13,724
In 1998 Mathan, M. (alias) Master Mathan, M. (BJP) won by a margin of 60,385 votes.

Palani : 11,59,677* (6,82,853) - Kumarasamy, P. (AIADMK) : 2,97,850
Ganesa Murthy, A. (MDMK) : 2,69,133; Kaarvendhan, S.K. (TMC) : 85,407; Others : 12,689; Invalid : 17,774
In 1998, Ganeshamurthi, A. (MDMK) won by a margin of 27,602 votes.

Perambalur (SC) : 10,64,321* (6,95,743) - Raja A. (DMK) : 3,30,675
Rajarethinam P. (AIADMK) : 2,62,624; Periyasamy D. (DPI) : 85,209; Others : 2,107; Invalid, 15,128
In 1998, Rajerathinam, P. (AIADMK) won by a margin of 60,436 votes.

Periyakulam : 11,21,725* (6,66,934) - Dinakaran (AIADMK) : 3,03,881
Selvendran P. (DMK) : 2,58,075; Mansoor Alikhan (PT) : 87,429; Others : 9,146; Invalid : 8,403
In 1998, Muthiah, R. (AIADMK) won by a margin of 70,663 votes.

Pollachi (SC) : 10,74,230* (6,13,153) - Krishnan C (MDMK) : 2,93,038

Thiyagarajan, M. (AIADMK) : 2,83,523; Rajan, K.N. (JD-S) : 9,914; Jothiraj, M. (PT) : 9,280; Ganesan, P. (IND) : 6,886; Invalid : 10,512
In 1998 Thiyagarajan M. (AIADMK) won by a margin of 95,400 votes.

Pudukottai : 12,18,297* (7,80,852) - Thirunavukarasu (MGR AIADMK) : 3,96,216 Singaravadivelu S. (NC) : 3,31,914; Palaniappan (alias) Puratch (PT) : 29453; Others : 12,421; Invalid : 10,848
In 1998, Raja Paramasivam (AIADMK) won by a margin of 30,520 votes.

Ramanathapuram : 11,15,127* (6,40,694) - Malaichamy K (AIADMK) : 2,65,253 Bhavani Rajenthiran, MSK (SM) (DMK) 2,58,607; Nazeera Parvin K. (PT) : 96,334; Others : 9,114; Invalid : 11,386
In 1998, Sathiamoorthy, V. (AIADMK) won by a margin of 24,092 votes.

Rasipuram (SC) : 11,61,474* (6,43,060) - Saroja V. (AIADMK) : 3,04,843 Uthayarasu S. (PMK) : 2,66,438; Natesan C. (TMC) : 46,564; Others : 11,156; Invalid : 14,059
In 1998, V. Saroja (AIADMK) won by a margin of 54,377 votes.

Salem : 12,57,383* (7,43,754) - Selvaganapthy, T.M., (AIADMK) : 3,63,669 Ramamurthy K. (TRC) : 3,38,278; Devadass, S.R. (TMC) : 19,604; Others : 9,905; Invalid : 12,298
In 1998, Ramamurthy K. (IND) won by a margin of 1,32,415 votes.

Sivaganga : 11,17,223* (6,23,958) - Sudarsana Nachiappan E.M. (INC) : 2,46,078 Raja H. (BJP) : 2,22,267; Chidambaram P. (TMC) : 1,27.528; Others : 15,758; Invalid : 12,327
In 1998, Chidambaram, P. (TMC) won by a margin of 59,141, votes.

Sivakasi : 12,57,935* (7,90,752) - Vaiko (MDMK) : 3,25,829 Ramasamy V. Justice (AIADMK) : 2,51,048; Gunasekaran A. (TMC) : 1,52,817; Thamaraikani R. (IND) : 36,977; Others : 12,790; Invalid : 11,291
In 1998, Vaiko (MDMK) won by a margin of 1,34,923 votes.

Sriperumbudur (SC) : 13,53,858* (7,44,842) - Krishnaswamy, A. (DMK) : 3,85,558; Venugopal, K. (AIADMK) : 3,10,556; Pushparaman., J. (TMC) : 28,292; Others: 4,670; Invalid : 15,776
In 1998, Venugopal K. (AIADMK) won by a margin of 23,795 votes.

Tenkasi (SC) : 10,44,090* (6,77,205) - Murugesan S. (AIADMK) : 2,39,241 Arumugam S. (BJP) : 2,38,354; Krishnasamy K. (PT) : 1,86,220; Others : 3,011; Invalid : 10,379
In 1998, Murugesan, S. (AIADMK) won by a margin of 97,267 votes.

Thanjavur : 10,49,837* (6,64,815) - Palanimanickam S.S. (DMK) : 2,95,191 Thangamuthu K. (AIADMK) : 2,62,177; Chidambaram PL.A. (TMC) : 69,025; Jayabalan (IND) : 12,239; Sreenivasan A. (AIFB) : 10,704; Others : 1,058; Invalid : 14,421
In 1998, Palanimanickam, S.S. (DMK) won by a margin of 48,204 votes.

Tindivanam : 11,28,742* (6,83,601) - Gingee N. Ramachandran (MDMK) : 3,23,234; Ramamoorthee K. (INC) : 3,13,884; S.P. Subramaniyan (TMC) : 40,879; Others : 5,604; Invalid : 0
In 1998, N. Ramachandran Gingee (MDMK) won by a margin of 31,132 votes.

Tiruchendur : 10,40,627* (5,43,932) - Jayaseelan, A.D.K. (DMK) : 2,37,630 Rajan, B.P. (AIADMK) : 1,77,964; Dhanuskodi Athithan, R. (TMC) : 1,09,035; Others : 10,443; Invalid : 8,860
In 1998, Ramarajan R. (AIADMK) won by a margin of 46,855 votes.

Tiruchengode : 15,27.064* (8,45,137) - Kannappan, M (MDMK) : 4,09,293
Palaniswami K. (AIADMK) : 4,04,737; Kanagasabapathy, T.M. (PT) : 11,535; Others : 8,450; Invalid : 11,122
In 1998, Palanisamy K. (AIADMK) won by a margin of 1,04,809 votes.

Tiruchirappalli : 12,45,971* (7,02,752) - A Rangarajan Kumaramangalam (BJP) : 3,77,450; Adaikkalaraj L. (INC) : 2,88.253; Rajasekaran M. (TMC) : 17,256; Others : 8,177; Invalid : 11,616
In 1998, Rangarajan Kumaramangalam (BJP) won by a margin of 23,795 votes.

Tirunelveli : 11,21,877* (6,10,090) - Pandian P.H. (AIADMK) : 2,49,975
Geetha Jeevan P. (DMK) : 2,23,481; Bhakthavatchalam, P.v. (PT) : 1,12,941; Others : 14,157; Invalid : 9,536
In 1998, Janarthanan, R. (AIADMK) won by a margin of 6,904 votes.

Tirupattur : 11,44,891* (7,46,109) - Venugopal, D. (DMK) : 3,50,703
Rajendran, A.R. (AIADMK) : 3,27,090; Jayamohan, A. (TMC) : 51,932; Others: 1,890; Invalid : 14,494
In 1998, Venugopal D. (DMK) won by a margin of 274 votes.

Vandavasi : 11,04,886* (6,79,991) - Durai M. (PMK) : 3,45,539
Krishnasswamy, M. (INC) : 2,86,342; Wahab, K.A. (TMC) : 36,844; Invalid : 11,266
In 1998, Durai M. (PMK) won by a margin of 65,075 votes.

Vellore : 11,49,169* (7,02,639) - Shanmugam, N.T., (PMK) : 3,24,547
Mohamed Asif (AIADMK) : 2,98,862; Thamizharasan, C.K. (TMC) : 44,551; Others : 21,415; Invalid : 13,264
In 1998, Shanmugam N.T. (PMK) won by a margin of 26,405 votes.

1998

Party	Seats won	Vote share
ADMK	18	25.9%
DMK	5	20.1%
PMK	4	6.1%
TMC	3	20.2%
BJP	3	6.9%
IND	6	20.8%

TRIPURA (2)

It had been the CPI (M) stronghold. Both seats were bagged by the party.

Tripura East (SC) : 8,54,764* (5,64,376) - Bajuban Reang (CPM) : 3,04,934
Jishnu Dev Varma (BJP) : 1,54,434; Kashiram Reang (INC) : 84,789; Samarendra Chakma (AMB) : 7,343; Debabrata Koloy (IND) : 5,751; Invalid : 8,125
In 1998, Baju Ban Riyan (CPM) won by a margin of 72,686 votes.

Tripura West : 9,41,291* (6,58,408) - Samar Chowdhury (CPM) : 3,72,553
Sudhir Ranjan Majumder (AITC) : 1,74,154; Pijush Kanti Biswas (INC) : 83,384; Others : 18,252; Invalid : 11,065
In 1998, Samar Choudhury (CPM) won by a margin of 18,876 votes.

* Total Electorates
Figures in ( ) are Votes polled

UTTAR PRADESH (85)

The Congress had been the leading party in Uttar Pradesh till 1971 so far as Lok Sabha elections are concerened. In 1977, it lost to BLD but regained the first position in 1980. While 1984 was the year of the INC, the Janata Dal came to the top slot in 1989.

Since 1991 and till 1998 the BJP had been the leading party.

The 1999 results however have been a great set back to the party (BJP).

The performance with Kalyan Singh as the Chief Minister was summed up by *The Times of India* in its Editorial 'BJP's Kalyan'.

(Total Lok Sabha Seats : 1952-1962 : 86
1967 onwards : 85)

Voter turn out in Uttar Pradesh has always been lower than the National average. In the 1952 election it was just 38.4%.

The Press ascribed the BJP's debacle primarily to the Chief Minister Kalyan Singh's non-performance.

"In both symbolic and arithmetic terms Uttar Pradesh occupies a central place in the political imagination of India but for the Bharatiya Janata Party, the state is the closest thing to *punya bhoomi*, the land which nurtured its lotus and facilitated the sangh parivar's phenomenal rise to power at the Centre. Today, however, despite the triumphant return of Atal Bihari Vajpayee to New Delhi, the *bagwa dhwaj* in UP is flying at half mast. So spectacular has been the BJP's setback in its northern stronghold that notwithstanding an impressive showing elsewhere in the country, the party's all-India seat tally is pretty much the same as it was last year and its nationwide vote percentage has slipped by a good 3 per cent. In 1998, the BJP and its allies won 60 seats in UP; today they have barely managed to hold on to half that number. Even though the Samajwadi Party confounded pollsters and emerged as the second biggest force in the state, its vote share too has fallen. Bahujan Samaj Party has increased its seat tally to 14 but it is really the Congress which has registered the most remarkable growth in its vote share. The party benefited from the support of Muslim voters — and from Mrs. Sonia Gandhi breathing life into what had become a moribund state organisation—but the fact that it had to build upon such a low vote base meant the Congress was able to triumph mainly in those constituencies from which it fielded senior leaders.

If there is one reason why the BJP fared so poorly this time around, it is the widespread dissatisfaction with the way in which the Kalyan Singh government is running the state. The sangh parivar came to power promising Ram but delivered a *rajya* completely devoid of the virtues associated with the hero of Ayodhya. Apart from alienating key sectors of the electorate such as government employees and teachers, the BJP has totally neglected developmental issues. Party leaders may have wanted to talk only about Kargil and the foreign origins of Mrs. Gandhi but it was governance—or rather the lack of governance—that most animated the electorate. UP's towns and cities are in a state of acute disrepair with roads colonised by potholes, mud and filth. The school system is in shambles, electricity and water supply is highly erratic and little has been done to improve employment prospects. As if these were not provocative enough, many BJP candidates added to voters anger by repeatedly asserting that 'local' problems should not bc raised during 'national' elections. Finally, infighting within the state unit position. It is no secret that upper caste BJP leaders resent the rule of a backward caste leader like Kalyan Singh and want desperately to ease him out. On his part, Singh maintained a Delphic silence in the face of the vigorous anti-BJP campaign waged by his former party colleague, Sachidand Sakshi. Sakshi is speaking quite openly about the possibility of a new state-wide 'backward caste' political formation linking Mulayam Singh Yadav of the SP and Kalyan Singh. Presumably, the fear of such a reconfiguration will help keep Singh's foes in the BJP at bay for a while but either way, the party's prospects in UP are grim so long as people's concerns are given short shrift

Region Wise Uttar Pradesh Results

Seats Won	1996	1998	1999
U.P. Hills (Total Seats : 4)			
BJP	2	4	3
Cong	2	0	1
Central U.P. (Total Seats : 15)			
BJP	10	10	2
Cong	0	0	2
SP	3	4	6
BSP	2	1	3
Ind/Oth	0	0	2
Western U.P. (Total Seats : 20)			
BJP	16	17	7
Cong	1	0	2
SP	3	3	8
BSP	0	0	1
Ind/Oth	0	0	2
Rohilkhand (Total Seats : 10)			
BJP	2	5	2
Cong	2	0	2
SP	4	4	3
BSP	1	0	1
Ind/Oth	1	1	2
Bundelkhand (Total Seats : 4)			
BJP	3	4	0
Cong	0	0	1
BSP	1	0	3
Eastern U.P. (Total Seats : 32)			
BJP	19	17	14
Cong	2	0	2
SP	6	9	9
BSP	2	3	6
Ind/Oth	3	3	1
Overall U.P. (Total Seats : 85)			
BJP	52	57	29
Cong	5	0	10
SP	16	20	26
BSP	6	4	14
Ind/Oth	6	4	6

- Bharatiya Janata Party fielded 51 of its 57 members of the dissolved Lok Sabha in Uttar Pradesh. Only 22 won.
- Of the four Bahujan Samaj Party ex-MPs in th fray, only Mayawati managed to win. High profile MPs like Arif Mohammad Khan and Akbar Ahmad Dumpy lost.

❖ Of the 20 Samajwadi Party members of the dissolved Lok Sabha, only 10 managed to get re-elected.

The fact that 51 out of total 85 MPs elected this time from UP were not members of the last Lok Sabha demonstrates how fed up the performance of their representatives as well as with frequent elections.

BJP's pathetic performance 29 compared to 57 last time—is being attributed to the people's anger at functioning of the BJP-led Government in the State, a churning in caste combinations in the State and, of course, to State BJP leaders working at cross-purposes, targeting their own collegues than their rivals.

Constituency-wise Results — 1999 and Winners of 1998

Agra : 12,50,358* (6,42,572) - Raj Babbar (SP) : 2,88,558
Bhagwan Shankar Rawat (BJP) : 1,75,576; Raisuddin (BSP) : 1,19,762; Ajay Singh (INC) : 38,033; Invalid : 146
In 1998, Bhagwan Shankar Rawat (BJP) won by a margin of 48,311 votes.

Akbarpur (SC) : 12,33,413* (7,46,458) - Mayawati (BSP) : 2,59,762
Ram Piyare Suman (SP) : 2,06,376; Bechan Ram Sonkar (BJP) : 1,82,752; Babu Lal (AD) : 53,472; Mata Prasad (INC) : 19,522; Others : 16,985; Invalid : 7,589
In 1998, Mayawati (BSP) won by a margin of 25,169 votes.

Aligarh : 12,53,174* (5,64,618) - Sheela Gautam (BJP) : 2,19,313
Sahab Singh (BSP) : 1,38,496; Sunil Singh (SP) : 1,35,232; Usha Rani Tomar (INC) : 42,630; Others : 18,426; Invalid : 10,521
In 1998 Sheela Gautam (BJP) won by a margin of 1,31,699 votes.

Allahabad : 14,10,588* (6,48,551) - Murli Manohar Joshi (BJP) : 2,19,114
Kunwar Rewati Raman Singh (alias) Maniji (SP) : 1,48,783; Reeta Bahuguna Joshi (INC) : 1,33,428; Ram Dular Singh Patel (BSP) : 1,09,383; Others : 37,808; Invalid : 35
In 1998, Murli Manohar Joshi (BJP) won by a margin of 38,582 votes.

Almora : 9,61,789* (4,03,872) - Bachi Singh Rawat (BJP) : 1,92,388
Harish Rawat (INC) : 1,80,929; Others : 24,288; Invalid : 6,267
In 1998, Bachi Singh Rawat (BJP) won by a margin of 81,903 votes.

Amethi : 11,00,861* (6,38,178) - Sonia Gandhi (INC) : 4,18,960
Sanjai Singh (BJP) : 1,18,948; Paras Nath Maurya (BSP) : 33,658; Kamarujjama Fauzi (SP) : 16,678; Others : 35,928; Invalid : 14,006
In 1998, Sanjai Singh (BJP) won by a margin of 23,283 votes.

Amroha : 12,22,635* (7,78,257) - Rashid Alvi (BSP) : 3,37,919
Chetan Chauhan (BJP) : 2,44,694; Pratap Singh (RLD) : 94,913; Chandra Pal Singh (SP) : 78,670; Others : 14,600; Invalid : 8,061
In 1998, Chetan Chauhan (BJP) won by a margin of 65,515 votes.

Aonla : 10,02,309* (5,92,306) - Kunwar Sarvraj Singh (SP) : 1,95,839
Rajveer Singh (BJP) : 1,78,213; Mahi Pal Singh Yadav (BSP) : 1,39,389; Chander Pal Singh Kashyap (INC) : 67,811; Others : 3,747; Invalid : 7,307
In 1998, Rajveer Singh (BJP) won by a margin of 8,022 votes.

Azamgarh : 12,15,261* (6,61,604) - Rama Kant Yadav (SP) : 2,27,616

* Total Electorates
Figures in ( ) are Votes polled

Akbar Ahmad Dumpy (BSP) : 2,00,637; Ram Surat (BJP) : 1,61,878; Chandrajeet (INC) : 36,434; Israr (IND) : 6,601; Ramdular (AD) : 5,892; Others: 13,822; Invalid : 8,724

In 1998, Akbar Ahmad Dumpy (BSP) won by a margin of 5,365 votes.

Baghpat : 13,21,056* (7,52,936) - Ajit Singh (RLD) : 3,58,038

Sompal (BJP) : 2,03,466; Tekchand (BSP) : 98,893; Mirajuddin (SP) : 59,801; Others : 21,637; Invalid : 11,101

In 1998, Somapl (BJP) won by a margin of 43,920 votes.

Bahraich : 12,26,455* (6,04,614) - Padma Sen Chaudhary (BJP) : 2,23,768

Arif Mohammad Khan (BSP) : 2,18,017; Ruvab Sayeeda (SP) : 98,801; Gyanendra Pratap Singh (INC) : 26,880; Mukesh Kumar (IND) : 11,772; Others : 17,350; Invalid : 10,026

In 1998, Arif Mohammad Khan (BSP) won by a margin of 38,376 votes.

Ballia : 12,87,896* (6,19,524) - Chandra Shekhar (SJP-R) : 2,35,946

Ram Krishna Urf Gopal (BJP) : 1,80,271; Ram Deo Verma "Mauryakant" (BSP): 1,42,647; Digvijay (INC) : 36,477; Others : 15,583; Invalid : 8,600

In 1998, Chandrashekher (SJP-R) won by a margin of 29,564 votes.

Balrampur : 11,64,924* (6,76,951) - Rizvan Zaheer alias Rajju Bhaiya (SP) : 2,55,267; Bhisham Shankar Tiwari alias Kaushal Tiwari (BJP) : 2,35,109; Badri Prasad Chaudhary (BSP) : 98,824; Mangal Deo Singh (INC) : 41,590; Nanak Chand (IND) : 10,731; Others : 24,758; Invalid : 10,672

In 1998, Rizwan Zaheer (SP) won by a margin of 57,259 votes.

Banda : 11,59,801* (5,89,303) - Ram Sajiwan (BSP) : 2,09,995

Shyam Charan Gupta (SP) : 1,81,364; Ramesh Chandra Dwivedi (BJP) : 1,38,907; Dada Ram Sajiwan Singh (INC) : 20,042; Kailash Nath Patel (AD) : 11,533; Others : 16.966; Invalid : 10,496

In 1998 Ramesh Chandra Dwivedi (BJP) won by a margin of 17,948 votes.

Bansgaon (SC) : 12,79,729* (6,08,738) - Raj Narayan Pasi (BJP) : 1,84,684

Subhawati Paswan (SP) : 1,74,996; Sadari Pahalwan (BSP) : 1,37,221; Kamal Kishor (INC) : 94,383; Others : 7,481; Invalid : 9,973

In 1998, Raj Narayan Pasi (BJP) won by a margin of 30,540 votes.

Bara Banki (SC) : 10,88,629* (6,30,500) - Ram Sagar (SP) : 2,10,958

Baij Nath Rawat (BJP) 1,55,667; Kamla Prasad Rawat (INC) : 1,25,743; Sant Bali Sidharth (BSP) : 1,09,466; Others : 19,171; Invalid : 9,495

In 1998 Baijnath Rawat (BJP) won by a margin of 13,776 votes.

Bareilly : 14,29,045* (6,63,548) - Santosh Gangwar (BJP) : 2,92,813

Master Chhote Lal Gangwar (SP) : 1,58,113; Islam Sabir (INC) : 1,27,992; Farukal Hassan (BSP) : 69,618; Others : 6,973; Invalid : 8,039

In 1998, Santosh Kumar Gangwar (BJP) won by a margin of 32,440 votes.

Basti (SC) : 11,79,647* (5,93,906) - Shriram Chauhan (BJP) : 1,74,361

Lal Mani Prasad (BSP) : 1,72,546; Kalpnath Sonkar (SP) : 1,44,220; Ram Jiyawan (INC) : 78,616; Others : 15,595; Invalid : 8,568

In 1998, Shriram Chauhan (BJP) won by a margin of 70,217 votes.

Bijnor (SC) : 12,76,384* (7,11,282) - Sheeshram Singh Ravi (BJP) : 2,14,266

Omwati Devi (SP) : 1,90,566; Veer Singh (BSP) : 1,83,676; Mangal Ram Premi (RLD) : 88,994; Others : 27,423; Invalid : 6,357

In 1998, Omwati Devi (SP) won by a margin of 9,212 votes.

Bilhaur : 12,61,014* (6,38,771) - Shyam Bihari Mishra (BJP) : 1,92,054
Raja Ram Pal (BSP) : 1,88,831; Sadhu Ram Kushwaha (SP) : 1,24,415; Naresh Bahadur (INC) : 1,12,070; Sohan Prakash (AD) : 12,950; Others : 2,130; Invalid : 6,321
In 1998, Shyam Bihari Mishra (BJP) won by a margin of 98,447 votes.

Badaun : 11,06,517* (6,10,270) - Saleem Iqbal Shervani (SP) : 2,36,496
Shanti Devi Shakya (BJP) : 1,95,182; Brijpal Singh (BSP) : 1,37,909; Shantee Devi (INC) : 26,418; Others : 8,078; Invalid : 6,187
In 1998, Saleem Iqbal Sherwani (SP) won by a margin of 39,658 votes.

Bulandshahar : 10,98,340* (4,99,074) - Chhatra Pal (BJP) : 1,80,102
Saeedul Hassan (INC) : 1,18,173; Naz Khan (BSP) : 84,282; Jugendra Singh Sirohi (SP) : 75,260; Imtiza Md. Khan (IND) : 23,680; Others : 13,260; Invalid : 4,317
In 1998, Chhatra Pal (BJP) won by a margin of 85,359 votes.

Chail (SC) : 13,10,550* (5,15,937) - Suresh Pasi (BSP) : 1,51,557
Amrit Lal Bharti (BJP) : 1,22,272; Ram Nihore Rakesh (INC) : 95,352; Shailendra Kumar (SP) : 89,223; Lakhan Singh Rajpasi (AD) : 34,559; Others : 13,783; Invalid : 9,191
In 1998 Shailendra Kumar (SP) won by a margin of 17,459 votes.

Chandauli : 13,39,194* (7,38,159) - Jawahar Lal Jaiswal (SP) : 2,65,412
Anand Ratan Maurya (BJP) : 1,91,883; Kamla Rajbhar (BSP) : 1,89,138; Siyaram (JD-S) : 14,945; Lalmani (PMSP) : 12,212; Kailash Nath Singh Yadav (Janata Party) : 12,049; Others : 41,047; Invalid : 11,473
In 1998, Anand Ratna Mourya (BJP) won by a margin of 6,482 votes.

Deoria : 12,76,208* (7,04,710) - Shri Prakash Maini (BJP) : 2,51,814
Mohan Singh (SP) : 2,09,673; Rajesh Kumar Singh (BSP) : 1,35,019; Chandra Bhushan Pandey (INC) : 69,343; Pramod Kumar Nishad (AD) : 14,492; Others : 13,798; Invalid : 10,571
In 1998, Mohan Singh (SP) won by a margin of 4,068 votes.

Domariaganj : 11,46,663* (6,24,312) - Ram Pal Singh (BJP) : 1,98,263
Mohd. Mukim (INC) : 1,62,696; Kamal Yusuf Malik (SP) : 1,51,444; Surendra Yadav (BSP) : 96,147; Others : 8,601; Invalid : 7,,161
In 1998, Ram Pal Singh (BJP) won by a margin of 74,091 votes.

Etah : 10,36,859* (5,95,040) - Kunwar Devendra Singh Yadav (SP) : 2,26,999
Mahadeepak Singh Shakya (BJP) : 1,74,475; Seth Sultan Alam (BSP) : 1,02,048; Rajendra Singh (INC) : 71,892; Others : 11,724; Invalid : 7,902
In 1998, Mahadeepak Singh (BJP) won by a margin of 12,140 votes.

Etawah : 11,27,199* (6,08,768) - Raghraj Singh Shakya (SP) : 2,33,065
Shiv Prasad Yadav (BSP) : 1,49,382; Sukhda Mishra (BJP) : 1,44,526; Sarita Bhadauria (INC) : 51,868; Others : 23,033; Invalid : 6,894
In 1998, Sukhda Mishra (BJP) won by a margin of 31,038 votes.

Faizabad : 12,28,649* (6,65,798) - Vinay Katiyar (BJP) : 1,93,191
Siya Ram Nishad (BSP) : 1,35,629; Nirmal Khatri (INC) : 1,06,237; Hira Lal Yadav (SP) : 85,213; Mitra Sen Yadav (IND) : 79,343; Dharam Raj Patel (AD) : 16,252; Others : 41,300; Invalid : 8,633
In 1998, Mitrasen Yadev (SP) won by a margin of 7,737 votes.

Farrukhabad : 12,42,368* (6,40,642) - Chandra Bhushan Singh (Munnoo Babu) (SP) : 2,22,984

Prof. Ram Buksh Singh Verma (BJP) : 1,60,422; Louise Salman Khursheed (INC) : 1,55,601; Devendra Singh (BSP) : 80,837; Others : 13,126; Invalid : 7,672
In 1998, Swami Sachchidanand Hari Sakshi (BJP) won by a margin of 31,159 votes.

Fatehpur : 11,71,111* (5,45,594) - Ashok Kumar Patel (BJP) : 1,42,911
Surya Bali Nishad (BSP) : 1,41,848; Vishambhar Prasad Nishad (SP) : 1,22,060; Vibhakar Shashtri (INC) : 94,032; Yuadunath (AD) : 17,586; Others : 19,951; Invalid : 7,206
In 1998, Ashok Kumar Patel (BJP) won by a margin of 46,436 votes.

Firozabad (SC) : 11,57,680* (5,82,774) - Ramjilal Suman (SP) : 2,89,459
Prabhu Dayal Kateria (BJP) : 2,06,091; Chandra Bhan Verma (BSP) : 58,676; Others : 19,086; Invalid : 9,462
In 1998, Prabhu Dayal Kateria (BJP) won by a margin of 39,950 votes.

Garhwal : 10,58,313* (4,74,229) - Maj. Gen. (retd) Bhuwan Chandra Kanduri (BJP) : 2,39,745
Satpal Maharaj (INC) : 2,10,063; Others : 22,373; Invalid : 2,048
In 1998, Mag. Gen. (Retd.) Bhuwan Chandra Khanduri (BJP) won by a margin of 1,74,947 votes.

Ghatampur (SC) : 11,08,686* (5,63,152) - Pyare Lal Shankhwar (BSP) : 1,56,582
Arun Kumari Kori (SP) : 1,56,477; Kamal Rani (BJP) : 1,55,987; Jagdish Chandra (AD) : 57,799; Ashkaran Shakhwar (INC) : 29,859; Others : 1,410; Invalid : 5,038
In 1998, Kamal Rani (BJP) won by a margin of 42,489 votes.

Ghazipur : 11,30,011* (7,41,960) - Manoj (BJP) : 2,40,592
Om Prakash (SP) : 2,29,559; Bachcha Yadav (BSP) : 1,71,681; Ishtiyaque Ansari (INC) : 40,151; Ram Badan (CPI) : 14,434; Others : 37,622; Invalid : 7,921
In 1998, Om Prakash (SP) won by a margin of 17,173 votes.

Ghosi : 12,15,936* (6,86,389) - Bal Krishna (BSP) : 2,07,105
Siddhartha Rai (JD-U) : 1,70,604); Dara Singh Chauhan (SP) : 1,68.747; Sudha Rai (INC) : 69,266; Atul Kumar Anjan (CPI) : 26,491; Baliram (AD) : 16,635; Others : 18,633; Invalid : 8,908
In 1998, Kalpnath Rai (SAP) won by a margin of 18,374 votes.

Gonda : 11,59,190* (5,87,694) - Braj Bhushan Sharan Singh (BJP) : 2,43,138
Kirit Vardhan Singh Urf Raja Bhaiya (SP) : 1,83,964; Deep Narain Pandey (INC) : 64,815; Ayodhya Naresh Pandey (BSP) : 32,583; Others : 52,498; Invalid : 10,696
In 1998, Kirti Vardhan Singh Urf Raza Bhaiya (SP) won by a margin of 25,571 votes.

Gorakhpur : 12,61,260* (6,58,451) -Aditya Nath (BJP) : 2,67,382
Jamuna Prasad Nishad (SP) 2,60,043; B.P. Yadav (SP) : 93,852; Jamal Ahmad (INC) : 20,026; Others : 9,242; Invalid : 7,906
In 1998, Aditya Nath (BJP) won by a margin of 26,145 votes.

Hamirpur : 10,63,370* (6,22,127) - Ashok Kumar Singh Chandel (BSP) : 2,17,732
Raj Narain (alias) Rajju Maharaj (SP) : 2,06,068; Ganga Charan Rajput (BJP) : 1,66,838; Rajendra Singh (INC) : 9,319; Others : 12,387; Invalid : 9,783
In 1998, Gangacharan S/o Ramswaroop (BJP) won by a margin of 16,924 votes.

Hapur : 15,77,173* (7,36,382) - Ramesh Chand Tomar (BJP) : 2,34,525
Trilok Tyagi (RLD) : 2,22,567; Khalid (BSP) : 1,93,221; Ram Asrey (SP) : 57,989; Others : 15,332; Invalid : 12,748
In 1998, Ramesh Chand Tomar (BJP) won by a margin of 1,61,962 votes.

Hardoi (SC) : 10,83,894* (5,59,499) - Jai Prakash (ABLTC) : 2,06,256
Usha Verma (SP) : 2,00,852; Girendra Pal Singh (BSP) : 1,22,728; Dileep Kumar Munna (INC) : 16,203; Others : 8,946; Invalid : 4,514
In 1998, Usha Verma (SP) won by a margin of 15,426 votes.

Haridwar (SC) : 11,83,848* (6,73,563) - Harpal Singh Sathi (BJP) : 2,36,844
Ramesh Kumar Burman (BSP) : 2,03,997; Shishpal (INC) : 1,39,724; Surendra Kumar Rakesh (SP) : 54,091; Invalid : 6,681
In 1998, Harpal Singh Sathi (BJP) won by a margin of 1,29,873 votes.

Hathras (SC) : 11,38,146* (4,67,558) - Kishan Lal Deler (BJP) : 1,78,253
Ganga Prasad Pushkar (BSP) : 1,09,846; Bangali Singh (SP) : 1,07,548; Ram Gopal (INC) : 62,712; Others : 1,399; Invalid : 7,800
In 1998, Kishan Lal Diler (BJP) won by a margin of 1,42,465 votes.

Jalaun (SC) : 11,64,671* (5,81,802) - Brij Lal Khabri (BSP) : 1,97,705
Bhanu Pratap Singh Verma (BJP) : 1,84,353; Ramesh Chandra Kori (SP) : 89,386; Ram Prasad Ahirwar (INC) : 70,394; Jai Ram Srivas (IND) : 22,362; Others : 10,655; Invalid : 6,947
In 1998, Bhanu Pratap Singh (BJP) won by a margin of 45,640 votes.

Jalesar : 11,20,995* (6,75,989) - Prof. S.P. Singh Baghel (SP) : 2,17,336
Ompal Singh Nidar (BJP) : 2,09,274; Ram Veer Upadhyay (BSP) : 1,49,628; Javed Ali Khan (INC) : 53,717; Others : 31,731; Invalid : 14,303
In 1998, Professor S.P. Singh Baghel (SP) won by a margin of 2,734 votes.

Jaunpur : 12,74,543* (7,02,988) - Chinmayanand (BJP) : 2,07,405
Paras Nath (SP) : 1,98,770; Lal Chand (BSP) : 1,81,928; Subhash Nishad (AD) : 44,769; Kamla Prasad Singh (INC) : 38,736; Others : 19,910; Invalid : 11,470
In 1998, Paras Nath Yadav (SP) won by a margin of 13,448 votes.

Jhansi : 13,19,190* (7,62,812) - Sujan Singh Bundela (INC) : 2,83,387
Rajendra Agnihotri (BJP) : 2,00,866; Hargovind Kushwaha (SP) : 1,31,773; Jaiprakash Sahu (Adovcate) (BSP) : 1,01,657; Others : 32,818; Invalid : 12,311
In 1998, Rajendra Agnihotri (BJP) won by a margin of 50,368 votes.

Kairana : 10,99,503* (7,00,065) - Amir Alam (RLD) : 2,06,345
Niranjan Singh Malik (BJP) : 1,68,073; Ram Kishan Kashyap (BSP) : 1,58,341; Munavvar Husan (SP) : 1,34,159; Others : 25,109; Invalid : 8,038
In 1998, Virendra Verma (BJP) won by a margin of 62,061 votes.

Kaiserganj : 11,15,142* (6,46,538) - Beni Prasad Verma (SP) : 2,33,934
Chamundeshwri Markandeya Pratap Chand (BJP) : 1,82,375; Sunder Singh (BSP) : 1,16,693; Surendra Nath Avasthi Putto Bhaia (INC) : 70,578; Others : 32,148; Invalid : 10,810
In 1998, Beni Prasad Verma (SP) won by a margin of 24,971 votes.

Kannauj : 12,33,412* (6,93,752) - Mulayam Singh Yadav (SP) : 2,91,617
Arvind Pratap Singh (ABLTC) : 2,12,478; Sughar Singh Pal (BSP) : 1,18,492; Digvijai Narain Singh (INC) : 27,082; Radhey Shyam (IND) : 10,268; Others : 24,148; Invalid : 9,667
In 1998, Pradeep Kumar Yadav (SP) won by a margin of 42,555 votes.

Kanpur : 14,17,761* (6,35,651) - Shri Prakash Jaiswal (INC) : 2,93,610
Jagatveer Singh Drone (BJP) : 2,59,151; Shyam Lal Gupta (SP) : 40,690; Man Singh Bagga (BSP) : 26,374; Others : 15,799; Invalid : 27
In 1998, Jagatveer Singh Dron (BJP) won by a margin of 1,36,009 votes.

Khalilabad : 12,15,784* (6,72,949) - Bhai Chandra Yadav (SP) : 2,36,834
Ram Prasad Chaudhary (BSP) : 2,06,809; Ashta Bhuja Prasad Shukla (BJP) : 1,60,362; Krishna Chandra Pandey (INC) : 41,048; Others : 19,432; Invalid : 8,464
In 1998, Indrajeet Mishra (BJP) won by a margin of 2,100 votes.

Kheri : 1,26,314* (7,17,065) - Ravi Prakash Verma (SP) : 2,02,373
Rajendra Kumar Gupta (BJP) : 1,97,858; Girish Chandra Maurya (BSP) : 1,80,776; Tej Narayan Trivedi (INC) : 94,028; Others : 30,125; Invalid : 11,905
In 1998, Ravi Prakash Verma (SP) won by a margin of 57,914 votes.

Khurja (SC) : 12,71,984* (4,89,206) - Ashok Kumar Pradhan (BJP) : 2,16,011
Smt. Satyawati Urf Satya Bahin (INC) 1,05,713; Phool Singh Tomar (BSP) : 99,481; Smt. Vimal Pal (SP) : 42,639; Others : 17,890; Invalid : 7,472
In 1998, Ashok Kumar Pradhan (BJP) won by a margin of 2,29,359 votes.

Lalganj (SC) : 13,13,829* (6,98,220) - Bali Ram (BSP) : 2,29,122
Daroga (SP) : 1,98,123; Jayanand (BJP) : 1,65,705; Lalit Devi (INC) : 56,773; Banarasi Ram (CPI) : 13,919; Others : 24,886; Invalid : 9,692
In Daroga Prasad Saroj (S) won by a margin of 16,996 votes.

Lucknow : 15,52,441* (7,53,943) - Atal Bihari Vajpayee (BJP) : 3,62,709
Karan Singh (INC) : 2,39,085; Bhagwati Singh (SP) : 78,826; Ijaharul Haque (BSP) : 43,948; Others : 29,375; Invalid : 0
In 1998, Atal Bihari Vajpayee (BJP) won by a margin of 2,19,222 votes.

Machhlishahr : 12,63,192* (6,62,703) - Chandra Nath Singh (SP) : 2,01,374
Ram Vilas Vedanti (BJP) : 1,80,250; Shiv Sharan Verma (BSP) : 1,37,303; Shriram Verma Patel (AD) : 64,589; Arun Kumar Singh (Munna) (INC) : 50,424; Others : 19,869; Invalid : 8,894
In 1998 Chinmayanand (BJP) by a margin of 41,534 votes.

Maharjganj : 11,29,627* (6,85,069) - Akhilesh Singh (SP) : 2,39,826
Pankaj Chaudhary (BJP) : 2,29,182; Talat Aziz (BSP) : 1,71,408; Jitendra Singh (INC) : 24,516; Others : 12,182; Invalid : 7,955
In 1998 Pakan Chaudharry (BJP) won by a margin of 26,940 votes.

Mainpuri : 11,09,097* (5,80,084) - Balram Singh Yadav (BJP) : 2,44,183
Darshan Singh Yadav (BJP) : 2,16,087; Balak Dass Shakya (BSP) : 75,107; Munshi Lal (INC) : 15,139; Others : 19,092; Invalid : 10,546
In 1998, Balram Singh Yadav (SP) won by a margin of 10,366 votes.

Mathura : 11,76,548* (5,40,511) - Chaudhary Tejvir Singh (BJP) : 2,10,212
Rameshwar Singh (RLD) : 1,68,485; Pt. Kamal Kant Upmanyu (BSP) : 1,18,720; Chaudhary Hari Singh Rawat (SP) : 19,816; Others : 12,923; Invalid : 10,355
In 1998, Tejvir Singh (BJP) won by a margin of 1,90,030 votes.

Meerut : 12,69,494* (7,54,487) - Avtar Singh Bhadana (INC) : 2,58,456
Amar Pal Singh (BJP) : 2,33,620; Hajji Yaqoob (BSP) : 2,27,133; Jagveer Singh (SP) : 13,050; Others : 11,805; Invalid : 10,423
In 1998, Amar Pal Singh (BJP) won by a margin of 58,805 votes.

Mirzapur : 13,56,017* (7,82,304) - Phoolan Devi (SP) : 2,90,849
Virendra Singh (BJP) : 2,06,373; Rajendra Tripathi (BSP) 1,34,973; Shyamdhar Mishra (INC) : 93,635; Lalit Mohan Silpkar Kasera (AD) : 19,557; Others : 25,737; Invalid : 11,180
In 1998, Birendra Singh (BJP) won by a margin of 52,777 votes.

Misrikh (SC) : 10,89,823* (6,19,588) - Sushila Saroj (SP) : 1,59,279
Ram Shankar Bhargav (BSP) : 1,55,072; Ram Pal Verma (ABLTC) : 1,46,658; Ram Lal Rahi (INC) : 1,16,571; Others : 34,739; Invalid : 7,269
In 1998, Ram Shanker (BSP) won by a margin of 1,495 votes.

Mohanlalganj (SC) : 11,50,176* (6,18,329) - Reena Choudhary (SP) : 1,82,034
Purnima Verma (BJP) : 1,46,676; Suresh Bahadur (BSP) : 1,39,237; Baldev Chowdhary (INC) : 80,459; Manjula Diwakar (CPI) : 32,618; Others : 27,230; Invalid : 10,075
In 1998, Reena Choudhary (SP) won by a margin of 11,188 votes.

Moradabad : 11,56,135* (6,46,930) - Chandra Vijay Singh Alias Baby Raja (ABLTC) : 2,53,321
Shaflqur Rahman Barq (SP) : 1,56,871; Mohammad Akil (BSP) : 1,23,714; Reena Kumari (INC) : 63,762; Zahid Hussain (NLP) : 20,729; Sudhir Kumar Singh (IND) : 12,391; Others : 9,526; Invalid : 6,616
In 1998, Safiqur Rehman Vark (SP) won by a margin of 36,481 votes.

Muzaffarnagar : 12,17,407* (6,91,547) - Saiduzzeman (INC) : 1,96,669
Sohanveer Singh (BJP) : 1,70,918; Rajpal Singh Saini (BSP) : 1,63,721; Harendra Singh (SP) : 1,12,499; Tej Pal (IND) : 10,605; Others : 27,939; Invalid : 9,196
In 1998, Sohanveer Singh (BJP) won by a margin of 22,724 votes.

Nainital : 13,96,787* (8,03,619) - Narayan Datt Tiwari (INC) : 3,50,381
Balraj Pasi (BJP) : 2,37,974; Naina Ahmad (BSP) : 1,23,509; Muzaffar Ali (SP): 63,293; Others : 18,762; Invalid : 9,700
In 1998, Smt. Ila Pant (BJP) won by a margin of 15,577 votes.

Padrauna : 12,10,405* (7,08,153) - Ram Nagina Mishra (BJP) : 1,96,651
Baleshwar Yadav (SP) : 1,69,913; Kunwar Ranjeet Pratap Narayan Singh (INC) : 1,55,861; Prasidha Naryan Chauhan (BSP) : 1,33,656; Mohd. Arshad Khan (NLP) : 16,028; Others : 23,057; Invalid : 12,807
In 1998, Ram Nagina Mishra (BJP) won by a margin of 50,775 votes.

Phulpur : 11,83,537* (6,90,973) - Dharam Raj Singh Patel (SP) : 1,83,282
Beni Madhav Bind (BJP) : 1,63,243; Tulsi Ram Yadav (BSP) : 1,50,173; Soneylal Patel (AD) : 1,27,780; Ram Pujan Patel (INC) : 32,376; Rehman Ali (SJPR) : 13,675; Others : 9,498; Invalid : 10,946
In 1998, Jang Bahadur Singh Patel (SP) won by a margin of 14,525 votes.

Pilibhit : 11,39,194* (7,56,275) - Maneka Gandhi (IND) : 4,33,421
Anis Ahmad alias Phool Baboo (BSP) : 1,93,566; Ram Saran Verma (SP) : 58,792; Raj Rai Singh (INC) : 50,086; Others : 12,139; Invalid : 8,271
In 1998, Maneka Gandhi (IND) won by a margin of 2,11,876 votes.

Pratapgarh : 11,89,143* (5,75,723) - Rajkumari Ratna Singh (INC) : 2,02,170
Abhaya Pratap Singh (BJP) : 1,96,158; Ashok Kumar (BSP) : 78,323; Shyad Ali (SP) : 39,921; Ram Manohar (AD) : 25,359; Others : 25,158; Invalid : 8,634
In 1998, Ram Vilas Vedanti (BJP) won by a margin of 68,465 votes.

Rae Bareli : 11,80,356* (6,96,302) - Captain Satish Sharma (INC) : 2,24,202
Gajadhar Singh (SP) : 1,50,653; Anand Prakash Lodhi (BSP) : 1,37,775; Arun Kumar Nehru (BJP) : 1,36,217; Others : 35,614; Invalid : 11,841
In 1998, Ashok Singh (BJP) won by a margin of 40,722 votes.

Rampur : 13,21,861* (8,20,796) - Begum Noor Bano Urf Mahtab Zamani Begum (INC) : 3,38,493; Mukhtar Abbas Naqvi (BJP) : 2,23,022; Ghanshyam Singh Lodhi (BSP) : 1,10,362; Abdul Salam (SP) : 92,867; Others : 45,680; Invalid : 10,372
In 1998, Mukhtar Abbas Naqvi (BJP) won by a margin of 4,936 votes.

Robertsganj (SC) : 14,43,467* (7,55,019) - Ram Shakal (BJP) : 2,00,826
Hari Prasad (alias) Ghamdi Singh (SP) : 1,84,989; Ramchandra Tyagi (BSP) : 1,58,136; Pakauri Lal (AD) : 93,721; Sudhakar Chamar (INC) : 88,168; Others : 17,608; Invalid : 11,662
In 1998, Ram Shakal (BJP) won by a margin of 26,742 votes.

Saharanpur : 12,61,869* (7,78,805) - Mansoor Ali Khan (BSP) : 2,35,659
Rasheed Masood (RLD) : 2,13,352; Nakli Singh (BJP) : 1,43,000; Nirbhay Paul Sharma (IND) : 1,09,489; Mohd. Irshad (SP) : 42,276; Others : 28,183; Invalid : 6,846
In 1998, Nakli Singh (BJP) won by a margin of 59,836 votes.

Saidpur (SC) : 13,09,952* (4,48,875) - Tufani Saroj (SP) : 1,53,292
Sharada Prasad (BSP) : 1,33,016; Vijay Sonkar Shastri (BJP) : 1,06,263; Sankatha Prasad Shastri (INC) : 28,384; Others : 17,738; Invalid : 10,182
In 1998, Vijay (BJP) won by a margin of 825 votes.

Salempur : 12,65,863* (6,47,355) - Babban Rajbhar (BSP) : 1,70,558
Hari Vansh Sahai (SP) : 1,61,508; Har Kewal Prasad (JD-U) : 1,50,690; Bhola Pandey (INC) : 1,16,820; Shri Ram Chaudhary (CPI-ML-L) : 12,519; Others : 24,380; Invalid : 10,880
In 1998, Harikewal Prasad (SAP) won by a margin of 39,021 votes.

Sambhal : 10,81,419* (6,27,689) - Mulayam Singh Yadav (SP) : 2,59,430
Ch. Bhupendra Singh (BJP) : 1,43,596; Budh Sain (BSP) : 1,37,268; Shri Pal Singh Yadav (INC) : 61,103; Others : 18,462; Invalid : 7,830
In 1998, Mulayam Singh Yadav (SP) won by a margin of 1,66,682 votes.

Shahabad : 11,28,589* (6,49,099) - Daud Ahmad (BSP) : 2,14,146
Raghvendra Singh (BJP) : 1,72,014; Lias Azami (SP) : 1,69,486; Ram Avtar Dixit (INC) 60,834; Asharfi Lal (AD) : 13,105; Others : 10,360; Invalid : 9,150
In 1998, Raghavendra Singh (BJP) won by a margin of 20,612 votes.

Shahjahanpur : 11,30,852* (6,82,896) - Kunwar Jitendra Prasad (INC) 2,07,167
Ram Murti Singh Verma (SP) : 1,89,175; Satyapal Singh Yadav (BJP) : 1,52,317; Satyapal Maurya (BSP) : 1,05,050; Others : 20,237; Invalid : 8,950
In 1998, Satya Pal Singh Yadav (BJP) won by a margin of 22,685 votes.

Sitapur : 11,14,886* (6,44,865) - Rajesh Verma (BSP) : 2,11,120
Janardan Prasad Misra (BJP) : 1,74,758; Mukhtar Anis (SP) : 1,31,650; Ammar Rizvi (INC) : 1,01,759; Others : 17,626; Invalid : 7,952
In 1998, Janardan Prasad Misra (BJP) won by a margin of 27,920 votes.

Sultanpur : 12,20,728* (6,22,094) - Jai Bhadra Singh (BSP) : 1,73,558
Ram Lakhan Verma (SP) : 1,58,959; Piyare (IND) : 1,29,525; Deepa Kaul (INC) : 82,385; Chandra Bhushan (IND) : 23,929; Algoo Ram (AD) : 12,718; Jalil Ahmad (NLP) : 10,311; Others : 19,019; Invalid : 11,690

In 1998, Devendra Bhadur Rai (BJP) won by a margin of 64,442 votes.

Tehri Garhwal : 12,51,582* (4,90,460) - Manvendra Shah (BJP) : 2,07,889
Vijay Bahuguna (INC) : 1,92,068; Munna Chauhan (SP) : 50,196; Vidya Sagar Nautiyal (CPI) : 16,631; Others : 16,463; Invalid : 7,263
In 1998, Manvendra Shah (BJP) won by a margin of 1,82,092 votes.

Unnao : 12,01,204* (5,99,341) - Deepak Kumar (SP) : 2,07,242
Mohd. Moin (BSP) : 1,69,467; Devi Bux (BJP) : 1,49,546; Anis-ur-Rehman (INC) : 46,258; Others : 17,888; Invalid : 8,940
In 1998, Devi Bux (BJP) won by a margin of 81,29 votes.

Varanasi : 14,07,844* (6,33,826) - Shankar Prasad Jaiswal (BJP) : 2,11,955
Rajesh Kumar Mishra (INC) : 1,59,096; Niranjan Rajbhar (AD) : 83,282; Salma Bashar (SP) : 78,442; Babu Lal Patel (BSP) : 75,059; Others : 16,523; Invalid : 9,469
In 1998, Shankar Prasad Jaiswal (BJP) won by a margin of 1,51,952 votes.

WEST BENGAL (42)

The Left has been in control for around two decades but the Trinamool Congress under Mamata Banerjee has been making serious erosions. The BJP in alliance won the Krishnagar and Dum Dum seats. The Congress was just present with 3 seats while TC wrested 8 seats. The CPI(M), RSP and CPI shared the other 29 seats with CPI(M) leading th Left alliance.

	Total Seats
1952	34
1957-1962	36
1967-1971	40
1977 onwards	42

Press Comments

As the tabulation of ballots for Sunday's elections in 42 parliamentary constituencies concluded, the ruling communists were dismayed reading the bottomline : Ms. Mamata Banerjee's Trinamool Congress and its ally, BJP, are dangerously making inroads into their rural bastions while the other rival, Congress, has hit the comeback trail.

After watching sharp swings in fortunes in the past 48 hours, the ruling left coalition led by the CPI (M) ended up with a tally of 29 seats, down from last year's 33.

Viewed in today's context, the days immediately ahead of the CPI(M) and its partners look fraught with uncertainties as both the Trinamool and the BJP gave an impressive account of themselves by wresting Nabadwip, Contai and Krishnanagar, three improtant rural parliamentary segments to take their tally to ten. The Trinamul-BJP combine also annexed three assembly segments from the leftists.

For the Communists, far more important than the numbers is the realisation that the Trinamool BJP alliance which has so far grown plugging into the popular anger in Calcutta and adjoining area has begun to shed the city only label and foraying into rural Bengal. Unlike in 1998, the partners have snatched three parliamentary seats from the CPI(M).

As it appears, the two Opposition blocs, the Trinamool-BJP alliance and the Congress are finding their feet either side of a divide between South and North Bengal. While, Ms. Banerjee's alliance has put its signature firmly on the political life of South

Bengal, the Congress, with Mr. Somen Mitra playing the driving force behind it, scripted a resurrection of sorts where it won all the three seats.

Also a matter of grave concern for the communists is the revelation that in most of the seats they managed to retain in rural Bengal the margins were appreciably lower, thanks to the concerted way the Trinamool - BJP combine and the Congress ate into their votes. Two cases can be cited to drive the point home: Indrajit Gupta of the Communist Party of India (CPI), who won the Midnapore seat for the fifth time in a row scraped past a seemingly feeble Opposition by a 12,373 margin. Similarly, Ms. Geeta Mukherjee, also of the CPI, won by a little over 33,000 ballots.

Constituency-wise Results — 1999 and Winners of 1998

Alipurduar (ST) : 10,44,238* (7,77,618) - Joachim Baxla (RSP) : 3,89,919
Dhirendra Narjinarai (BJP) : 2,36,786; Basanti Baraik (INC) : 1,19,309; Others : 14,848; Invalid : 16,765
In 1998, Joachim Baxia (RSP) won by a margin of 1,95,599 votes.

Arambagh : 11,36,153* (9,43,586) - Anil Basu (CPM) : 5,03,920
Chunilal Chakraborty (BJP) : 3,87,199; Idrish Ali (INC) : 40,816; Others : 1,565; Invalid : 10,086
In 1998, Anil Basu (CPM) won by a margin of 1,87,300 votes.

Asansol : 12,76,297* (8,29,147) - Bikash Chowdhury (CPM) : 3,77,265
Ajit Ghatak (Moloy Ghatak) (AITC) : 3,39,401; Manik Upadhyay (INC) : 89,261; Others : 9,365; Invalid : 13,855
In 1998, Bikash Chowdhury (CPM) won by a margin of 26,149 votes.

Balurghat (SC) : 8,51,433* (8,40,989) - Barman Ranen (RSP) : 3,75,669
Subhash Ch. Barman (BJP) : 3,12,748; Bikash Barman (INC) : 1,43,034; Others: 9,447
In 1998, Ranen Barman (RSP) won by a margin of 1,72,175 votes.

Bankura : 10,42,063* (7,41,303) - Acharia Basudeb (CPM) : 3,81,720
Natabar Bagdi (IND) : 2,74,722; Bula Chatterjee (INC) : 35,512; Others : 31,977; Invalid : 17,372
In 1998, Acharia Basudeb (VPM) won by a margin of 1,11,583 votes.

Barasat : 13,02,147* (10,43,590) - Ranjit Panja (TC) : 5,18,520
Saral Beb (AIFB) : 4,21,620; Debi Ghoshal (INC) 76,751; Others : 14,394; Invalid : 12,305
In 1998, Ranjit Kumar Panja (WBTC) won by a margin of 66,707 votes.

Barrackpore : 10,40,092* (8,45,189) - Tarit Baran Topdar (CPM) : 3,99,269
Jayanta Bhattacharya (TC) : 3,58,494; Ashok Sukla (INC) 59,732; Others : 13,224; Invalid : 14,470
In 1998, Tarit Baran Topdar (CPM) won by a margin of 27,957 votes.

Basirhat : 10,71,551* (8,64,988) - Ajoy Chakraborty (CPI) : 4,07,903
M. Nuruzzam,an (TC) : 3,25,316; Abu Tayed M.M. Hossin (INC) : 1,18,612; Others : 4,464; Invalid : 8,693
In 1998, Ajay Chakraborty (CPI) won by a margin of 1,20,076 votes.

Berhampore : 12,10,965* (9,37,642) - Adhir Ranjan Chowdhury (INC) : 4,34,073
Pramothes Mukherjee (RSP) : 3,38,682; Sabyasachi Bagchi (BJP) : 1,34,569;

* Total Electorates
Figures in ( ) are Votes polled

Others : 19,047; Invalid : 11,271
In 1998, Promothes Mukherjee (RSP) won by a margin of 1,23,369 votes.

Birbhum (SC) : 10,43,436* (7,34,173) - Ram Chandra Dome (CPM) : 3,73,687
Madanlal Choudhury (BJP) : 2,16,531; Asit Kumar Mal (INC) : 1,26,305; Others : 7,037; Invalid : 10,613
In 1998, Dome Ram Chandra (CPM) won by a margin of 1,61,512 votes.

Bolpur : 10,43,436* (7,92,871) - Somnath Chatterjee (CPM) : 4,64,199
Suniti Chattarajee (TC) : 2,77,810; Sushil Banerjee (INC) : 37,093; Others : 2,852; Invalid : 10,917
In 1998, Somnath Chatterjee (CPM) won by a margin of 2,51,092 votes.

Burdwan : 12,16,274* (9,84,338) - Sar Nikhilananda (CPM) : 5,98,170
Anup Mukherjee (BJP) : 2,96,487; Rajkrishna Dawn (INC) : 67,096; Cahmaru Oram (JMM) : 9,353; Manab Bandopadhyay (IND) : 648; Invalid : 12,584
In 1998, Sar Nikhilananda (CPM) won by a margin of 2,72,253 votes.

Calcutta North-East : 9,24,253* (6,58,631) - Ajit Panja (TC) : 2,97,491
Md. Salim (CPM) : 2,55,917; Tapas Roy (INC) : 84,516; Others : 20,707
In 1998, Ajit Kumar Panja (WBTC) won by a margin of 64,173 votes.

Calcutta South : 12,02,629* (8,05,268) - Mamata Banerjee (TC) : 4,69,103
Subhankar Chakraborty (CPM) : 2,55,095; Partha Roy Chowdhury (INC) : 51,735; Others : 29,188; Invalid : 147
In 1998, Mamata Banerjee (WBTC) won by a margin of 2,24,081 votes.

Contai : 9,90,917* (8,23,688) - Neetish Sengupta (TC) : 3,95,048
Sudir Giri (CPM) : 3,82,915; Ajit Khanra (INC) : 34,070; Others : 3,415; Invalid: 8,240
In 1998, Sri Sudhir Giri (CPM) won by a margin of 74,860 votes.

Coochbehar (SC) : 11,15,895* (9,02,471) - Amar Roy Pradhan (AIFB) : 4,43,148
Ambika Charan Ray (TC) : 3,34,983; Sabita Roy (INC) : 90,378; Papiya Barman (BSP) : 17,188; Others : 6,132; Invalid : 10,642
In 1998, Amar Roy Prodhan (FBL) won by a margin of 1,23,166 votes.

Darjeeling : 12,76,267* (5,89,959) - S.P. Lepcha (CPM) : 2,56,826
Nar Bahadur Khatiwara (INC) : 1,44,857; Tarun Roy (TC) : 1,27,603; R.B. Rai (IND) : 31,719; Others : 19,466; Invalid : 9,488
In 1998, Ananda Pathak (CPM) won by a margin of 1,22,556 votes.

Diamond Harbour : 11,38,628* (8,57,918) - Samik Lahiri (CPM) : 4,02,761
Sardar Amjad Ali (AITC) : 3,31,598; Daulat Ali Sheikh (INC) : 1,06,344; Others: 3,639; Invalid : 13,576
In 1998, Samik Lahiri (CPM) won by a margin of 60,956 votes.

Dum Dum : 15,88,614* (12,09,926) - Tapan Sikdar (BJP) : 6,14,471
Anil Bhattacharya (CPM) : 4,79,910; Ramesh Bhattacharjee (INC) : 85,648; Others : 11,085; Invalid : 18,812
In 1998, Tapan Sikdar (BJP) won by a margin of 1,36,152 votes.

Durgapur (SC) : 12,11,190* (8,85,076) - Sunil Khan (CPM) : 4,61,940
Anil Kumar Saha (BJP) : 3,43,977; Haradhan Mondal (INC) : 58,407; Others : 4,767; Invalid : 15,985
In 1998, Khan Sunil (CPM) won by a margin of 1,78,443 votes.

Hooghly : 11,51,891* (9,30,275) - Rupchand Pal (CPM) : 4,40,674
Tapan Das Gupta (AITC) : 4,28,189; Dilip Nath (INC) : 48,068; Others : 2,319; Invalid : 11,025

In 1998, Rupchand Pal (CPM) won by a margin of 6,116 votes.

Howrah : 13,82,042* (9,93,635) - Swadesh Chakraborty (CPM) : 4,90,537
Kakoli Ghosh Dastidar (AITC) : 3,87,088; Subhash Chandra Bandyopadhyay (INC) : 90,592; Others : 13,182; Invalid : 12,236
In 1998, Bikram Sarkar (WBTC) won by a margin of 6,536 votes.

Jadavpur : 14,03,150* (10,04,718) - Krishna Bose (AITC) : 4,85,366
Kanti Ganguly (CPM) : 4,18,601; Maya Ghose (INC) : 79,672; Others : 7,559; Invalid : 13,520
In 1998, Krishna Bose (WBTC) won by a margin of 78,201 votes.

Jalpaiguri : 11,01,416* (8,43,416) - Minati Sen (CPM) : 4,05,785
Kalyan Chakraborty (TC) : 2,96,848; Girija Sankar Roy (INC) : 99,994; Others : 29,168; Invalid : 11,621
In 1998, Minati Sen (CPM) won by a margin of 1,74,975 votes.

Jangipur : 10,88,094* (7,85,797) - Abul Hasnat Khan (CPM) : 3,52,580
Mainul Haque (INC) : 2,91,263; Syed Mushtaque Murshed (TC) 1,20,770; Others : 10,880; Invalid : 10,304
In 1998, Abul Hasnat Khan (CPM) won by a margin of 72,501 votes.

Jhargram (ST) : 9,91,326* (8,03,200) - Rupchand Murmu (CPM) : 4,02,325
Dakhin Murmu (TC) : 2,93,644; Biswanath Murmu (JKP-N) : 84,332; Others : 11,399; Invalid : 11,500
In 1998, Rupchand Murmu (CPM) won by a margin of 2,87,188 votes.

Joynagar (SC) : 11,18,073* (8,15,536) - Sanat Kumar Mondal (RSP) : 3,96,383
Krishna Pada Majumder (BJP) : 2,84,082; Jagat Pada Sanpui (INC) : 46,173; Renu Patha Halder (IND) : 74,016; Others : 1,875; Invalid : 13,007
In 1998, Sanat Kumar Mandal (RSP) won by a margin of 1,76,061 votes.

Katwa : 11,81,236* (9,30,036) - Mahboob Zahedi (CPM) : 4,61,502
Amal Kumar Dutta (AITC) : 3,53,140; Tuhin Samanta (INC) : 91,204; Others : 12,503; Invalid : 11,687
In 1998, Zahedi Mahboob (CPM) won by a margin of 1,38,707 votes.

Krishnagar : 10,82,103* (8,45,489) - Satyabrata Mookherjee (BJP) : 3,66,954
Dilip Chakraborty (CPM) : 3,44,720; Ashim Saha (INC) : 1,06,137; Others : 16,130; Invalid : 11,548
In 1998, Ajoy Mukhopadhyay (CPM) won by a margin of 40,672 votes.

Malda : 10,46,857* (8,23,415) - A.B.A. Ghani Khan Choudhury (INC) : 3,25,883
Sailen Sarkar (CPM) : 3,01,280; Muzaffar Khan (BJP) : 1,72,575; Others : 14,058; Invalid : 9,619
In 1998, Abul Barkat Ataul Ghani Khan Choudhury (INC) won by a margin of 49,082 votes.

Mathurapur (SC) : 10,76,801* (8,28,713) - Radhika Ranjan Pramanik (CPM) : 3,82,962
Gobinda Chandra Naskar (AITC) : 3,31,237; Monoranjan Halder (INC) : 89,719; Prahlad Kumar Purkait (IND) : 14,691; Invalid : 10,104
In 1998, Radhika Ranjan Pramanik (CPM) won by a margin of 1,01,876 votes.

Midnapore : 10,99,385* (8,62,567) - Indrajit Gupta (CPI) : 4,14,545
Manoranjon Dutta (BJP) : 3,85,772; Samir Roy (INC) : 47,013; Others : 5,162; Invalid : 10,075
In 1998, Indrajit Gupta (CPI) won by a margin of 2,75,519 votes.

Murshidabad : 11,72,646* (8,36,120) - Moinul Hassan (CPM) : 3,91,366

Mannan Hossain (INC) : 2,68,006; Sagir Hossain (TC) : 1,42,275; Others : 25,748; Invalid : 8,725
In 1998, Moinul Hassan (CPM) won by a margin of 1,90,466 votes.

Nabadwip (SC) : 13,19,014* (10,14,379) - Ananda Mohan Biswas (AITC) : 4,59,319; Asim Bala (CPM) : 4,20,184; Biswas Shashanka Shekhor (INC) : 1,08,464; Susil Kumar Sarkar (BSP) : 8,775; Others : 5,342; Invalid : 12,295
In 1998, Asim Bala (CPM) won by a margin of 41,154 votes.

Panskura : 9,86,713* (8,24,564) - Gita Mukherjee (CPI) : 4,01,431
Gouri Ghosh (AITC) : 3,54,573; Rajani Kanta Boloi (INC) : 59,147; Others : 979; Invalid : 8,434
In 1998, Gita Mukherjee (CPI) won by a margin of 1,79,543 votes.

Purulia : 10,07,771* (6,91,712) - Birsingh Mahato (AIFB) : 3,51,143
Tapati Mahato (BJP) : 1,76,273; Jepal Majhata (INC) : 1,39,345; Others : 14,425; Invalid : 10,526
In 1998, Birsingh Mahato (FBL) won by a margin of 1,57,137 votes.

Raiganj : 11,44,551* (8,78,745) - Priya Ranjab Dasmunsi (INC) : 4,09,331
Subrata Mukherjee (CPM) : 3,34,076; Biplab Mitra (TC) : 1,10,049; Others : 22,260; Invalid : 3,029
In 1998, Subrata Mukheree (CPM) won by a margin of 6,281 votes.

Serampore : 13,25,375* (9,25,201) - Akbar Ali Khandoker (AITC) : 4,11,406
Sudarsan Roy Chaudhury (CPM) : 3,63,642; Pradip Bhattacharya (INC) : 1,33,155; Others : 3,103; Invalid : 13,895
In 1998, Akbor Ali Khandoker (WBTC) won by a margin of 44,611 votes.

Tamluk : 10,97,800* (9,18,889) - Lakshman Chandra Seth (CPM) : 4,55,168
Nirmalendu Bhattacharjee (AITC) : 4,00,342; Manik Bhowmik (INC) : 44,622; Others : 9,550; Invalid : 9,207
In 1998, Lakshman Chandra Seth (CPM) won by a margin of 87,952 votes.

Uluberia : 11,01,093* (8,15,957) - Hannan Mollah (CPM) : 3,98,671
Sudipta Roy (AITC) : 3,30,813; Sisir Kumar Sen (INC) : 71,867; Others : 4,892; Invalid : 9,714
In 1998, Hannan Mollah (CPM) won by a margin of 1,13,530 votes.

Vishnupur (SC) : 10,71,389* (8,46,339) - Sandhya Bauri (CPM) : 4,83,084
Adhibas Duley (TC) : 3,01,514; Mallika Mandal (INC) : 29,237; Ajit Saha (JKP-N) : 17,109; Others : 3,558; Invalid : 11,837
In 1998, Sandhya Bauri (CPM) won by a margin of 1,71,313 votes.

1998

Party	Seats won	Vote share
CPI (M)	24	35.4%
TC	7	24.4%
RSP	4	4.5%
CPI	3	3.6%
Ind	4	32.1%

Since 1967 the voter turn out has always been above the national average.

ANDAMAN & NICOBAR (1)

Andaman & Nicobar Islands : 2,31,976* (1,47,077) - Bishnu Pada Ray (BJP) : 76,891; Manoranjan Bhakta (INC) : 62,944; Others : 5,956; Invalid : 1,286
In 1998, Manoranjan Bhakta (NCP) won by a margin of 544 votes.

CHANDIGARH (1)

Chandigarh : 5,84,656* (2,82,721) - Pawan Kumar Bansal (INC) : 1,32,914 Krishan Lal Sharma (BJP) : 1,27,393; Mata Ram Dhiman (BSP) : 7,781; Others: 14,633
In 1998, Satya Pal Jain (BJP) won by a margin of 10,366 votes.

DADRA & NAGAR HAVELI (1)

Dadra & Nagar Haveli : 98,376* (73,499) - Delkar Mohanbhai Sonjibhai (IND) : 29,853; Bhurkud Dilipbhai Navjibhai (BJP) : 14,975; Patel Amrutbhai Babubhai (SHS) : 14,029; Dhodia Gulabbhai Nanjibhai (INC) : 10,601; Bhurkud Prabhudhai Puniyabhai (IND) : 2,447; Invalid : 1,594
In 1998, Delkar Mohanbhai Sanjbhai (BJP) won by a margin of 8,717 votes.

DAMAN & DIU (1)

Daman & Diu : 72,216* (51,810) - Patel Dahyabhai Vallab (INC) : 25,136 Tandel Devjibhai Jogib (BJP) : 21,910; Ramesh Pamsi (IND) : 3,422; Dhirajkumar H. Solanki (SHS) : 332; Invalid : 1,010
In 1998 Devjibhai J. Tandel (BJP) won by a margin of 1,236 votes.

PONDICHERRY (1)

Pondicherry : 7,01,990* (4,44,162) - M.O.H. Farook (INC) : 1,65,108 M. Ramadass (PMK) : 1,40,920; P. Kannan (TMC-C) : 1,11,737; Others : 26,397
In 1998, S. Arumugham (DMK) won by a margin of 36,774 votes.

LAKSHADWEEP (1)

Lakshadweep (ST) : 37,620* (30,172) - P.M. Sayeed (INC) : 16,133 K.P. Muthukoya (JD-U) : 12,924; Hussain Faburikage (JD-S) : 542; Ameer Biyyammada (IND) : 281; Invalid : 312
In 1998, P.M. Sayeed (INC) won by a margin of 964 votes.

DELHI (7)

The INC had come to power replacing the BJP. But no performance led to the party total collapse. All the 7 seats Lok Sabha were won by the BJP. Manmohan Singh lost to Prof. Vijay Kumar of BJP. Both Madan Lal Khurana and Sahib Singh were back although no one got a minsiterial berth.

---

* Total Electorates
Figures in ( ) are Votes polled

	Voter turn out			
	1991	1996	1998	1999
New Delhi	47.9	51.7	50.20	41.79
South Delhi	46.9	48.5	49.27	42.12
Outter Delhi	45.8	48.1	48.98	41.43
East Delhi	48.2	50.5	51.44	44.39
Chandni Chowk	57.1	57.5	61.76	54.09
Delhi Sadar	53.6	60.2	58.45	52.55
Karol Bagh	50.3	53.7	54.53	45.20
Total	**48.5**	**50.63**	**51.29**	**48.83**

Constituency-wise Results — 1999 and Winners of 1998

Chandni Chowk : 3,76,603* (2,04,454) - Vijay Goel (BJP) : 74,001
Jai Prakash Aggarwal (INC) : 72,006; Shoabib Iqbal (JD-S) : 52,721; Harbhajan Singh (IND) : 2,576; Others : 3,149; Invalid : 1
In 1998, Vijay Goel (BJP) won by a margin of 4,349 votes.

Delhi Sadar : 5,29,456* (2,78,267) - Madan Lal Khurana (BJP) : 1,43,168
Jagdish Tytler (INC) 1,29,316; Others : 3,852; Hepjool Rehman (IND) : 1,931
In 1998 Madan Lal Khurana (BJP) won by a margin of 48,494 votes.

East Delhi : Lal Behari Tiwari (BJP) won by a margin of 1,28,946 votes over Deep Chand of the Congress.

Karol Bagh (SC) : 5,71,402* (2,58,282) - Anita Arya (BJP) : 1,28,946
Meira Kumar (INC) 1,16,501; Others : 7,173; Ram Swaroop (IND) : 5,662
In 1998, Meira Kumar (INC) won by a margin of 4,849 votes.

New Delhi : 5,42,395* (2,26,758) - Jag Mohan (BJP) : 1,24,626
R.K. Dhawan (INC) : 96,733; Raja Kumar Azad (IND) : 1,579; Others : 3,818; Invalid : 2
In 1998, Jagmohan (BJP) won by a margin of 32,647 votes.

Outer Delhi : 31,01,838* (12,87,504) - Sahib Singh Verma (BJP) : 7,09,692
Deep Chand Sharma (INC) 5,07,220; Brahm Singh (BSP) : 41,911; Others : 28,664; Invalid : 17
In 1998, Krishan Lal Sharma (BJP) won by a margin of 98,350 votes.

South Delhi : 11,92,698* (4,99,910) - Vijay Kumar Malhotra (BJP) : 2,61,150
Manmohan Singh (INC) : 2,32,231; Modh Sarif (IND) : 2,846; Others : 4,630; Invalid : 53
In 1998 Sushma Swaraj (BJP) won by a margin of 1,16,713 votes.

13th Lok Sabha : Anatomy of the Vote in Delhi

The Focus this week in the Capital has been on the 7-0 win of the BJP nominees in the city as also a convincing victory of the Naitonal Democratic Alliance (NDA) all over the country. The Congress, on the other hand, has fared rather badly, though in terms of vote percentage the party has improved its performance significantly as compared to the last elections.

While analysing the results, one can safely reach the conclusion that the vote this

* Total Electorates
Figures in ( ) are Votes polled

time was for secularism. People all over the country have opted for the NDA which had projected a common minimum programme with a secular agenda. Therefore, in terms of seats, it is the NDA that has grown while the BJP with its non-secular predilections has not grown at all.

It is as if the body has grown while there is no growth of the core. Prior to the elections, the BJP had put a moratorium on its own principled demands like the construction of Ram temple, abolition of Article 370 and a uniform civil code. By opting for the NDA, where the BJP is the main partner, the people have put a moratorium on these demands for ever.

In real terms, the strength of the BJP has remained the same at 182 despite heavy losses in Uttar Pradesh, while each of its major electoral partners—the DMK, TDP, Biju Janata Dal, Trinamool Congress and INLD have shown a growth in the elections.

Coming to Delhi, the BJP has been able to improve its performance by bagging all seven as compared to six last time. It had fielded its best team in Delhi and the two weak links perceived by the High Command—Krishan Lal Sharma and Mrs Sushma Swaraj—were sent elsewhere. Incidentally, both lost in Chandigarh and Bellary respectively, although Mrs Swaraj may find herself accommodated in the Union Council of Ministers.

The reasons for the Congress receiving the worst drubbing since 1977 are not difficult to diagnose. Lacklustre governance, arbitrary selection of candidates, limited organisational network and failure of the Congress president Mrs Sonia Gandhi to address even a single meeting in the Capital—all contributed in distancing the voter from the party.

It was for the first time that the premier Congress leader did not address a meeting in the Capital of the country. From the days of Jawaharlal Nehru, Delhi was always the place from which the Congress gave a clarion. The association of the Nehru-Gandhi family with Delhi has been historical.

Mrs. Indira Gandhi always addressed several meetings in Delhi and would take pride in the fact that her own mother Mrs Kamala Nehru belonged to Bazar Sitaram in the walled city. Such was the Nehru-Gandhi equation with the city.

Mrs. Sonia Gandhi too has always cited her proximity to the Capital on quite a few occasions. At the one-day AICC session a few months ago, held at the Talkatora Indoor Stadium, Mrs. Sonia Gandhi had recalled how she got married in this city, how she became the mother of two children here and how late Indira Gandhi breathed her last in her arms. She was here only when the news of her husband's asassination was flashed. She incidentally is also the voter here and Delhi is her home.

However, for reasons best known to those at the helm of affairs in the Congress, no public meeting of Mrs Gandhi could take place. It is essential that political parties form associations with the electorate and the failure to hold a meeting in the city in a way did alienate a section of the electorate from the party.

The Delhi Congress has been struggling to put its acts together for the past decade. The party has been unable to fill the vacuum in the leadership after the marginalisation of H.K.L. Bhagat. Bhagat paid the price when the Congress fared badly in the 1993 Assembly polls even though the then high command had overruled him in the selection of candidates in key constituencies.

With intense factionalism that was witnessed in the rank and file of the party after Bhagat's exit, no local leader could sustain himself as a major force for long. Over the years, factionalism only grew and in order to iron out things, the High Command decided to foist Mrs. Shelia Dikshit, "an outsider" and the local Congress leaders accepted her without even a whimper.

Mrs Dikshit led the party to victory in the 1998 Asembly polls and was rewarded with Chief Ministership. The various factions of the Congress watched helplessly and endorsed her candidature. It is totally another thing that Mrs. Dikshit has not been successful in projecting the positive achievements of her tenure in an effective manner and has at the same time, been unable to endear herself to a large section of the MLAs and party functionaries.

In deciding the tickets she played an important role and was instrumental in securing nominations for Deep Chand Sharma from Outer Delhi, H.K.L. Kapoor from East Delhi and Jagdish Tytler from Delhi Sadar. Three other seats were given to R.K. Dhawan, Manmohan Singh and Ms Meira Kumar, all members of the Congress Working Committee.

The seventh seat was allotted to a local stalwart Jai Prakash Aggarwal even though the Janata Dal (Secular) Shoiab Iqbal and Naib Imam of the Jama Masjid had indicated to the High Command that if the seat was given to M.M. Aggarwal, senior vice president of the DPCC, the Muslims would support the Congress.

The net result was that despite having the support of 56 out of 70 MLAs in the Delhi Assembly, the party was unable to win even a single seat. Jagdish Tytler did put up a valiant fight in the Delhi Sadar constituency and Jai Parkash Aggarwal gasped for vital support from party functionaries in Paharganj and Ballimaran Assembly segments of the Chandni Chowk parliamentary constituency.

The party lost from the Assembly segments of the Chief Minister, her cabinet colleagues—Mahinder Singh Saathi, Yoganand Shastri, Narendra Nath, A. K. Walia, DPCC chief Subhash Chopra and Deputy Speaker Mrs Kiran Chaudhary.

In all, the Congress lost from 53 out of 70 Assembly segments of Delhi.

In the post poll scenario, the Congress MLAs are baying for the blood of the Chief Minister and have been demanding her replacement.

However, Mrs Dikshit apparently does not have any threat from within the local Congress which continues to be divided on factional lines. No Delhi leader at present enjoys the strength and the stature to organise the MLAs to replace her. The decision on whether she would stay or not would entirely depend on Mrs. Sonia Gandhi.

Therefore, the threat to her would become real only if the High Command shares the view that her governance was a major factor in the rout in Delhi.

The 1999 parliamentary polls have demonstrated that the vote was neither for Vajpayee and nor against Sonia Gandhi. If it had been for Vajpayee, then the reverses suffered by the BJP in UP, Vajpayee's home state, would not have been there. And if it had been against Sonia, the Congress victory in Karnataka and party's performance in Maharashtra, (where her foreign origin was the main cause of the split in the Congress) would not have been there.

The victory has been of the people, who while opting for either of the three formations—the NDA, Congress and Left—have upheld the secular credentials of the country.

The BJP, despite being the leading partner of NDA, has not shown any growth in terms of seats and may have to do serious thinking regarding its future strategies. May the people always win. —*Pankaj Vohra*

Statistics and Actual Vote Support

In elections, statistics other than those of seats won or lost by various parties often reveal a picture which is very different from their real strength on the ground.

The election data released by the Election Commission on verdict-99 reveals that some parties which have been 'routed' have actually increased their vote support. And some whose graph in terms of seats has gone up have actually lost ground. The contrast between the Congress(I) and the BJP is a case in point.

The Congress(I) which has started beating its breast over its debacle should perhaps take a closer look at the statistics to draw some cheer. As compared to the 1998 general election when it polled 25.82 per cent of the total votes polled in the country, the party's vote base has actually gone up to 28.42 per cent. In 1998, the party contested 477 seats whereas in 1999 it fielded candidates only in 453 seats.

Of course, the increase in the percentage of the Congress(I) could be due to electoral adjustments with three important regional parties—the AIADMK in Tamil Nadu, the Rashtriya Janata Dal in Bihar and the Indian National Lok Dal in Uttar Pradesh. But even in Andhra Pradesh where it fought on its own and got a severe drubbing, its vote percentage has actually gone up. Like in 1988, it had no electoral alliance with any party. The electoral understanding between the Telugu Desam and the BJP proved a lethal political combination for the Congress(I).

In 1998, the Congress(I) bagged 22 seats in Andhra Pradesh by polling 38.46 per cent votes and in 1999 despite securing 42.81 per cent popular vote, the party managed to win only five Lok Sabha seats! This is the lowest-ever tally for the Congress(I) in the State. The Telugu Desam-BJP combine together secured 49.6 per cent of votes polled and swept the State.

Bihar is yet another example where the RJD vote-share actually went up from 26.58 per cent to 29.71 per cent and yet received a rude electoral shock. Even the Congress(I) vote-share in the State went up from 7.27 per cent to 8.75 per cent. The RJD-Congress(I)-CP(M) combine which had total understanding ended up with a tally of just 10 seats as compared to 22 seats in the 1998 election.

Statistical details on the performance of the BJP also make interesting reading. The BJP's vote-share has actually gone down from 25.59 per cent to 23.07 per cent. On the face of it this is a serious setback for the BJP, but in 1999 election, the party contested only 338 seats as compared to 388 in 1998.

Despite a loss of about nine per cent vote and 28 seat loss in Uttar Pradesh alone, the party has managed to increase its tally from 181 to 182. Elections to five Lok Sabha elections—four in Bihar and one Assam—are due on October 28 and the BJP is contesting in four constituencies. So the final picture for the BJP may not be all that bad.

Statistics also reveal the continuing decline of the CPI as a political force. In the 1998 election, the party polled 1.75 per cent total vote at the national level and in the current election it has further gone down to 1.45 per cent. In the last election, the CPI narrowly escaped the ignominy of being de-recognised as a 'national party' as it failed to secure the required six per cent votes in more than four States/UT.

The Commission accords the status of 'national' and 'State' party to parties on the basis of either the votes polled or a certain number of seats won in the Lok Sabha/Assembly. The CPI escaped the embarassment by qualifying under the second category. This time too it is the second criteria which will come to the rescue of the CPI.

As per the second category, a party is entitled for recognition if it has one member in the Lok Sabha for evey 25 members of the House or any fraction of that number elected from that State/Union Territory or at least one member to the Legilative Assembly for that State/UT for every 30 members of that Assembly or any fraction of that number.

A party which qualifies under either of the criteria in four States/UT is entitled to be recognized as a national party. In 1996, the Bahujan Samaj Party qualified to be recognised as a national party by fulfilling the criteria. Interestingly, in the current election the all-India vote percentage of the BSP has actually gone down from 4.67 per cent to 4.23 per cent.

6

Last Election of the Millennium

Records, Analysis and Highlights

I. Prime Ministers

(i)*Atal Bihari Vajpayee*—He is the first non-Congres Prime Minister to become the Prime Minister for the third time (1996, 1998 and 1999)

He has a number of victories from different constituencies spread over four states - Balrampur (UP) 1957; Gwalior (Madhya Pradesh) 1971; New Delhi 1977, 1980; Vidisha (Madhya Pradesh) 1991; Lucknow (UP) 1998 and 1999. He won twice from two constituencies simultaneously from different states in 1991 and 1996. Member of Rajya Sabha for 2 terms, Lost elections twice from Balrampur (1967) and Gwalior (1984). Contested as BJS/BJP candidate

(ii) *Chandra Shekhar* (Former Prime Minister)—He has 8 victories to his credit.

(iii) *H.D. Deve Gowda* (Former Prime Minister in 1996)—He lost in Hassan (Karnataka) in 1999.

II. Members of Parliament

(i) *P. M. Sayeed* elected on Congress ticket 10 times from Lakshadweep.

(ii) *Inderjit Gupta* of the CPI elected 10 times from West Bengal : 1960, 1962 Calcutta South West; 1967 Alipur; 1971 Alipur; 1980 and 1984 Basirhat; 1989, 1991 Midnapur; 1996, 1998 and 1999 Jadavpur.

(iii) *Madhav Rao Scindia* and *Chandra Shekhar* have won 8 times.

(iv) MPs in 1999 from two constituencies.

(a) *Mrs. Sonia Gandhi* Bellary (Karnataka), Amethi (UP)

(b) *Mulayam Singh Yadav* Sambhal (UP)

III. Notable Winners and Losers

(i) G. Puttaswamy Gowda (Congress) defeated former Prime Minister H.D. Deve Gowda (JD-S) from Hassan constituency in Karnataka, with a margin of 1,41,757 votes.

(ii) I.D. Swami (BJP) defeated former Haryana Chief Minister Bhajan Lal (Congress), who was defeated for the first time in his career, from Karnal with a margin of 1,47,854 votes.

(iii) Vijay Kumar Malhotra (BJP) defeated former Union Finance Minister Manmohan Singh (Congress) from South Delhi.

(iv) P. Chidambaram former Finance Minister lost from Sivaganga in Tamil Nadu

(v) Atal Bihari Vajpayee (BJP) defeated Karan Singh (Congress) former Union Minister from Lucknow with a margin of more than one lakh and twenty three thousand votes.

(vi) L.K. Advani (BJP) defated T.N. Seshan (Congress) former Chief Election Commissioner, from Gandhinagar (Gujarat) with a margin of about one lakh and eighty nine thousand votes.

(vii) Vadnal Rajan (BJP rebel) defeated Karnataka Chief Minister J.H. Patel from Chennagiri Assembly seat (Karnataka). Patel finished third.

(viii) N. Bhaskara Rao, former Chief Minister Andhra lost to B. Dattareya of BJP from Secunderabad with a margin of about one lakh votes.

IV. Families

(a) **Father and Son** : Congress leader from Kerala, K. Karunakaran, won from Mukundapuram in the Lok Sabha while his son K. Muralidharan (Cong) has been elected from Kozhikode. Karunakaran defeated E.M. Sreedharan, son of E.M.S. Nambudiripad, Marxist stalwart.

In Karnataka, H.D. Deve Gowda (JD-S) lost in Hassan while his son H.D. Revenna came to grief in Holenarsipur. Another son, H.D. Kumaraswamy, lost both Lok Sabha (Kanakapura) and Assembly (Santhur) elections.

(b) **Father and Daughter** : Mebhooba Mufti of the J&K People's Democratic Party (PDP) lost to Umer Abdulla (National Conference) in Srinagar while her father Mufti Mohammed Sayeed (PDP) was defeated by Ali Mohommed Naik (National Conference) in Anantnag.

(c) **Sons** : In Rajasthan, Jagat Singh (Cong), son of former Union Minister Natwar Singh, lost to Vishwendra Singh (BJP) in Bharatpur while Manvendra Singh (BJP), son of External Affairs Minister Jaswant Singh, lost to Sona Ram (Cong) in Barmer. In Punjab, Akali Dal's Sukhbir Singh Badal, son of Chief Minister Parkash Singh Badal, lost in Faridkot. In Haryana, Ajay Chautala, son of Chief Minister Om Prakash Chautala, defeated Dharamvir (Cong) in Bhiwani.

(d) **Wives** : Jayanti Patnaik, wife of former chief minister J.B. Patnaik, lost to former IGP Anadi Charan Sahu (BJP) in Berhampur. But Hemavati Gomang (Cong), wife of Orissa Chief Minister Giridhar Gomang, won in Koraput against Jayaram Pangi (BJD) by 2.7 lakh votes.

(e) **Brother** : In a high-profile contest in Madhya Pradesh, Chief Minister Digvijay Singh's brother Laxman Singh (Cong) defeated TV star Nitish Bharadwaj (BJP) in Rajgarh.

V. War and Votes

Sudha Yadav (BJP) wife of BSF Deputy Commandant Sukhbir Singh Yadav who died defending Kargil, defeated Rao Inderjit Singh (Congress) by 2.03 lakhs votes from Mahendargarh (Haryana).

VI. Sportsmen

(i) Rashid Alvi (BSP) defeated Chetan Chauhan in Amroh (UP).

(ii) Kirti Azad (BJP) defeated Md Alo Ashraf Fatmia of RJD in Darbhanga (Bihar).

VII. Stars

Among the stars who won are

(i) Vinod Khanna (BJP) in Gurdaspur, Punjab;

(ii) Sunil Dutt (Cong) in Mumbai North-West, Maharashtra;

(iii) Raj Babbar (SP) in Agra, UP;
(vi) Ambareesh (Cong) in Mandya, Karnataka;
(v) Shashikumar (JD-U) in Chitradurga, Andhra Pradesh; and
(vi) Krishnam Raju (TDP) in Narsapur, Andhra Pradesh.

Those who lost include S. Chandrashekhar (JD-U) in Chitradurga-Murali Marxist backed independent in Alappuzha, Kerala, Biju Phukan (AGP) in Dibrugarh, Assam, Mansur Ali Khan PT in Periyakulam, Tamil Nadu - Mahesh Kanodia (BJP) in Patna, Gujarat.

Successful Women Candidates (1999)

Table 6.1 : Partywise Number

Party	No. of Successful candidates
BJP	15
Congress	15
Left Parties	04
SP	03
TDP	03
Trinamul Congress	02
Others	05
Total	47

Seats and Votes

The Congress, despite having won less number of seats than the BJP, secured higher percentage of votes than the latter in the just concluded Lok Sabha elections. In terms of percentage of votes polled on the seats contested, the BJP leads the table despite contesting lesser number of seats than the Congress.

Releasing statistical data relating to these elections at a Press conference, the Deputy Election Commissioner Subas Pani said that the Congress with 28.42 per cent secured at the national level, was ahead of the BJP whose tally stood at 23.07 per cent. However, the BJP had contested a lesser number of seats (339) than the Congress (453).

The BJP, in turn, showed a better performance in terms of votes secured in the constituencies where it had fielded its candidates. Its share stood at 39.67 per cent as against 35.40 of the CPI-M. The Congress came third with 33.99 per cent.

The election witnessed a spate of multi-cornered contests despite remedial measures taken by the EC in the recent past to restrict the number of candidates. Rajasthan had the privilege of witnessing the solitary straight contest in the country, whereas UP topped the list of states with the highest number of candidates (32) contesting elections from one of its seats. While 29 constituencies witnessed a triangular contest, 44 others had quadrangular line-up.

Out of the remaining constituencies, 72 saw five candidates each pitted against one another while 179 constituencies had six to eight candidates in the fray. However, there were more than 10 candidates trying their luck in 142 constituencies while the remaining 92 had 9 to 10 nominees.

Notwithstanding the clamour of the political parties for 33 per cent reservation for women, the number of women candidates contesting the Lok Sabha elections stood at an abysmally low 277 out of which only 47 emerged victorious.

The Congress had fielded the maximum number of women (50) and was followed by the BJP (25). The Samajwadi Party came next, having fielded 12 candidates.

While both the Congress and the BJP have won 15 such seats each, the Left parties bagged four seats. The Samajwadi party and the Telugu Desam Party's tally stood at three each while Trinamul Congress would have two MPs in the new House.

The Lakshadweep constituency registered the highest number of voters having cast their votes while Srinagar recorded the lowest turnout with a count of barely 11.93 per cent.

The four other constituencies with more than 80 per cent voter turnout include Tumluk, Bankura, Contai and Arambagh, all in West Bengal. Other seats with low turnout were Anantnag with 14.34 per cent turnout and Baramullah, 27.79 per cent.

[Courtsey - *Hindustan Times*]

Table 6.2 : Statewise Party Performance in Lok Sabha Elections - 1999

Party	Contested	Won	Success Percentage
1	2	3	4
Andhra Pradesh : 42 Seats			
All India Majlis-e-ithehad-ol-muslimen	1	1	100
Telugu Desam Party	34	29	85.29
Indian National Congress	42	5	11.9
Bharatiya Janata Party	9	7	77.9
Arunachal Pradesh : 2 Seats			
Indian National Congress	2	2	100
Assam : 14 seats			
Communist Party of India (Marxist-Leninist) Liberat	3	1	33.3
Indian National Congress	14	10	64.28
Independents	11	1	9.09
Bharatiya Janata Party	11	2	18.18
Bihar : 54 seats			
Rashtriya Janata Dal	36	7	19.44
Janata Dal (United)	23	18	73.91
Indian National Congress	16	4	18.75
Bharatiya Janata Party	29	23	79.31
CPM	-	1	
Ind.	-	1	
Goa :2 seats			
Bharatiya Janata Party	2	2	100
Gujarat : 26 seats			
Indian National Congress	26	6	23.07
Bharatiya Janata Party	26	20	76.92
Haryana : 10 seats			
Indian National Lok Dal	5	5	100
Bharatiya Janata Party	5	5	100
Himachal Pradesh : 4 seats			
Himachal Vikas Congress	1	1	100
Bharatiya Janata Party	3	3	100
Jammu and Kashmir : 6 seats			
National Conference	6	4	66.66
Bharatiya Janata Party	6	2	33.33

1	2	3	4
Kerala : 20 seats			
Communist Party of India (Marxist)	12	8	66.66
Kerala Congress (M)	1	1	100.00
Kerala Congress	1	1	100.00
Indian National Congress	17	8	47.05
Muslim League	2	2	100.00
Karnataka : 28 seats			
Janata Dal (United)	10	3	30.00
Indian National Congress	28	18	64.28
Bharatiya Janata Party	19	7	36.84
Madhya Pradesh : 40 seats			
Indian National Congress	40	11	27.5
Bharatiya Janata Party	40	29	72.5
Maharashtra : 48 seats			
Peasants and Workers Party of India	2	1	50.00
Nationalist Congress Party	38	6	15.78
Shiv Sena	22	15	68.18
Bharipa Bahujan Mahasangh	4	1	25.00
Janta Dal (Secular)	2	1	50.00
Indian National Congress	42	10	23.80
Bharatiya Janata Party	27	13	48.1
Republican Party of India (a)	1	1	100.00
Manipur : 2 seats			
Manipur State Congress Party	1	1	100
Nationalist Congress Party	NA	1	NA
Meghalaya			
Nationalist Congress Party	1	1	100
Indian National Congress	2	1	50
Mizoram : 1 seat			
Mizo National Front	1	1	100
Nagaland : 1 seat			
Indian National Congress	1	1	100
Orissa : 21 seats			
Biju Janata Dal	12	10	83.33
Indian National Congress	20	2	10
Bharatiya Janata Party	9	9	100
Punjab : 13 seats			
Shiromani Akali Dal (Simranjit Singh Mann)	1	1	100
Shiromani Akali Dal	9	2	22.22
Indian National Congress	11	8	72.72
Communist Party of India	1	1	100
Bharatiya Janata Party	3	1	33.3
Rajasthan : 25 seats			
Indian National Congress	25	9	36
Bharatiya Janata Party	25	16	64
Sikkim : 1 seat			
Sikkin Democratic Front	1	1	100

1	2	3	4
Tamil Nadu : 39 seats			
Communist Part of India (Marxist)	2	1	50.00
Pattali Makkal Katchi	7	5	71.42
Marumalarchi Dravida Munnetra Kazhagam	5	4	80.00
Indian National Congress	11	2	18.18
Dravida Munnetra Kazhagam	19	12	63.15
Bharatiya Janata Party	6	4	66.6
All India Anna Dravida Munnetra Kazhagam	24	10	41.66
M.G.R. Anna D.M. Kazhagam	1	1	100.00
Tripura : 2 seats			
Communist Party of India (Marxist)	2	2	100
Uttar Pradesh : 85 seats			
RLD	7	2	28.57
Samajwadi Party	85	26	30.58
Bahujan Samaj Party	80	14	17.5
Indian National Congress	76	10	13.15
Independents	1	1	100
Bharatiya Janata Party	77	29	37.66
Samajwadi Janta Party (Rashtriya)	1	1	100
Loktantrik Congress Party	2	2	100
West Bengal : 42 seats			
Communist Party of India (Marxist)	32	21	65.62
All India Forward Bloc	3	2	66.66
Revolutionary Socialist Party	4	3	75
All India Trinamool Congress (AITC)	28	8	28.57
Indian National Congress	41	3	7.31
Bharatiya Janata Party	13	2	15.38
Communist Party of India	3	3	100
Union Territories			
Andaman & Nicobar : 1 seat			
Bharatiya Janata Party	1	1	100
Chandigarh			
Indian National Congress	1	1	100
Daman & Dau : 1 seat			
Indian National Congress	1	1	100
Dadra & Nagar Haveli : 1 seat			
Independent	1	1	100
Delhi : 7 seats			
Bharatiya Janata Party	7	7	100
Lakshadweep			
Indian National Congress	1	1	100
Pondicherry : 1 seat			
Indian National Congress	1	1	100

Table 6.3 : Performance of Political Parties in Reserved Constituencies (13th Lok Sabha)

S.No.	Party	Seats won	Percentage of seats won
1.	BJP	48	40%
2.	Congress	18	15%
3.	CPI (M)	7	5.8%
4.	TDP	6	5%
5.	JD (U)	6	5%
6.	SP	5	4.1%
7.	BSP	4	3.3%
8.	BJD	3	2.5%
9.	RSP	3	2.5%
10.	DMK	2	1.7%
11.	AIADMK	2	1.7%
	Others	16	13.3%
	Total	**120**	

Total reserved seats for SC & ST = 120

Table 6.4 : Party-wise State-wise performance in 13th Lok Sabha

	State/Territory	Reserved Seats (SC + ST)	Seats won by BJP	Seats won by Congress	Seats won by others
1.	Andhra Pradesh	8	1	1	TDP = 6
2.	Arunachal Pradesh	-	-	-	
3.	Assam	3		2	Others = 1
4.	Bihar	13	8		JD (U) = 4, RJD = 1
5.	Goa	-	-	-	-
6.	Gujarat	6	6	-	-
7.	Haryana	2	1	0	Others = 1
8.	Himachal Pradesh	1	-	-	Others = 1
9.	Jammu & Kashmir	-	-		
10.	Karnataka	4	1	1	JD (U) = 2
11.	Kerala	2	-	1	CPI (M) = 1
12.	Madhya Pradesh	15	12	3	
13.	Maharashtra	7	2	2	Others = 3
14.	Manipur	1	-	-	Othres = 1
15.	Meghalaya	-	-		
16.	Mizoram	-	-	-	
17.	Nagaland	1	-	1	
18.	Orissa	8	4	1	BJD = 3
19.	Punjab	3	-	2	CPI = 1
20.	Rajasthan	7	4	3	
21.	Sikkim	-	-	-	
22.	Tamil Nadu	7	-	-	DMK = 3, AIADMK = 2 PMK= 1, MDMK = 1
23.	Tripura	1	-	-	CPI (M) = 1
24.	West Bengal	10	-	-	CPM = 5,. RSP = 3, Others = 2
25.	Uttar Pradesh	18	8		SP = 5, BSP = 4, Others = 1
26.	Andaman & Nicobar Island	-	-	-	
27.	Chandigarh	-	-	-	
28.	Dadra & Nagar Haveli	1	-	-	Othjers = 1
29.	Daman & Diu	-	-	-	
30.	Delhi	1	1	-	
31.	Lakshadweep	1	-	1	
32.	Pondicherry	-	-	-	

Table 6.5 : Regionwise Analysis of Party Performance

	BJP			Congress			CPI(M)			CPI			JD			Shiv Sena			S.P.			BSP			DMK			AIADMK			TDP		
Region	98	99	G/L	98	99	G/L	98	99	G/L	98	99	G/L	98	99	G/L	98	99	-	98	99	G/L	98	99	G/L	98	99	G/P	98	99	G/L	98	99	G/L
North	83	58	-25	6	14	+8	-	-	-	-	-	-	-	-	-	-	-	-	20	26	+6	4	14	+10	-	-	-	-	-	-	-	-	-
South	20	18	-2	41	33	-8	6	9	+3	5	-	-5	-	-	-	-	-	-	-	-	-	-	-	-	6	12	+6	18	10	-8	12	29	+17
East	29	36	+7	24	21	-3	26	23	-3	4	3	-1	-	-	-	-	-	-	-	-	-	-	-	-	-	-	-	-	-	-	-	-	-
West	60	80	+20	78	36	-34	6	9	+3	-	-	-	-	-	-	6	15	+9	-	-	-	-	-	-	-	-	-	-	-	-	-	-	-

Table 6.6 : Analysis of Party Position in the North (1998 and 1999)

State/Union Territory	BJP			Congress			SP			BSP		
	1998	1999	Gain/Loss	1998	1999	Gain/Loss	1998	1999	Gain/Loss	1998	1999	Gain/Loss
Chandigarh	1	-	-1	-	1	+1	-					
Delhi	6	7	+1	1	-	-1	-					
Haryana	1	5	+4	3	-	-3	-					
Himachal Pradesh	3	4	+1	1	-	-1	-					
Jammu& Kashmir	2	2	-	1	-	-1	-					
Punjab	3	1	-2	-	8	+8						
Uttar Pradesh	57	29	-28	-	5	+5	20	26	+6	4	14	+10
Total	**83**	**58**	**-25**	**6**	**14**	**+8**	**20**	**26**	**+6**	**4**	**14**	**+10**

Table 6.7 : Analysis of Party Performance in the South Region (1998 and 1999)

State/ Union Territory	BJP			Congress			CPI(M)			CPI			JD			AIADMK			DMK			TDP		
	1998	1999	G/L	1998	1999	G/L	1998	1999	G/L	1998	1999	G/L	1998	1999	G/L	1998	1999	G/L	1998	1999	G/L	1998	1999	G/L
Andhra	4	7	+3	22	5	-17	-	-	-	2	-	-2	-	-	-	-	-	-	-	-	-	12	29	+17
Karnataka	13	7	-6	9	18	+9	-	-	-	-	-	-	3	3	-	-	-	-	-	-	-	-	-	-
Tamil Nadu	3	4	+1	-	2	+2	-	1	+1	1	-	-1	-	-	-	19	10	-8	5	12	+7	-	-	-
Lakshadweep	-	1	-	-1	-	-	-	-	-	-	-	-	-	-	-	-	-	-	-	-	-	-	-	-
A&N.Islands	-	1	-	-1	-	-	-	-	-	-	-	-	-	-	-	-	-	-	-	-	-	-	-	-
Pondicherry	-	-	-	-	-	-	-	-	-	-	-	-	-	-	-	-	-	-	1	-	-1	-	-	-
Kerala	-	-	-	8	8	-	6	8	+2	2	-	-2	-	-	-	-	-	-	-	-	-	-	-	-
Total	**20**	**18**	**-2**	**41**	**33**	**-8**	**6**	**9**	**+3**	**5**	**-**	**-5**	**3**	**3**	**-**	**18**	**10**	**-8**	**6**	**12**	**+6**	**12**	**29**	**+17**

G/L : Gain & Losses

Table 6.8 : Analysis of Party Performance in the Eastern Region (1998 and 1999)

State/ Union Territory	BJP			Congress			CPI(M)			CPI			RJD			AGP		
	1998	1999	G/L	1998	1999	G/L	1998	1999	G/L	1998	1999	G/L	1998	1999	G/L	1998	1999	G/L
Assam	1	2	+1	10	10	-	-	-	-	-	-	-	-	-	-	5	-	5
Arunachal Pradesh	-	-	-	-	2	+2	-	-	-	-	-	-	-	-	-	-	-	-
Manipur	-	-	-	-	-	-	-	-	-	1	-	-1	-	-	-	-	-	-
Meghalaya	-	-	-	2	1	-1	-	-	-	-	-	-	-	-	-	-	-	-
Mizoram	-	-	-	-	-	-	-	-	-	-	-	-	-	-	-	-	-	-
Nagaland	-	-	-	1	1	-	-	-	-	-	-	-	-	-	-	-	-	-
Tripura	-	-	-	-	-	-	2	2	-	-	-	-	-	-	-	-	-	-
Sikkim	-	-	-	-	-	-	-	-	-	-	-	-	-	-	-	-	-	-
West Bengal	1	2	+1	1	3	+2	24	21	-3	3	3	-	-	-	-	-	-	-
Orissa	7	9	+2	5	2	-3	-	-	-	-	-	-	-	-	-	-	-	-
Bihar	20	23	+3	5	3	-2	-	-	-	-	-	-	17	7	-10	-	-	-
Total	**29**	**36**	**+7**	**24**	**22**	**-2**	**26**	**23**	**-3**	**4**	**3**	**-1**	**17**	**7**	**-10**	**5**	**-**	**5**

Table 6.9 : Performance of Major Political Parties in 1998 and 1999 Lok Sabha Polls

Western Region

State/Union	BJP			Congress			CPI(M)			JD			CPI			Shiv Sena			NCP		
Territory	1998	1999	G/L	1998	1999	G/L	1998	1999	G/L	1998	1999	G/L	1998	1999	G/L	1998	1999	G/L	1998	1999	G/L
Goa	-	2	+2	2	-	-2	-	-	-	-	-	-	-	-	-	-	-	-	-	-	-
Daman& Diu	1	1	-	-	-	-	-	-	-	-	-	-	-	-	-	-	-	-	-	-	-
Gujarat	19	20	+1	7	6	-1	-	-	-	-	-	-	-	-	-	-	-	-	-	-	-
Madhya Pradesh	30	29	-1	10	11	+1	-	-	-	-	-	-	-	-	-	-	-	-	-	-	-
Maharashtra	4	13	+9	33	10	-23	-	-	-	-	-	-	-	-	-	6	15	+9	-	6	+6
Dadva& Nagar Havali	1	-	-1	-	-	-	-	-	-	-	-	-	-	-	-	-	-	-	-	-	-
Rajasthan	5	16	+11	18	9	-9	-	-	-	-	-	-	-	-	-	-	-	-	-	-	-
Total	**60**	**81**	**+21**	**70**	**36**	**-34**	-	-	-	-	-	-	-	-	-	**6**	**15**	**+9**	-	**6**	**+6**

Table 6.10 : Progressive Performance of Political Parties at State Level

Party	1991	1996	1998	1999	Gain / Losses in 1999 as compared with 1998
1	2	3	4	4	6
Andhra Pradesh (42)					
Congress	25	22	22	5	- 17
BJP	-	-	4	7	+ 3
CPI	1	2	2	-	- 2
CPI (M)	1	1	-	-	-
JD	-	-	1	-	-
TDP	13	16	12	29	+ 17
Independents and others	1	1	1	-	- 1
MIM			1	1	
Arunachal Pradesh (2)					
Arunachal Congress	Formed in 1998		2	Nil	- 2
Congress	2	-	-	2	+ 2
Independent and others	-	2	-	-	-
Assam (14)					
BJP	2	1	1	2	+1
Congress	8	5	10	10	No change
CPI	-	-	-		
CPI (M)	-	-	-		
JD	1	1			
AGP	1	5	-		
Congress (S)	-	-	1		- 1
PTCA	-	-	1		- 1
Independents and others	2	2	1	1	
CPI (MLL)	-	-	-	1	+1
One election due on Oct. 28, 1999					
Bihar (54)					
BJP	5	18	20	23	+3
Congress	1	2	6	03	-3
CPI	8	3	-		
CPI(M)	1	1	-		
JD+JNP	31	23	1	17 (JDU)	+16
INC(U)	-	6	10 (Samata)		
Independants and others	8	1	0		
RJD	-	-	17	7	-10
	54	54	54	54	
Delhi (7)					
BJP	5	5	6	7	+1
Congress	2	2	1	-	-1

1	2	3	4	4	6
Goa (2)					
INC	2	-	2	-	-2
MGP	-	1	-	-	-
UGDP	-	1	-	-	-
BJP	-	-	-	2	+2
Gujarat (26)					
BJP	20	16	19	29	+1
Congress	5	10	7	6	-1
JD (G)	1	-	-		
Haryana (10)					
BJP	-	4	1	5	+4
Congress	9	2	3	-	-3
INLD				5	+5
HVP	1	3	1	-	-1
Independents and others	-	1			
Himachal Pradesh (4)					
BJP	2	-	2	3	+1
HVC	-	-	-	1	+1
Congress	2	4	1	-	-1
Note: (In 1998 election was not held in 1998)					
Jammu & Kashmir (6)					
BJP	Election	1	1	2	+1
NC	not	-	2	4	+2
Congress	held	4	1	-	-1
JD	-	1	-	-	
(Election Results for 2 seats not declared in 1998 election)					
Karnataka (28)					
Congress		9		18	+9
BJP		13		7	-6
JD(U)		Did not exist		3	-
Janata Dal		3		-	-3
Lok Shakti		3		with JDU	
Kerala (20)					
Congress	13	7	8	8	-
CPI(M)	3	5	6	8	+2
MUL	2	2	2	2	-
KEC-M	0	0	1	1	-
KEC	-	-	-	1	+1
CPI	-	2	2	-	-2
JD/JP	-	1	-	-	
KCM	-	1	-	-	
RSP	1	1	1	-	-1
Independent	1	1	-	-	

1	2	3	4	4	6
Madhya Pradesh (40)					
BJP	17	27	30	29	-1
Congress	27	8	10	11	+1
BSP	1	2	-	-	-
Cong.(T)	-	1	-	-	No longer exists
MPVP	-	2	-	-	(No longer exists)
Maharashtra (48)					
Shiv Sena	4	15	6	15	+9
BJP	5	18	4	13	+9
Congress	38	15	33	10	-23
NCP	Did not exist			6	+6
Independents & others	4	-	5	4	-1
			(PWP 1 RPI 4)		
CPI	1	-	-	-	
Manipur (2)					
MSCP			1	1	-
Congress	1	2	-		
CPI	-	-	1	Vacant=1	
Meghalaya (2)					
Congress		2		1	-1
NCP		Did not Exist		1	+1
Mizoram (1)					
Congress	1	1	-	-	-
Independent & others	-	-	1 (UPF)	1	-
Nagaland (1)					
Congress			1	1	-
Orissa (21)					
BJD	-	-	9	10	+1
BJP	-	-	7	9	+2
Congress	13	16	5	2	-3
CPI(M)	1	1	-	-	
JD	6	4	-		
CPI	1	-	-	-	
Punjab (13)					
Congress	12	2	-	8	+8
SAD	0	8	8	2	-6
BJP	-	-	3	1	-2
Others				2	-
BSP	1	3	0	-	-

* Elections were held in 1992. Almost all Akali groups boycotted elections.

1	2	3	4	4	6
Rajasthan (25)					
BJP	11	12	5	16	+11
Congress	13	12	18	9	-9
Independent & others	-	1	2	-	-2

1	2	3	4	4	6
Sikkim (1)					
SDF		1	1	1	-
Independent & others	1	-	-	-	
Tamil Nadu (39)					
DMK		17	5	12	+7
AIADMK	11	-	18	11	-7
PMK		-	4	5	+1
BJP	-	-	3	4	+1
MDMK		-	3	3	-
Congress	28	-	-	2	+2
Others		-	-	2	+2
CPI	-	2	1	-	-1
TMC	-	20	3	-	-3
JP	-	-	1	-	-1
Independent	-	-	1	-	-1
Uttar Pradesh (85)					
BJP	52	52	57	29	-28
SP		16	20	26	+6
BSP	01	06	04	14	+10
Congress	5	5	-	10	+10
Independent & others	-	4	2	6	+4
CPI	1	-			
JD	22	2	-	-	
JP/JD(S)	4	-	-		
Samata	-	-	2	-	-2
West Bengal (42)					
CPM			24	21	-3
TC			7	8	+1
Congress			1	3	+2
BJP			1	2	+1
CPI			3	3	-
AIFB			2	2	-
RSP			4	3	-1
Union Territories					
Chandigarh					
BJP		1		-	-1
Congress		-		1	+1
Dadar Nagar Haveli					
Independent				1	+1
BJP		1			-1
Daman & Diu					
BJP		1		-	-1
Congress				1	+1
Lakshadweep					
Congress		1		1	
Pondicherry					
Congress				1	+1
DMK		1			-1
A & N. Islands					
BJP				1	+1
Congress		1		-	-1

Congress in the 13th Lok Sabha

While the Congress continues to be the main opposition in the Lok Sabha, its strength has been significantly reduced. Apart from it, the composition of Congress MPs has also undergone many changes.

Several stalwarts who made effective parliamentarians and could be depended upon to take on the Treasury benches have fallen by the wayside.

The most obvious change in the Congress parliamentary party (CPP) is, of course, the leader.

Mr Sharad Pawar, who led the Congress party as leader of Opposition in the 12th Lok Sabha, but revolted against the party leadership on election-eve, will no longer be occupying his former place in the House. He retains his membership of the Lok Sabha but will change seats.

Several other Congress leaders who occupied the front benches will not be present. P. Shiv Shankar, deputy leader who was among the leading speakers of his party, has lost the election.

Balram Jakhar who could be depended upon by the party to participate in debates on agriculture, has also failed to get re-elected. K. Natwar Singh had opted out of this election and so will not be a member of the new Lok Sabha. Vijay Bhaskar Reddy, Bhajan Lal and Motilal Vora who are among other senior leaders will be conspicuous by their absence from the Congress benches.

Party spokesperson Ajit Jogi, chief whip P.J. Kurien and P.C. Chacko, who relished a good "fight" and were at the forefront of any battle in the House, are among those who failed to make the grade. Prithviraj Chavan, also figures in the list of Congress losers. The party was banking upon its senior leader Manmohan Singh to pin down the Treasury benches, especially on economic matters, but his defeat means a loss of yet another capable speaker for the Congress.

This loss will be made up by the return of senior leaders like Narain Dutt Tiwari and Jitendra Prasad along with another veteran P. M. Sayeed and former ministers Rajesh Pilot and Madhavrao Scindia. They will need to marshall all their talent in this Lok Sabha if they are to make their presence felt.

BJP : The Growth Curve

In 1951 Shyam Prasad Mookerjee resigned from Jawahar Lal Nehru's cabinet and formed the Jana Sangh. The JanaSangh is the political ancestor of what is now known as the Bharatiya Janata Party.

In the first elections to the Lok Sabha held in 1952, the Jana Sangh polled just 3.1% votes, its performance being limited to Uttar Pradesh, Madhya Pradesh and West Bengal. In the next five years the party gained a hold in Maharashtra and secured 5.9% votes in the Lok Sabha elections of 1957. The party continued to extend its hold in U.P. and M.P., the 1962 score having risen to 6.4% of the votes.

In 1967 the Jana Sangh under Balraj Madhok secured the highest non-congress votes (9.5%). The year 1971 however registered a decline and the % vote slided down to 7.4%. (The JS merged with Janata Party in the post-emergency phase. The JS was revived as BJP for the 1984 elections). The worst came in 1984 when the presence in Lok Sabha was reduced to just 2 members. The revival came in 1989 under L.K. Advani The BJP bagged 86 seats in the Lok Sabha the score further went up to 120 in 1991 under the Presidentship of M.M. Joshi. The vote percentage also increased to 20.1%

Since then the BJP has never looked back. The 1996 elections gave the party 161 seats in the Lok Sabha which further increased to 182 in 1998. The 25.16% vote share was a clear indication that the party was no longer just a party with a narrow urban base limited to the Hindi heartland. It has become a major national party.

While in 1984, the party's presence had been restricted to Madhya Pradesh, Rajasthan, Gujarat and Delhi, the 1998 BJP influence had extended to twenty States. It captured 57 seats from Uttar Pradesh, 30 from Madhya Pradesh and 20 from Bihar. In Delhi it captured 6 out of the seven seats. With just 1 seat, it had opened its account in States of Assam, Haryana, West Bengal, Chandigarh, Dadra and Nagar Haveli and Daman and Diu.

The 1998 elections to the Lok Sabha had been contested by the BJP in collaboration with its regional allies. The party's base had expanded both in the rural as well as the urban sector. Kerala and the North East are territories where the party has yet to establish its credentials in terms of Lok Sabha seats.

In 1986, the BJP was only the third largest party. In 1991 it was the largest opposition party. In 1996 it was still the single largest party but could not muster enough allies to form the government. It occupied the Treasury Benches for 13 days but resigned as it could not secure a majority in the Confidence Vote.

1998 was different. The BJP formed the government with a number of allies. (BJP-led government was a 13 party alliance). The government however lost the vote of confidence in April 1999 after one of the allies, the AIADMK withdrew support.

The BJP base is still dominated by forward and middle castes. It has been gaining increasing popularity among the OBCs and even the SCs. It is becoming more acceptable to the Muslims but only in select parts.

The BJP was perceived as a force in over 300 seats. In the 1998 elections it had lost by a margin below 5% in 56 seats and was runner-up in 122 constituencies. Its standing among women as well as among the educated voters has shown a consistent increase.

Table 6.11 : 1999 Lok Sabha Election at a Glance

Bhartiya Janata Party (BJP)	182
Telugu Desam Party	29
Janata Dal (United)	21
Shivsena	15
Dravida Munnetra Kazhagam	12
Biju Janata Dal	10
All India Trinamool Congress	8
Indian National Lok Dal	5
Pattali Makkal Katchi	5
Marumalarchi Dravida Munnetra Kazhagam	4
Shiromani Akali Dal	2
Himachal Vikas Congress	1
Loktantrik Congress	2
M.G.R. Anna D.M. Kazhagam	1
Manipur State Congress Party	1
NDA + TDP	**298**
Indian National Congress	114
All India Anna Dravida Munnetra Kazhagam	10
Rashtriya Janata Dal	7
Muslim League	2
Rashtriya Lok Dal	2

Kerala Congress (M)	1
INC + Allies	**136**
Communist Party of India (MARXIST)	33
Communist Party of India	4
Revolutionary Socialist Party	3
All India Forward Bloc	2
Kerala Congress	1
Left Parties	**43**
Samajwadi Party	26
Bahujan Samaj Party	14
Nationalist Congress Party	8
Jammu and Kashmir National Conference	4
Other Party	1
Independent	5
All India Majlis-e-Ittehadul Muslimeen	1
Samjwadi Janata Party (Rashtriya)	1
Sikkim Democratic Front	1
Peasants and Workers Party of India	1
Janata Dal (Secular)	1
SAD (M)	1
BBM	1
Communist Party of India (Marxist-Lenninist) (Liber)	1
Others	**66**
Total	**543**

Table 6.12 : Party Position in the 13th Lok Sabha as compared with the 12th Lok Sabha

S.No.	Party	Seats 1998	Seats 1999	Gain and Loss in 1999 as compared with 1998
1	2	3	4	5
1.	BJP	182	182	no change
2.	INC	140	114	- 26
3.	CPM	32	33	+1
4.	Samajwadi Party	20	26	+ 6
5.	AIAMDK	18	10	-8
6	RJD	17	7	-10
7.	Samata	12	with JDU	
8.	TDP	12	29	+ 17
9.	BJD	9	19	+ 1
10.	JD (U)]	6	20	
11.	JD (S)]		(JD + Lok Shakti)	
12.	CPI	9	4	- 5
13.	SAD	8	2 + 1 (Mann)	- 6
14.	TC	7	8	+ 1
15.	DMK	6	12	+ 6
16.	Shiv Sena	6	15	+ 9
17.	RSP	5	3	- 2
18.	BSP	5	14	+ 5
19.	HLD (R)	4	Does not exist	
20.	RPI	4	-	- 4
21.	PMK	4	5	+ 1
22.	Lok Shakti	3	with JDU	
23.	MDMK	3	4	+ 1

1	2	3	4	5
24.	TMC	3	-	- 3
25.	AIFB	2	2	No change
26.	IUML	2	2	No change
27.	Arunachal Congress	2	-	- 2
28.	National Conference	3	4	+ 1
29.	HVP	1	-	- 1
30.	ASDC	1	-	- 1
31.	AICC (S)	1	-	- 1
32.	KC (M)	1	1	No change
33.	SDF	1	1	No change
34.	MIM	1	1	No change
35.	PWP	1	1	-
36.	UMFA	1	-	- 1
37.	MSC	1	1	No change
38.	TR (C)	1	-	- 1
39.	JP	1	-	- 1
40.	SJP	1	1	-
41.	RSJP	1	1	-
42.	UPF	1	-	- 1
43.	MPVP	2	-	Does not exist
44.	Independents	4	4	No change
45.	INLD	-	5	+ 5
46.	Lok Tantrik Contress	-	2	+ 2
47.	MGDK	1	1	No change
48.	MSCP	-	1	+ 1
49.	RLD	-	2	+ 2
50.	CPI (MLL)	-	1	+ 1
51.	KEC	-	1	+ 1
52.	NCP	-	8	+ 7

Table 6.13 : Success Rate of Political Parties - 1999

Party 1	Contested 2	Won 3
Bharatiya Janata Party	339	182
Indian National Congress	453	114
Communist Party of India (Marxist)	72	33
Janata Dal (United)	60	21
Bahujan Samaj Party	225	14
Communist Party of India	54	4
Janata Dal (Secular)	96	1
Telugu Desam	34	29
Samajwadi Party	151	26
Shivsena	63	15
Dravida Munnetra Kazhagam	19	12
All India Anna Dravida Munnetra Kazhagam	29	10
Biju Janata Dal	12	10
All India Trinamool Congress	29	8
Natonalist Congress Party	132	7
Rashtriya Janata Dal	61	8
Pattali Makkal Katchi	8	5
Indian National Lok Dal	5	5
Jammu & Kashmir National conference	6	4
Marunmalarchi Dravida Munnetra Kazhagam	5	4
Revolutionary Socilaist Party	5	3

1	2	3
All India Forward Bloc	15	2
Muslim League Kerala State Committee	12	2
Shiromani Akali Dal	9	2
Samajwadi Janata Party (Rashtriya)	14	1
Manipur State Congress Party	2	1
Himachal Vikas Congress	1	1
Kerala Congress	1	1
Kerala Congress (M)	1	1
Sikkim Democratic Front	1	1
Rashtriya Lok Dal	15	2
Akhil Bhartiya Lok Tantrik Congress	4	2
Communist Party of India (Marxist-Lenninist) (Liberation)	56	1
Bharipa Bajujan Mahasangha	4	1
Peasants and Workers Party of India	2	1
All India Majlis-e-Ittehadul Muslimeen	1	1
M.G.R. Anna D.M. Kazhagam	1	1
Shiromani Akali Dal (Simranmjit Singh Mann)	1	1
Independent	1945	6
Total	**3943**	**543**

Formation of New Government (October 16, 1999)

On October 16, 1999 the seventy member NDA ministry was sworn in with Atal Bihari Vajpayee as the Prime Minister. The following were the Portfolios of new Union Ministers

Prime Minister
Atal Bihari Vajpayee

Cabinet Ministers
1. Mr. L.K. Advani: Home
2. Mr. Ananth Kumar: Culture, Youth Affairs and Sports
3. T.R. Baalu: Environment and Forests
4. Ms. Mamata Banerjee: Railways
5. George Fernandes: Defence
6. Jagmohan: Urban Development
7. Satyanarain Jatiya: Urban Employment and Poverty Alleviation
8. Ram Jethamalani: Law, Justice and Company Affairs
9. Manohar Joshi: Heavy Industries and Public Enterprises
10. Murli Manohar Joshi:Human Resource Development and Science and Technology
11. P.R. Kumaramangalam : Power
12. Pramod Mahajan : Parliamentary Affairs and Water Resources
13. Murasoli Maran : Commerce and Industry
14. Ram Naik : Petroleum and Natural Gas
15. Nitish Kumar : Surface Transport
16. Juel Oram : Tribal
17. Ram Vilas Paswan : Communications
18. Naveen Patnaik : Mines and Minerals
19. Sunderlal Patwa : Rural Development
20. Suresh Prabhu : Chemicals and Fertilizers

21. Kashiram Rana : Textiles
22. Shanta Kumar : Consumer Affairs and Public Distribution
23. Jaswant Singh : External Affairs
24. Yashwant Sinha : Finance
25. Sharad Yadav : Civil Aviation

Ministers of State (Independent charge)

1. Ms Maneka Gandhi : Social Justice and Empowerment
2. Arun Jaitley : Information and Broadcasting
3. M. Kannapan : Non-conventional Energy Sources
4. Dilip Ray : Steel
5. Vasundhara Raje : Small-scale Industries
6. N.T. Shanmugham : Health and Family Welfare
7. Ms. Uma Bharati : Tourism

Ministers of State

1. Ramesh Basi : Chemicals and Fertilizers
2. Bijoya Chakravarty : Water Resources
3. Shriram Chauhan : Parliamentary Affairs
4. Bandaru Dattatreya : Urban Development
5. Jaisingh Rao Patil : HRD
6. Santosh Gangwar : Science and Technology
7. Chaman Lal Gupta :Civil Aviation
8. Vallabhai Kathiriya : Heavy Industries and Public Enterprises
9. Faggan Singh Kulaste : Parliamentary Affairs
10. V. Dhananjay Kumar : Finance
11. Bangaru Laxman : Planning and Programme Implementation
12. Sumitra Mahajan : HRD
13. Subhash Maharia : Rural Development
14. Babulal Marandi : Environment and Forests
15. Jayawanti Mehta : Power
16. Munni Lal : Labour and Employment
17. Omar Farooq Abdullah : Commerce and Industries
18. Ajit Kumar Panja : External Affairs
19. Hiran Pathak : Defence
20. Devendra Pradhan : Surface Transport
21. E. Ponnuswami : Petroleum
22. A. Raja : Rural Development
23. O. Rajagopal : Law, Justice and Company Affairs
24. Raman : Commerce and Industries
25. N.G. Ramachandran : Textiles
26. Vidaya Sagar Rao : Home
27. S.B.P.P.K Satyanarayanan Rao : Agriculture
28. Bachi Singh Rawat : Defence
29. Syed Shahnawaz Hussain : Food Processing
30. Tapan Sikdar : Communication

31. Digvijay Singh : Railways
32. T.H. Chaoba Singh : Culture, Youth Affairs, Sports
33. V. Sreenivasa Prasad : Consumer Affairs and Public Distribution
34. I.D. Swami : Home
35. Ms Rita Verma : Mines and Minerals
36. Balasaheb Vikhe Patil : Finance
37. Hukumdeo Narayan Yadav : Agriculture

(Unallocated portfolios to be looked after by the Prime Minister. Ms. Vasundhara Raje to also assist the Prime Minister in handling the Ministries of Personnel, Public Grievances and Pensions, Department of Energy and Department of Space. Dilip Ray and Santosh Gangwar to also assist the Minister of Parliamentary Affairs.)

[*UNI*]

The cabinet included 8 women, 7 Scheduled Castes and 3 Scheduled Tribes MPs. Bihar was represented by 11 members —the highest followed by Tamil Nadu, Maharashtra and Madhya Pradesh, 8 each. Six Ministers were from Uttar Pradesh. Assam, Manipur, Himachal Pradesh and Kerala each had one Minister. O.P. Rajagopal is a Rajya Sabha Member. He had lost election from Kerala. He is the only exception of a defeated candidate given a ministerial berth.

Notable mission were Ramakrishna Hegde and Sikander Bakht.

Table 6.14 : Party Numbers and Cabinet Berths

Party	M.Ps	Cabinet Ministers	Minister of State
National Conference	4		1
MDMK	4		2
PMK	5		2
TC	8	1	1
BJD	10	1	1
DMK	12	2	1
SS	15	2	1
JD (U)	20	4	2
BJP	182	15	31

TDP (29), INLD (5) and SAD (2) have not joined.

Table 6.15 : State Wise Distribution of Ministries

State	M.Ps (BJP Allies)	Cabinet Ministers	Miniter of State
1	2	3	4
J and K	6		2
Haryana	10		1
Delhi	7	1	
Uttar Pradesh	30	2	4
Bihar	40	5	5
West Bengal	10	1	2
Orissa	19	2	2
Assam and NE	4	2	
A.P.	36	4	
Karnataka	9	1	2
T.N.	25	3	4
Maharashtra	28	5	3

1	2	3	4
Madhya Pradesh	29	2	5
Rajasthan	16	1	2
H.P.	4	1	
Gujarat	20	2	2
Punjab	3	-	-
Others	5		1

Under represented : Uttar Pradesh

Bihar and Maharashtra shared between them a quarter of the Ministerial berths.

Table 6.16 : Age Profile of Ministers

Age Profiles	BJP	Allies
Below 40 years	4	2
40-59	14	6
51-59	11	7
60-65	11	6
66 and above	6	3

Agenda Before the Government *(Text of Prime Minister's Address to the Nation, Oct. 16, 1999)*

Following is the text of the Prime Minister, A.B. Vajpayee's address to the Nation here today :

"My dear countrymen,

"I address you today to perform a very pleasant duty: to thank all of you for your positive and clear mandate to the National Democratic Alliance and its friendly parties in this election.

"The NDA represents the aspriations of every region of our great nation and every section of our vibrant society. The NDA, in fact, reflects the spirit of India in all its diversity. It also mirrors the fundamental unity in this diversity.

"We may have been sent to Parliament under the banners of different parties. But we all have a common commitment: to give India a stable and good Government.

"We are all guided by the lofty principles of secularism, social justice, social harmony and women's empowerment. Ours is a Government wedded to a common ideal: to create a kinder, gentler and more tolerant society, free from all discrimination, fear and insecurity.

"Free and fair elections are the lifeblood of a democracy. It is matter of great pride for all of us that our Nation has once again demonstrated its unshakable commitment to democracy.

"Our Nation continues to march on the path she adopted when she became a Republic in 1950. With the successful completion of the last election of this century, India stands taller in the eyes of all democracy-loving people of the world.

"It has been a long campaign. A lot of heat and dust were generated during this general election. But now that the election is over, we should put the acrimony and bitterness of the last couple of months behind us. And get down to the task of nation-building. There is not a moment to lose.

"The Opposition's role in a democracy is no less important than that of the Government. It is a role mandated by the people and comes with a lot of responsibility.

"Constructive criticism is an essential input for good policies and programmes. Consensus on National issues is necessary for effective action.

"I look forward to both constructive criticism and consensus on national issues.

"My countrymen, the world rushes ahead—whether or not we look up from our narrow concerns. Neither do the tasks that confront us abate. The number of young women and men to whom jobs must be provided continues to increase. Children still go to bed hungry. A sense of insecurity prevails. The soul of India rebels against this reality.

"Starting today, our Government has set itself the task of implementing our agenda for a proud, prosperous India. It is my solemn pledge to all of you that nothing shall prevent us from the task of good governance. We talk of the 21st century. In just ten weeks from today, India, along with the rest of the world, will enter a new era of challenges and opportunities.

"We are pledged to the emergence of a 'new' India in the new century. We can redeem this pledge through collective effort, by resolutely meeting the challenges and seizing the opportunities of the 21st century. We may have been sent to Parliament under the banners of different parties. But we have all been sent for a common task: to make India a strong, vigorous, prosperous and caring country.

"To meet the challenges, we have to act now. In the coming days, our Government proposes to:

❖ Speed up economic reforms and focus attention on infrastructure development. The new century demands a new mindset.

❖ Introduce new laws for financial sector reforms so that India can keep pace with the rest of the world.

❖ Evolve a programme for achieving fiscal rectitude by improved expenditure management, deep tax reforms and a new mechanism for speedier restructuring and disinvestment of public sector units.

❖ Promote investment, including foreign direct investment, by adoption of suitable measures and removing bottlenecks that lead to costly delays.

❖ Re-arrange priorities of development by redeploying resources and strengthening institutions for providing to all : safe drinking water, primary health services, primary education, rural roads, housing to rural homeless. In this task, we seek the participation of the private sector.

"My countrymen, all these tasks can be completed if we work together. Let us proceed, as the Gita counsels us.

'Bodhyanta Parasparam' imparting Wisdom to each other.

"The opportunities are unlimited. We can use one of them to our national advantage if we stand united—both in properity and in the face of adversity. India's greatest asset is her unity, and my Government is determined to maintain this unity at all cost.

"One of our immediate tasks will be to firmly put down terrorism, which has come to cast its cruel shadow on innocent people. Our message is loud and clear: the life of every Indian citizen under our dispensation is precious. In our fight against terrorism, we will be guided by the principle of 'zero tolerance'.

The same principle of 'zero tolerance' will apply while dealing with corruption that has bred contempt for the law. One of the first legislations we will take up is the Lok Pal bill so that the rot can be checked from the top.

"A broad consensus already exists on electrol reforms to weed out muscle and money power. We propose to soon introduce in Parliament a comprehensive electoral reform bill.

"We often talk of the future belonging to our youth. But, for decades their problems, especially that of unemployment, have remain unattended. We believe that our young women and men will be the architects of the 'new' India of the 21st century.

"I am confident that a buoyant national economy will create tremendous employment opportunities. I am equally confident that our focus on education and health will prepare today's youth for tomorrow's challenges.

"The Government of free India had set itself the noble task of wiping every tear from every eye, of ending centuries-old discriminations and social inequities. Somewhere along the journey from freedom to the eve of this century, Government lost track of that task.

"Illiteracy is a curse and a denial of human dignity. As is gender discrimination or, for that matter, lack of something as basic and essential as drinking water and primary health care.

"My dear countrymen, India today needs a government that cares. India needs a Government that will reach out to the last person in the last row.

"Our Government pledges itself to narrowing the gap between our performance and your expectation. The mandate of '99 is a bond of trust between people and Government. We shall not betray this trust. With the help of a billion people proud of being India, there is nothing that we cannot achieve, no problem we cannot tackle, no challenge we cannot face and, no opportunity we cannot seize."

7

The Electoral System

Views and Provisions

The Sum-off Suggestion

The deficiencies of the electoral system as prevalent in India have been the subject matter of comments by a number of political thinkers. The system is an adaptation of the British model and suffers from the major deficiency that the winning candidate does not always reflect the majority will.

Various countries have adopted variations of this model. There is for example the system of proportional representation or the list system. Yet another model would be to have a mixture of both the first-past-the-post and proportional representation system.

The Chief Election Commissioner had yet another model in mind. He spoke about it in an interview. The excerpts:

I believe the Indian Constitution is a fine document. But some fine-tuning is still required. The commission has been arguing for these reforms, but the political parties, though they talk about reforms, have done very little. My only hope is that the next Lok Sabha will address these matters.

What Kind of Reforms Would You Like to See?

There are areas — for instance, vote of no-confidence, stability of Parliament, and having neutral governments under governors in states going to elections — where reforms are needed. I wouldn't like to go into details.

I favour run-off elections instead of the prevailing first-past-the-post method. For example, if in a constituency, 40 per cent voting takes place and there are six candidates, the one who gets 10 per cent is declared winner and he claims the mandate. In a run-off election, the top two candidates should go for repoll the next day.

It can be done without incurring any extra cost. This will ensure that the winning candidate has the majority vote, and will change the ideological position of different political parties. Because, to get the majority vote, they cannot project demands of only a section of the electorate.

The Law Commission's Recommendations

Electoral reforms also figured in the report submitted by the Law Commission. *The Times of India* reported the recommendations in its September 21 issue.

The Law Commission recommended to the Union government that Independent candidates be barred from contesting elections to the Lok Sabha and legislative assemblies. It also suggested that a legislature should have a full five-year term.

In its 170th report, the Commission, headed by former Supreme Court judge B.P. Jeevan Reddy, said that in order to contain defections, a "pre-poll coalition" or "front of political parties" should be treated as a "political party".

It also suggested inclusion of a chapter in the Representation of the People Act to regulate the formation and functioning of political parties to avoid their splintering and to ensure internal democracy and maintenance of funds.

The Commission favoured scrapping of explanation-1 to section 77(1) of the Represntation of the People Act to make the electoral system more representative, fair and transparent.

Section 77 exempts a candidate from declaring poll expenses incurred by him beyond the fixed limit. The Supreme Court has already declared that "section 77 is breeding corruption" and has recommended its scrapping.

The Commission also suggested provisions to make it obligatory for every candidate to declare his/her assets and of his/her spouse had dependent relations as well as provide particulars regarding criminal cases pending against them.

On state funding of political parties, the Commission has reiterated the recommendations of the Indrajit Gupta Committee subject to certain changes. Similar provisions are in vogue in several democratic countries.

The panel also recommended that in case of electoral offences and certain other serious offences, framing of a charge by the court should itself be a ground for disqualification in addition to conviction. The Commission has proposed amendments to the relevant provisions of the Criminal Procedure Code to check false complaints. It emphasised the desirability of adopting a rule that only a candidate obtaining 50 per cent or more votes be declared elected, and holding of "run off" elections wherever necessary.

Any party, which receives less than five per cent of the total vote in elections to the Lok Sabha and assemblies "shall not be entitled to any seat", the Commission said. It suggested a new rule in the Rules of Procedure and Conduct of Business for Lok Sabha to ensure stability of government.

Other salient features of the recommendations include use of electronic voting machines and restrictions on "no-confidence motion", the release said.

The Commission has also recommended a "list system" on the German model and also delved into the concept of "negative vote".

Reacting to the commission's recommendations, Congress spokesman Kapil Sibal said these issues should be discussed threadbare after the formation of the 13th Lok Sabha. "It is the duty of all political parties to make the electoral process cleaner and, therefore, it is necessary to have a constructive attitude. The recommendations should not be thrown to the winds as has been done in the past," he said.

On the other hand, NCP general secretary Devendra Dwivedi said the Law Commission should not "*suo motu* tender advice in areas which fall within the purview of other institutions". "The commission lacks expertise to go into the mechanisms of either the Parliamentary system or the electoral process. This increasing tendency of institutional trespass is a matter of concern."

BJP vice-president J.P. Mathur said he was surprised at the commission's recommendation that independent candidates should be barred from contesting elections to the Lok Sabha and legislative assemblies. He said any person on the voters list had three rights — to vote, to propose another person's name for contesting elections or to contest the elections himself. "Why should a voter be denied the third right?" he asked.

He said the other recommendations would have to be studied carefully and a proposal acceptable to all political parties evolved.

EC Guidelines and Code of Conduct

The Election Commission is to play the role of the Umpire or should it also have the powers to lay down the rules of the game?

The Election Commission was enthusiastically keen that apart from conducting the elections in a manner laid down in the Representation of the People Act, it must also ensure a level playing field for all the contestants.

The politicians had agreed to a code of conduct. What if it was violated by any individual? Did the EC have the authority to seek compliance or punish the defaulter? Before this question is answered, let us have a look at the Code itself.

I. General Conduct

(1) No party or candidate shall indulge in any activity which may aggravate existing differences or create mutual hatred or cause tension between different castes and communities, religious or linguistic.

(2) Criticism of other political parties, when made, shall be confined to their policies and programme, past record and work. Parties and candidates shall refrain from criticism of all aspects of private life, not connected with the public activities of the leaders or workers of other parties. Criticism of other parties or their workers based on unverified allegations or on distortion shall be avoided.

(3) There shall be no appeal to caste or communal feelings for securing votes. Mosques, Churches, Temples or other places of worship shall not be used as forum for election propaganda.

(4) All parties and candidates shall avoid scrupulously all activities which are "corrupt practices" and offences under the election law, such as the bribing of voters, intimidation of voters, personation of voters, canvassing within 100 metres of a polling station, holding public meetings during the period of 48 hours ending with the hour fixed for the close of the poll, and the transport and conveyance of voters to and from polling station.

(5) The right of every individual for peaceful and undisturbed home life shall be respected, however much the political parties or candidates may resent his political opinions or activities. Organising demonstrations or picketing before the houses of individuals by way of protesting against their opinions or activities shall not be resorted to under any circumstances.

(6) No political party or candidate shall permit its or his followers to make use of any individuals land, building, compound wall etc. without his permission for erecting flag-staffs, suspending banners, pasting notices, writing slogans etc.

(7) Political parties and candidates shall ensure that their supporters do not create obstructions in or break up meetings and processions organised by the other parties. Workers or sympathisers of one political party shall not create disturbances at public meetings organised by another political party by putting questions orally or in writing or by distributing leaflets of their own party. Processions shall not be taken out by one party along places at which meetings are being held by another party. Posters issued by one party shall not be removed by workers of another party.

II. Meetings

(1) The party or candidate shall inform the local police authorities of the venue and time of any proposed meeting well in time so as, to enable the police to make necessary arrangements for controlling traffic and maintaining peace and order.

(2) A party or candidate shall ascertain in advance if there are any restrictive or prohibitory orders in force in the place proposed for the meeting. If such orders exist, they shall be followed strictly. If any exemption is required from such orders it shall be applied for and obtained well in time.

(3) If permission of license is to be obtained for the use of loudspeakers or any other facility in connection with any proposed meeting, the party or candidate shall apply to the authority concerned well in advance and obtain such permission or license.

(4) Organisers of a meeting shall invariably seek the assistance of the police on duty for dealing with persons disturbing a meeting or otherwise attempting to create disorder. Organisers themselves shall not take action against such persons.

III. Processions

(1) A party or candidate organising a procession shall decide before hand the time and place of the starting of the procession, the route to be followed and the time and place at which the procession will terminate. There shall ordinarily be no deviation from the programme.

(2) The organisers shall give advance intimation to the local police authorities of the programme so as to enable the latter to make necessary arrangements.

(3) The organisers shall ascertain if any restrictive orders are in force in the localities through which the procession has to pass, and shall comply with the restrictions unless exempted specially by competent authority. Any traffic regulations or restrictions shall also be carefully adhered to.

(4) The organisers shall take steps in advance to arrange for passage, of the procession so that there is no block or hindrance to traffic. If the procession is very long, it shall be organised in segments of suitable lengths, so that at convenient intervals, especially at points where the procession has to pass road junctions, the passage of held-up traffic could be allowed by stages thus avoiding heavy traffic congestion.

(5) Processions shall be regulated as to keep as much to the right of the road as possible and the direction and advice of the police on duty shall be strictly complied with.

(6) If two or more political parties or candidates propose to take processions over the same route or parts thereof at about the same time, the organisers shall establish contact well in advance and decide upon the measures to be taken to see that the processions do not clash or cause hindrance to traffic. The assistance of the local police shall be availed of for arriving at a satisfactory arrangement. For this purpose, the parties shall contact the police at the earliest opportunity.

(7) The political parties or candidates shall exercise control to the maximum extent possible in the matter of processionists carrying articles which may be put to misuse by undesirable elements, especially in moments of excitement.

(8) The carrying of effigies purporting to represent members of other political parties or their leaders, burning such effigies in public and such other forms of demonstration shall not be countenanced by any political party or candidate.

IV. Polling Day

All political parties and candidates shall :

(i) co-operate with the officers on election duty to ensure peaceful and orderly polling and complete freedom to the voters to exercise their franchise without being subjected to any annoyance or obstruction;

(ii) supply to their authorised workers suitable badges or identity cards;

(iii) agree that the identity slips supplied by them to voters shall be on plain (white) papers and shall not contain any symbol, name of the candidate or the name of the party;

(iv) refrain from serving or distributing liquor on polling day and during the twenty-four hours preceding it;

(v) not allow unnecessary crowds to be collected, near the camps set up by the political parties and candidates near the polling booths so as to; avoid confrontation and tension among workers and sympathisers of the parties and candidate;

(vi) ensure that the candidate's camps shall be simple. They shall not display any posters, flags, symbols or any other propaganda material. No eatables shall be served or crowds allowed at the camps; and

(vii) co-operate with the authorities in complying with the restrictions to be imposed on the plying of vehicles on the polling day and obtain permits for them which should be displayed prominently on those vehicles.

V. Polling Booth

Except the voters, no one without a valid pass from the Election Commission shall enter the polling booths.

VI. Observers

The Election Commission is appointing observers. If the candidates or their agents have any specific complaint or problem regarding the conduct of the elections they may bring the same to the notice of the observer.

VII. Party in Power

The party in power whether at the Centre or in the State or States concerned, shall ensure that no cause is given for any complaint that it has used its official position for the purposes of its election campaign, and in particular-

(i) (a) the Ministers shall not combine their official visit with electioneering work and shall also not make use of official machinery or personnel during electioneering work;

(b) govt. transport including official aircrafts, vehicles, machinery and personnel shall not be used for furtherance of the interest of the party in power;

(ii) public places such as maidans etc. for holding election meetings, and use of helipads for air-flights in connection with elections, shall not be monopolised by itself. Other parties and candidates shall be allowed the use of such places and facilities on the same terms and conditions on which they are used by the party in power;

(iii) rest houses, dak bungalows or other Government accommodation shall not be monopolised by the party in power or its candidates and such accommodation shall be allowed to be used by other parties and candidates in a fair manner but no party or candidate shall use or be allowed to use such accommodation (including premises appertaining thereto) as a campaign office for holding any public meeting for the purposes of election propaganda;

(iv) issue of advertisement at the cost of public exchequer in the news papers and other media and the misuse of official mass media during the election period for partisan coverage of political news and publicity regarding achievements with a view to furthering the propsects of the Party in Power shall be scrupulously avoided;

(v) ministers and other authorities shall not sanction grants/payments out of discretionary funds from the time elections are announced by the Commission; and

(vi) from the time the elections are announced by the Commission, Ministers and other authorities shall not-

(a) announce any financial grants in any form or promises thereof; or

(b) lay foundation stones etc. of projects or schemes of any kind; or

(c) make any promise of construction of roads, provision of drinking water facilities etc; or

(d) make any ad-hoc appointments in Government, Public Undertakings etc. which may have the effect of influencing the voters in favour of the party in power.

(vii) Ministers of Central or State Govt. shall not enter any polling station or place of counting except in their capacity as a candidate or voter or authorised agent.

Supreme Court on Guidelines

The Election Law itself makes a difference between 'offences' and guidelines. For example the Shiv Sena supremo Bal Thackeray had been disenfranchised for an offence. On the other hand the opponents freely criticized the private lives, not connected with the public activities of the leaders of other parties. Appeals to communal feelings were made in places of worship. Convoys of cars much in excess of what the EC approved accompanied the leaders when they went to file nominations. Distribution of liquor on the night preceeding the poll was widely reported in the press in many constituencies. All these violations remained unpunished. The EC at best appealed to the political parties to observe the guidelines as in the case of indecent aspersions cast on private lives of opponents.

The matter regarding observance of guidelines on publications of opinion and exit polls brought the issue before the Supreme Court.

The guidelines do not have any statutory backing. The EC argued that these were in larger public interest. The stand of the government was that the guidelines were ultra-vires vis-a-vis the Constitution.

In the final judgement, it was ruled that the Supreme Court could not act as the executing court.

The EC suffered a serious set back to its authority but the trouble was of its own making. It should have known the difference between a directive and an offence.

"If ever there was one institution which could have pricked the bubble of "the Seshan effect" on the Election Commission, it was the Supreme Court. The hour of reckoning for the Election Commission came when a Constitution bench of the apex court, told the Commission that its penchant for issuing guidelines and bans was not based on legitimate authority. The court saw through the Commission's game to use the judicial shoulder for placing its unlicensed gun to shoot at all comers. The message to the Election Commission was clear: Understand what its powers are under the law and the Constitution and issue orders and guidelines that are enforceable. The court's logic was simple and devastating — If the EC had the powers to issue guidelines, why should it come to the court for enforcing them? The issuing of guidelines touched the limits of absurdity when the Life Insurance Corporation was told to conduct its annual meeting indoors and not announce its decisions and benefits to policy holders until the end of elections. In the process, such larger objectives as prevention of rigging and poll violence are not getting the attention they deserve.

That opinion polls and exit polls have become part of the democratic process all over the world is indisputable. How much they influence the voter and affect the outcome is disputable. The real mischief was done when the Election Commission stretched the poll process to almost three months and staggered the polling to four phases lasting more than a month. Time was when this country's electorate went to the polls on a single day to complete both the Lok Sabha and State Assembly elections. It is absurd that candidates are allowed only three weeks to campaign for elections while the Commission itself takes double that time to conduct the poll and announce the results. The Supreme Court judgement has come as a timely reminder to democratic institutions not to exceed their constitutional brief and heap unauthorised power on themselves."

(*Hindustan Times*)

Criminalisation of Politics

Contesting elections has always been an expensive business. Even in the Pre-independence era, Congress tickets were mostly given to leaders who could manage their own finances. There were practising advocates, landlords and many other professionals for whom the Congress association was a mission. They worked for the party and even spent their own earnings for party benefits.

After independence there was a sea change in the situation. Politics was now a rewarding business. The quota permit Raj was an added attraction. One could be Congressman and also make money by cornering quotas and selling them out at premium.

As the cost of electioneering increased the professionals were gradually replaced by people who joined Congress more to seek a career rather than serve the country. Ingenuous ways and means were developed as the salary one earned as an MLA or MP was not enough even to run the family kitchen. Add to it the expenses involved in keeping the vote banks in the constituency happy, and there was no way out except to make politics a business preposition.

In the absence of any other source of income, once elected, several MLAs and MPs started finding out ways and means to keep in business. Soon it became clear that money power alone may not be enough in dealing with the rivals. In came the muscle power.

Survival demanded that votes be won irrespective of the methods to be employed. Canvassing alone or the Manifestos were not enough. Some people had to be kept away from the polling booths. Some booths had to be captured. This job was entrusted to known criminals under the patronage of political aspirants.

The slide did not stop even at this stage. The criminals instead of working for their political masters, decided to be candidates themselves. They knew all the tricks of the trade. Besides that, a postion as MLA or MP could be their shield from police harassment for their usual and normal criminal occupations. Criminalisation of politics gradually assumed big proportions.

As the electoral process got vitiated more and more, the Election Commission came out with provisions that disqualified people convicted for offences from contesting the elections.

The relevant provisions are as follows:

Criminalisation of Politics — Participation of Criminals in the Electoral Process as Candidates — Disqualification on Conviction for Offences - Effect of Appeal and Bail - Regarding

Whereas, the country is facing the serious problem of criminalisation of politics in which criminals, i.e., persons convicted by courts of law for certain offences, are entering into election fray and contesting as candidates; and

Whereas, section 8 of the Representation of People Act, 1951, lays down the conditions under which a person would be disqualified on grounds of conviction for contesting elections of Parliament and Legislature of a State; and

Whereas; any person convicted of any offence listed under sub-section (1) of section 8 of the Representation of the People Act, 1951 shall be disqualified for a period of six years from the date of such conviction; and

Whereas, a person convicted for the contravention of any of the laws listed under sub-section (2) of section 8 of the Representation of the People Act, 1951 and sentenced to imprisonment for not less than 6 months shall be disqualified from the date of such conviction and shall continue to be disqualified for a further period of 6 years after his release; and

Whereas, under sub-section (3) of section 8 of the Representation of the People Act, 1951, a person convicted of any other offence and sentenced to imprisonment for not less than 2 years shall be disqualified for a further period of 6 years since his release; and

Whereas, sub-section (4) of section 8 of the Representation of the People Act, 1951 states that none of the above mentioned disqualification will take effect in case of a person who on the date of the conviction is a Member of Parliament or the Legislature of a State, till 3 months have elapsed from that date or, if within that period an appeal or application for revision is brought in respect of the conviction or the sentence, until that appeal or application is disposed of by the court; and

Whereas, it has been often observed that even those persons who are not the sitting members of Parliament or State Legislatures on the date of conviction, contest election if they have filed an appeal or application for revision and have been granted bail during pendency of such appeals/revision; and

Whereas, the Commission has carefully examined and considered the question whether such persons who have been convicted of offences mentioned in the said section 8 of the Representation of the People Act, 1951, can contest elections during the period when they are released on bail, pending disposal of their appeals or applications for revision; and

Whereas, the Commission has observed that this very question has come to be considered by several Hon'ble High Courts and they have taken the view that the release on bail does not wipe off the disqualification under the said section 8 of the Representation of the People Act, 1951; and

Whereas, it has been observed that the Hon'ble Madhya Pradesh High Court, while dealing with the case of *Purshottamlal Kaushik Vs. Vidya Charan Shukla* (66 Election Law Reports-110) held in that case as follows:

"It is obvious that the decision of the returning officer must depend on facts as they existed on the date of scrutiny since it is beyond human comprehension to visualise subsequent events and to base the decision of validity of nominations on the unknown future events. The "improper rejection" of a nomination within the meaning of expression used in section 100(1) (c) and 'important acceptance' in section 100 (1) (d) (i) of the R.P. Act, 1951, must, therefore, mean whether the rejection or acceptance of the nomination by the returning officer was improper with reference to section 36(2) (a) on the basis of facts existing on the date of scrutiny which alone were available to him and were relevant for deciding the validity of the nomination.

The question now is of the effect of suspension of the sentence by the appellate Court. Section 389 Cr.P.C. which gives this power to the first court till filing of appeal and then to the appellate court enables suspension of execution of the sentence or order appealed from. It is only the execution which is suspended and nothing more with the result that the sentence awarded is not to be suffered during the pendency of the appeal even though it subsists and the appellant is released on bail. There is no indication in section 8(2) of the R.P. Act that the disqualification thereunder remains in abeyance during the pendency of appeal against conviction. On the other hand, section 8(3) gives the contrary indication by laying down an exception only in case of sitting members. Suspension of execution of the sentence or order and grant of bail under section 389 Cr. P.C. has the only effect of avoiding sufferance of sentence pending appeal, but then in order to attract the disqualification under section 8(2) it is not necessary to suffer any part of the sentence awarded. This has also been held by the Supreme Court in *Sarat Chandra's case* (Supra): This decision also indicates that suspension of sentence does not wipe out the conviction and sentence. It was held that a reprieve is a temporary suspension of the sentence which does not wipe it out; all that it does is to have an effect on the execution of the sentence. If suspension of sentence during pendency of an appeal does not have the effect of wiping it out, it is difficult to accept the contention that the disqualification under section 8(2) remains arrested or in abeyance during operation of the suspension order pending appeal against the conviction and sentence. This is more so, when in section 8(2) there is nothing to support this view and section 8(3) gives contrary indication"; and

Whereas, the Hon'ble High Court of Judicature at Allahabad also took a similar view in the case of *Shri Sachindra Nath Tripathi Vs. Doodnath* (84 Election Law Reports 46), and while declaring the election as void of Shri Doodnath, who stood convicted by the trial court for offences under Section 302 and 307 IPC, and who stood released on bail during the election period, held that:

"The disqualification, which is an automatic effect of conviction, springs up right at the time of pronouncement of conviction, finding which is yet to be reversed or set aside.

......It is to be seen as to what is the effect of bail, granted to the respondent before the date of filing the nomination paper. If no bail is granted and the execution of the sentence is not suspended by the stay orders, then the accused will remain in jail and the only effect of granting bail is that he is released from the confinement. Grant of bail does not interfere with the finding of conviction and that cannot render the disqualification, automatically emerging from conviction, inoperative"; and

Whereas, the same question again came to be considered in a more recent case before the Hon'ble Himachal Pradesh High Court in *Vikram Anand Vs Rakesh Singha* etc. etc. (Election Petition Nos. 1, 4 and 5 of 1994), and the Hon'ble High Court, while declaring the election as void of the returned candidate (Shri Singha), who stood convicted in a criminal case under section 148, etc., of the IPC and sentenced to imprisonment for 5 years and who had been released on bail during the pendency of appeal to the Hon'ble Supreme Court, held in its judgement dated 13.09.1994 as follows:

......Despite suspension of sentence and release on bail, the order of conviction remains in operation holding the person guilty of such offence or offences for which he has been awarded sentence of imprisonment for not less than two years, as such the disqualification as provided under sub-section (3) of section 8 of the Act continues. In order to attract disqualification under sub-section (3) of section 8 of the Act, the execution of the order of conviction and sentence of improisonment or any part thereof is not required. What is necessary is the actual conviction and sentence imposed by the Court for not less than two years, which order remains in operation despite stop put to execution of the order of sentence during the pendency of appeal by releasing the convicted person on bail and suspending the sentence awarded to him.'

......after examining the legal position, this court has come to the conclusion that when the appellate Court passes an order of suspension of sentence and/or release on bail of a convicted person, the order of his conviction still remains in existence and the disqualification, suffered by him as a result of conviction and sentence, for a period of not less than two years as envisaged under sub-section (3) of section 8 of the Act, is not automatically suspended and it continues to be in operation.'; and

Whereas, it has also been observed that when the Hon'ble Supreme Court dismissed the criminal appeal filed by Shri Rakesh Singha, it also dismissed his election appeal holding that Shri Singha was disqualified *ab initio* for contesting election under section 8(3) of the Representation of the People Act, 1951;

Now, therefore, the Election Commission has, after taking due note and paying due regard to the above judicial pronouncements of the Hon'ble Supreme Court and the Hon'ble High Courts, come to the considered view that the disqualification under section 8 of the Representation of People Act, 1951 for contesting elections to Parliament and State Legislatures, on conviction for offences mentioned therein, take effect from the date of conviction by the trial court, irrespective of whether the convicted person is released on bail or not during the pendency of appeal (subject, of course, to the exception in the case of sitting members of Parliament and State Legislatures under sub-section (4) of the said section 8 of the Representation of the People Act, 1951).

Accordingly, the Election Commission, in exercise of its power of superintendence, direction and control of elections to Parliament and State Legislatures vested by Article 324 of the Constitution, hereby directs that all the Returning Officers, at the time of scrutiny of nominations, must take note of the above legal position and decide accordingly about the validity or otherwise of the candidature of contestants disqualified under the said section 8 of the Representation of the People Act, 1951.

Role of Money Power in Indian Elections

The Money Power has been the bane of the Indian political system. While the Election Commission has set limits of Election expenses that may be incurred by the candidates, there is no limit on the expenses that the political party may incur in promotion of the candidature. It is this lacuna that has made elections so expensive and beyond the reach of ordinary but honest people who may like to join the legislatures. The political parties are also not bound to disclose all their sources of revenue through which they manage their campaigns. Helicopters and chartered planes are frequently used and paid for by the party. The usual explanation is that money is received through donations. The crores of Rupees needed for funding the elections are shown to have been received in cash (less than five thousand) from sympathisers and friends of the party or candidate. Receipts for this amount need not come through cheques.

The Prime Minister is by law allowed the facility of travel by IAF planes. Four former Prime Ministers (or their parties) have yet to pay the amount due for having used IAF planes.

Table 7.1 : Limits of Election Expenses for All Parliamentary and Assembly Constituencies

Name of State/ Union Territory		Maximum limit of election expenses in any one	
		Parliamentary Constituency	Assembly Constituency
State			
1.	Andhra Pradesh	15,00,000	6,00,000
2.	Arunachal Pradesh	10,00,000	3,00,000
3.	Assam	15,00,000	6,00,000
4.	Bihar	15,00,000	6,00,000
5.	Goa	8,00,000	3,00,000
6.	Gujarat	15,00,000	6,00,000
7.	Haryana	15,00,000	6,00,000
8.	Himachal Pradesh	15,00,000	4,00,000
9.	Jammu & Kashmir	15,00,000	—
10.	Karnataka	15,00,000	6,00,000
11.	Kerala	15,00,000	6,00,000
12.	Madhya Pradesh	15,00,000	6,00,000
13.	Maharashtra	15,00,000	6,00,000
14.	Manipur	15,00,000	3,00,000
15.	Meghalaya	13,00,000	3,00,000
16.	Mizoram	12,00,000	3,00,000
17.	Nagaland	15,00,000	3,00,000
18.	Orissa	15,00,000	6,00,000
19.	Punjab	15,00,000	6,00,000
20.	Rajasthan	15,00,000	6,00,000
21.	Sikkim	10,00,000	3,00,000
22.	Tamil Nadu	15,00,000	6,00,000
23.	Tripura	15,00,000	3,00,000
24.	Uttar Pradesh	15,00,000	6,00,000
25.	West Bengal	15,00,000	6,00,000
Union Territories			
1.	Andaman and Nicobar Islands	10,00,000	—
2.	Chandigarh	8,00,000	—
3.	Dadra & Nagar Haveli	6,00,000	—
4.	Daman and Diu	6,00,000	—
5.	Delhi	15,00,000	5,00,000
6.	Lakshadweep	6,00,000	—
7.	Pondicherry	12,00,000	3,00,000

Politics and Criminals

With a view to arrest increasing criminalisation of politics certain provisions have been made in the Representation of the People Act, 1951. The relevant provisions read as follows:

Representation of The People Act, 1951
(Part II - Acts of Parliament)

Sec.8. Disqualification on conviction for certain offences -[(1) A person convicted of an offence punishable under:

(a) Section 153 A (offence of promoting enmity between different groups on ground of religion, race, place of birth, residence, language, etc., and doing acts prejudicial to maintenance of harmony) or section 171E (offence of bribery) or section 171 F (offence of undue influence or personation at an election) or sub-section (1) or (2) of section 376 sub-section (D) (offences relating to rape) or section 498A (offence of cruelty towards a woman by husband or relative of a husband) or sub-section (2) or sub-section (3) of section 505 (offence of making statement creating or promoting enmity, hatred or ill-will between classes or offence relating to such statement in any place of worship or in any assembly engaged in the performance of religious worship or religious ceremonies) of the Indian Penal Code (45 of 1860), or

(b) the Protection of Civil Rights Act, 1955 (22 of 1955), which provides for punishment for the preaching and practice of "untouchability", and for the enforcement of any disability arising therefrom; or

(c) section 11 (offence of importing or exporting prohibited goods) of the Customs Act, 1962 (52 of 1962); or

(d) sections 10 to 12 (offence of being a member of an association declared unlawful, offence relating to dealing with funds of an unlawful association or offence relating to contravention of an order made in respect of a notified place) of the Unlawful Activities (Prevention) Act, 1967 (37 of 1967); or

(e) the Foreign Exchange (Regulation) Act, 1973 (46 of 1973); or

(f) the Narcotic Drugs and Psychotropic Substances Act, 1985 (61 of 1985); or

(g) section 3 (offence of committing terrorist acts) or section 4 (offence of committing disruptive activities) of the Terrorist and Disruptive Activities (Prevention) Act, 1987 (28 of 1987); or

(h) section 7 (offence of contravention of the provisions of sections 3 to 6) of the Religious Institutions (Prevention of Misuse) Act, 1988 (41 of 1988); or

(i) section 125 (offence of promoting enmity between classes in connection with the election) or section 135 (offence of removal of ballot papers from polling stations) or section 135A (offence of booth capturing) or clause (a) of sub-section (2) of section 136 (offence of fraudulently defacing or fraudulently destroying any nomination paper) of this Act (or)

(j) section 6 (offence of conversion of a place of worship) of the Places of Worship (Special Provisions) Act, 1991

shall be disqualified for a period of six years from the date of such conviction.

(2) A person convicted for the contravention of-

(a) any law providing for the prevention of hoarding or profiteering; or

(b) any law relating to the adulteration of food or drugs; or

(c) any provisions of the Dowry Prohibition Act, 1961 (28 of 1961); or

(d) any provisions of the Commission of Sati (Prevention) Act, 1987 (3 of 1988).

and sentenced to imprisonment for not less than six months, shall be disqualified from the date of such conviction and shall continue to be disqualified for a further period of six years since his release.

(3) A person convicted of any offence and sentenced to imprisonment for not less

than two years [other than any offence referred to in sub-section (1) or sub-section (2) shall be disqualified from the date of such conviction and shall continue to be disqualified for a further period of six years since his release].

(4) Notwithstanding anything [in sub-section (1) or sub-section (2) or sub-section (3)] a disqualification under either sub-section shall not in the case of a person who on the date of the conviction is a member of Parliament or the Legislature of a State, take effect until three months have elapsed from that date or, if within that period an appeal or application for revision is brought in respect of the conviction or the sentence until that appeal or application is disposed of by the court.

Explanation - In This Section

(a) "law providing for the prevention of hoarding or profiteering" means any law, or any order, rule or notification having the force of law, providing for -

(i) the regulation of production or manufacture of any essential commodity;

(ii) the control price at which any essential commodity may be bought or sold;

(iii) the regulation of acquisition, possession, storage, transport, distribution, disposal, use or consumption of any essential commodity;

(iv) the prohibition of the withholding from sale of any essential commodity ordinarily kept for sale;

(b) "Drug" has the meaning assigned to it in the Drugs and Cosmetics Act, 1940 (23 of 1940).

(c) "essential commodity" has the meaning assigned to it in the Essential Commodities Act, 1955 (10 of 1955)

1. Ins. by Act 42 of 1991.s. 8 (w.e.f. 18.9.1991).

2. Sub-section (3) renumbered as sub-section (4) by Act 1 of 1989. s. 4 (w.e.f. 15.3.1989).

3. Subs. by s. 4.ibid- "in sub-section (1) and sub-section (2)" (w.e.f. 15.3.1989).

8

The New Government

Press Reactions

A Decisive Verdict

By giving the BJP-led omnibus alliance a comfortable working majority in the 13th Lok Sabha, the electorate has returned a verdict that is more decisive than in 1998. The combine, which has as many as 24 partners, has succeeded in winning enough numbers to form a government, thanks to the strategic alliance it had struck with regional parties having a dominant presence in the various States, the Telugu Desam in Andhra Pradesh and the DMK in Tamil Nadu, for instance. What is significant, however is that the BJP's own tally has remained just about the same as in the previous Lok Sabha and the fresh accretions this time have come from its allies, old and new. The surprise elements lay in the substantial gains made by Mulayam Singh Yadav's Samajwadi Party and Kanshi Ram's Bahujan Samaj Party which besides the Congress(I), have claimed their own slice of the anti-BJP electoral cake. The split in the anti-BJP vote has apparently not gone to that party's advantage as it has done in Maharashtra for instance, at least in the context of the Lok Sabha. If the BJP-Shiv Sena combine in Maharashtra could secure an impressively higher tally, it was primarily because of the erosion caused in the Congress(I)'s vote base by Sharad Pawar's Nationalist Congress Party. This, however, has not worked in the Assembly poll, where the ruling coalition has ended up capturing fewer seats than the combined strength of the Congress(I) and the NCP.

The one State where the incumbency factor has worked very favourably is Andhra Pradesh, where N. Chandrababu Naidu's Telugu Desam (TDP), together with the BJP, has won over three-fourths of the 42 Lok Sabha seats. (*The Hindu*)

The Real Victors

One remarkable feature of the elections is the increase in the number of small parties and the Lok Sabha seats won by them. The other is that as many as 200 Lok Sabha seats overall changed hands — an index of voter disenchantment with politicans of all hues. Regional and caste-based parties have done well, a surprising outcome of the third national elections in three years. It was widely assumed —and opinion polls reflected that assumption —that voters had had enough of the comings and goings of central governments and would vote for stability by backing national parties. This has not been so. Far from small parties yielding seats to the two big national parties, the BJP and Congress, the reverse has happened. The BJP has stayed where it was in 1998 with the same seat tally; the Congress has done worse and actually lost seats. And the real gainers among small parties are the regional and caste-based parties which have wrested seats in Uttar Pradesh, for example, from the BJP and in Andhra Pradesh from the Congress.

One reason for greater political fragmentation in the 13th Lok Sabha is that no national issues emerged during the campaign although the BJP in particular tried to talk-up a pan-India wave. Evidently the electorate was not greatly impressed by the BJP's chest-thumping on Kargil. Nor did the Congress succeed in capturing the national imagination in any way. Both these major national parties made no serious effort to sell or educate the electorate on economic reforms, a truly national issue if ever there was one. It was a colossal missed opportunity. And the more is the pity from the point of view of the NDA government for it will have to take a number of tough decisions to speed up the GDP growth and give birth to the so-called second generation of reforms. Many signs point to the fact that voters are no longer swayed by demagogues and grand visions. They are focussed on what will or will not improve their living conditions. When local issues matter, parties attuned to those issues which make themsleves accessible to local groups or form tactical alliances to give themselves clout, such parties have tended to benefit.

These were not municipal polls as one TV pundit sourly remarked. But voters were not looking at the horizon, they were looking squarely at what was right before them. They generally did not like what they found. Good governance or rather the almost universal lack of it loomed large. So large, in fact that dissatisfaction with state governments has been decisive in the Lok Sabha verdict right across the country in Karnataka, Rajasthan, Punjab, Bihar, UP and even Maharashtra (where the Congress split saved the ruling alliance from ignominy). There are several implications here for the Centre too. The next stage of economic reform depends crucially on the states. Regional parties and caste-based parties in the states will pay the predominant role for better or worse on major policies. They can build a consensus or wreck central government initiatives. Therefore the Centre must not allow itself to function as the Delhi durbar of old but as a partner to bring about change in the states. (*Indian Express*)

Coalition Era

The results of the 13th Lok Sabha elections clearly show that coalition politics is here to stay. The success the National Democratic Alliance has achieved should be seen as an endorsement of the policy of consensus that the BJP tried to pursue in the 12th Lok Sabha. It was thoughtful of the party to have broadened the base of the coalition it led by welcoming into its fold new parties. Small wonder that in comparison to the Congress, the BJP appeared more accommodative, realistic and capable of successfully managing political contradictions. More than anything else, it is the knack of leading a coalition that was on test in these elections and the BJP has definitely won on this score. Which means that the party is shouldering the responsibility of pursuing consensual politics. There is no other way the BJP can manage the affairs of the nation. After all, the party is dependent on the support of 24 heterogeneous parties which are united only in their opposition to the Congress. It is a truism that Atal Bihari Vajpayee, who has emerged as the tallest national leader, alone has the stature to take up this challenge. The victory is clearly his and that of the accommodative spirit the BJP displayed during the 16 months of its tenure.

It was not for want of a desire to rule by consensus that the Vajpayee government fell. Hence, it should not be difficult for a liberal politician like Vajpayee to see the new House as one grand coalition and treat it as such. If the BJP is comfortable in a grouping which has the DMK, the Shiv Sena and the Janata Dal(U) as its constituents, it should not be a problem for it to seek cooperation from the Congress. There is, perhaps, no other way it can manage some of the political, economic and foreign policy issues facing the nation. In the past, the BJP showed considerable political dynamism when it pursued the economic reforms agenda which had been willy-nilly set in motion by the Congress. Unfortunately the Congress, which should have reciprocated in equal measure, was guided more by petty political gains than the larger national interest. Whether it was on the Insurance Bill or disinvestment in the public sector, the Congress attitude was one of disinterestedness, if not outright non-cooperation. As a result, the reforms process could not make the desired headway. Politics was allowed to keep the two apart even when Indian soldiers fought a pitched battle to evict the Pakistani intruders from the snowcapped Kargil heights.

On the foreign policy front, Vajpayee has spoken about carrying forward his ill-fated bus diplomacy. This is possible only if it has the requisite support in the House. The issue of signing the Comprehensive Test Ban Treaty has been hanging fire for want of a consensus. The Vajpayee government has taken some initiative to sort it out with the Americans although the progress External Affairs Minister Jaswant Singh has achieved in his talks with the Clinton administration is not yet known. This will surely be one of the priority items for the new government. Needless to say, any forward movement on CTBT is possible only if the government evolves a consensus in the new House. The voters have definitely given their mandate for such an approach. It is now the turn of the National Democratic Alliance to live up to its image as practitioners of the politics of consensus. (*Indian Express*)

Promises to Keep

If there is a single coherent message delivered by the electorate in this election, it is that populist gestures that are not backed by true intent are double-edged weapons. In Punjab, the rout of the Akali-BJP combine owes to a considerable extent to its promises of free electricity and water to farmers. So many years after the Green Revolution, the leaders do not seem to have fathomed the reality that the rural electorate is no longer impoverished. It will not gratefully pick up every scrap they deign to cast at it. The farmer is now prosperous enough — and politically mature enough—to regard freebies with suspicion. What he wants is not free services but reliable services. He wants to pay—and he wants the government to replace the power transformer that has burned out in his village. He knows that an administration bled dry by freebies will never be able to improve infrastructure. Ergo, such an administration is not in his interest. A case in point is that of the Punjab Agricultural University, which ushered in the Green Revolution in India and laid to rest the ghost of PL-480 in the Sixties. Today, underfunded by the state government, it has little left over even for basic research at a time when agriculture has come to imply terminator genes, international trade regimes and patent law. When the ambit and implications of the sector are increasing, the trailblazer of agricultural research in India is out for the count. The people of Punjab have clearly voted against the pauperisation of the state, which was once the exemplar of progress.

There are instances elsewhere as well. In Rajasthan, anti-incumbency sentiment owes to the state government's promise to introduce reservation for Jats. About a month ago, the Jat Mahasabha expressed its dissatisfaction over the tardiness of the government in no uncertain terms, and the vote has swung significantly in favour of the BJP. Similarly, in Andhra Pradesh, the people seem to have shrugged off the freebies and subsidies promised by the Congress(I). The poor showing of the CPI(M), at least in the initial phases of counting in West Bengal are also part of the pattern. While the party has implemented major land reforms in the state and kept farmers happy, the land can support only so many people. Meanwhile, the CPI(M)'s old commitment to militant labour politics has ensured the flight of capital from the state. When capital goes, enterprise usually follows. The result is a state whose people are chronically unemployed or underemployed and which routinely loses its best entrepreneurial talent to more progressive states.

The lesson of this election, then, is that the people are no longer vulnerable to gimcrackery. The penetration of the media has ensured that the electorate knows when political leaders are out to pauperise them under the pretence of helping out. They understand that any largesse will be paid for from funds earmarked for infrastructure and they would rather have the government provide them with an enabling environment rather than free services. The populists should have known better. In this political climate, even Mrs. Gandhi's *garibi hatao* would not have stood a chance. (*Indian Express*)

On Expected Lines

The electoral trends so far generally seem to confirm the belief, which had been prevalent right from the start of the campaign and was largely confirmed by the various opinion polls, that the alliance led by the BJP would secure a majority but not a very substantial one. If the final outcome endorses this assessment, it would show yet again that the electorate is not unduly influenced by the points which the contending parties make with great vigour in the conviction that they are virtually irrefutable. In the present context, it would appear that the arguments proffered by the BJP about its government's role in the Kargil conflict and the suitability of Mr. Atal Bihari Vajpayee as Prime Minister did make an impact, but not as much of it as the party and its partners might have hoped. By the same token, the adverse comments which the saffron lobby made time and again about Mrs. Sonia Gandhi's foreign origin, sometimes descending even to the level of describing her as a security risk, were also virtually ignored by the voters. Otherwise, the Congress would not have fared as well as it has done in Punjab and Karnataka, where the anti-incumbency factor appears to have taken a toll of the BJP and its allies, the Akalis and the Janata Dal (United).

A similar factor was also evidently at work in Rajasthan and Madhya Pradesh to the detriment of the Congress. The rout which the Congress suffered in Delhi may have revived the national capital's reputation as a saffron city, but one has to remember that only a year ago, the city had given almost exactly the opposite verdict. What such outcomes demonstrate, therefore, is that the voters make up their own minds, quite independently of the arguments for or against a party which are made with such passion by the contenders in the field. Arguably, it is not that the points made by the parties such as stability or the experience — or the lack of it—of a leader are not taken into account, but they are assessed along with so many other factors, both local and ideological apart from the infighting within a party, that the end result is not always what the propagandists may have expected. There are other considerations as well. In Delhi, for instance, the low turnout may have affected the Congress more than a cadre-based disciplined party like the BJP. Dutifully, at the end of the day all the parties will say that they will learn from these results, but they rarely do. (*The Hindustan Times*)

Setback for Congress

. . . . Earlier, the enthusiastic response to Mrs. Sonia Gandhi's public meetings had evidently enthused the Congress rank and file. Considering that the party had fared quite well in last November's elections and the assumption of the party president's post by Mrs. Sonia Gandhi had infused a sense of purpose in the organisation, it was reasonable to presume that the party's fortunes were on the mend. The final results, however, which showed that the number of seats won by it has fallen well below the figure of 141 won in 1998 must have come as something of a shock to the party and its supporters. There may have been a slight increase in its voting percentage from 25.8 in 1998 to 27, but the fact that its tally of seats is the lowest ever is a cause for serious concern, calling for "introspection", as the leaders have acknowledged. There has also been the usual advocacy for the induction of young people and the "retirement" of the old.

But while all of this is valid, what is perhaps even more important for the Congress is to spell out its policies in clear and unambiguous terms, as Nehru used to do in Parliament and at public meetings with indefatigable energy many times in a year. There may not be anyone of his stature and clarity of vision in today's organisation, but unless the party as a whole rises to fill this vacuum, it will have a hard struggle in front of it. Some of the results, like the huge margin of success in Amethi and the fine showing in Karnataka, show that there is no reason to feel depressed by the present setback. But apart from determined efforts to rev up the organisation, the party will revamp have to shed the habit of waiting for others to commit mistakes to retrieve its position, as has happened in UP and also in Karnataka, and earlier in Delhi and Rajasthan. As the turn-around in the BJP's favour in the last two states has shown, such successes are ephemeral. Only a clear enunciation of policy—on secularism, liberalisation, coalitions et al-by a vigorous and young party can ensure success of a more permanent nature. (*The Hindustan Times*)

Second Chance

. . . . The feeling of relief will be widely shared since yet another unclear verdict would have been regarded as little short of a disaster in a country which has witnessed too vigorous an assertion of democracy in the last three years. The business community will be particularly pleased because of the distinct possibility of the installation of a government which will not be on tenterhooks from day one, as the last government was. Although the NDA has more constituents than the earlier alliance, which may be regarded by its opponents as a built-in recipe for instability, none of them are likely to show their impatience right from the beginning, as the AIADMK did last time, if only because it is known that the electorate will not look kindly on such a trouble-maker.

The BJP, too, must have learnt a few important lessons in the art of managing a coalition in the last one year to be able to run the show without any major tremors. The party and its partners might have preferred a more secure majority but its absence is probably a blessing in disguise, for the advantage of an adequate but not substantial majority is that it will keep the hardliners in the Sangh parivar in check. It is quite on the cards that if the NDA's tally had gone well beyond 300, as some of the earlier projections had suggested, then the saffron lobby would have been far more active in pushing its agenda, thereby embarrassing the Vajpayee government and alienating many of the BJP's allies, most of whom, except the Shiv Sena, belong to what is known as the secular camp. At present, with the hardliners expected to lie low if only to let the new government settle down, the latter should focus solely on governance, something which had been sadly neglected in the last few years because of the preoccupation of virtually all the parties with elections. Indeed, if there is a message from the voters in this election, it is the need for ruling politicians to concentrate on the task of administration rather than on manipulating caste, communal and other sectarian factors to reach the winning post.

Both Uttar Pradesh and Bihar are prime examples of ruling parties squandering their goodwill through infighting and misgovernance while hoping that primordial loyalties will save them. In Karnataka, Punjab and Orissa, too, indifferent administration was the reason for the rejection of the ruling parties. On the other hand, Chandrababu Naidu's success in Andhra Pradesh has shown that a greater emphasis on development than on politics can pay dividends. The second chance which Mr Vajpayee has now been given can be better utilised, therefore, if he chooses to distance himself from the customary jousting which is the staple of Indian politics and concentrate instead on pursuing policies which will help to dispel the gloom and uncertainty that continue to prevail about India's economic direction. The Prime Minister's wider acceptability places him in a unique position to fulfill the promises which, till now, have only been the stuff of rhetoric in India. He can also play a major role in lowering the political temperature, which the electoral combats of the last three years had helped to raise to unacceptable levels.

There is also little need to promise dramatic changes in the statute book either to keep out any adversary from certain official postions or overhaul the system altogether. It is possible, of course, that if the government lasts this time without much trouble, the earlier pledges about switching to a presidential form or having a fixed-term Lok Sabha will not be repeated. These have often been an expression of unease about the frequent changes of government than of a real need. Above all, since it is no secret that nothing other than Mr. Vajpayee's moderate image has helped his party and his allies to return to power, the best way for them to retain it is to shun extremism and stick to the middle path. In achieving this, the fact that the BJP's allies have more than 100 seats between them places them in a position where they can exercise a restraining influence. The role of the Telugu Desam and the DMK will be more crucial in this respect because of their experience in governance than that of the Janata Dal (United) which is still something of an unknown quantity apart from being a new ally. The opposition, too, should remember that the phrase of playing a constructive role should not be honoured in its breach, as has often been the case in the past. (*The Hindustan Times*)

British Press

The British press has largely agreed that the elections in India have been a victory for regional parties and signalled that the Indian electorate was willing and able to throw out politicians who had failed to deliver.

The Daily Telegraph said: "It seems India voted along regional lines ... the real victory belongs to the BJP's regional allies...."

The Times said though the BJP would be the single largest party in Parliament, "it has been brought to power by its regional allies". The paper questioned the "viability of such a fragmented coalition" saying that "the 24-party National Democratic Alliance (NDA) might prove to be an unwieldy monster in government".

The Guardian in an editorial said that a significant trend established by this election was "the burgeoning strength of regional parties at the expense of the Centre". It added: "...most importantly of all, the elections revealed a growing impatience with incompetent and self serving politicians". The paper said that the election ignored the `people's agenda' which it said was summed up in the phrase "good governance". The paper concluded that if national politics were to remain relevant, "meeting this challenge is Vajpayee's most urgent task".

The Financial Times said that, with a diminished Congress, Atal Bihari Vajapyee "ought...to be ideally placed to push through the budget cuts and privatisation that India needs". But the paper said that the nature of the coalition makes the BJP "somewhat more reliant than before on its allies among the regional parties". This, it said, "could make for difficulties, especially over the all important reduction of the budget deficit". The paper has praise for Chandrababu Naidu, who, it says, "put up a strong showing". This, said the *FT*, suggests "Indian voters will buy reform if it is sold to them properly".

Other European Reactions

The western business and government establishments are, at best, "cautiously optimistic" about the prospects of political stability in the immediate future with the BJP-led National Democratic Alliance winning a clear majority in Parliament after five short-lived governments and three general elections in three years.

Belgium's *Le Soir* speculates about the prospects of the Prime Minster, A.B. Vajpayee, compromising with his powerful allies in "what is bad omen for the stability of a country that has voted for the third time since 1996 and is going to have its sixth government in six years".

La Libre Belgique wonders about the fate of the "two Gandhis" elected to Parliament—"Sonia, the Congress party president and her sister-in-law and intimate enemy, Maneka, who is allied with the Hindu nationalist party". It points out that Ms. Maneka Gandhi—described as an 'environmentalist' - had lost family favour after her husband Sanjay Gandhi's death in 1980.

Ms. Sonia Gandhi, is described as being "devoid of administrative or political experience" and as an "Italian-born heiress to India's leading political dynasty", who has lived in India for thirty years. Both the Congress(I) and BJP are reported to have campaigned on the twin agenda of political stability and social harmony but the Indian voters "punished the Congress for bringing down the last Government" and many Indians were "unable to accept Ms. Sonia Gandhi as prime minister because she was born in Italy." Ms. Maneka Gandhi is described being "part of Prime Minister Vajpayee's BJP-led coalition" and the Congress party's "sworn enemy".

The Financial Times editorial states: "On the surface India's election does not seem to have moved the country's politics very much. The election of the BJP-led coalition with roughly the same majority as the last one presumably leaves it similarly vulnerable to parliamentary defeat.

"In fact, as the exuberant response of the Bombay stock market has shown, there are some grounds for hoping that the new administration may enjoy a longer life than its predecessors. If so, it will have a chance to proceed with economic reforms that could secure India a still higher (economic) growth rate" and the paper hopes that the popular Vajpayee, "can push through the budget cuts and privatisation that India needs".

The editorial states that "estimates by the Asian Development Bank suggest that at seven per cent India will have the fastest-growing economy in Asia next year. A concentrated efforts at reform could make still higher growth sustainable, especially since India's demographic profile with a generally young population is favourable".

The European commentators have harped on the theme that a healthy economic growth, backed by reforms, is vital for stability and prosperity in India. It has been noted that "the electorate in Punjab rejected a policy of free electric power after they saw the effect on State finances. The Telugu Desam Party of Naidu, the reformist Chief Minister of Andhra Pradesh, put up a strong showing. This suggests that Indian voters will buy reforms if it is sold to them properly. Vajpayee must take note".

A common European perception reflected in the media and official comments is that stability is now in India's reach. It is argued that with the rise of powerful regional parties in the world's biggest democracy, parliamentary arithmetic in India has changed. It is stated that while Vajpayee in his last administration was hostage to the whims of almost any of his eighteen partners, this time only two of his allies carry enough weight to cause serious concern.

New Ideas, not Gandhis

"New ideas, not new Gandhis", is what the Congress party needs if it is to become a serious contender for power, noted *The Times* newspaper in its editorial on the Indian election. "Since the death of Indira Gandhi in 1984, the Congress has been little more than a vehicle for personality politics, the locus of an obsession with the Gandhi family," the paper says. "The foreign roots of the current Italian-born Sonia Gandhi should not be blamed for the defeat. Nor should salvation be sought in the rise of Priyanka Gandhi Wadhera, Sonia's 27-year-old daughter," it adds.

The paper hopes for a stable government, and says "India needs time to recover from three years of elections that have sapped resources and interest in politics: it is to be hoped that the new government will be strong enough to offer that vital breathing space."

The Times as well as other British newspapers have all been struck by the fact that the elections were fought on the basis of personalities, rather than on the basis of concrete programmes. "This unedifying election ignored the issues that matter most to Indians: education, healthcare, utilities, economic opportunity, bureaucracy and corruption. This is the people's agenda. It can be summed up in one word: good governance." The paper says "if national politics is to remain relevant, meeting challenge is Vajpayee's most urgent task."

The *Financial Times*, reflecting the feelings of foreign investors, says the new government ought to "be ideally placed to push through the budget cuts and privatisation that India needs." It notes that the Asian Development Bank has said that with a 7 per cent growth rate India could have the fastest growing economy in Asia next year. But, it says "a concentrated effort at reform could make still higher growth sustainable, especially since India's demographic profile with a generally young population is favourable."

The *Financial Times*, as well as the other British newspapers, all point out that the election has left the BJP even more dependent on its coalition allies than previously. The *Financial Times* notes that "this could make for difficulties, especially over the all important reduction of the budget deficit which is needed to free up savings for productive investment and reduce interest rates." The newspaper notes the success of Chandrababu Naidu in Andhra Pradesh, and says that it suggests "Indian voters will buy reform if it is sold to them properly."

The Guardian speculates on the stability of the new government "Increased majority or not, Vajpayee will remain in thrall to the conflicting, competing interests of his disparate coalition partners, all of whom will seek rewards for their support. It is legitimate to wonder how long Vajpayee can keep this lot happy." The paper also touches on the low voter turnout, which it says "implies disillusionment with the endless political shenanigans in Delhi." It adds, "most important of all, the election revealed a growing impatience with incompetent, self-serving politicians."

South-East Asian Reactions

The results of the Lok Sabha polls have been welcomed by political observers and somc business leaders in South-East Asia as a sign of possible administrative stability in New Delhi.

The positive reaction by India's business sector has been duly noticed, especially in Singapore which was the first country in the region to have felt "bullish" about building economic ties with New Delhi some years ago. The spotlight was not, however, on the question whether such "bullishness" could be revived in the wake of some recent frustrations.

In Indonesia, India's latest democratic exercise was seen as a manifestation of the success of the system. The elite opinion in Jakarta, which now finds itself in the throes of a crisis over Indonesia's resurgence of representative governance, was characterised by an extraordinary dose to India-friendly disposition in what was seen as New Delhi's sustained track record of democracy.

Commenting on "Vajpayee's victory" in the context of the "greater challenges before the world's largest democracy in the third millennium", *The Jakarata Post* outlined in an editorial an altogether new role for India in catalysing democracy in Asia. Of India's capabilities, the paper said, "With ties with its neighbours on the mend, its economy strengthened and internal stability ensured, India is now in its best position in years to help spread the seeds of democracy in many Asian countries and play a more significant role in the international political arena".

This perception of India as a possible harbinger of democracy in Asia was put in a different context, too, with the paper suggesting that "Vajpayee's new government, scheduled to be formed next week, should not delay in fulfilling its promise to sign the Comprehensive Test Ban Treaty". New Delhi should adhere to its professed line that its "nuclear tests were only for national security and nuclear deterrence purposes".

With the theme of a possible international niche for Indian democracy dominating the new political consciousness of the Indonesian elite, *Kompas*, an influential paper in the native language, said, "While Indonesia has only recently again started experiencing democratic life... over four decades, India has always practised democracy since Independence." Noting that the latest electoral exercise in "the largest democracy in the world" has now "successfully come to an end," the paper said, "The winning party should now concentrate on fulfilling its promises... which include maintaining peace and stability in the region and at the international level", it should also "work for improving the living standards and welfare of the people of India".

9

Views and News

Elections and Results

The CPI(M)

The election results had clearly demonstrated certain trends among the voters so far as their preference for various parties were concerned.

The Congress, which at one time vehemently opposed the coalition concept had come round to the view that under the present circumstances its dream of single party rule at the centre was not even a distant possibility. However, its dismal performance in terms of number of MPs (including its allies and sympathisers like the Left parties) had put it out of court.

The NDA which was a pre-poll alliance had secured clear majority and much more than the magic number of 272. There was no other choice except the NDA and yet the Congress and the Third Front leaders did not seem reconciled to the verdict. Like spoil sports, they were attacking the NDA government without being in any position to offer a viable alternative. Their frustration and blinkered vision was clearly visible in their post-poll utterances and statements.

Harkishan Singh Surjeet

Maintaining that the ruling party would be much more precariously placed this time, CPI-M general secretary Harkishan Singh Surjeet said that while the BJP has not been able to improve upon its tally even marginally, the representation of the allies has gone up. In his view, the increased strength of the allies gives them more leverage.

Still struggling to come to terms with the fact that some of its erstwhile friends have aligned with the BJP, Surjeet warned that in doing so these parties may have invited the danger of the communal virus spreading in their respective States.

Writing in the party weekly *People's Democracy*, Surjeet said that while the future would show how the colaition would work, the people would have to brace themselves for a more vigorous struggle against the "not-so-hidden agenda" of the communal forces. This agenda, he said, is likely to be pursued more vigorously this time by the saffron brigade.

Many of the allies would be forced to oppose the BJP's pursuit of the Hindutva agenda in Government. As most of them represent regional aspirations, their outlook and perceptions could come in conflict and contradict the BJP's position.

The CPI-M leader recalled that during the campaign itself, allies like the DMK and the TDP had sought to distance and demarcate themselves from the BJP.

Sonia Gandhi and Others

The Congres(I) president, Ms. Sonia Gandhi, called for introspection tc assess the reverses suffered by the party in the Lok Sabha elections. In a statement, she "unhesitatingly" accepted the verdict of the people while admitting that the results had not been up to expectations.

The results did cause reverberations in the party but for the moment, at least, Ms Gandhi's leadership does not appear to be under threat. There is no other consensus leader around whom the partymen can rally; besides, the party is still reeling from its poorest performance ever. Key players in the Congress(I) seem to be waiting to gauge the mood of fellow leaders before making any move.

But Ms. Gandhi will have to fight to regain her hold on the party if younger leaders assert themselves. The AICC(I) establishment insisted that Ms. Gandhi should not be held solely responsible for the sharp decline in seats since both the leader and the party contributed to a victory or defeat.

When it was pointed out that this was not the view in 1996 and 1998, when the party presidents, P.V. Narasimha Rao and Sitaram Kesri, were held responsible and forced to quit after the party's numbers declined in the Lok Sabha, the spokesman, Kapil Sibal, said the party was still to anlayse the results.

In fact, in 1998 under Kesri's leadership, the party had won 142 Lok Sabha seats but he was unceremoniously ousted to make way for Ms. Gandhi. But Sibal claimed today that "if Ms. Gandhi had not campaigned for the party then, we would have got fewer seats".

The former President of the INC Sitaram Kesri, in a T.V. interview was extremely critical of the role played by the advisors like Arjun Singh. He however justified the retention of Sonia Gandhi as President on the plea that there was no other available option. Manmohan Singh was tried but was pushed out with a small 'jhatka' by the RSS. He claimed that he was familiar with the mentality of the grassroot workers of the Congress party and leaders who met the workers only by appointment were totally ignorant of the grassroot realities. The party spokesman Kapil Sibal ceased to be at his job for 'professional' reasons. Ajit Jogi was backed after his defeat at the polls. Mani Shanker continued to show his optimism. Others like Renuka Chowdhry kept on hoping rather wishing that the alliance would break under the pressure of its contradictions as the regional allies would not allow the leading partner, the BJP to cut into their popularity base within the States.

Karunanidhi

Karunanidhi of the DMK was firm about his party adhering to NDA agenda.

The common manifesto of the NDA was itself based on consultations Vajpayee had "with all of us."

Further, the NDA itself, as a "new political formation", had committed itself to fresh initiatives and efforts for building a "resurgent" India. Fidelity to this, common document would mark the DMK's approach, clarified Karunanidhi.

On the presence of "more demanding partners" (such as the AIADMK) earlier which had made the Vajpayee coalition shaky and on whether the Government would be stable this time, Karunanidhi said, "let us hope for good things." Declining to comment on poll reverses and surprises in several other States, Karunanidhi, to another query, said it was not a question of whether 18 or 24 partners figured in the NDA in ensuring the stability of a coalition Government. "It is the intention and attitude of the partners that matter," he added.

The DMK chief also hinted that the issue of admitting new partners into the NDA was quite open. "Are you ready?" shot back Karunanidhi when asked about the possibility of new entrants, in the context of the TDP's attitude towards the NDA.

M.L. Sondhi

Prof. M.L. Sondhi, now Chairman of the Indian Council for Social Science Research made a detailed analysis of the election results and also spelled out the future agenda for the NDA listing the priorities.

A product of the London School of Economics, Prof. Sondhi was with the Foreign Service before he resigned and plunged into politics as a JS candidate from Delhi. He had been teaching at the Jawahar Lal Nehru University all these years. He wrote:

The results of the 1999 elections have upset many expectations of the political pundits who predicted a confused outcome, if not victory for the emerging 'largest party'. So much accustomed to the triumphalism of the past, they failed to perceive the new psychological equilibrium produced by Vajpayee's active role model in Indian politics.

Leaving aside UP and Punjab as special cases of pathological infighting, the prudence and deliberation with which the BJP has defied apocalyptic predictions in Maharashtra, Madhya Pradesh, Bihar, Tamil Nadu, Gujarat and Andhra Pradesh, and has crossed declared 'red lines' almost everywhere else, is a tribute to the masterful integration of 'strategy' and 'conscience'. This is the Vajpayee factor that makes his policies distinctive from the abrasive real politik of other political *dramatis personae*. The number of votes for the BJP, right up to the Andaman islands, is cause for trepidation for the other all-India party, the Congress.

Many illusions are being fostered to save the Congress face, but it is clear that the strength and impact of this party have been grossly overstated. The grotesque exaggerations of many of the party's spokesmen and sympathisers during the election campaign created a polarised environment in which the Congress leadership played a spoiler's role. The outstanding exception was Dr. Karan Singh who conducted a scholarly and sophisticated campaign. They underestimated the challenge from a Prime Minister whose confidence stemmed not only from his government's international reputation as an outward looking force, but who, despite pockets of resistance from his own side, came through as the vehicle for India's political and cultural adjustment to scientific, technological and economic advance.

The Congress is no longer an ideology-driven organisation, it does not represent the Indian mainstream, and it has failed to democratise itself. Hence, it would be premature to talk of a real resurgence in a systematic sense of the Congress in UP, Karnataka or Punjab, since its dyanstic model will exacerbate political feuding at both national and regional levels.

Surveying the developments under way, there are grounds for cautious optimism in favour of the Vajpayee-led National Democratic Alliance. The task of running a coalition might indeed appear formidable, but the outcome will depend on the speed with which the mandate for economic reforms and strategic independence is translated into practice. Let us look at the following five items and how they relate to the political scenario:

1. Respect for the electoral mandate: The platform of the NDA promises to provide

impressive momentum to the processes of economic reform and modernisation. The NDA takes robust attitude to a dramatic economic turnaround whereas the Congress and the Left, nostalgic for the pre-glasnost days in the Soviet Union, still speak a language opposed to the economic underpinning of a civil society. They draw heart from the chinese experiment in marrying incompatibles, which will lead, according to China-watchers, not to synthesis, but to chaos. The electoral verdict and its pattern is overwhelmingly in favour of democratic values.

2. The mandate to consolidate institutional structures for economic reforms: Vajpayee has clearly stated in a recent interview that he wishes to take reforms 'to a new plane': indeed he has hinted at a 'hundred days' programme. Some policy recommendations could be adopted immediately to meet the multiple objectives of high and efficient growth, low inflation and rapid poverty alleviation: (a) get the Finance Ministry out of determining interest rates, (b) get the market in, and (c) let the Ministry of Finance and the Reserve Bank coordinate policies to make interest rates market-determined.

As economic writer Surjit S. Bhalla has observed "Freeing the interest rate regime would be a win-win policy for Vajpayee's government. Growth will go up enormously. Inefficiencies will be eliminated, jobs will increase, poverty rates will go down, inflation will stay low, and India's competitiveness and exports should witness a boom." (d) to prevent inter-ministry battles either a reform-czar ministry or individual should be set or appointed to give a cohesive framework to reforms, as well as (e) an advisory committee of the best professionals on various aspects of reform.

3. Mandate to consolidate a strategic vision: The Vajpayee government clearly has a mandate to stabilise India's external environment, which can be firmed up by garnering support across the political spectrum. A domestic consensus is coming into being for a new strategic direction for the next five years, composed of both peaceful regional and global environment, and also for immediate security issues. His policy spectrum of underground nuclear tests, missile development, withstanding the pressure of sanctions, ousting the Kargil intruders and ensuring the diplomatic isolation of Pakistan has been most impressive. India's interests will continue to include a nuclear inventory of both quantity and quality. The CTBT is not an end in itself. India's identity and federal cohesion can be secured by broadening the base of its strategic reliance.

4. Mandate for India as a mature and outward-looking internationalist force: Even as a 'caretaker' Prime Minister, Vajpayee worked with vigour and success in taking crucial economic and strategic decisions disproving the thesis of a 'power-vacuum' at the Centre. In the controversy over India's telecom policy implementation, he was guided by the needs of reform and liberalisation. When facing external military threats he reflected the strength of India's democratic system, and his own pragmatism and discretion in behaving like a responsible decision-maker leading a nuclear India.

His great moral achievement has been to restore India's image as a mature and outward-looking internationalist force. With the US he has opened a political space for both domestic prosperity and international leverage, but will have to manage the Indo-US relationship for it to function as a factor for stability, and resist the allure of 'appeasement'.

5. Mandate for legitimising 'Indian' secularism and strengthening democracy: The Indian identity has been problematic since at least the last century, moving between tradition and modernity, secularism and culture, mainstream and subaltern. The last BJP-led government began the process of legitimising an alternative verison of Indian

secularism—*sarva dharma sambhava* i.e., recognising the religious ethos of this country as expressed through no matter which religion, community or sect.

Despite the brouhaha created by the dispossessed Congress and Left elites, the functioning of the BJP-led government has been neither 'theocratic'—there are no Hindu priests with a canonical right to wield political power—nor fascist. The only spell of fascist rule in this country, with suspension of the right to habeas corpus, full media censorship, suppression of all political freedoms took place under Indira Gandhi's leadership, and she remains an icon for many Congress leaders.

We may indeed congratulate ourselves for following a relatively peaceful electoral procedure for changing governments. But there are disturbing trends pointing to a devaluation of the spirit of democracy—an obsessive concern with a numerical majority to the exclusion of norms, institutions and restraints. Politicians openly boast of rigging seats, of using criminal and mafia organisations to gather votes, and seek to electorally institutionalise dynasticism. In fact, the key issue for Vajpayee today is the unfinished task of taking democracy forward into the next millennium. (*Courtsey*: *Hindustan Times*)

Mayawati

In Uttar Pradesh, Mayawati senmed more concerned with performance of SP rather than the debacle suffered by the BJP. She attributed the improvement in the Samajwadi party's poll performance to the "support" it got from Chief Minister Kalyan Singh.

Talking to newspersons Ms Mayawati said Kalyan Singh overtly helped the SP candidates and in certain cases ensured defeat of the official BJP nominee by blatant misuse of the Government machinery. In some cases, Ms Mayawati said, even the district administration officials were instructed by the Chief Minister to ensure victory of the SP contestants.

She said that the defeated BJP candidate and two-time MP, Ramvilas Vedanti, had exposed Kalyan Singh and had even decided to sit in dharna demanding his removal.

She said that even the helicopter used by Sakshi Maharaj, the expelled BJP leader who was denied ticket from Farrukhabad parliamentary seat and who campaigned for the SP candidates, was provided by Chief Minister Kalyan Singh. Mr. Singh, she alleged, identified his "enemies" within the party and ensured their defeat in an organised manner.

Denying that the Congress won 12 seats due to the Sonia-Priyanka factor, Ms Mayawati said that it won "due to money power and a manipulated media".

Former BSP minister and Mayawati loyalist RK Choudhary explained: "(BSP leader) Kanshi Ram and Mayawati diligently followed the slogan - each one's share according to his strength. Thus, they gave 17 per cent tickets to Muslims, 38 per cent to backwards, 20 per cent to Dalits, and 10 per cent to upper castes. They also developed leadership across the state in the castes neglected by other political parties such as Pal, Shakya, Baghel, Maurya, Pushkar, and Saini among the backwards, and Sankhawar, Passi, Dhobi, Valmiki, and Khatiks among Dalits. This paid dividends."

Then, having decided to fight the Lok Sabha election alone, the BSP leadership took three major steps:

❖ Early selection of candidates in consultation with the district office-bearers.

❖ Setting up a poll management system by dividing Vidhan Sabha segments into sectors of 20 polling booths, each handled by six workers.

❖ Identifying winning seats, which included those 16 in which the BSP had ended second in 1998.

The result was spectacular. The party won 14 seats and finished second in another

14. Of the 16 it concentrated on, it won seven: Shahabad, Sitapur, Ghosi, Lalganj, Banda, Jalaun and Saharanpur.

"Our awareness rallies have not gone waste," says Choudhary, adding that, perhaps for the first time, Dalits cast their votes in constituencies like Ballia, Gonda and Pratapgarh.

The basic strategy was to evolve a constituency-specific "winning caste combination". This explains the party's fielding a Brahmin in Jalesar and a Thakur in Sultanpur (which the BSP won primarily because there was no other Thakur in the fray.)

Mayawati herself said that the performance was because of hard work. Away from the media glare, she campaigned in all 85 constituencies by road. The party did not hire filmstars or resort to any gimmicks. In the end, she convinced her flock that she could best protect their interests; as a result, others joined the bandwagon.

Mulayam Singh Yadav

The SP leader had his own reasons for the BJP's performance. His contention was that the performance could have been still worst for his adversary, the NDA but for the Congress strategy in Uttar Pradesh.

Samajwadi Party president Mulayam Singh Yadav said that the Congress had "helped" the Bharatiya Janata Party-led alliance come to power.

Addressing newspersons after the constitution of the 13th Lok Sabha, Yadav said he "regretted" the CPI(M) also took a stand that helped the Congress. He said he could not believe the Left party could go "against" its own resolutions.

Yadav said he would not comment on how long the new Government would last. For at least six months, he said, he would like to keep quiet. "Let them take oath. Let the portfolios be distributed," he said.

The Samajwadi Party president said 20 to 25 seats were won by the BJP as the Congress was trying to defeat the Samajwadi Party. Prime Minister Atal Bihari Vajpayee and Congress president Sonia Gandhi attacked each other "just to show off", he said. In fact they were friendly towards each other.

The Samajwadi leader said that Murli Manohar Joshi would not have won in Allahabad but for the Congress's "role". The same was the reason behind the success of the BJP candidate in Dumriaganj. While the Congress did all possible things to make things easier for the BJP, it was left to the Samajwadi Party to fight the BJP he said.

Yadav said his party would challenge in the poll verdict in Ghatampur and Hardoi where the party candidates had lost by small margins. He said that the Congress had gone to the polls with 146 members in the last Lok Sabha and had come to the level of 112. The Samajwadi Party had 20 members earlier and had raised its tally to 26.

Saeed Naqvi

Sonia's strategy of saying no to coalitions was critically commented upon by the political analyst Saeed Naqvi in Indian Express:

So the Congress has got its just desserts for having been so fawning and obsequious about Sonia Gandhi. Let me tell you a simple story. Somewhere in it may be a clue to what I think of her politics.

I feel sorry that Vasant Sathe walked straight into the trap I laid for him during one of those TV election specials becuase he remains my favourite Congressman. The poor fellow gave away the game the most senior Congressman nurture as a deep secret.

On the panel were two Congressmen, Vasant Sathe and Jairam Ramesh to take stock of the situation just before the counting began. To wind up the situation I asked them a simple question: "Supposing, for argument's sake, the Congress emerges as the largest single party, would it be willing to form a coalition government?" Ramesh said: "If such a situation arose we shall have to consider coalitions".

But Sathe, in full glare of TV camera, raised both his hands like he were warding off some evil: "No, no, no" he exclaimed. "We are all sunk if we ever go into a coalition".

Let us consider the attitude towards coalitions that Sonia Gandhi's Congress has maintained from the very outset.

Remember the Ides of March, 1998. The election results were in. The BJP was deftly putting together a coalition. Chandrababu Naidu, with 12 MPs, was hesitating. The President, who was consulting various leaders, also met the Congress President, Sitaram Kesri, who asked for time. Supposing the wily old Congress President was buying time to put together some sort of a backward caste-driven power structure which would have included the dreaded Yadavs from UP and Bihar, where do you think would Sathe have stood in such a bargain? "No, no, no," he would have said, "we shall be sunk in a coalition". That Sathe is a metaphor for a large body of the Congress party became quite clear on that occasion. Kesri's name plates were pulled out in a matter of hours. Sonia Gandhi was installed as party president.

Her moment of glory was the Pachmarhi session of the Congress in September 1998. Under her leadership, the party said "no to coalitions" even though the Yadavs were imploring her to let them in.

"No" to coalitions at this juncture made a great deal of sense because in the assembly elections due in November in Madhya Pradesh, Rajasthan and Delhi, the contest was a direct one between the Congress and the BJP. No coalitions were required. Considering that the Congress trounced the BJP in the three contests, the decision taken at Pachmarhi was a brilliant one.

Instead of treating the outcome of the three elections as a particular happening, thinkers around Sonia Gandhi, somewhat in the Sathe mould, enunciated a general principle: the Congress would return to power on its own. Even this carried credit so long as Sonia was seen as the architect of a Congress party revival.

But her implausible pursuit of prime ministerial power caused not just Sharad Pawar's revolt, but raised eyebrows all around. Sonia Gandhi does not wish to supervise cabinet meetings with the likes of the Yadavs breathing down her neck; Sonia Gandhi would like to be prime minister. How does one reconcile the irreconcilable? It was some cheek on her part to really believe that even though her party had threatened to bury Mulayam Singh Yadav in UP, the Samajwadi party leader, driven by some inexplicable higher purpose, would still support her elevation to prime ministership.

Many Congressmen have developed an amnesia about the fact that Sonia Gandhi by saying no to coalitions on that occasion, was once again enabling the BJP to continue in power during the period when the NDA extracted the advantages from Kargil.

Then followed the current campaign. Sonia Gandhi was the prime ministerial candidate but it was still unclear whether she was still averse to coalitions or enthusiastic about them in graduated measure.

What are the implications of this sustained ambiguity? Sonia Gandhi allowed herself to be pitted against Atal Bihari Vajpayee as the prime ministerial candidate. To become prime minister, sans coalitions, she would have had to be within striking distance of

272 seats. This, clearly, was an absurd proposition.

What then, was the game? Well, as Jairam Ramesh said, "we may have to consider a coalition" provided the numbers favour such a scenario.

But if Vasant Sathe is allowed to write Sonia Gandhi's speech in such circumstances, it would read something like this: "We must rediscover the elan of the Congress for which Mahatma Gandhi, Jawaharlal Nehru, Indira Gandhi and Rajiv Gandhi made so many sacrifices. This we can do only by not falling prey to the lure of office by entering into unprincipled coalitions. We shall soon see that a coalition of 24 disparate elements, where Mandal and Kamandal have joined hands in crude pursuit of power, cannot take the country forward".

What would have been the implications of this hypothetical statement? It would have enabled the BJP and allies to come to power for the third time.

The Indian electorate has spared Sonia Gandhi the occasion to play such a role. The point I am making is this; after the Mandalisation of politics, the BJP reacted swiftly and sought to accommodate all tiers in the Hindu society into the power structure.

The BJP, for all its weaknesses, is a politically alert organisation. Look how it created space for powerful regional parties in its framework. The Congress, under the leadership of political illiterates like Sonia Gandhi, has persisted with its self-defeating upper casteism.

K. Pankajakshan

K. Pankajakshan, General Secretary of the RSP bashed both the CPI(M) and the CPI. The Forward Bloc had been rather soft on the two Left majors but the RSP demanded an attitudinal change.

"Until and unless an attitudinal change is made by them no viable and cohesive Left Front or for that matter Left unity worth the name can be achieved."

According to the party, only if the Left parties unite together on policies and programmes, they can effectively exhort and work towards the formation of a Third Front which includes the Left, democratic and secular forces. And, it is such a Third Front with the Left parties as its core, which can counter the 'corrupt' Congress and the 'communal' BJP and their retrograde, anti-people policies.

The RSP, which saw the ingredients of such a front in parties like the Samajwadi Party and the Nationalist Congress Party, however, agreed that there were a number of economic issues on which the SP and the Left parties did not have a similar stand.

While assessing the post-poll scenario and its impact on the national scene, the RSP underlined that the two Communist parties' advocacy for supporting the Congress in the name of resisting the BJP proved to be futile. This line, it emphasised, not only did not do any good for the CPI-M or the CPI but it also caused considerable damage to the advancement of the Left movement as such.

The absence of a united Left was a major hurdle in the advancement of progressive Left forces in the country, with the divergence of views between the two Communist parties and other Left parties standing in the way of Left unity, he said.

Asserting that Left unity does not simply mean the unity among the major parties of the Left, Pankajakshan claimed that a concerted effort has to be made to include all like-minded parties in the broad Left political spectrum.

Mammen Mathew

The defeat of Laloo Yadav in Bihar was a big political event. *The Hindustan Times* discussed the issue. Writing about the 'big loser' Mammen Mathew wrote:

Ram Vilas Paswan can puff out his chest. It was his addition of anti-establishment, anti-Yadav, Dalit votes to the BJP's upper caste formation and the Samata Party's Kurmi support base that swept out Laloo Prasad Yadav in Bihar, despite the latter's Muslim-Yadav combination steadfastly holding firm.

Propelled into power in 1990 by chance, Laloo Yadav had consolidated his hold in Bihar through the Mandal magic and by stopping LK. Advani's Rath Yatra. The formidable combination of OBCs and Muslims enabled his Janata Dal to bag most of Bihar's 54 seats in the 1991 general election.

Yet Laloo frittered away this base quickly. Keen to stem any challenge that might arise to his leadership in the Janata Dal, he began to consciously consolidate the Muslim-Yadav base, ignoring and even alienating the Kurmis whose leader Nitish Kumar was his potential rival. The increasing Yadavisation goaded Nitish Kumar to float his own outfit, Samata, in 1994: the Kurmi-Koeri castes combined with the CPI-ML electorally in the 1995 Assembly election, but failed to make any headway.

The Laloo magic started to fade in 1996 itself. Samata and BJP aligned to win 30 seats in that year's election, and 32 in 1998. But till then, it was more a battle of attrition. However, the Samata-BJP combine received a fillip once Paswan joined the National Democratic Alliance (NDA), and blunted Laloo's MY edge. Paswan convinced confused Dalit voters to throw in their lot with the anti-Laloo combine. Indeed, but for the absence of Muslims, the BJP-Samata-Janata Dal (U) alliance mirrors, to some extent, the social alliance the Congress had forged before the advent of Mandal.

The Dalit-forward-backward phalanx now theoretically embraces a spectrum of over 80 castes against a handful in the Left-Laloo-Congress camp. Yet, despite the BJP's tremendous performance, its own vote share has declined by four per cent—and the Congress' has increased by five per cent. This is exactly where Paswan managed to damage Laloo. His Dalit support provided the winning edge. That the RJD and Congress could manage just eight out of 40 seats in north and central Bihar is proof.

Muslim alienation was also crucial, especially at Madhepura where Laloo failed to woo the Muslim-dominated segment of Alamnagar. This had given a lead of 9,000 to Sharad Yadav in 1998 and, this time, boosted him by four times that. Again, Kishanganj constituency is 70 per cent Muslim, yet elected BJP candidate Shahnawaz Hussain.

As the results came trickling in, silence enveloped the chief minister's residence at 1, Anne Marg. Indeed, Laloo Yadav has reasons to worry—with the Assembly election only three months away, the BJP-Samata-JD(U) combine, on the basis of this performance could win 160 Assembly seats.

Rashtriya Janata Dal insiders blame their leader for the debacle, claiming his penchant to field deserters from other parties caused tremendous heartburn—party workers and leaders refused to cooperate with those who had recently joined the party. They also say the alliance with the Congress proved costly, for it led to a polarisation of the anti-Laloo vote. So far, as an option to BJP-Samata, the Congress had been helping fracture this.

Detractors, however, admit that though Laloo is down, it would be foolish to declare him out. For one, the result could help create a sympathy wave for him in the Assembly election. To pre-empt this, the victorious combine had better start delivering at once.

Atal Bihari Vajpayee

And finally the Prime Minister Atal Bihari Vajpayee called on political parties for making a new beginning to unitedly face the challenges now confronting the country "It is time that the bitterness generated during the elections subsides. It is time that we created an atmosphere for consensus." Towards this end, he proposes to evolve a mechanism which would enable the government and the Opposition parties to exchange views and search for solutions in a spirit of accommodation.

Mr. Vajpyaee, said that the Opposition would be taken into confidence to bring about a consensus on matters related to the economy which figure at the top of his list of priorities. He mentioned in particular the need to speedily clear the backlog of pending Bills. These include the Insurance Regulatory Authority (IRA) Bill, the Money Laundering Prevention Bill, the Foreign Exchange Management Act, the Companies Act and so forth. Mr. Vajpayee would also like to ensure the swift passage of the new telecom policy and to get as wide an agreement as he can secure on the future of public sector undertakings, on providing a fillip to the private sector and on creating a climate that would be conducive for bringing in foreign investment. About opposition, Vajpayee said that they will have to rethink their position. They will have to take a close look at potentially profitable PSUs which can be revived. But those which do not fall under this category cannot simply be "finished" since salaries must continue to be paid. It is in this larger context that privatisation will have to be viewed.

Equally urgent for the Prime Minister is the need to strengthen rural infrastructure. He said that efforts will have to be stepped up to build roads, provide education, health care, electricity and other basic amenities. He pointed to a new problem that has arisen in the country. "It is difficult to judge where a village ends and a city begins. Both are expanding. Indeed, some villages fall within the jurisdiction of a municipality."

The Prime Minister added: "There is a new realisation in the villages. They look at the amenities that are available in the city. They are aware of the city lifestyle. And they wonder why they are denied access to them."

He said that his government intended to provide more resources and more power to panchayats and zilla parishads to enable them to better shoulder the task of development. But the real problem, he said, was that the implementation of development schemes left much to be desired.

Mr. Vajpayee said that strange as it may sound, money was not really a problem. The fact is that the money allocated to projects was either not spent well or not spent at all.

Another problem is that in any development project the Centre and the states have to share the costs. However, states are reluctant to give their share. The result is that the funds set aside by the Centre lie unattended.

Consensus, Vajpayee said, was also vital to initiate electoral reforms. A committee to look into all aspects of the electoral system and the functioning of Parliament would be set up soon. It could take up a number of suggestions made by the law commssion which, he said, were 'excellent'.

On issues related to foreign policy, Vajpayee, in an answer to a question related to President Bill Clinton's proposed visit to India, said the American President was welcome to come but a "postive atmosphere needed to be created." He mentioned in particular the move to lift sanctions and at the same time to give the President authority on the Pressler rules. This would allow him to lift sanctions on military sales to Pakistan. Such a step, the Prime Minsiter said, would compel India to divert its resources for purchasing arms since the country's security concerns would have to be met regardless of the costs.

At the same time, he said, India must build on the enormous goodwill it has earned thanks to the restraint and maturity it showed during the Kargil crisis. Despite intense provocation,India chose not to cross the Line of Control. India's peaceful intentions were thus demonstrated to the entire world.

On resuming the dialogue with Pakistan, Vajpayee said that a change of attitude in Islamabad was imperative. The change has to be evident on the ground. "How can you tolerate cross-border terrorism?" he asked. He said Pakistan has not fully realised that many people are disturbed at the way that country "did Kargil after Lahore". The restoration of trust was required. "Talks can begin at the official level any day. But without trust they would be of no avail." Once the element of trust finds its rightful place in the relations betweeen the two countries, they can talk on all issues, including Kashmir.

The Prime Minister said he was keen to step up regional cooperation, especially in the area of trade. He said that an "unnecessary debate" was created about sugar imports from Pakistan. The most extraordinary interpretations were given: the sugar was paid for in dollars; these dollars were used to buy arms; and these arms killed our jawans and so forth. The fact of the matter, Vajpayee said, was that the balance of trade is in India's favour. He was of the firm belief that trade should increase among SAARC countries.

Mr. Vajpayee said that soon after the formation of the government he would be talking to the Opposition on India's stand on CTBT. He expressed confidence that it was possible for them to forge a consensus taking into full account the country's security needs and its international obligations.

10

Lok Sabha Elections (1952-99)

The Lok Sabhas since 1952 - A Brief Resume

There have been thirteen Lok Sabhas since the first ever elections held in 1952. The first three Lok Sabhas had a full five years term.

The term of the fourth Lok Sabha would have expired in 1972 but the elections were preponed to 1971. The year 1969 witnessed a split in the Congress and Mrs. Indira Gandhi, the then Prime Minister sought a fresh mandate from the people

In the fourth General Elections, held in 1967 the faction led by Mrs. Indira Gandhi got 350 seats while the split group Congress (O) got just 16 seats.

The term of the fifth Lok Sabha constituted in 1971 would have under normal circumstances expired in 1976. But in between came the Allabhabad High Court judgement. Indira Gandhi responded to the adverse verdict against her by imposing emergency and during this period, the term of the Lok Sabha was extended by one year.

The sixth Lok Sabha elections were held in 1977. The Congress lost the majority having won just 154 seats against 297 seats won by the newly formed Janata Party. The Janata Party comprised a number of parties. Besides Congress (O), there were the Jana Sangh, Socialist Party and the Congress for Democracy.

The combination could not last long. Morarji Desai could not carry the team together and was succeeded by Charan Singh as the Prime Minister from the Janata Party. Charan Singh had the unique distinction of having been the Prime Minister and yet never faced the Lok Sabha in that capacity. The final fall came in 1979 and fresh elections were held in 1980.

The seventh Lok Sabha lasted till 1984. The then Prime Minister Indira Gandhi was assasinated and the succeeding Prime Minister Rajiv Gandhi decided to have fresh elections in 1984. He wanted to cash the sympathy wave and the Congress was back in the eighth Lok Sabha with 415 seats out of a total of 515 seats contested by the party.

The year proved dismal for the BJP. It was reduced to just 2 members in the Lok Sabha. Rajiv Gandhi entered the Lok Sabha with a new vision. However, the odds were heavy against him. It was not easy to break the power brokers lobby, more so because money was needed to run the party and it could not be arranged without recourse to give and take between the government and the private donors.

It is alleged that placed under these compulsions a new strategy was evolved. Instead of raising money from private persons and corporates, the party preferred cuts in government deals with foreign firms. One such deal which cost the Congress party its next term was the Bofors deal. The eighth Lok Sabha was dissolved on 27th November 1989.

In Ninth Lok Sabha again these was a non-Congress majority. Although the

Congress had secured 195 seats the largest seats by a single party, Rajiv Gandhi declined to form the government in the absence of an outright mandate. The Janta Dal headed by V.P. Singh had won only 143 seats but formed the government with the understanding that has government would have support from BJP, CPI, CPI(M) and some others from outside.

The Ninth Lok Sabha lasted for only 16 months and eleven days. In between there were two Prime Ministers-V.P. Singh and Chandra Shekhar.

The Ninth Lok Sabha was dissolved on March 6, 1991. In the elections to the 10th Lok Sabha held in 1991, Congress improved its tally. It had 251 MPs. The number was short of an absolute majority but the Prime Minister P.V. Narsimha Rao managed to survive the full term.

The Congress did not have the requisite majority and yet survived the full term. The structural demolition of the Masjid at Ayodhya Ram Janmabhoomi took place during Narsimha Rao's tenure and JVM bribery case was also a product of this era. The 1996 elections to the 11th Lok Sabha resulted in a hung parliament. The BJP had 161 members and the Congress only 140. The BJP was given a chance to form the government but it could not cobble a majority and resigned after just 13 days of power handing over the reigns of the government to the United Front.

The eleventh Lok Sabha was unable to survive for the full term although in between the UF Prime Minister Deve Gowda had to be replaced by I.K. Gujaral as the Congress price for outside support.

Twelfth Lok Sabha elections were held in 1998. The BJP had a score of 182 MPs. With the support of MPs from other parties, some of whom were part of the government Atal Bihari Vajpayee was able to run the government but only for 13 months. This time the government headed by Atal Bihari Vajpayee lost the confidence vote by just 1 number and fresh elections had to be held. No party or combination was able to satsify the President that it had the support of 272 members. Sonia Gandhi's efforts to bring all non-BJP MPs under one banner did not click as the Congress was averse to coalition and the SP headed by Mulayam Singh was unwilling to let the Congress be in power and decimate its Muslim vote bank in Uttar Pradesh. A detailed account of the fall of the government forms another chapter in the book.

The Thirteenth Lok Sabha was again without any single party securing an absolute majority. But this time the BJP had contested elections as part of the National Democratic Alliance and the alliance did have the requisite number.

Once again it is a combination of parties in power. The Congress had 114 members against 182 of the BJP. There is a fair chance that the Lok Sabha this time will have a full term. But politics often defies logical forecasting.

Table 1 reflects the party position at a glance in the 13 Lok Sabhas.

Table 2 provides information regarding the performance of each party in each State in the previous 12 Lok Sabhas, covering data on seats won, percentage of votes obtained, and running up parties.

Table 3 present party position in North-East.

Table 4 to 12 include data on diverse issues like total candidates, voters, performance of women, independents, qualifications, occupations of Members and expenditure etc.

Table 10.1 : Party Position in the Thirteen Lok Sabhas (1952 - 1999)

Lok Sabha	Period	Total Seats	Congress	BJS/BJP	CPI	CPI (M)	Janta Party	Others
First	1952-57	489	364	3	16	Did not exist	Did not exist	106
Second	1957-62	494	371	4	27	Do	Do	92
Third	1962-67	494	361	14	29	Do	Do	90
Fourth	1967-71	520	283	35	23	19	Do	160
Fifth	1971-76	518	350	22	23	25	-	98
Sixth	1976-79	542	154	-	7	22 (BJS, Congress, and other parties)	297	62
Seventh	1979-84	542	353	52	11	36 JP (S) 41	JP (JP) 31	118
Eighth	1985-89	522	415	2	6	22	10	67
Ninth	1989-91	543	197	86	12	33	143 (Janata Dal)	72
Tenth	1991-95	543	251	119	14	35	39 (Janata Dal)	85
Eleventh	1996-98	543	140	161	12	32	47 (Janata Dal)	151
Twelfth	1998-99	543	141	182	9	32 17 Rashtria Janata Dal	6 (Janata Dal)	146
Thirteenth	1999-	543	114	182	4	32	21 JD(U)	190

Note : 1999 elections : TDP 29 (Andhra Pradesh) NCP 8 (Maharashtra 6, Manipur 1, Meghalaya 11)
Shiv Sena 15 (Maharashtra) SP 26 (Uttar Pradesh TC 8 (West Bengal)
DMK 12 (Tamil Nadu) BSP 14 (Uttar Pradesh)
AIADMK 10 (Tamil Nadu) BJP 10 (Orissa)
RJD 7 (Bihar)

Table 10.2 : Party Performance Statewise : 1952-99

Year	Leading Party	Seats won	Vote (%)	Runner-up	Seats won	Vote (%)
Andhra Pradesh						
1952	Congress	14	40.1	PDF	7	28.2
1957	Congress	37	51.5	CPI	2	12.0
1962	Congress	34	48.0	CPI	7	21.0
1967	Congress	35	46.8	SWA	3	13.8
1971	Congress	28	55.7	TPS	10	14.3
1977	Congress	41	57.4	BLD	1	32.3
1980	Congress	41	56.2	INCU	1	7.2
1984	TDP	30	44.8	Congress	6	41.8
1989	Congress	39	51.0	TDP	2	34.5
1991	Congress	25	45.6	TDP	13	32.3
1996	Congress	22	39.7	TDP	16	32.4
1998	Congress	22	38.5	TDP	12	32.0
1999	TDP	29	-	BJP	5	-
Assam						
1952	Congress	11	45.7	SOC	1	19.2
1957	Congress	9	51.7	PSP	2	20.0
1962	Congress	9	45.1	PSP	2	19.1
1967	Congress	10	45.8	PSP	2	12.8
1971	Congress	13	57.0	APHC	1	3.0
1977	Congress	10	50.6	BLD	3	35.8
1980	Congress	2	51.0	ICS	0	31.8
1985	AGP	7	33.4	Congress	4	23.6
1991	Congress	8	28.5	BJP	2	8.6
1996	Congress	6	31.6	AGP	5	27.2
1998	Congress	10	39.0	BJP	1	24.5
1999	Congress	10	-	BJP	2	-
Bihar						
1952	Congress	45	45.8	SOC	3	21.3
1957	Congress	41	44.5	JHP	6	7.5
1962	Congress	39	43.9	SWA	7	18.2
1967	Congress	34	34.8	SSP	7	17.8
1971	Congress	39	40.1	CPI	5	9.9
1977	BLD	52	65.0	AIJKD	1	0.6
1980	Congress	30	36.4	Janata Party	8	23.6
1984	Congress	48	51.8	CPI	2	8.2
1989	Janata Dal	32	37.7	BJP	8	11.7
1991	Janata Dal	31	34.1	CPI	8	7.6
1996	Janata Dal	22	31.8	BJP	18	205
1998	BJP	20	24.0	RJD	17	20.6
1999	BJP	23	-	JD(U)	18	-

Year	Leading Party	Seats won	Vote (%)	Runner-up	Seats won	Vote (%)
Delhi						
1952	Congress	3	49.4	KMPP	1	7.3
1957	Congress	5	54.3	BJS	0	19.7
1962	Congress	5	50.7	BJS	0	32.7
1967	BJS	6	46.7	Congress	1	38.8
1971	Congress	7	64.4	BJS	0	29.6
1977	BLD	7	68.2	Congress	0	30.2
1980	Congress	6	50.4	Janata Party	1	37.9
1984	Congress	7	68.7	JP	0	18.8
1989	BJP	4	26.2	Congress	2	43.4
1991	BJP	5	40.2	Congress	2	39.6
1996	BJP	5	49.6	Congress	2	37.3
1998	BJP	6	50.7	Congress	1	42.6
1999	BJP	7	-	Congress	0	-
Gujarat						
1962	Congress	16	52.6	SWA	4	25.0
1967	SWA	12	39.9	Congress	11	46.9
1971	Congress	11	44.9	INCO	11	39.7
1977	BLD	16	49.5	Congress	10	46.9
1980	Congress	25	54.8	Janata Party	1	36.9
1984	Congress	24	53.2	BJP	1	18.6
1989	BJP	12	30.5	Janata Dal	11	27.8
1991	BJP	20	50.4	Congress	5	29.0
1996	BJP	16	48.5	Congress	10	38.7
1998	BJP	19	48.3	Congress	7	36.5
1999	BJP	20		Congress	6	-
Haryana						
1967	Congress	7	44.1	BJS	1	19.9
1971	Congress	7	52.6	BJS	1	11.2
1977	BLD	10	70.4	Congress	0	18.0
1980	Congress	5	32.6	JPS	4	33.5
1984	Congress	10	55.0	LKD	0	19.1
1989	Janata Dal	6	38.9	Congress	4	46.2
1991	Congress	9	37.2	HVP	1	3.4
1996	BJP	4	19.7	HVP	3	15.2
1998	HLD	4	25.9	Congress	3	26.0
1999	BJP	5	-	INLD	5	-
Himachal Pradesh						
1952	Congress	3	52.4	KMPP	0	12.3
1957	Congress	4	47.3	PSP	0	11.8
1962	Congress	4	68.7	RPI	0	6.5
1967	Congress	6	48.4	BJS	0	19.1
1971	Congress	4	75.8	BJS	0	10.6
1977	BLD	4	57.2	Congress	0	38.6
1980	Congress	4	52.1	Janata Party	0	36.4
1984	Congress	4	67.6	BJP	0	23.3
1989	BJP	3	45.3	Congress	1	42.0
1991	Congress	2	46.2	BJP	2	42.8
1996	Congress	4	54.3	BJP	0	39.6
1998	BJP	3	51.4	Congress	1	41.9
1999	BJP	3	-	HVP	1	-

Year	Leading Party	Seats won	Vote (%)	Runner-up	Seats won	Vote (%)
Jammu and Kashmir						
1967	Congress	5	50.5	JKNC	1	24.9
1971	Congress	5	54.1	Independent	1	32.2
1977	Congress	3	16.4	JKNC	2	33.9
1980	JKNC	3	36.9	Congress	1	18.7
1984	JKNC	3	46.2	Congress	3	30.2
1989	JKNC	3	46.8	Congress	2	38.9
1996	Congress	4	27.5	BJP	1	18.8
1998	JKNC	3	36.4	BJP	2	28.6
1999	JKNC	4	-	BJP	2	-
Karnataka						
1952	Congress	10	53.4	KMPP	1	23.0
1957	Congress	23	55.5	KMPP	1	18.7
1962	Congress	25	52.7	LSS	1	3.3
1967	Congress	18	49.0	SWA	5	14.3
1971	Congress	27	70.9	INCU	0	16.4
1977	Congress	26	56.8	BLD	2	39.9
1980	Congress	27	56.3	Janata Party	1	22.9
1984	Congress	24	51.6	Janata Party	4	35.1
1989	Congress	27	48.9	Janata Dal	1	28.3
1991	Congress	23	42.1	BJP	4	28.8
1996	Janata Dal	16	34.9	BJP	6	24.6
1998	BJP	13	27.0	Congress	9	36.2
1999	Congress	18	-	BJP	7	-
Kerala						
1952	Congress	6	35.1	Independent	4	36.2
1957	CPI	9	37.5	Congress	6	34.8
1962	CPI	6	35.5	Congress	6	34.3
1967	CPI	9	24.6	SSP	3	8.2
1971	CPM	6	19.8	CPI	3	9.1
1977	Congress	11	29.1	CPI	4	10.4
1980	Congress	6	19.1	Congress	5	26.3
1984	Congress	13	33.3	KCJ	2	5.5
1989	Congress	14	41.7	CPM	2	22.9
1991	Congress	13	38.8	CPM	3	20.7
1996	Congress	7	38.0	CPM	5	21.2
1998	Congress	8	38.7	CPM	6	21.0
1999	CPM	8	-	Congress	8	-
Madhya Pradesh						
1952	Congress	27	51.6	Independent	2	11.9
1957	Congress	35	52.1	ABHM	1	4.8
1962	Congress	24	39.6	BJS	3	17.9
1967	Congress	24	40.8	BJS	10	29.6
1971	Congress	21	45.6	BJS	11	33.6
1977	BLD	37	57.9	Congress	1	32.5
1980	Congress	35	47.2	Janata Party	4	31.3
1984	Congress	40	57.1	BJP	0	30.0
1989	BJP	27	39.7	Congress	8	37.7
1991	Congress	27	45.3	BJP	12	41.9
1996	BJP	27	41.3	Congress	8	30.9
1998	BJP	30	45.7	Congress	1039.4	
1999	BJP	29	-	Congress	11	-

Year	Leading Party	Seats won	Vote (%)	Runner-up	Seats won	Vote (%)
Maharashtra						
1952	Congress	40	50.1	Independent	3	12.0
1957	Congress	38	48.7	PSP	5	8.7
1962	Congress	41	52.9	Indepndent	2	14.2
1967	Congress	37	48.5	PWP	2	7.5
1971	Congress	42	63.1	Forward Block	1	2.5
1977	Congress	20	47.0	BJS	19	31.4
1980	Congress	39	53.3	Janata Party	8	20.4
1984	Congress	43	51.2	ICS	2	12.1
1989	Congress	28	45.4	BJP	10	23.7
1991	Congress	38	48.4	BJP	5	20.0
1996	BJP	18	21.8	Congress	15	34.8
1998	Congress	33	43.6	Shiv Sena	6	19.7
1999	Shiv Sena	15	-	BJP	13	-
Orissa						
1952	Congress	11	42.5	GP	5	26.2
1957	Congress	7	40.0	GP	7	29.1
1962	Congress	14	55.5	GP	4	17.4
1967	SWA	8	30.9	Congress	6	33.3
1971	Congress	15	38.5	SWA	3	15.9
1977	BLD	15	51.8	Congress	4	38.2
1980	Congress	20	56.1	JPS	1	19.6
1984	Congress	20	57.5	Janata Party	132.0	
1989	Janata Dal	16	49.5	Congress	3	38.4
1991	Congress	13	44.1	Janata Dal	6	34.6
1996	Congress	16	44.9	Janata Dal	4	30.1
1998	BLD	9	27.5	BJP	7	21.2
1999	BJP	10	-	BJP	9	-
Punjab						
1952	Congress	16	42.8	SAD	2	11.4
1957	Congress	21	51.3	CPI	1	16.8
1962	Congress	14	41.3	BJS	3	15.2
1967	Congress	9	37.3	ADFS	3	22.6
1971	Congress	10	46.0	CPI	2	6.2
1977	SAD	9	42.3	BLD	3	12.5
1980	Congress	12	52.5	SAD	1	23.4
1984	SAD	7	37.2	Congress	6	37.6
1989	SADM	6	29.2	Independents	3	12.7
1991	Congress	12	49.2	BSP	1	19.3
1996	SAD	8	28.7	BSP	39.0	
1998	SAD	8	32.9	BJP	1	11.7
1999	Congress	8	-	SAD	2	-
Rajasthan						
1952	Congress	9	41.1	Independents	6	29.2
1957	Congress	19	53.6	Independents	3	27.6
1962	Congress	14	37.6	Independents	3	24.4
1967	Congress	10	40.0	SWA	8	27.0
1971	Congress	14	50.4	BJS	4	12.4
1977	BLD	24	65.2	Congress	1	30.6
1980	Congress	18	42.6	Janata Party	4	31.7
1984	Congress	25	52.7	BJP	0	23.7
1989	BJP	13	29.6	JD	11	25.7

Year	Leading Party	Seats won	Vote (%)	Runner-up	Seats won	Vote (%)
1991	Congress	13	44.0	BJP	12	40.9
1996	BJP	12	41.7	Congress	12	40.5
1998	Congress	18	44.5	BJP	5	41.7
1999	BJP	16	-	Congress	9	-
Tamil Nadu						
1952	Congress	35	36.4	Independents	15	23.1
1957	Congress	31	46.5	Independents	8	39.8
1962	Congress	31	45.3	DMK	7	18.5
1967	DMK	25	35.8	SWA	6	9.2
1971	DMK	23	35.3	Congress	9	12.5
1977	ADMK	18	30.5	Congress	14	22.3
1980	Congress	20	31.6	DMK	16	23.0
1984	Congress	25	40.5	ADMK	12	18.4
1989	Congress	27	39.9	ADMK	11	17.1
1991	Congress	28	42.8	ADMK	11	18.1
1996	DMK/TMC	37	52.6	CPI	2	2.2
1998	ADMK	18	25.9	DMK	5	20.1
1999	DMK	12	-	PMK	5	-
Uttar Pradesh						
1952	Congress	81	53.0	SOC	2	12.9
1957	Congress	70	46.3	Independents	9	21.5
1962	Congress	62	38.2	BJS	7	17.6
1967	Congress	47	33.4	BJS	12	22.2
1971	Congress	73	48.6	BJS	4	12.3
1977	BLD	85	68.1	Congress	0	25.0
1980	Congress	51	35.9	JPS	29	29.0
1984	Congress	83	51.0	Lok Dal	2	21.6
1989	Janata Dal	54	35.9	Congress	15	31.8
1991	BJP	51	32.8	Janata Dal	22	21.3
1996	BJP	52	33.4	SP	16	20.8
1998	BJP	57	36.5	SP	20	28.7
1999	BJP	29	-	SP	26	-
West Bengal						
1952	Congress	24	42.1	CPI	5	9.5
1957	Congress	23	48.2	CPI	6	19.0
1962	Congress	22	46.8	CPI	9	29.4
1967	Congress	14	39.7	CPM	5	15.7
1971	CPM	20	34.3	Congress	13	28.2
1977	CPM	17	26.2	BLD	15	21.5
1980	CPM	28	39.9	Congress	4	36.5
1984	CPM	18	35.9	Congress	16	48.2
1989	CPM	27	38.4	Congress	4	41.4
1991	CPM	27	35.2	Congress	5	36.2
1996	CPM	23	36.7	Congress	9	40.1
1998	CPM	24	35.4	Trinamool	7	24.4
1999	CPM	21	-	Trinamool	8	-

Table 10.3 : Party Performance in North-East

State/Party	1996 Won	1996 Votes	1998 Won	1998 Votes	1999 Won
Arunachal Pradesh					
Congress	0	28.8%	0	23.9%	2
BJP	0	17.4%	0	21.8%	-
Ind./Others	2	—	2	52.5%	-
Manipur					
Congress	2	40.2%	0	18.6%	-
CPI	0	04.0%	1	20.5%	-
Ind./Others	—	—	1	25.4%	2
Meghalaya					
Congress	1	53.7%	2	47.6%	1
BJP	0	09.1%	0	09.0%	-
Ind./Others	1	—	0	25.5%	1
Mizoram					
Congress	1	42.5%	0	34.9%	1
MNF	0	37.6%	0	26.9%	-
Ind./Others	—	—	1	35.0%	-
Nagaland					
Congress	1	62.3%	1	86.7%	1
NPC	0	35.2%	—	—	-
Ind./Others	—	—	0	13.3%	-
Tripura					
Congress	0	34.1%	0	42.1%	-
CPM	2	54.4%	2	48.8%	2
Ind./Others	—	—	0	08.2%	-

Table 10.4 : Twelve Genral Elections : A View of Candidates, Votes and Polling Stations

Year	Elective Seats	Candidates	Electorate	Voter turnout	Poling stations
1952	489	1,864	173,213,635	62.2%	196,084
1957	494	1,591	193,652,069	62.2%	220,244
1962	494	1,985	216,372,215	55.0%	238,244
1967	520	2,369	249,372,215	61.3%	267.555
1971	518	2,784	274,094493	55.3%	342,944
1977	542	2,439	321,174,327	60.5%	358,208
1980	542	4,620	355,590,700	56.9%	434,442
1984	542	5,481	399,816,294	64.0%	505,751
1989	543	6,160	498,906,429	62.0%	579,810
1991	543	8,699	514,126,380	61.0%	594,797
1996	543	13,9520	592,572,288	57.9%	767,462
1998	543	4,750	605,884,103	62.0%	773,494

Table 10.5 : Seats Fought and Won by Major Parties

Party	1984		1989		1991		1996		1998	
	Fought	Won	Fought	Won	Fougth	Won	Fought	Won	Fought	Won
Congress	517	415	510	197	227	483	140	529	141	474
BJP	229	2	225	85	119	471	161	471	179	384
CPI & CPM	130	28	114	45	49	102	44	118	41	129
Janta Dal	219	10	244	143	56	302	46	196	6	190

Table 10.6 : Female and Male Contestants during Last Twelve Lok Sabhas

Year	No. of seats	No. of contest ants	Male			Female		
			Con-testd	Elec-ted	% win-ning	Cont-ested	Elec-ted	% win-ning
1952	489	1,874	—	—	—	—	—	—
1957	494	1,518	1,473	467	31.7	45	27	60.0
1962	494	1,985	1,915	459	24.0	70	35	50.0
1967	520	2,369	2,302	490	21.3	67	30	44.8
1971	518	2,784	2,698	499	18.5	86	21	24.4
1977	542	2,439	2,369	523	22.1	,70	19	27.1
1980	542	4,620	4,478	514	11.5	142	28	19.7
1984	542	5,574	5,406	500	6.2	164	42	25.6
1989	543	6,160	5,962	502	8.5	198	27	13.6
1991	543	8,699	8,374	492	5.9	325	39	12.0
1996	543	13,9520	13,3530	504	3.8	599	39	06.7
1998	543	4,750	4,476	500	11.2	274	43	15.7

Table 10.7 : Performance of Independent Candidates during Last Twelve Lok Sabha Elections

Year	No. of independents	Elected	Deposits forfeited	Percentage forfeiture
1952	0849	36	0503	59.25
1957	0667	73	0342	51.27
1962	0480	20	0379	78.96
1967	0865	35	0747	86.36
1971	1,134	14	1,066	94.00
1977	1,224	09	1,190	97.22
1980	2,821	08	2,791	98.94
1984	3,792	05	3,746	98.79
1989	3,712	12	3,671	98.90
1991	5,687	05	5,660	99.52
1996	10,6350	09	10,6030	99.70
1998	1,915	06	1,898	99.11

Table 10.8 : Age Profile of Members from First to Eleventh Lok Sabha

Age Group	1st	2nd	3rd	4th	5th	6th	7th	8th	9th	10th	11th
25-30 yrs.	28 (6.0)	13 (2.6)	11 (2.3)	22 (4.4)	16 (3.1)	18 (3.5)	9 (1.7)	7 (1.3)	14 (2.92)	8 (1.48)	43 (8.04)
31-35 yrs.	54 (11.6)	60 (12.3)	34 (7.1)	37 (7.5)	28 (5.0)	26 (5.0)	43 (8.3)	36 (6.8)	16 (3.34)	26 (4.81)	0 (11.21)
36-40 yrs.	58 (12.5)	91 (18.7)	64 (13.7)	68 (13.7)	62 (12.3)	62 (11.9)	71 (13.7)	60 (11.3)	55 (11.48)	52 (9.63)	5 (15.89)
41-45 yrs.	68 (14.7)	71 (14.6)	79 (16.6)	84 (17.0)	76 (15.0)	69 (13.3)	75 (15.5)	73 (13.7)	72 (15.03)	84 (15.56)	83 (15.51)
46-50 yrs.	74 (16.0)	64 (13.1)	73 (15.4)	85 (17.0)	99 (19.6)	94 (18.1)	70 (13.5)	77 (14.5)	78 (16.28)	91 (16.85)	4 (13.83)
51-55 yrs.	93 (20.3)	76 (15.6)	69 (14.5)	69 (14.0)	94 (18.6)	94 (18.1)	84 (16.2)	74 (13.9)	79 (16.49)	76 (14.07)	2 (13.46)
56-60 yrs.	47 (10.1)	70 (14.4)	58 (12.2)	55 (11.0)	57 (11.3)	66 (12.7)	87 (16.8)	80 (15.1)	65 (13.57)	71 (13.15)	51 (9.53)
61-65 yrs.	29 (6.2)	25 (5.1)	58 (12.2)	39 (7.9)	35 (6.9)	41 (8.0)	41 (7.9)	74 (13.9)	53 (11.06)	69 (12.78)	42 (7.89)
66-70 yrs.	10 (2.0)	12 (2.4)	21 (4.4)	25 (5.0)	25 (4.9)	33 (6.4)	24 (4.6)	30 (5.7)	34 (7.10)	41 (7.59)	21 (3.93)
71-75 yrs.	1 (0.2)	4 (1.0)	6 (1.2)	10 (2.0)	9 (1.7)	11 (2.1)	1 (2.1)	11 (2.1)	11 (2.30)	17 (3.15)	3 (0.56)
76-80 urs	-	-	1 (0.2)	1(0.2)	2 (0.4)	4 (0.7)	3 (0.6)	6 (1.1)	1 (021)	4 (0.74)	1 (0.19)
81-85 yrs.	-	-	1 (0.2)	1 (0.2)	1 (0.2)	1 (0.2)	1 (0.02)	3 (0.6)	-	1 (0.19)	-
86-90 yrs.	-	-	-	-	-	-	-	-	1 (0.21)	-	-
Total	**462**	**486**	**475**	**496**	**504**	**519**	**519**	**531**	**479**	**540***	**542***
Total number of seats	**499**	**500**	**503**	**523**	**521**	**544**	**544**	**544**	**522**	**544**	**544**

Note : The figures in brackets represent percentages.
* Information about the age of rest of members was not available.

Table 10.9 : Educational Background of Members from First to Eleventh Lok Sabha

Educational Background	1st	2nd	3rd	4th	5th	6th	7th	8th	9th	10th	11th
Under Matriculates	112 (23.2)	120 (25.4)	141 (28.7)	54 (11.5)	119 (23.1)	52 (9.8)	53 (10.0)	42 (7.9)	21 (4.1)	21 (3.91)	16 (3.23)
Matriculates/Higher Secondary or Inter-mediate Certificate holders	88 (18.4)	90 (19.1)	87 (17.7)	101 (22.1)	82 (16.0)	132 (24.9)	118 (22.3)	112 (21.0)	111 (21.68)	101 (18.81)	72 (14.52)
Graduates	177 (37.1)	160 (33.9)	157 (32.0)	172 (35.4)	178 (34.6)	205 (38.7)	213 (40.3)	238 (44.6)	222 (43.36)	245 (45.62)	27 (45.77)
Post-Graduates (including technical qualifications)	85 (17.8)	92 (19.5)	98 (20.0)	113 (24.7)	127 (24.7)	132 (24.9)	136 (25.8)	131 (24.6)	137 (26.70)	150 (27.93)	50 (30.24)
Doctoral Degree or other high academic qualification holders	15 (3.5)	9 (2.1)	7 (1.6)	17 (3.7)	8 (1.5)	9 (1.7)	8 (1.5)	10 (1.9)	21 (4.1)	20 (3.72)	31 (6.25)
Total	**477**	**471**	**490**	**457**	**514**	**530**	**528**	**533**	**512**	**537**	**496**
Total No of Seats	**499**	**500**	**503**	**523**	**521**	**544**	**544**	**544**	**522**	**544**	**544**

Note : The figures in brackets represent percentages.

Table 10.10 : Occupation of Members in Eleven Lok Sabhas

Prior Occupation	1st	2nd	3rd	4th	5th	6th	7th	8th	9th	10th	11th
Agriculturistis	97 (22.5)	141 (29.1)	129 (27.4)	154 (30.6)	168 (33.2)	189 (36.0)	206 (39.3)	203 (38.3)	204 (40.40)	160 (29.57)	0 (38.74)
Artistes	-	-	-	1 (0.2)	-	-	1 (0.2)	5 (0.9)	3 (0.59)	6 (1.11)	8 (1.48)
Civil and Military Services	16 (3.7)	19 (4.0)	4 (0.9)	16 (3.2)	17 (3.4)	9 (1.7)	5 (0.9)	16 (3.0)	9 (1.78)	19 (3.51)	13 (2.40)
Diplomats	-	-	-	-	-	-	-	-	2 (0.40)	4 (0.74)	1 (1.84)
Economists	-	-	-	-	-	-	-	-	3 (0.59)	-	-
Engineers and Technologists	-	-	4 (0.9)	7 (1.4)	6 (1.2)	5 (0.9)	6 (1.1)	4 (0.8)	8 (1.58)	10 (1.85)	9 (1.66)
Former Rulers	5 (1.1)	7 (1.4)	10 (2.1)	7 (1.4)	2 (0.4)	3 (0.6)	1 (0.2)	3 (0.6)	-	6 (1.11)	-
Industrial Workers/Trade Unionists	-	-	1 (0.2)	1 (0.2)	-	9 (1.7)	4 (0.8)	7 (1.3)	5 (0.99)	5 (0.92)	8 (1.48)

Table 10.11 : Muslim Representation in Lok Sabha

Year	1952	1957	1962	1967	1971	1980	1984	1989	1991	1996
Muslim Representation	36	24	32	29	27	46	41	33	28	26

Table 10.12 : Representation of Women

The evolution of Indian democracy over the twelve Lok Sabha elections has witnessed a very slow improvement in the proportion of women representatives in Parliament.

General Election	Year	Total no. of seats	No. of women members	% of the total
First	1952	499	22	4.4
Second	1957	500	27	5.4
Third	1962	503	34	6.8
Fourth	1967	523	31	5.9
Fifth	1971	521	22	4.2
Sixth	1977	544	19	3.5
Seventh	1980	544	28	5.1
Eighth	1984	544	44	8.1
Ninth	1989	517	27	5.2
Tenth	1991	544	39	7.2
Eleventh	1996	544	40*	7.4
Twelfth	1998	543	43	7.9

*One member was nominated by the President.

Table 10.13 : Expenditure on Lok Sabha Elections

Year	Rs. in crore
1952	10.5
1957	5.9
1962	7.8
1967	11.2
1971	14.4
1977	29.8
1980	37.1
1984	81.5
1989	154.2
1991	359.1
1996	597.5
1998	664.5
1999	850

11

Chronology of Events

Pre-poll, Poll and Post-Poll

April 1999 14 Jayalalitha arrives in Delhi.

- ❖ Meets the President and informs that her party was no longer supporting the BJP led coalition.

15 Prime Minister moves Motion of Confidence.

17 Confidence vote is held.

- ❖ The government loses by a single vote.

28 Election Commission to hold all-party meeting on May 3.

- ❖ Prime Minister A.B. Vajpayee in his address to the nation appeals to voters for a decisive mandate and not a fractured. BJP urges the President to direct EC to one conduct early poll.
    - ❖ 'Can an Indian become Italy's Prime Minister'?- Andhra Pradesh Chief Minister N. Chandrababu Naidu on Sonia Gandhi. (Indian Express, April 28, 1999)

29. Senior Janata leader Ram Vilas Paswan not averse to tie up with BJP-Samata in Bihar for ensuring the defeat of his arch rival Laloo Prasad Yadav.

- ❖ B.J.P. and allies to have common election manifesto—B.J.P. Chief Keshubhai Thakre.
    - ❖ Congress terms Prime Minister's speech on April 28 as an act of impropriety.

30. Keep caretaker government in check, Congress requests President.

- ❖ Sonia's foreign origin should not be a campaign issue—A.B. Vajpayee

May, 1 Advantage to BJP if elections held in June—Sharad Pawar, Senior Congress Leader.

- ❖ We will never support Hindutva, but a tie-up with BJP can reduce tension.

2 A.B. Vajpayee and L.K. Advani ask party workers not to be over confident.

- ❖ B.J.P.'s image as anti-Muslim Party blunted—Vajpayee
    - ❖ No. BSP-Congress del in Punjab.

3 The Election Commission holds meeting with political parties to discuss election dates.

- ❖ Bofors Issue: President of India sanctions prosecution of Madhavsingh Solanki, former External Affairs Minister.

- ❖ Home Secretary B.P. Singh and ten other Senior Officers shifted.
- ❖ Buta Singh a Former Union Minister and Independent MP in the last Lok Sabha and 4 Hegde loyalist MLAs join Congress.

May, 4 September End-Oct. beginning to be the election time: announces Election Commission.

- ❖ Several senior officers of Govt. of India shifted.

5 Congress's strong protest to the President of India on the transfers by the BJP caretaker government

- ❖ Goa Assembly election to be held on June-4, announces the Election Commission.
  - ❖ AIADMK General Secretary Jayalalitha lists reasons for withdrawing support: Defence Minister's anti-national activities, withdrawal of free power supply to farmers, hike in PDS prices, betrayal of Tamil Nadu's interests in Cauvery dispute.

6 Senior TMC leader and five time Lok Sabha Member N. Dennis joins the Congress

- ❖ BSP leader Kanshi Ram rules out pact with Congress. If BJP wins, face poll 2000 A.D.—Sonia Gandhi.

7 36 BJP MLA's of UP send resignation letters to President Thakre demanding replacement of Kalyan Singh as U.P. Chief Minister.

- ❖ Severe blow to S.P. of Mulayam Singh in Maharasthra. Hussai Dalwai President of the State Unit, Harbans Singh Vice-President and other promiment members join Congress.

7 TDP leader and a former Union Minister Renuka Chaudhary joins Congress.

8 A former Haryana Minister Dr. Om Parkash Sharma of the Indian National Lok Dal (INLD) joins Congress.

- ❖ It will be coalition again: Laloo Prasad Yadav.
  - ❖ Stars predict a fractured verdict.

9 Madhya Pradesh Chief Minister Digvijay Singh expresses the need for Cong. and Left parties alliance

- ❖ MGR-ADMK ready to tie-up with DMK.

10 Former Rajya Sabha Member and TDP leader Khaleel-ur-Rehman joins Congress.

- ❖ The Supreme Court issues notice to West Bengal Chief Minister Jyoti Basu on plot allotment to V.I.Ps from his discretionary quota.
  - ❖ S.P. accusses Congress of destroying Third Front No tie up with it even if BJP gains.

11 West Bengal governor Dr. A.R. Kidwai resigns.

- ❖ How did Sonia Gandhi vote as an Italian in 1980 elections-B.J.P spokesman
  - ❖ Controversy over Sonia's origin meaningless-Congress.
- ❖ The Supreme Courts acquits 19 of the 26 accused in the Rajiv Gandhi assassination case. Death sentence to 3 confirmed and 3 others given life imprisonment.

May, 12 Congress Working Committe and Leader of Opposition in Lok Sabha meets J. Jayalalitha, AIADMK Chief.

- ❖ The Republican Party of India (RPI) announces its inclination to tie up with the Congress and not the Samajwadi Party (SP)
  - ❖ B.J.P. rules out any truck with 'casteist' S.P.

13 Mata Prasad, Governor Arunachal Pradesh removed by the government. He had refused to resign. His tenure had been expired last year.

14 Supreme Court rejects Jaya plea on special courts. G.S. Tohra senior Akali dal leader and former President of the S.G.P.C. expelled from the party for six years for his alleged anti-party activities.

- ❖ E.C. can probe Sonia's voter status only on a plea—M.S. Gill, Chief Election Commissioner.

15 B. Raman, an ex. Intelligence Chief, a retired Additional Secretary of the Cabinet Secretariat suggests that Sonia Gandhi because of her birth not being in India, but not a Italy, voluntarily step down from the race for Prime Ministership of India.

- ❖ Shiromani Akali Dal (SAD) splits. G.S. Tohra group to elect new party chief.
  - ❖ The BJP and its allies to go to poll under the banner of a new front— National Democratic Alliance.
- ❖ Tushar Gandhi, great-grandson of Mahatma Gandhi leaves the S.P. and joins the Congress.

16 Three members of the Congress Working Committee—Sharad Pawar, P.A. Sangma and Tariq Anwar send a 4-page letter to Sonia Gandhi Congress President, opposing her being projected as Prime Minister, she being not an Indian citizen by birth.

17 Sonia Gandhi resigns from the presidentship of Congress but Congress Working Committee rejects it.

- ❖ The Congress Working Committee rejects the demand of the three members who do not attend the special meeting called to discuss their letters. T.M. Congress Chief Mamata Bannerji supports the damand of three members of the Congress Working Committee.

18 The Chief Ministers of four Congress ruled States lead the rising chorus for the withdrawal of Mrs. Gandhi's resignation as party president.

- ❖ I stick to my stand—Sharad Pawar.

19 No plan to form a third front comprising non-BJP and non-Congress parties—Sharad Pawar.

- ❖ I had told Sonia Gandhi not to propose herself as the Prime Ministerial candidate as there were a number of experienced congressmen who were more eligible for the post—P.A. Sangma.
  - ❖ Pressure on CWC to expel rebel tris.

20 Tris-Sharad Pawar, P.A. Sangma and Tariq Anwar expelled for six years by the Congress Working Committee. Former Kerala Chief Minister A.K. Antony and Working Committee member favours suspension and not expulsion.

- ❖ It is my happiest moment: Sharad Pawar on his expulsion.
  - ❖ Sonia Gandhi's foreign issue to feature in manifesto—Prime Minister A.B. Vajpayee.

May, 21 Several leaders of Maharashtra join Sharad Pawar group. New Front soon—Sharad Pawar

- ❖ AICC meeting fixed for May 25 to persuade Sonia Gandhi to take back her resignation.

22 Rajya Sabha Member Suresh Kalmadi (in 1998 elections he had left Congress) joins Congress and merges his Maharashtra Vikas Agadi with the Congress Party.

- ❖ Janata Dal leader Ram Vilas Paswan personally favours the stand taken by Sharad Pawar and two others.

23 PM alerts Sonia on threat to her life. Congress sees fascist plot. C.W.C. members Pranab Mukherjee and Arjun Singh meet the PM in this regard.

- ❖ 28 out of 77 MLA's and 13 MLC's out of 26 of Maharashtra attend Pawar's meeting. First Phase of poll notified.

24 Sonia Gandhi withdraws her resignation as president of the Indian National Congress

- ❖ Sonia and Pawar loyalists expel each other's members in Maharashtra Legislative Assembly and Council.

25 Congress Parliamentary Party will choose its PM:Sonia rebels will be given a befitting reply. Sonia Gandhi at the AICC session at New Delhi.

26 Air strikes to flush out infiltrators begin in the Kargil sector in J&K.

27 Sharad Pawar group floats Nationalist Congress Party.

28 Some Bihar Congress leaders join Pawar group. Former Lok Sabha Member Vasant Pawar resigns from the Congress and joins N.C.P.

29 Cong.-bashing kicks off TD campaign. BJP defeat is one-point agenda of CPM—CPM leader Surjeet.

- ❖ Trinamool Congress- Vajpayee is still its choice.
  - ❖ BJP for coalition government even if it gets majority of its own—Venkaish Naidu BJP general Secretary
- ❖ Scnia as PM will be a national disaster-J.H. Patel Karnataka C.M.

30 Ruling Akali Dal in Punjab splits. Expelled senior leader G.S. Tohra forms a new party.

31 George is a danger-sack him says Jaya

June, 1 NCP working on third front with like-minded parties, says Sharad Pawar.

2 D.M.K. formally joins BJP led NDA

3 Former AICC general secretary Devandva Nath Dwivedi quits Congress and joins NCP

- ❖ MPCC split formal. Forty five out of 75 Congress members of the Maharashtra State Assembly and 14 of 26 in the legislative council quit Congress and form new group supporting Sharad party.

June, 4 Voting for the Goa Assembly with electronic machines held.
❖ Over 70 per cent voters cast votes in Goa Assembly.

5 D.M.K. Chief M. Karunanidhi vows to protect miniorities.

6 Congress wins Goa Assembly elections. Party position as under.

Congress 21	BJP 10	MGP 4
UGDP 2	Ind. 1	GRC 2

7 No friction likely in our ties with Lok Shakti - BJP Legislative party, Karnataka.

8 Communication Minister Jagmohan shifted to the Urban Development Ministry and Ram Jethmalani to Law.

9 Two senior TDP leaders of Andhra join Congress.

10 A special court at Chennai frame charges against Jayalalitha and others in the Tansi Land deal case.

11 Basu, Chief Minister of Bengal and CPI(M) leader for early polls in view of Kargil.

12 The Maharashtra Assembly speaker and Council Chairman recognise the breakaway group of Sharad Pawar's Congress (R) in the Maharashtra Legislature.

13 Senior BJP leader Sushma Swaraj, formerly a Union Cabinet Minister and an M.P. from South Delhi Parliamentary Constituency firm on not contesting 13th Lok Sabha election.

14 VHP President Ashok Singhal attacks Congress Chief and welcomes NCP leader Sharad Pawar for raising the issue of foreign birth of Sonia Gandhi.

15 Punjab Chief Minister Prakash Singh Badal retained as President of the Akali Dal.
❖ Senior Janata leader Ram Vilas Paswan for tie up with BJP-Samata.

16 TMK not to enter into electoral alliance with AIADMK.

17 Samajwadi Party of Mulayam Singh Yadav and National Congress Party of Shard Pawar join hands.

18 The Samata Party invites S.P. and NCP to join BJP-led alliance.
❖ Congress president Sonia Gandhi blames BJP on Kargil.

19 AIADMK invites TMC to join the front led by it.

20 Shiv Sena Chief Bal Thackeray criticises NCP-SP alliance.

21 B.S.P. rules out truck with any party in U.P.

22 Kargil unlikely to affect poll schedule—Chief Election Commissioner M.S. Gill.
❖ BJP withdraws supports to Bansi Lal Government in Haryana and pulls out of H.V.P.—BJP combination running the government—Party position.
❖ HVP-35, BJP 14, INLD 22, Cong. 12, Independents 10

23 Law Minister Jethmalani writes to the President and disputes EC bar on Sena Chief Bal Thackeray.

24 Lok Sabha elections to be held in time-C.E.C.

25 Govt. to consider Rajya Sabha Session demand for a discussion on Kargil issue.

- ❖ Bansilal Chief Minister Haryana of the H.V.P. survives vote of confidence with the help of Congress. 55 votes in favour and 35 against.

June, 26 Congress AIADMK talks.

27 Laloo Prasad Yadav re-elected Rashtriya Janata Dal president.

28 Congress president Sonia Gandhi launches attack on BJP for its failure to check Pak intrusions in Kargil. Govt. convenes party meet at Kargil-No secret deal, no third party mediation—Prime Minister.

29 Congress demand Rajya Sabha session on Kargil.

30 Law Ministry proposes state funding for coming polls but Election Commissioner disposes.

July, 1 Rashtriya Janata Party led by party chief Shanker Singh Vaghela merges with the Congress.

2 Election Commission gets Govt. nod for election as per schedule.

3 Roshan Baig, Karnataka JD Minister of State for Toursim and Wakf resigns to join J.D.

- ❖ Kim Gangte Manipur CPI leader, and a member of the dissolved Lok Sabha joins Samata Party.
- ❖ BJP National President Kushabau Thakre says that India must cross LOC and retrieve POK.
- ❖ Political Party meet convened by the E.C. agree to the poll schedule.

4 Shakuni Chandhuri, Samata Party MP of Bihar in the dissolved Lok Sabha decided to join RJD.

- ❖ Pakistan Prime Minister contacts President Clinton on Kargil.
- ❖ Atal Bihari Vajpayee Prime Minister says 'no to the invitation of President Clinton-time not opportune for the meeting.
- ❖ R.J.D. Chief Laloo Prasad Yadav wants National Government at the Centre in view of Kargil

5 After a 3 hour meeting between US president Clinton and Pak Prime Minister Nawab Sharif, in a joint statement from Washington, Pakistan promises to withdraw from Kargil.

- ❖ The Congress and the Left urge government not to accept mediators on Kargil
- ❖ The Nationalist Congress Party (NCP) gets itself registered.
- ❖ Meghalaya PCC renominates former Mizoram governor and Member of the dissolved Lok Sabha P.R. Kyndiah as its candidate for the Shillong Parliamentary seat.
- ❖ AIADMK leader J. Jayalalitha launches election campaign with Anti-BJP. vow.

6 Defence Minister George Fernandes deserved to be tried over Kargil-Laloo Prasad Yadav, R.J.D. Chief.

7 Thirteen Chief Minister of States oppose calling the Rajya Sabha Session to discuss Kargil, Seven favour and other remian neutral in the meeting called by the Prime Minister.

- ❖ Senior JD leader and former President of the Party's North East Regional Co-ordination Committee, Dulal Chandra Baruah resigns.

July, 8 BJP would not dump allies even if it gets majority in the ensuing Lok Sabha elections - BJP chief, Kushabau Thakre.

9 Coalition govt. best bet after elections- RJD.

❖ Two Janata Dal Member of the 11th Lok Sabha, Qamarul Islam and Raja Rangappa join Congress.

10 Govt advice needed for calling Rajya Sabha Session—President R.K. Narayanan in a letter to Vishwa Bandhu Gupta, a former MP.

11 The Election Commissioner announces a five-phase election programme beginning September 4. In general, all parties welcome CE's decision.

❖ Pakistan begins withdrawing forces from Kargil.

❖ At a meeting convened to brief political parties, on the latest situation in Kargil, Prime Minister Atal Bihari Vajpayee rules out any third mediation or intervention on Kashmir or in the ongoing conflict along the LOC.

❖ On the issue of convening Rajya Sabha meeting, the PM states that the question continued to elude consensus.

❖ We have learnt a lesson from Kargil - Prime Minister. We should remain vigilent.

12 Congress and BJP hail EC's decision on elections.

❖ J.D. accpets it reluctantly

❖ E.C. spells out do's and don'ts for political parties.

13 Election Commissioner's programme of spreading election to one month finds favour with about 39% people in the 'Net Poll' of the '*Hindustan Times*'. Congress prepares a questionnaire on Kargil and trains guns on government over this issue.

14 Congress withdraws support to H.V.P. Party Bansi Lal Govt in Haryana. Govt reduced to minority.

❖ Congress and AIADMK enter into electoral alliance in Tamil Nadu. Congress to contest 12 Lok Sabha Seats, AIADMK (23), CPM (2), CPI (2) and Indian National League (I). E.C. warns State governments against transfer of officials. Former Tamil Nadu Election Commissioner T.N. Malaisamy joins AIADMK

❖ Former Union Minister and RJD MP Jai Narayan Prasad joins Samata Party.

15 Maharashtra State Assembly dissolved by Shiv Sena BJP Govt. six month ahead of its usual time for holding simultaneous Assembly and Lok Sabha elections in Sept. 1999

❖ Janata Party President Subramanian Swami and the person usually considered responsible for the fall of BJP govt. and an ally of AIADMK, snaps ties with AIADMK on account of being ignored by Jayalalitha, AIADMK chief.

16 EC tells parties to avoid plastic poll material.

17 Kargil war is over—George Fernandes Defence Minister

❖ EC Summons Andhra Chief Secretary regarding launching some welfare schemes on the eve of announcement of election dates.

18 Year-round vigil planned in Kargil.

❖ Haryana Governor asks CM Bansilal to prove majority by 21 July.

- ❖ Two MLA-one of BJP and another of Janatântrik Bahujan Samaj Party of Uttar Pradesh join Congress.
- ❖ BJP state unit decides to nominate all MP's of the dissolved Lok Sabha to contest elections.

July, 19 Consensus continues to elude Janata Dal regarding its relations with the BJP, Sharad Pawar's NCP and the National Democratic Alliance etc.

20 Twelve Ministers and five party legislatures of the ruling Haryana Vikas Party demand Chief Minister Bansi Lal's resignation.

- ❖ Kargil not to be made an election issue BJP Chief Thakre
- ❖ RPI to have poll alliance with NCP.
- ❖ Karnataka BJP unit not to have tie up with Karnataka JD. Proxy voting for armed forces-BJP seeks supports from Congress.

21 In the wake of several desertions from his party. Bansi Lal Chief Minister Haryana heading HVP government resigns. Governor asks him to continue till further arrangements. Bansi Lal Government- a coalition government of H.V.P. and BJP was formed about 39 months ago. A few days earlier, BJP had quit the government and Bansilal Govt. had won the confidence vote with the support of Congress MLA's.

- ❖ Janata Dal splits into two mutually hostile groups over the issue of ideology and alliances.
- ❖ Sharad Yadav Party president announces the 'reunification of the Dal parivar' merging the Samata Party and Lok Shakti and aligning with the BJP-led National Democratic Alliance (NDA).
- ❖ Pro NDA-Sharad Yadav, I.K. Gujral, J.H. Patel, Ram Vilas Paswan and Kamala Sinha.
- ❖ Anti-NDA—H.D. Deve Gowda, Madhu Dandavate, S.R. Bommai, S. Jaipal Reddy, Bapu Kaldate, Srikant Jena, Siddaramiah, C.M. Ibrahim and Mrinal Gore.
- ❖ The of the Janata Dal removes Sharad Yadav from the post of president and elects H.D. Deve Gowda as the new Chief.
- ❖ Trinamool Congress to be the part of Govt. if BJP returns to power-Mamata Banerjee.
- ❖ Survey gives BJP allies 284, BJP 187, Congress 117, Vajpayee first choice for PM, 42%, Sharad Pawar 18%, L.K. Advani 16% and Sonia Gandhi 14% as choice.

22 Karnataka governor Khurshid Alam Khan accepts the recommendations of the J.H. Patel led Janata Dal Ministry and dissolves the Ministry. The House had five more months to complete its term.

- ❖ Deve Gowda group of the Janata Dal urges EC to allot to it the party symbol 'Wheel'.
- ❖ Janata Dal president Sharad Yadav suspends Deve Gowda former Prime Minister and Jaipal Reddy former Union Minister

- ❖ Congress Legislature Party leader Mehbhooba Mufti quits Congress.
  - ❖ Chief Election Commissioner M.S. Gill asks the Prime Minister and Chief Ministers to speak for India during their speeches and not for party on August 15.

July, 23 Indian National Lok Dal (INLD) Chief Om Prakash Chautala asked to take the oath of office of the Chief Minister Haryana in place of Bansi Lal who resigned on July 21, 1999. The new combination in the Legislative Assembly is as: INLD (22), BJP (11), Newly formed Haryana Vikas Party(D) (15) and independents (6)-Total effective Legislative strength-69.

- ❖ Karnataka Unit of BJP against the entry of the JD faction represented by J.H. Patel into the National Democratic Alliance.

24 The government of India appoints a four member committe to 'review the events leading to the Pakistani aggression in Kargil. The Committee to be headed by the defence expert K. Subrahmanyam.

- ❖ Maharashtra Chief Minister Narayan Rane sacks five Independent ministers.
  - ❖ Om Prakash Chautala of INLD sworn in as Chief Minister Haryana.

25. Drass cleared of intruders.

- ❖ Former Union Minister and Member of the dissolved Lok Sabha Mufti Mohammad Sayeed quits Congress. Former Director CBI. K.Vijayrama Rao and former judge of the Andhra High Court and former Chairman of the Minorities Commission Sardar Ali Khan join TDP.
  - ❖ Six Independent legislatures including the five sacked Ministers in Maharashtra on 24.7.99 join NCP.

26 Haryana speaker refuses to recognise the 15 Member H.V.P. splinter group.

- ❖ Election Commission tells parties to avoid plastic material in polls.
  - ❖ The Republican Party of India (RPI) formally splits in Maharashtra on the issue of extending support to NCP and INC.
- ❖ Former J&K, MP Janak Roy Gupta joins Congress.

27 Arunachal Pradesh Assembly dissolved on the recommendations of the State Cabinet.

- ❖ Haryana Chief Minister Om Prakash Chautala wins vote of confidence by 54-32 votes.
  - ❖ George Fernandes Chief of the Samata Party to BJP Chief Kushabhau Thakre-Admit JD into NDA or court me out.

28 BJP refutes that George Fernandes gave any ultimatum to it on the issue of admitting JD into NDA.

- ❖ Shiv Sena Chief Bal Thackeray disqualified by the President to vote for two years and to contest elections for six years
  - ❖ EC seeks clarification from the Central Government on the telecom policy.

July, 29 Sonia Gandhi to contest polls-Ajit Jogi-Congress spokesperson. The Samata Party and the Lok Shakti threaten BJP to quit NDA.

30 The Jamiat-ul-Ulema-e-Hind-a prominent Muslim organisation throws its weight behind Congress.

- ❖ Former Prime Minister Inder Kumar Gujral decides to contest the Lok Sabha polls from Jalandhar.

31 JD-Lok Shakti-Samata issue does not figure in the meeting of National Democratic Alliance.

- ❖ Trinamool Congress Chief Mamata Benerjee welcomes the move to include one J.D. faction in the N.D.A.

August, 1 Samata Party president George Fernandes states that his party and the Lok Shakti of Rama Krishna Hegde would leave the NDA if Sharad Yadav & Co. are not made part of it.

- ❖ The Rajasthan Jat Mahasabha resolves to vote against the Congress for its breach of trust on quota to Jats and other communities.
- ❖ SAD fields Mrs. Prabhijot Kaur, widow of former governor Rajasthan Darbara Singh from Jalandhar.
- ❖ SAD renominates seven of nine MP's in the dissolved Lok Sabha.

2 Former Prime Minsiter Inder Kumar Gujral decides not to contest the ensuing Lok Sabha elections.

- ❖ DMK reaches poll pact with PMK and TRC in Tamil Nadu
- ❖ CPI and CPM agree on seat-sharing in Andhra Pradesh.

3 Changes in poll schedule made in view of local festivals and constraints in law and order. Elections to begin from September 5 in place of September 4.

- ❖ BJP finalises list of 138 candidates.

4 BJP enters into pact with Sena in Maharashtra and DMK in Tamil Nadu.

5 The Wadhwa Commission of Enquiry to probe the killing of Australian missionary and his two sons in Orissa in January 1999 absolves the Sangh Pariwar.

- ❖ EC rejects NCP request for *Charkha* symbol
- ❖ CPI releases its first list.

6 Ex-Union Minister Karan Singh returns to the Congress after 18 years. He quits his Rajya Sabha seat that he had won with the support of Dr. Farooq Abdullah's National Conference.

- ❖ The '*Outlook*' opinion poll indicates clear majority for the BJP in the coming elections. Fiftyone per cent of those who polled finds A.B. Vajpayee as the best leader to lead the country.
- ❖ The Samajwadi Party (SP) releases its first list of 28 candidates.
- ❖ Ramakrishna Hegde asks BJP unit of Karnataka to shun 'greed' for seats.
- ❖ MDMK in Tamil Nadu climbs down as BJP offers its own seat.

7 EC freezes J.D.Symbol.

August, 8 Lok Sabha should have fixed term: Prime Minister Atal Bihari Vajpayee at an election rally of BJP at New Delhi

- ❖ Separate symbols to JD factions allotted-Janata Dal (United) of Sharad Yadav gets symbol of 'arrow' and the other group of Janata Dal (secular) led by former Prime Minister H.D.Deve Gowda gets the symbol of 'Kisan'.

9 Congress releases its first list of 72 candidates.

- ❖ Janata Dal (United) to strengthen NDA—Prime Minister A.B. Vajpayee.
  - ❖ Congress leader Natwar Singh opts out.

10 Congress to field Manmohan Singh former Finance Minsiter from South Delhi constituency.

- ❖ B.S.P. to contest all the 85 seats in U.P.

11 BJP and TDP forge poll pact.

- ❖ EC orders for shifting of some officials in MP, Orissa and Maharashtra
  - ❖ BJP central leaderships okay seat sharing with Sharad Yadav's Dal

12 CPM releases its election manifesto emphasises that the BJP rules was a disaster.

- ❖ BJP and INLD share 5 seats each to contest

13 Congress releases its election manifesto-Congress to take the Bofors investigation to its logical conclusion.

14 Union Minister of State for Health, Dalit Ezhilmalar resigns, quits PMK and joins AIADMK.

15 Maharashtrawadi Gomantak Party leader Ramakant Khalap a former Union Minister in the Janata Dal Government splits the party and joins the Congress.

- ❖ Maharashtra Minister of State for Transport Babasaheb Dhabekar resigns from the ministry stating that he cannot associate with the BJP Sena combine
  - ❖ BJP. Maharashta Legislative Council Member Pandurang Hazare joins the NCP and to contest Lok Sabha seat from Ramtek.

16 NDA releases its election manifesto-Only Indians by birth for high offices.

- ❖ A former Union Minister and Dalit leadder Chand Ram joins BJP.
  - ❖ A former BJP of the last dissolved Lok Sabha from Farrukhabad in UP, Mahamandaleshwar Swami Sachchidanand Hari Sakshi resigns from the party and states that he would work against BJP. He said that the denial of ticket to him was an insult to the Sadhu Samaj.
- ❖ A former Chief Election Commissioner T.N. Seshan to contest on Congress ticket from Gandhinagar (Gujarat) against L.K. Advani.

17 BJP and JD(U) arrive at poll pact in Bihar.

- ❖ Indian spells out draft N. Doctrine
  - ❖ AIFB, CPI release their manifesto
- ❖ BJP objects to Kapil Sibal as EC council
  - ❖ EC asks Prasar Bharati to observe neutrality in its programmes.

August, 18 Sushma Swaraj of the BJP, a former Central Cabinet Minister and Delhi Chief Minister to contest against Congress President Sonia Gandhi from the BELLARY Lok Sabha constituency in Karnataka.

- ❖ S. Jaipal Reddy, a former Janata Dal Cabinet Minister joins Congress.

19 Leave Kargil out of poll campaign—EC.

- ❖ Congress announces that Sonia Gandhi will contest from Amethi
  - ❖ Ms Uma Bharati of the BJP to contest from Bhopal and not from Khajuraho, her earlier constituency.

20 EC bars advertising campaigning on T.V.

- ❖ Former Tripura Congress Chief Minister Sudhir Ranjan Majumdar joins Trinamul Congress.

21 RJD to contest 34 seats and Congress 14 in Bihar.

22 Samajwadi Chief Mulayam Singh Yadav to contest from two seats - Kannauj and Sambalpur from UP.

- ❖ Resentment in Congress and CPI over announcement of Laloo Prasad Yadav RJD Chief's redistribution of seats.
  - ❖ Jayalalitha AIADMK Supremo fails to keep date with Congress President for a joint public election meeting.
- ❖ Congress leader of Bihar not happy with RJD's unilateral announcement on seats.
  - ❖ NCP releases its election manifesto.
- ❖ CPI quits RJD front in Bihar.

23 Those who cannot protect the border have no right to seek votes—Sharad Pawar.

- ❖ Sharad Pawar will be made Deputy PM under a NCP, BJP Secret Part-BSP Supremo Kanshi Ram.

25 Congress will provide quota for Jats-Sonia Gandhi

- ❖ Website for direct contact with Sonia
  - ❖ Another workshop for Ayodhya temple—Mahant Ramcharan Das Chariman Ram Janamabhoomi Nyas.
- ❖ No support to Sonia Gandhi at Bellary-Former Prime Minister and Janata Dal (Secular) President H.D. Deve Gowda.

26 Congress complains to EC to restrain Sushma Swaraj, rival candidate of Sonia Gandhi from referring to the latter as foreigner.

- ❖ We are not averse to coalition government says Manmohan Singh.

27 We will rethink about Coalition—Sonia Gandhi.

- ❖ Vijayantimala, former Congress MP and actress of yesterday quits Congress.
  - ❖ No bar on Kargil debate : E.C.

28 Promod Mahajan, Information and Braodcasting Minister regrets that his remarks about Sonia Gandhi had created some misunderstanding.

- ❖ R.J.D. releases its election manifesto.

August, 29 Fake ballot boxes found in Bihar.

- ❖ BJP has not compromised on its ideology—L.K. Advani
  - ❖ Congress set to become the largest single party: Lokmat CMCR IMS Survey.
- ❖ Bihar J.D.(U) Chief Ram Jiwan Singh quits party

30 Prime Minister urges restraint regarding remarks on Sonia Gandhi, Congress President.

- ❖ Keep private lives out of poll campaigns - EC.
  - ❖ S.S. Ahluwalia former Congress MP joins BJP.

31 Hindustan Times-A.C. Nielsen Survey predicts BJP Front Victory

- ❖ EC not being even-handed alleges Samata
  - ❖ Andhra Pradesh High court stays EC order prohibiting election - related advertisement by political parties on the electronic media
- ❖ Bengal Congress leader and State INTVC Chief Subrata Mukherjee joins the Trinamul Congress.

September, 1 Raipur Congress candidate Dr. Somnath Sahu withdraws on account of denial of ticket to Senior Party leader V.C. Shukla.

1 Prime Minister Atal Bihari Vajpayee expresses anguish over Congress leader Gulam Azad's remarks on his personal life.

2 End character bashing-Move onto serious issues—EC.

- ❖ A private panel releases criminal records of 46 AP. candidates.

3 First phase of polling ends.

- ❖ The Naib Imam of Jama Masjid Delhi asks Muslims to maintain equidistance from the Congress and the BJP.

4 Delhi Fatehpuri Masjid Imam appeals to vote for honest government.

5 Moderate turn-out in first phase of polls.

- ❖ EC. directs the Orissa Govt. not to shift DIG for the time being.
  - ❖ EC, G.V.G. Krishnamurthy goes twice to the polling station to cast his vote on account of non-recording of his new address in the voting register.

6 EC order repoll in 184 booths.

- ❖ 40 per cent voters turn-out in the capital.

6 The Madras High Court stays EC ban on TV. polls.

7 EC moves SC. on the stay order granted by Madras and Andhra High Courts for enforcement of its August 20 guidelines on publication and dissemination of results of opinion polls and exit polls.

- ❖ BJP Anantnag nominee and 2 others killed in blast.

8 The centre opposes the Election Commission's guidelines imposing restrictions on publication of opinion polls and exit polls and questions their legal validity.

9 Supreme Court declines to grant any interim stay on the Election Commission's plea for enforcement of its guidelines banning the publication of opinion polls during the first phase of Lok Sabha elections.

- ❖ Seventeen BJP workers injured in a grenade explosion in Doda (J&K)

September, 10 JD(U) candidate from Anantnag Mohammad Maqbool Dhar escapes bid on life by heavily armed militants.

Hundreds of teachers in Assam refuse to take election duties.

11 Maharashtra Minister of State for Revenue and BJP candidate for the Satrara Assembly seat and four other arrested in connection with the murder of an NCP Zilla Parishad leader.

12 Congress president Sonia Gandhi to be probed on FERA violations after elections: A.B. Vajpayee.

- ❖ NDA for the creation of Vanachal: L.K. Advani
  - ❖ Congress to fulfill its promise of Chhatisgarh—Sonia Gandhi
- ❖ Maharashtra Revenue Minister of BJP quits cabinet and states that he was falsely implicated.
  - ❖ Repoll ordered in 80 polling booths.

13 Sonia Gandhi control of Indira Gandhi National Centre for Arts Trust New Delhi fraudulent-BJP

- ❖ Former Union Home Minister Mufti Muhammad Sayeed and Jammu and Kashmir Medical Education Minister Sheikh Mustafa Kamal escape bid on life.

14 SC dismisses EC plea on exit poll.

- ❖ EC withdraws its guidelines banning the publication and telecast of exit/opinion polls after the SC's judgement.

15 Exit Polls—NDA leading comfortably

16 The Jammu&Kashmir Chief Electoral Officer orders an enquiry that State Chief Minister had warned that force would be used to get voters out for polling.

17 Ruling National Conference Legislative Assembly Member from Kupwara escapes bid on life.

- ❖ Anantag BJP Lok Sabha contestant quits, accuses replacement of foul play.
  - ❖ Arunachal CM among 4 elected unopposed to state Assembly.

18 Violence mars third phase of polling: 47 Killed, Bihar leads with 37 deaths, 53 per cent poll.

20 EC team to probe into the issue of duplicate ballots in Bihar. We will amend Constitution to protect the Minorities and Dalits—PM A.B. Vajpayee.

21 Patna High Court directs the Intelligence Bureau to file an affidavit in a reply to the statement made in PIL by the Janata Dal (United) regarding printing of excess ballot papers

- ❖ EC rejects George Fernandes charges regarding printing of excess ballot papers for certain Bihar constituencies.
  - ❖ The centre draws attention of EC to Bihar Governor's request for transfer of controversial officials.
- ❖ Bihar Governor meets the President and the Home Minister regarding the transfer of controversial officials.

21 Bihar Industry Minister Baidyanath Pandey resigns from the cabinet of Rashtriya Janata Dal and joins the Janata Dal (United).

	❖ Suspected ULFA militants kidnap BJP candidate Pannalal Biswas in Assam.
September, 21	Karnataka declines to give Cauvery water to Tamil Nadu.
	❖ Star News-Insight Exit Poll foretells big victory for NDA.
22	A.B. Vajpayee blames the RJD Government in Bihar for poll violence in the state.
	❖ Ensure 'foolproof' safety measures: Patna High Court to Election Commission.
23	Delhi High Court sanctions action against the Indira Gandhi National Centre for Arts (NCA) Trust headed by Congress President Sonia Gandhi, for allegedly changing its character from a public to a private trust.
	❖ EC seeks extra forces for Bihar.
24	Dr. Pannalal Oswal, BJP candidate from the Dhubri Lok Sabha constituency in Assam abducted and killed by the United Liberation Front of Assam (ULFA)
	❖ BJP asks CEC to provide adequate security to its candidates. Karnataka government rejects Cauvery Panel's advice to release water for Tamil Nadu.
25	In the fourth phase of Lok Sabha elections, 5 persons killed and 2 Ministers held in Bihar
	❖ D.D. exit poll gives clear lead to NDA.
26	Communists are the palanquin bearers of Sonia - L.K. Advani
	❖ Assam fit case for Central Rule: Sonia
	❖ RJD rigged polls in 19 constituencies in which polls were held in Bihar in the fifth phase - Ram Vilas Paswan, Janata Dal (United Leader)
27	EC. orders repolling in 559 booths (481 in Bihar)
28	The INSIGH exit poll predicts gains for Congress Allies in the fourth phase of the polls.
29	Poll in four Lok Sabha constituencies namely Purena, Rajmahal Bhagalpur and Khagariafor Bihar to be on Oct. 28 on account of heavy rains.
	❖ Militants attempt to blast J&K Secretariat.
30	Punjab and Haryana High Court issues notice to Election Commissioner JM Lyngdoh for reportedly issuing directions that led to preventing Haryana CM O.P. Chautala from casting his vote on September 5.
	❖ NDA to get 28 Bihar seats- Poll Survey of Lokmat-CMCR
October, 1	We are experts at coalitions now. I am contesting only becuase my work was cut short—A.B. Vajpayee Prime Minister.
	❖ Shoot at sight orders issued against poll offenders at Amethi Lok Sabha constituency.
2	Coalition if need be-Congress spokesman Kapil Sibal
3	Thirty eight persons die in the final phase of Election-17 in Manipur 7 in Tripura.
	❖ Polling officer found dead in guest house in Balasore, Orissa

❖ Two exist polls predict majority for NDA.

October, 4 About 14% polling in Anantnag Parliamentary constituency. One election agent of National Conference and 25 others injured by terrorist blasts.

❖ Sharad Yadav, president JD(U) and candidate from Madhepura against Laloo Prasad Yadav (RJD) asks E.C. to countermand election in the constituency on account of rigging on a large scale otherwise he would go on a fast unto-death.

❖ 270 polling booths which include 166 from Bihar to have repolling.

5 Nearly 1500 counting centres across the country set up.

❖ 13th Lok Sabha to be constituted on Oct. 10, 1999- EC.

❖ Sharad Yadav begins fast unto death.

6 NDA set to win the 13the Lok Sabha Election

❖ A.B. Vajpayee and Sonia Gandhi win.

❖ B.J.P. wins all the seven seats in Delhi.

7 Sonia Gandhi calls for introspection

❖ Comfortable majority for NDA.

❖ Karnataka Chief Minister faces his own defeat and his party's defeat in Assembly elections and resigns

8 NDA gives free hand to Vajpayee go to recast government

❖ TDP sends letter of support

❖ Manmohan Singh quits Rajya Sabha seats following his defeat in Lok Sabha.

❖ National Conferance to join Govt.

9 Congress and NCP agree to talk on Maharashtra political situation.

10 TDP Support from out side.

❖ Vajpayee elected N.D.A. leader.

❖ 13th Lok Sabha constituted.

❖ We have got to take hard decisions—A.B. Vajpayee

❖ Three All India General Secretaries Pranab Mukherjee, Mrs. Ambika Soni and Oscar Fernades assume moral responsibility for defeat and quit.

11 President invites the Prime Minister to form Government at the centre.

12 Pakistan Prime Minister Nawab Sharif over thrown by the Army Chief Genral Pervaiz Musharraf who was sacked earlier in the day. Probably all this resulted from Kargil debacle of Pakistan.

❖ Meghalaya UDP govt. collapses as the Congress withdraws support.

❖ Sonia Gandhi shoulders blame for party defeat

❖ Vajpayee sends list of Ministers to the President.

❖ Former BJP MP Sakshi Maharaj joins S.P.

❖ Sonia elected Chairperson of CPP

13 70-Member Atal Ministry (25 Cabinet Ministers) sworn in

❖ Arun Jaitely, Sharad Yadav, Ram Vilas Paswan, Mamata among new Ministers.

❖ Ramakrishna Hegde and Sikander Bakht do not find place in the new Cabinet.

- ❖ Syed Shahnawaz Hussain, BJP's lone Muslim Member in the Lok Sabha taken as Minister of state
  - ❖ JD(U)-BJP pact ends in Karnataka.
- ❖ SAD and INLD of the NDA, opt to stay out of NDA government.

October, 19 Sonia Gandhi decides to be the leader of opposition in the Lok Sabha and retain the Amethi seat.

22 Balyogi is elected Lok Sabha Speaker for the Second Term.

28 Elections held at remaining six Lok Sabha seats (Four in Bihar, one in Assam, One in Manipur).

12
The Epilogue

The 13th Lok Sabha elections marked a new low in the fortunes of the Indian National Congress. The State Assembly elections held in 1998 under the presidentship of Sonia Gandhi had raised new hopes but the expectations turned out to be highly exaggerated.

The Congress miscalculated in as much as it interpreted the State Assembly results (1998) as a break through. The party decided to go it all alone condemning the very concept of coalitions. The strategy did not work.

The INC had been banking heavily on the charisman of Sonia Gandhi. She drew large crowds, won both the Bellary and the Amethi seats and even Priyanka Gandhi and Rahul Gandhi attracted wide attention from the voters. However turning attendance at party sponsored meetings to votes is a different game. For that the party needs a dedicated core of field workers. The Congress proved very poor in this area and has paid dearly for its miscalculations.

In retrospect it could be said that turning the election into Sonia versus Atal Bihari was not a good strategy for the Congress. Atal Bihari had been in politics far too long and was shining brightly in the reflected glory of the Kargil. He was backed by a hard core of committed party workers. The Hindi heartland had been his favourite playground and in company with right allies, his charisma had spread to almost all parts of the country. The BJP was no longer the untouchable having put on back burner all the contentious issues. The Hindutva agenda that at one time used to scare away other regional political parties had been overshadowed by Atal Bihari's political liberalism. His leadership was now acceptable. This paid rich dividends to the NDA.

Atal Bihari was the undisputed leader. He had no rivals unlike other Non-Congress Prime Ministers in the past. Morarji Desai, V.P. Singh, Deve Gowda or even I.K. Gujaral had rivals and competitors. Atal Bihari had none in the BJP or even in the NDA.

The regional parties had their own appeal and followings. But at the National level it was only the BJP led NDA to which the voters could look up to. The war with Pakistan had given Atal Bihari Vajpayee an all India status and his popularity was no longer limited to the Hindi heartland.

The NDA was a unique combination of various thoughts. It had with itself, secularists, socialists, progressive thinkers and people of divergent ideologies all came together to give the country a stable government.

The NDA comprised political elements from all parts and regions of the country. It was the alliance that symbolised the coming together of both the regional and the national aspirations.

During best times, the Congress had experimented with the State politics being run from the Centre. Chief Ministers in Congress governed States were moved in and out like pawns in the games of the chess at the whims and likings of the leaders in New Delhi.

The phenomenon had now backfired. The State Chief Ministers now wanted a say in central policy making rather than being dictated from the Centre. The NDA was quick to scent the change. The Congress was unprepared.

The 1999 elections established the role of government's real performance as the ultimate determining factor. The incumbency myth was broken. Andhra Pradesh continued to be with the TDP. Non-performance costed Punjab to Akalis and the Bihar to Laloos dearly. The BJP stronghold U.P. was another non-governing State severely punished by the voters. State government performance in Madhya Pradesh, Rajasthan and Delhi severly affected the Congress.

Factionalism also brought dissaster in Uttar Pradesh and Delhi. Kalyan Singh and Sheila Dixit were unable to hold their flock together and paid dearly irrespective of their party affiliations.

Structural changes pay dividends much longer than cosmetic dress ups. West Bengal proved the point. The land reforms introduced in West Bengal have given the CPI(M) a strong grip. In Punjab even the lure of free power to the farmers did not put the Akalis back to power.

Do not take the voters for granted. The message was loud and clear even in the CPI(M) dominated West Bengal. Mamata Bannerjee and the NDA have started making dents in what was being considered the bastion of the Communist party. The CPI too has learnt the lesson although after the event. Political pundits would become irrelevant if they did not make forecasts. Some would give the NDA two years while the rest even lesser.

There are inbuilt contradictions within the NDA. The TDP is not a part of the government. Sikhs and Muslims have yet to find suitable representation. The Muslims and now the Christians feel scared about the BJP being pressurised by VHP, Bajrangdal or the RSS to pursue more vigourously the Hindutva Agenda.

A more rational view point is that the partners are more likely to stay together for more than one reason. The constituents do not have a personal agenda like Ms. Jayalalitha had in the previous set up. There will be regional pressures no doubt but they should be manageable for the alliance partners knowing that their survival is more important than giving a few concessions here or there. Also that even if Bengal gets some more railway lines that others, it is still a part of India.

Atal Bihari has also become all the more wiser politician by now. He has talent in his team. He has to make full use of the available talent. He has to take tough decisions.

Projections may go wrong but the government seems stable for the next three years. If within this time, it can show perceptable changes, its continuance is assured it must perform and perform well.